Exploring Modern Techniques in
HTML & CSS:

Where Design Meets Code

By
Mike Zephalon

About Author

Mike Zephalon was born in Toronto, Canada, and developed a passion for technology and programming at an early age. His journey into the world of coding began when he was just a teenager, experimenting with simple scripts and exploring the vast possibilities of web development. Mike pursued his studies at the University of Toronto, where he majored in Computer Science. During his time at university, he became deeply interested in JavaScript, captivated by its versatility and power in building dynamic, interactive web applications.

Over the years, Mike has worked with several tech startups and companies, where he honed his skills as a front-end developer. His dedication to mastering JavaScript and its frameworks has made him a respected voice in the developer community. Through his books and tutorials, Mike aims to empower new and experienced developers alike, helping them unlock the full potential of JavaScript in their projects.

Table of Contents

1. Foundations of HTML and CSS

Introduction

The advent of the internet has revolutionized how we access, share, and present information. At the core of web development are two foundational technologies: HTML (HyperText Markup Language) and CSS (Cascading Style Sheets). These languages work together to create visually appealing and functional websites that cater to diverse user needs. In this detailed introduction, we will explore the fundamentals, purpose, and capabilities of HTML and CSS, along with their evolution and best practices in 2025.

1. Understanding HTML: The Backbone of Web Content

HTML, or HyperText Markup Language, is the standard markup language used to structure web content. From simple text to complex multimedia applications, HTML provides the scaffolding upon which web pages are built.

1.1 What is HTML?

HTML is a markup language that uses tags to define elements on a web page. These elements can include headings, paragraphs, images, links, forms, tables, and more. HTML's primary function is to provide a semantic structure to content, making it understandable to browsers and accessible to users.

1.2 Key Features of HTML:

Semantic Elements: HTML5 introduced semantic tags like <header>, <footer>, <article>, and <section>, which enhance readability and accessibility.
Media Integration: Tags like <audio> and <video> allow seamless integration of multimedia.
Forms and Input: HTML supports various input types and attributes, enabling interactive and user-friendly forms.
Global Attributes: Attributes like class, id, and style provide additional functionality and flexibility.

1.3 The Structure of an HTML Document

An HTML document typically consists of:

```
<!DOCTYPE html>
<html lang="en">
<head>
   <meta charset="UTF-8">
   <meta name="viewport" content="width=device-width, initial-scale=1.0">
   <title>Document Title</title>
</head>
<body>
   <h1>Welcome to HTML</h1>
   <p>This is a paragraph.</p>
</body>
</html>
```

<!DOCTYPE html>: Specifies the document type and version (HTML5 in this case).
<html>: The root element containing all other elements.
<head>: Contains metadata, such as the title and links to external resources.

<body>: Contains the visible content of the web page.

1.4 Evolution of HTML

HTML has evolved significantly since its inception in 1991. HTML5, introduced in 2014 and widely adopted by 2025, brought notable improvements, including:

Enhanced support for multimedia and graphics.
Better semantics for improved SEO and accessibility.
Support for offline capabilities via the <canvas> element and web storage.

2. CSS: Styling the Web

While HTML provides structure, CSS (Cascading Style Sheets) controls the presentation. It determines how HTML elements are displayed, offering endless possibilities for creative and responsive designs.

2.1 What is CSS?

CSS is a style sheet language used to describe the look and formatting of a document written in HTML. It separates content from presentation, enabling developers to manage styles more efficiently.

2.2 Key Features of CSS:

Selectors: Define which HTML elements the styles apply to.
Box Model: Governs layout and spacing with properties like margin, padding, border, and content.
Responsive Design: Media queries allow designs to adapt to different screen sizes and devices.
Animations and Transitions: CSS enables dynamic effects without relying on JavaScript.

2.3 CSS Syntax

A CSS rule consists of a selector and a declaration block:

```
selector {
   property: value;
}
```

For example:
```
h1 {
   color: blue;
   font-size: 24px;
}
```
This rule sets the color of <h1> elements to blue and the font size to 24 pixels.

2.4 Types of CSS

Inline CSS: Applied directly to an HTML element using the style attribute.

```
<p style="color: red;">This is red text.</p>
```

Internal CSS: Defined within a <style> tag in the <head> section.

```
<style>
  p { color: green; }
</style>
```

External CSS: Linked via an external stylesheet, making it reusable across multiple pages.

```
<link rel="stylesheet" href="styles.css">
```

2.5 The Evolution of CSS

CSS has evolved through three major versions, with CSS3 being the current standard. By 2025, CSS capabilities include:

Grid and Flexbox Layouts: Streamlining responsive and complex layouts.
Custom Properties (CSS Variables): Reusable values for consistent styling.
Advanced Selectors: Enhanced specificity and targeting of elements.
Support for Dark Mode: Media queries like prefers-color-scheme adapt styles based on user preferences.

3. HTML and CSS Together: Building Modern Web Pages

The synergy between HTML and CSS is at the heart of web development. HTML structures the content, while CSS ensures it is visually appealing and user-friendly.

3.1 Responsive Web Design

Responsive design ensures that websites function well across various devices and screen sizes. CSS techniques for responsiveness include:

Media Queries:

```
@media (max-width: 600px) {
body { background-color: lightgray; }
}
```

Flexbox and Grid: Flexible layouts for dynamic resizing.
Viewport Meta Tag: Optimizes scaling for mobile devices.

```
<meta name="viewport" content="width=device-width, initial-scale=1.0">
```

3.2 Accessibility and SEO

Use semantic HTML for better accessibility and search engine indexing.
Ensure high contrast and legible fonts for visually impaired users.
Add alt attributes to images and ARIA roles for assistive technologies.

3.3 Debugging and Optimization

Utilize browser developer tools for debugging styles and structure.
Optimize CSS and HTML by removing unnecessary code and compressing files.
Leverage content delivery networks (CDNs) and caching for faster load times.

4. Tools and Best Practices

4.1 Tools for HTML and CSS Development

Code Editors: Visual Studio Code, Sublime Text, or Atom for efficient coding.
Frameworks and Libraries: Bootstrap, Tailwind CSS, and Bulma for rapid development.
Preprocessors: SCSS and LESS extend CSS with variables, nesting, and mixins.
Validation Tools: W3C Validator ensures standards-compliant code.

4.2 Best Practices

Maintain clean and organized code with comments and consistent formatting.
Use external stylesheets for scalability and reuse.
Avoid inline styles for easier maintenance.
Test across different browsers and devices to ensure compatibility.

Whether you want to build a web page to advertise your business, blog about a hobby, or maintain an online community, HyperText Markup Language (HTML) and Cascading Style Sheets (CSS) are the foundations upon which you will build.

HTML and CSS work together but each has a different role in making a web page. A web page is made up of lots of different types of content (text, images, links, video, and audio). HTML structures that content and CSS styles it. Together, they tell the browser how and what to render.

These two technologies are simple to get started with and provide enough power and expressivity that they let you get your ideas out there to the vast audience on the web.

Navigate to a website and what you see is the rendered output of content marked up with HTML and styled with CSS. As a browser user, you have access to the source code of a web page. In Chrome, for example, you can view a page's source code by pressing the keys Ctrl + U on a PC or command + option + U on a Mac. Alternatively, you can right-click with a mouse and choose View Page Source. Try it yourself. As an example, the following two figures show what the Packt website's Web Development portal looks like when rendered in the browser and as source code respectively.

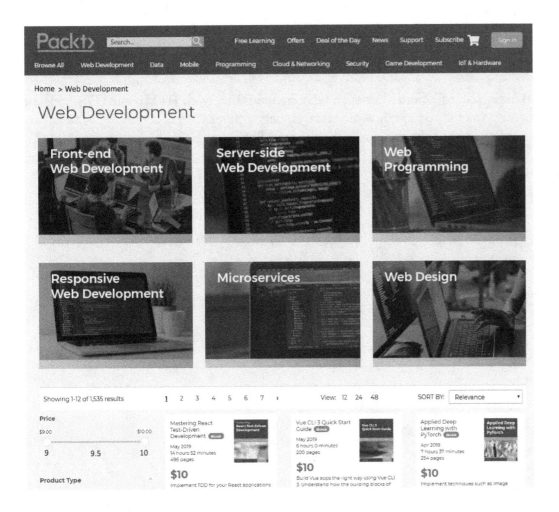

Figure: The Packt Publishing site's Web Development portal

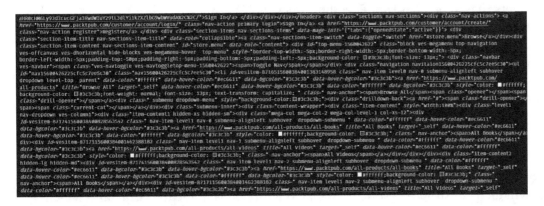

Figure: The HTML source code of the Packt site

By learning to write the HTML and CSS that make up the source code, we can create our own modern website.

In this chapter, we will develop an understanding of how a web page renders by following the process from initial request to completed composition. We will learn how to build a simple web page using HTML and then we will learn how to style that page with CSS.

By the end of this chapter, you will have been introduced to two of the core technologies of the web – HTML and CSS – and you will understand their roles in creating websites. You will have created a page from scratch and you will have used selectors to target parts of that web page for styling.

How a web page renders

When we navigate to a web page in our favourite browser, what happens? How do HTML and CSS translate to the page we see in front of us? In other words, how does a web page render?
The following figure shows a flowchart of the process, which is then further explained:

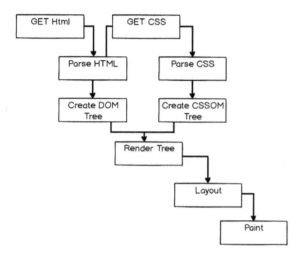

Figure: Flow chart of the web page render process

To summarize the process:

The user starts by navigating to a URL, possibly via a hyperlink or by typing the URL into the address bar of their browser.
The browser will make a GET request to the disk or a network. It will read the raw bytes from that location and convert them to characters (based on character encoding, such as UTF-8).
The browser then parses these characters according to the HTML standard to find the tokens that are familiar as HTML elements, such as <html> and <body>.
Another parse is then made to take these tokens and construct objects with their properties based on the rules appropriate to that token. At this point, the objects are defined.
Finally, the browser can define the relationships between these objects and construct the HTML DOM (Document Object Model) for the web page.

At this point, we have a DOM but not a rendered web page. The next task is to construct the CSSOM (CSS Object Model). Again, the browser will load any style sheet resources it needs to, which were found while parsing the document. It will then construct the styles associated with nodes in the tree structure, which gives us the CSSOM.

With the information gathered in the DOM and the CSSOM, the browser can create a render tree. The render tree is constructed by combining information from the CSSOM and the HTML DOM. Nodes in the HTML DOM that will not be rendered (for instance, those with the display: none; style) are excluded from the render tree. Those that are rendered are enriched with their computed style rules.

Now the browser has all the information it needs, it can begin to calculate the positions of elements in the rendered viewport. This is called the layout stage. The browser lays elements out based on their size and position within the browser viewport. This stage is often also called reflow. It means the browser must recalculate the positions of elements in the viewport when elements are added to or removed from the page or when the viewport size is changed.

Finally, the browser will rasterize or paint each element on the page, depending on their styles, shadows, and filters to render the page the user will see.

In this section, we have given a brief and simplified summary of the rendering of a web page. Think about how many resources might be loaded on a relatively complicated website and with JavaScript running events and we can see that much of this process happens frequently and not in such a linear manner. We can start to see the complexities of what a browser is doing when it renders your web page.

In the next section, we will start to look at how we create a web page by learning about the syntax of HTML, which helps us structure and contextualize our content. We will learn about the syntax of HTML and the elements we can use, and we will apply this knowledge to create a simple web page.

Understanding HTML

HTML is a markup language used to describe the structure of a web page.

Consider a snippet of text with no markup:

HTML HyperText Markup Language (HTML) is a markup language used to describe the structure of a web page. We can use it to differentiate such content as headings lists links images Want to https://www. packtpub.com/web-development Learn more about web development.

The preceding snippet of text makes some sense. It may also raise some questions. Why does the snippet begin with the word HTML? Why is there a URL in the middle of a sentence? Is this one paragraph? Using HTML, we can differentiate several bits of content to give them greater meaning. We could mark the word HTML as a heading, <h1>HTML</h1>, or we could mark a link to another web page using <a href="https://www.packtpub.com/web-development">Learn more about web development</a>.

There have been several versions of HTML since its first release in 1993 at the beginning of the web. Throughout the rest of this chapter, and indeed the rest of this book, we will be looking at and working with the current version of the HTML language, HTML5, which is the 5th major version of HTML. When we use the term HTML, we will refer specifically to HTML5 and if we need to talk about a different version we will do so explicitly.

In the next section, we will look at the syntax of HTML in more detail.

Syntax

The syntax of HTML is made up of tags (with angle brackets, <>) and attributes. HTML provides a set of tags that can be used to mark the beginning and end of a bit of content. The opening tag, closing tag, and all content within those bounds represent an HTML element. The following figures show the HTML element representation without and with tag attributes respectively:

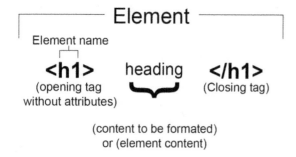

Figure: HTML element representation without tag attributes

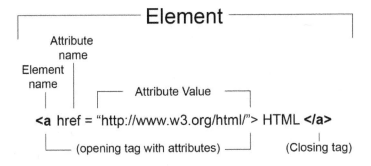

Figure: HTML element representation with tag attributes

A tag has a name (for instance, p, img, or h1), and that name combined with attributes will describe how the browser should handle the content. Many tags have a start and end tag with some content in between, but some tags don't expect any content, and these can be self-closing.

An opening tag can have any number of attributes associated with it. These are modifiers of the element. An attribute is a name-value pair. For example, href="https://www.packtpub. com/web-development" is an attribute with the name of href and the value of https:// www.packtpub.com/web-development. An href attribute represents a hypertext reference or a URL, and when this attribute is added to an anchor element, <a>, it creates a hyperlink that the user can click in the browser to navigate to that URL.

To provide information within an HTML document to be ignored by the parser and not shown to the end user, you can add comments. These are useful for notes and documentation to aid anyone who might read or amend the source of the HTML document. A comment begins with <!-- and ends with -->. Comments, in HTML, can be single or multiline. The following are some examples:

<!-- Comment on a single line -->

This comment is over multiple lines.
Comments can be used to inform and for detailed documentation.
You can use comments to provide helpful hints to other developers working on the web page but they will be ignored by the browser when parsing the page.

Let's see what the previous snippet of text content looks like when it is given some meaning with HTML:

<h1>HTML</h1>

<p>

HyperText Markup Language (HTML) is a markup language

used to describe the structure of a web page.

</p>

<p>

We can use it to differentiate such content as:

</p>

```
<ul>

<li>headings</li>

<li>lists</li>

<li>links</li>

<li>images</li>

</ul>

<p>

Want to <a href="https://www.packtpub.com/web-

development">learn more about web development?</a>

</p>
```

If we were to look at this HTML code rendered in a browser, it would look like the following figure:

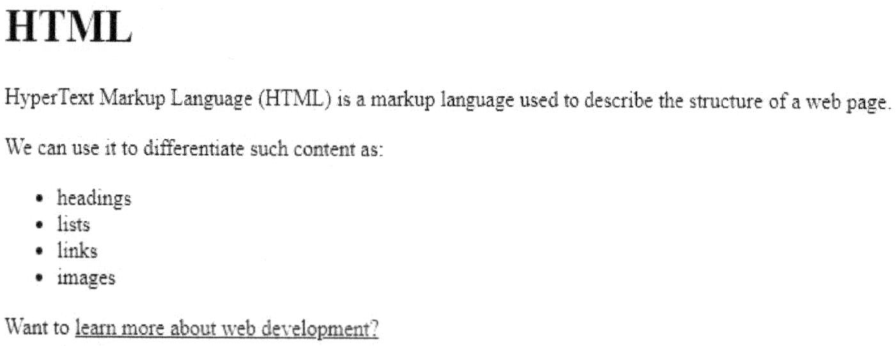

HTML

HyperText Markup Language (HTML) is a markup language used to describe the structure of a web page.

We can use it to differentiate such content as:

- headings
- lists
- links
- images

Want to learn more about web development?

Figure: HTML rendered in the Google Chrome web browser The first line shows the HTML text content with a start tag, <h1>, and an end tag, </h1>. This tells the browser to treat the text content as an h1 heading element.

The next line of our code snippet has a <p> start tag, which means the content until the corresponding end tag, </p> (on the last line), will be treated as a paragraph element. We then have another paragraph and then an unordered list element that starts with the <ul> start tag and ends with the </ul> end tag. The unordered list has four child elements, which are all list item elements (from the <li> start tag to the </li> end tag).

Type	Description	Example

Type	Description	Example
Metadata	Content hosted in the head of an HTML document. Doesn't appear in the web page directly but is used to describe a web page and its relationship to other external resources.	`<meta name="viewport" content="width=devicewidth,initial-scale=1.0">`

Flow	Text and all elements that can appear as content in the body of an HTML document.	`<body>`
		`<h1>Heading</h1> <p>Some content…</p>`
		`</body>`

Sectioning	Used to structure the content of a web page and to help with layout. Elements in this category are described in Chapter 2, Structure and Layout.	`<aside></aside>`
		`<article class="blog-post">`
		`<section></section>`
		`</article>`

Phrasing	Elements such as those used for marking up content within a paragraph element. Chapter 3, Text and Typography, will be largely concerned with this content type.	`<p><em>Emphasized text</em> and some normal text.</p>`
Type	Description	Example
Heading	Elements used to define the headings of a section of an HTML document. The h1-6 elements represent headings with h1 having the highest ranking.	`<h1>Main Heading</h1>` `<h2>Subheading</h2>`
Embedded	Embedded content includes media, such as video, audio, and images.	`<img src="media/kitten.png" alt="A cute kitten">`
Interactive	Elements that a user can interact with, which include media elements with controls, form inputs, buttons, and links.	`<input type="password" name="password" required>`

The last element in the example is another paragraph element, which combines text content and an anchor element. The anchor element, starting from the <a> start tag and ending at the </a> end tag, has the learn more about web development? text content and an href attribute. The href attribute turns the anchor element into a hyperlink, which a user can click to navigate to the URL given as the value of the href attribute.

As with our example, the contents of a paragraph element might be text but can also be other HTML elements, such as an anchor tag, <a>. The relationship between the anchor and paragraph elements is a parent-child relationship.

HTML elements

HTML5 defines more than a hundred tags that we can use to markup parts of an HTML document. These include the following:

The document root element: <html>
Metadata elements: <base>, <head>, <link>, <meta>, <style>, and <title>
Content sectioning elements: <address>, <article>, <aside>, <body>, <footer>,

\<header>, \<h1>, \<h2>, \<h3>, \<h4>, \<h5>, \<h6>, \<main>, \<nav>, and \<section>

Block text elements: \<blockquote>, \<dd>, \<details>, \<dialog>, \<div>, \<dl>, \<dt>, \<figcaption>, \<figure>, \<hr>, \<li>, \<menu>, \<ol>, \<p>, \<pre>, \<summary>, and \<ul>

Inline text elements: \<a>, \<abbr>, \<b>, \<bdi>, \<bdo>, \
, \<cite> , \<code>, \<data>, \<dfn>, \<em>, \<i>, \<kbd>, \<mark>, \<q>, \<rp>, \<rt>, \<ruby>, \<s>, \<samp>, \<small>, \<span>, \<strong>, \<sub>, \<sup>, \<del>, \<ins>, \<time>, \<u>, \<var>, and \<wbr>

Media elements: \<area>, \<audio>, \<img>, \<canvas>, \<map>, \<track>, \<video>, \<embed>, \<iframe>, \<object>, \<picture>, \<portal>, \<source>, \<svg>, and \<math>

Scripting elements: \<noscript> and \<script>

Table elements: \<caption>, \<col>, \<colgroup>, \<table>, \<tbody>, \<td>, \<tfoot>, \<th>, \<thead>, and \<tr>

Form elements: \<button>, \<datalist>, \<fieldset>, \<form>, \<input>, \<label>, \<legend>, \<meter>, \<optgroup>, \<option>, \<output>, \<progress>, \<select>, and \<textarea>

Web component elements: \<slot> and \<template>

We don't have to know all of these tags to use HTML well; some fulfil more common use cases than others. Each has a distinct purpose and provides a different semantic meaning and throughout this book, we will go into some detail about how to use these elements.

Content types

When starting with HTML, it can be easy to find the number and variety of elements overwhelming. It may be helpful to think about HTML in terms of content types.
The following table has a description and example of the different content types that can describe an element:

Let's run through an example of how an element can fit into these category types using the \<img> element. If we want to embed an image in our web page, the simplest way is to use the img element. If we want to create an img element, an example of the code looks like this: \<img src="media/kitten. png" alt="A cute kitten">.
We set the src attribute on the img element to an image URL; this is the source of the image that will be embedded in the web page.

Unless your image has no value other than as a decoration, it is a very good idea to include an alt attribute. The alt attribute provides an alternative description of the image as text, which can then be used by screen readers if an image does not load, or in a non-graphical browser.

An img element is a form of embedded content because it embeds an image in an HTML document. It can appear in the body of an HTML document as the child element of the body element, so it would be categorized as flow content.

An image can be included as content in a paragraph, so it is a type of phrasing content. For example, we could have inline images appear in the flow of a paragraph:

\<p>

Kittens are everywhere on the internet. The best thing about kittens is that they are cute. Look here's a kitten now:

\<img src="media/kitten.jpg" alt="A cute kitten">.
See, cute isn't it?

```
</p>
```

This code would render the following figure, with the image embedded in the paragraph and the rest of the text flowing around it:

Kittens are everywhere on the internet. The best thing about kittens is that they are

cute. Look here's a kitten now: . See, cute isn't it?

Figure: Image with text flowing around it

In certain circumstances, an img element is a type of interactive content. For this to be the case, the image must have a usemap attribute. The usemap attribute allows you to specify an image map, which defines areas of an image that are treated as hyperlinks. This makes the image interactive.
An img element does not act as metadata and it does not provide a sectioning structure to an HTML document. Nor is it a heading.

Elements can appear in more than one category and there is some overlap between the relationships of the categories. Some of these elements are very common and are used often, but some of these elements have very specific purposes and you may never come across a use case for them.
The content types can be useful for understanding how elements work together and which elements are valid in where. For further reference, we can see where each available element is categorized in the W3C's documentation on HTML5: https://html.spec.whatwg.org/multipage/ dom.html#kinds-of-content.

The HTML document

A web page is made up of an HTML document. The document represents a hierarchical tree structure similar to a family tree. Starting from a root element, the relationship between an element and its contents can be seen as that of a parent element and a child element. An element that is at the same level of the hierarchy as another element is a sibling to that element. We can describe elements within a branch of the tree as ancestors and descendants.

This structure can be represented as a tree diagram to get a better idea of the relationship between elements. Take, for example, this simple HTML document:

```
<html>

<head>

<title>HTML Document structure</title>

</head>

<body>

<div>

<h1>Heading</h1>
```

```
<p>First paragraph of text.</p>

<p>Second paragraph of text.</p>

</div>

</body>

</html>
```

Here, the root is an html element. It has two children: a head element (containing a title) and a body element containing some more content. It can be represented as a tree diagram as follows:

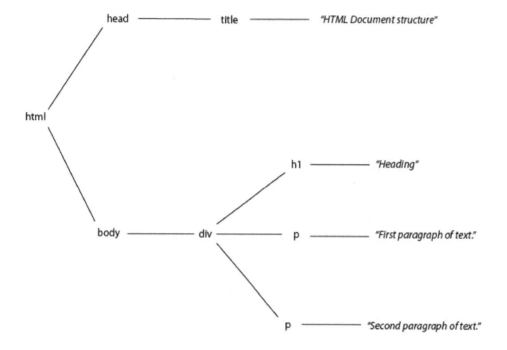

Figure: A representation of the HTML document as a tree diagram
In the browser, this code would render the following web page:

Figure: HTML rendered in the Google Chrome web browser

The <html> element is the parent of both the <head> and <body>, which (as children of the same parent) are siblings. <body> has one child, a <div> tag, and that has three children: an <h1> element and two <p> elements. The <h1> element is a descendant of <body> but not of <head>.

Understanding this structure will become more important when we look at CSS selectors and how we target parts of the HTML document later in this chapter.

Structuring an HTML document

An HTML5 document normally starts with a doctype declaration and has a root html element with two children – the head element and the body element.

The doctype declaration tells the browser it is dealing with an HTML5 document. The doctype is <!DOCTYPE html> and appears as the first line of the document. It is recommended to always add a doctype to make sure your HTML document renders as expected.

One of the nice things about HTML5 is that it simplifies doctype declaration. Before HTML5, there were two commonly used variations of web markup – HTML4 and XHTML1 – and they both had strict, transitional, and frameset versions of their doctype declarations. For example, the HTML 4 strict declaration looked like this: <!DOCTYPE HTML PUBLIC "-//W3C//DTD HTML 4.01// EN" "http://www.w3.org/TR/html4/strict.dtd">.

After the doctype, we have the html element, which is the root of the HTML document.

It is strongly recommended that you add a lang attribute to your html element to allow the browser, screen readers, and other technologies, such as translation tools, to better understand the text content of your web page.

The two children of the html element are as follows:

The head element, which includes the title and metadata providing information about assets to load and how web crawlers and search engines should handle the page.

The body element, which mostly represents the content rendered for a human browser user to consume. This includes articles, images, and navigation. In code, the structure we have described looks like this:

```
<!doctype html>

<html lang="en">

<head><title>Page Title</title></head>

<body></body>

</html>
```

This code would result in a blank web page with no content or metadata.

Metadata

The head is home to most machine-read information in an HTML document. The browser, screen readers, and web crawlers can get a lot of information from metadata and handle the web page differently depending on that information.

The following elements are considered metadata content:

base: This lets you set a base URL
link: This determines the relationship between a page and a resource (such as an external style sheet)
meta: This a catch-all for metadata
title: This is the name of your web page as it appears in the browser tab and search results and is announced by screen readers
The meta element can represent many different types of metadata, including some used by social networks to represent a web page.

Some common usages include the following:

Setting character encoding for a page – <meta charset="utf-8">
Setting the viewport for a browser on a mobile device – <meta name="viewport" content="width=device-width, initial-scale=1">
These elements give web developers ways to tell a browser how to handle the HTML document and how it relates to its environment. We can describe our web page for other interested parties (such as search engines and web crawlers) using metadata.

Our first web page

In our first example, we will create a very simple web page. This will help us to understand the structure of an HTML document and where we put different types of content.

Exercise – creating a web page

In this exercise, we will create our first web page. This will be the minimal foundation upon which future chapters can build.

The steps are as follows:
To start, we want to create a new folder, and then open that folder in Visual Studio Code (File | Open Folder…).
Next, we will create a new plain text file and save it as index.html.

In index.html, we start by adding the doctype declaration for HTML5:

<!DOCTYPE html>
Next, we add an HTML tag (the root element of the HTML document):

<html lang="en">
</html>

In between the opening and closing tags of the html element, we add a head tag. This is where we can put metadata content. For now, the head tag will contain a title:

<head>
<title>HTML and CSS</title>
</head>

Below the head tag and above the closing html tag, we can then add a body tag. This is where we will put the majority of our content. For now, we will render a heading and a paragraph:

```
<body>
<h1>HTML and CSS</h1>
<p>

How to create a modern, responsive website with HTML and CSS

</p>

</body>
```

The result of this exercise should look like the following figure when opened in a browser:

HTML and CSS

How to create a modern, responsive website with HTML and CSS

Figure: The web page as displayed in the Chrome web browser

Activity– video store page template

We've been tasked with creating a website for an online on-demand film store called Films on Demand. We don't have designs yet but want to set up a web page boilerplate that we can use for all the pages on the site. We will use comments as placeholders to know what needs to change for each page that is built on top of the boilerplate template. For visible content in the body element, we will use lorem ipsum to get an idea of how content will flow.

The steps are as follows:
Create a file named template.html.

We want the page to be a valid HTML5 document. So, we will need to add:
The correct doctype definition.

Elements to structure the document: The html element, the head element, and the body element.
A title element that combines the Films on Demand brand with some specifics about the current page.
Metadata to describe the site: We'll set this to Buy films from our great selection. Watch movies on demand.
Metadata for the page character set and a viewport tag to help make the site render better on mobile browsers.

We want to add placeholders for a heading (an h1 element) for the page, which we will populate with lorem ipsum, and a paragraph for the content flow, which we will also populate with the following lorem ipsum text:

"Lorem ipsum dolor sit amet, consectetur adipiscing elit. Nullam quis scelerisque mauris. Curabitur aliquam ligula in erat placerat finibus. Mauris leo neque, malesuada et augue at, consectetur rhoncus libero. Suspendisse vitae dictum dolor. Vestibulum hendrerit iaculis ipsum, ac ornare ligula. Vestibulum efficitur mattis urna vitae ultrices. Nunc condimentum blandit tellus ut mattis. Morbi eget gravida leo. Mauris ornare lorem a mattis ultricies. Nullam convallis tincidunt nunc, eget rhoncus nulla tincidunt sed. Nulla consequat tellus lectus, in porta nulla facilisis eu. Donec bibendum nisi felis, sit amet cursus nisl suscipit ut. Pellentesque bibendum id libero at cursus. Donec ac viverra tellus. Proin sed dolor quis justo convallis auctor sit amet nec orci. Orci varius natoque penatibus et magnis dis parturient montes, nascetur ridiculus mus."

In this section, we've looked at HTML, the markup language that structures and gives context to the content of a web page. We have looked at the syntax of HTML, created our first web page, and learned about the structure of an HTML document. When we've looked at our web page in a browser, it has been rendered with the default styling provided by the browser. In the next section, we will look at how we can customize the styling of our web page using CSS. We will learn how to add styles, how to specify what parts of a page they apply to, and some of the properties we can style.

Understanding CSS

CSS is a style sheet language used to describe the presentation of a web page.
The language is designed to separate concerns. It allows the design, layout, and presentation of a web page to be defined separately from content semantics and structure. This separation keeps source code readable and lets a designer update styles separately from a developer who might create the page structure or a web editor who is changing content on a page.

A set of CSS rules in a style sheet determines how an HTML document is displayed to the user. It can determine whether elements in the document are rendered, how they are laid out on the web page, and their aesthetic appearance.

In the next section, we will look at the syntax of CSS.

Syntax

A CSS declaration is made of two parts: a property and a value. The property is the name for some aspect of style you want to change; the value is what you want to set it to.

Here is an example of a CSS declaration:
color: red;

The property is color and the value is red. In CSS, color is the property name for the foreground color value of an element. That essentially means the color of the text and any text decoration (such as underline or strikethrough). It also sets a current color value.

For this declaration to have any effect on an HTML document, it must be applied to one or more elements in the document. We do this with a selector. For example, you can select all the <p> elements in a web page with the p selector. So, if you wanted to make the color of all text in all paragraph elements red, you would use the following CSS ruleset:

p {
color: red;

}

The result of this CSS ruleset applied to an HTML document can be seen in the following figure:

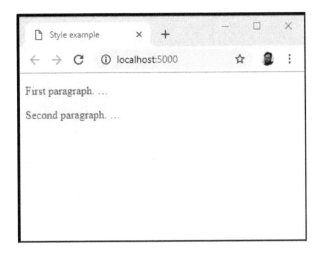

Figure: Result of a CSS rule applied to <p> elements in HTML

The curly braces represent a declaration block and that means more than one CSS declaration can be added to this block. If you wanted to make the text in all paragraph elements red, bold, and underlined, you could do that with the following ruleset:

p {

color: red;

font-weight: bold;

text-decoration: underline;

}

The result of this CSS ruleset applied to an HTML document can be seen in the following figure:

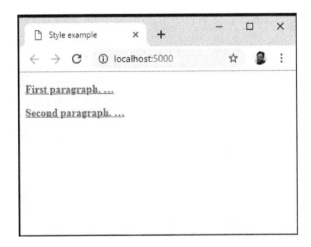

Figure: Several CSS declarations applied to <p> elements in HTML

Multiple selectors can share a CSS ruleset. We can target these with a comma-separated list. For example, to apply the color red to p elements, h1 elements, and h2 elements, we could use the following ruleset:

p, h1, h2 {

color: red;

}

Multiple CSS rulesets form a style sheet. The order of these CSS rules in a style sheet is very important as this is partly how the cascade or specificity of a rule is determined. A more specific rule will be ranked higher than a less specific rule and a higher-ranked rule will be the style shown to the end user. We will look at cascade and specificity later in this chapter:

CSS Rule Set

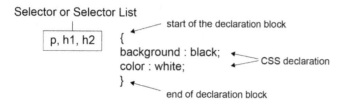

Figure: A CSS ruleset explained

Adding styles to a web page

There are several ways we can add CSS to a web page:

Via an element's style attribute (inline styles)
With a style element in the head or body of the HTML document
By linking an external style sheet to the HTML document with a link element

Each of these methods has pros and cons. Inline styles apply only to that element and have high specificity but we can't access pseudo-classes and pseudo-elements this way. They can make maintenance and updates time-consuming. Both the link and style elements provide greater separation of concerns, keeping the CSS separated from the HTML, which can be beneficial for organization and maintaining a clean code base. We will try out each of these methods in the following exercises.

Exercise– adding styles

In this exercise, we will add styles to a web page using the link element, the style element, and the style attribute.

Here are the steps:

Let's start with a simple web page:

<!DOCTYPE html>

<html lang="en">

```html
<head>

<meta charset="utf-8">

<title>Adding styles</title>

</head>

<body>

<h1>Adding styles</h1>

<p>First paragraph</p>

<p>Second paragraph</p>

</body>

</html>
```

Before adding any styles, the web page will look like this:

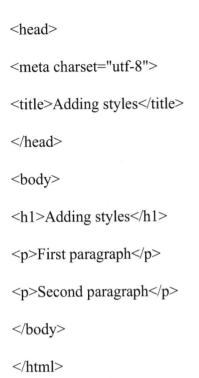

Figure: The unstyled web page

We'll make the text more readable by creating an external CSS file that we can link to our web page. To do that we save a file named styles.css in the chapter folder.

Add the following CSS to styles.css:

```css
body {

font-family: Arial, Helvetica, sans-serif;

font-size: 18px;

padding: 0;
```

```
margin: 1rem;

}

h1 {

margin: 0;

margin-bottom: 1rem;

}

p {

margin: 0;

margin-bottom: .5rem;

}
```

Next, we need to link the file to the web page. We do this with a link element added to the tag <head> of the web page beneath the tag <title>:

```
<link href="styles.css" rel="stylesheet">
```
Using a style element, added just before the end tag of body, we can set a different color for all paragraph elements:

```
<style>

p {

color: red;

}

</style>
```

The result will look similar to the following figure, with all paragraphs colored red:

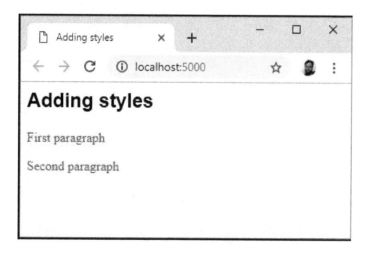

Figure: The web page with styles applied

Finally, we will give the first paragraph a different style using an inline style attribute, setting the color to blue and adding a line-through text decoration as follows:

First paragraph

The result will be like the one shown in the following figure:

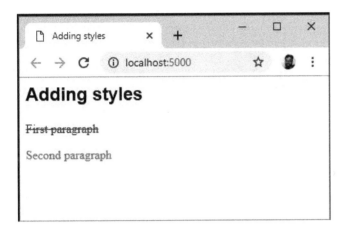

Figure: The web page with inline style applied

We've looked at how we can add styles to a web page. In the next section, we will look at the different CSS selectors we can use to apply our styles to parts of the HTML document.

CSS selectors

To target elements in the HTML document with CSS, we use selectors. There are a lot of options available to help you select a wide range of elements or very specific elements in certain states.
Selectors are a powerful tool and we will look at them in some detail as the different options available can help with both web page performance and making your CSS more maintainable.
For example, you can use a selector to target the first letter of a heading, like you might expect to see in a medieval book:

h1::first-letter {

font-size: 5rem;

}

Or, you could use a selector to invert the colors of every odd paragraph in an article:

p {

color: white;

```
background-color: black;

}

p:nth-of-type(odd) {

color: black;

background-color: white;

}

p {

color: white;

background-color: black;

}

p:nth-of-type(odd) {

color: black;

background-color: white;

}
```

We will explore a variety of the options available to us when creating selectors.

Element, ID, and class

Three commonly used selectors are as follows:

Element type: For example, to select all p elements in an HTML document, we use the p selector in a CSS ruleset. Other examples are h1, ul, and div.

A class attribute: The class selector starts with a dot. For example, given the <h1 class="heading">Heading</h1> HTML snippet, you could target that element with the. heading selector. Other examples are. post and. sub-heading.

An ID attribute: The id selector starts with a hash symbol. For example, given the <div id="login"> <!-- login content --> </div> HTML snippet, you could target this element with the #login selector. Other examples include #page-footer and #site-logo.

The universal selector (*)

To select all elements throughout an HTML document, you can use the universal selector, which is the asterisk symbol (*). Here is an example snippet of CSS that is often added to web pages; a value is set on the html element and then inherited by all descendant elements:

```
html {

box-sizing: border-box;

}

*, *:before, *:after {

box-sizing: inherit;

}
```

Using the inherit keyword and the universal selector, we can pass a value on to all the descendants of the html element. This snippet will universally apply the border-box model to all elements and their pseudo-elements (that's the reason for :before and :after). You'll learn more about the box model and layout in the next chapter.

Attribute selectors

Attribute selectors let you select elements based on the presence of an attribute or based on the value of an attribute. The syntax is square brackets, [], with the suitable attribute inside. There are several variations that you can use to make matches:

[attribute] will select all elements with an attribute present; for example, [href] will select all elements with an href attribute.

[attribute=value] will select all elements with an attribute with an exact value; for example, [lang="en"] will select all elements with a lang attribute set to en.

[attribute^=value] will select all elements with an attribute with a value that begins with the matching value; for example, [href^="https://"] will select all elements with an href attribute beginning with https://, which links to a secure URL.

[attribute$=value] will select elements with an attribute with a value that ends with the matching value; for example, [href$=".com"] will select all elements with an href attribute that ends with .com.

[attribute*=value] will select elements with an attribute with a value that has a match somewhere in the string; for example, [href*="co.uk"] will select all elements with an href attribute matching.co.uk. http://www.example.co.uk?test=true would be a match, as would https://www.example.co.uk.

Pseudo-classes

To select an element when it is in a particular state, we have several pseudo-classes defined. The syntax of a pseudo-class is a colon, :, followed by a keyword.
There are a great number of pseudo-classes, but most developers' first experience of them is when styling links. A link has several states associated with it:

When an anchor element has an href attribute, it will have the :link pseudo-class applied to it
When a user hovers over the link, the :hover pseudo-class is applied to it

When the link has been visited, it has the :visited pseudo-class applied to it

When the link is being clicked, it has the :active pseudo-class applied to it

Here is an example of applying styling to the various pseudo-class states of an anchor element:

a:link, a:visited {

color: deepskyblue;

text-decoration: none;

}

a:hover, a:active {

color: hotpink;

text-decoration: dashed underline;

}

In the following figure, we can see the first link with the :link or :visited styles applied and the second link with the :hover or :active styles applied:

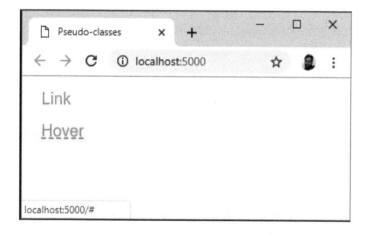

Figure: Link with and without the hover state

The cascade can cause some issues with styling links. The order in which you specify your CSS rules for each state of the link is important. If, for example, we applied the a:hover rule before the a:link rule in the previous example, we would not see the hover effect. A mnemonic exists for remembering the order: love-hate. The l is for :link, the v is for :visited, the h is for :hover, and the a is for :active.

Some other useful pseudo-classes for selecting elements in a particular interactive state include: checked, :disabled, and :focus.

Several pseudo-classes help us select a pattern of children nested under an element. These include :first-child, :last-child, :nth-child, :nth-last-child, :first-of-type, :last-of-type, :nth-of-type, and :nth-last-of-type.

For example, we can use :nth-child with an unordered list to give a different style to list items based on their position in the list:

```
<style>

ul {

font-family: Arial, Helvetica, sans-serif;

margin: 0;

padding: 0;

}

li {

display: block;

padding: 16px;

}

li:nth-child(3n-1) {

background: skyblue;

color: white;

font-weight: bold;
}

li:nth-child(3n) {

background: deepskyblue;

color: white;

font-weight: bolder;

}

</style>

<!-- unordered list in HTML document -->

<ul>

<li>Item 1</li>

<li>Item 2</li>
```

```
<li>Item 3</li>

<li>Item 4</li>

<li>Item 5</li>

<li>Item 6</li>

<li>Item 7</li>

</ul>
```

The following figure shows the result. The :nth-child pseudo-class gives you a lot of flexibility because you can use keywords such as odd and even or functional notation such as 3n - 1:

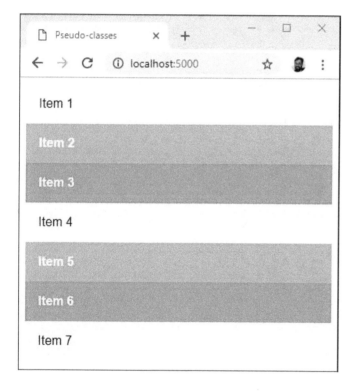

Figure: Using the :nth-child pseudo-class

Pseudo-elements

Pseudo-element selectors are preceded by two colons (::) and they are used to select part of an element. The available pseudo-elements include ::after, ::before, ::first-letter, ::first-line, ::selection, and ::backdrop. These pseudo-elements give us a handle we can use to add stylistic elements without adding to the HTML document. This can be a good thing if the pseudo-element has no semantic value and is purely presentational, but it should be used with care.

Combining selectors

What makes CSS selectors particularly powerful is that we can combine them in several ways to refine our selections. For example, we can select a subset of li elements in an HTML document that also has a .primary class selector with li.primary.

We also have several options, sometimes called combinators, for making selections based on the relationships of elements:

To select all the li elements that are descendants of an ul element, we could use ul li.
To select all the li elements that are direct children of an ul element with the primary class, we might use ul.primary > li. This would select only the direct children of ul.primary and not any li elements that are nested.
To select a li element that is the next sibling of li elements with the selected class, we could use li.selected + li.
To select all of the li elements that are the next siblings of li elements with the selected class, we could use li.selected ~ li.

The following figure shows the difference between using li.selected + li and li.selected ~ li. In other words, the difference between the following two CSS declarations is applied to a list where the fourth list item has a .selected class applied to it:

li.selected + li {

background: deepskyblue;

color: white;

font-weight: bolder;

}

li.selected ~ li {

background: deepskyblue;

color: white;
font-weight: bolder;

}

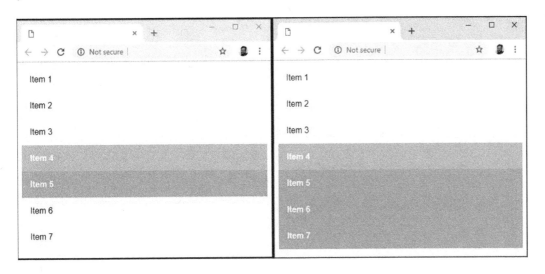

Figure: Selecting the next adjacent sibling compared to selecting all of the next siblings Let's try out some of the selectors we've learned about in an exercise.

Exercise– selecting elements

In this exercise, we will differentiate list items by styling the odd items. We will use a class selector to style a selected item and a next-siblings combinator to style the elements after the selected item.

The steps are as follows:
We will start with a simple web page with a ul list element and nine list items:

```
<!DOCTYPE html>

<html lang="en">

<head>

<meta charset="utf-8">

<title>Selectors</title>

</head>
<body>

<ul>

<li>Item 1</li>

<li>Item 2</li>

<li>Item 3</li>

<li>Item 4</li>

<li>Item 5</li>

<li>Item 6</li>

<li>Item 7</li>
<li>Item 8</li>

<li>Item 9</li>

</ul>

</body>

</html>
```

So that we can style a selected item differently, we will add a selected class to the fifth list item:

```
<li class="selected">Item 5</li>
```

Next, we will add a style element to the head element with the following CSS:

```
<head>

<meta charset="utf-8">

<title>Selectors</title>

<style>

ul {

font-family: Arial,

Helvetica, sans-serif;

margin: 0;

padding: 0;

}

li {

display: block;

padding: 16px;

}

</style>

</head>
```

This will remove some of the default styling of the unordered list in the browser. It will remove margins and padding on the list and set the font style to Arial (with Helvetica and sans-serif as a fallback).
Next, we will style the odd list items with the :nth-child pseudo-class. We can use the odd keyword for this. With this style, any odd list item will have a blue background and white text:

```
li:nth-child(odd) {

background-color: deepskyblue;

color: white;

font-weight: bold;
```

}

This gives us the stripy effect that we can see in the following figure:

Item 1

Item 2

Item 3

Item 4

Item 5

Item 6

Item 7

Item 8

Item 9

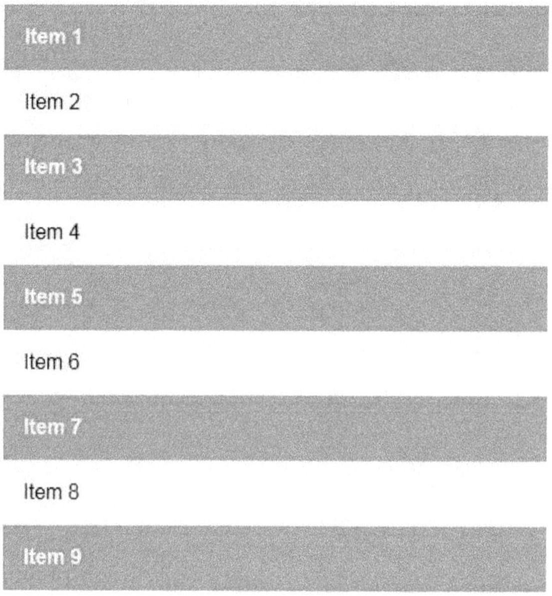

Figure: Stripy list using :nth-child(odd)

We can style the selected class selector:

li.selected {

background-color: hotpink;

}

This overrides the striped effect for those items with the selected class selector, as seen in the following figure:

Item 1

Item 2

Item 3

Item 4

Item 5

Item 6

Item 7

Item 8

Item 9

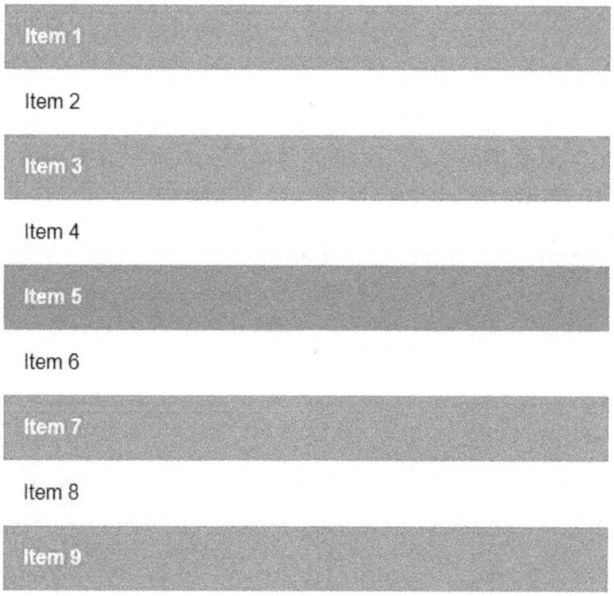

Figure: Stripy list with a selected item

Finally, we will style all of the odd-numbered list items after the selected item using the all-next-siblings combinator. In this case, the list items numbered 7 and 9 will have an orange background because they are the odd-numbered list items that are also siblings after the selected item (the list item numbered 5):

li.selected ~ li:nth-child(odd) {

background-color: orange;

}

The result is seen in the following figure:

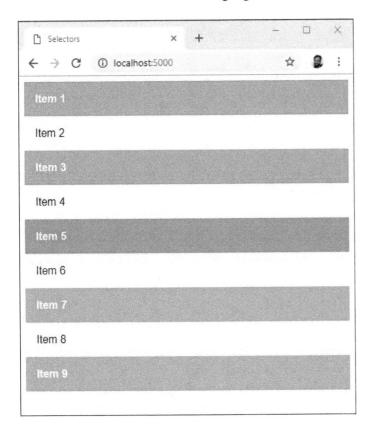

Figure: Combining selectors to style a list

Style sheets can have a large number of style rules and combinations of selectors. It is good to understand why one rule takes precedence over another one. This is where CSS specificity comes in.

CSS specificity

If we have two CSS declarations that affect the same style property of an element, how do we know which of those declarations will take precedence?
Several factors decide the ranking of a CSS declaration and whether it is the style the browser will apply. The term for these factors is specificity.

A style attribute that adds inline styles to an element has the highest specificity value. An ID selector has a greater specificity value than a class selector and a class selector or attribute selector has a greater specificity value than an element type. We can calculate the specificity value by giving points to each of these specificity values.

The most common way of representing this is as a comma-separated list of integers, where the leftmost integer represents the highest specificity. In other words, the leftmost value is the inline style attribute; next is an ID selector; next is a class selector, pseudo-class, or attribute selector; and the rightmost value is an element.

An inline style would have the 1, 0, 0, 0 value. An ID selector would have the 0, 1, 0, 0 value. A class selector would have the 0, 0, 1, 0 value, and an h1 selector would have the 0, 0, 0, 1 value.

Let's look at a few examples with more complex selectors:

li.selected a[href] has two element selectors (li and a), a class selector (.selected), and an attribute selector ([href]), so its specificity value would be 0, 0, 2, 2:

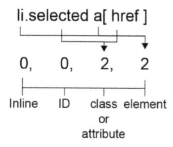

Figure: Calculating the specificity of li.selected a[href]

#newItem #mainHeading span.smallPrint has two ID selectors, a class selector (.smallPrint), and a span element, so its specificity value would be 0, 2, 1, 1:

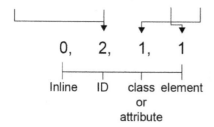

Figure: Calculating the specificity of #newItem #mainHeading span.smallPrint

Comparing the two selectors, we can see that the selector in the second example is more specific than the selector in the first example.

The special case of !important

The !important keyword can be appended to the value of any CSS declaration. It sets the specificity of that rule to have a special value of 1, 0, 0, 0, 0, which will give it precedence over any style including inline styles.

As an example of where it can be useful, we might want to create a style rule that is reusable and lets us hide content on a web page. If we apply this class to an element, we want that element to be hidden and not be rendered on the web page. However, consider the following example:

```
<style>

div.media {

display: block;

width: 100%;

float: left;

}

.hide {

display: none;

}

</style>

<div class="media hide">

...Some content

</div>
```

We might expect our div element to be hidden because the .hide class appears second in the style sheet. However, if we apply the specificity calculations we've learned about, we can see that div. media scores 0, 0, 1, 1, and .hide only scores 0, 0, 1, 0. The div.media rule for the display property with a block value will override the none value of the .hide class. We can't really use this instance of the .hide class as we don't know whether it will have any effect.

Now, consider the same .hide class but using the !important keyword:

Adding the !important keyword will make this .hide class much more reusable and useful as we can pretty much guarantee that it will hide content as we desire.

CSS custom properties

A relatively new addition to CSS, CSS custom properties (often called CSS variables) allow you to store a value with a name and reuse that value in multiple different CSS rules.

A CSS variable is defined as a name and a value inside a CSS ruleset. The name is prefixed with a double hyphen, --. The value can be any valid CSS value. The selector part of the ruleset will specify the scope of the variable. The :root selector is often used to define variables for the whole document but the scope could be targeted to a specific part of the document.

When applying a CSS variable we use the var() function. An optional fallback value can be given for cases where the variable has not been set.

For example, we could set a --color-primary variable with the color hex value of #FC9C9C on the :root of the document and then later access that variable to set the color of all paragraphs in the document:

```
:root {

--color-primary: #FC9C9C;

}

p {

color: var(--color-primary, #FF0000);

}
```

The benefit of storing a value as a variable is that you can provide a semantic name for a variable and have that used in many different places keeping, for example, the colors for a theme consistent, more maintainable, and easier to update in the future.

We've learned a lot about the syntax and fundamentals of CSS in this chapter. Let's apply some of this knowledge to an activity.

Activity– styling the video store template page

In the previous activity, we were tasked with creating boilerplate HTML for a web page for the Films on Demand website. In this activity, we are going to add some style to that template page.
The steps are as follows:

We will start with the template from Activity, which we will save as template.html:

```
<!DOCTYPE html>

<html lang="en">

<head>

<meta charset="utf-8">

<title>

Films on Demand –

<!-- Title for page goes here -->

</title>

<meta name="description"

content="Buy films from our great

selection. Watch movies on
```

demand.">

<meta name="viewport"

content="width=device-width,

initial-scale=1">

</head>

<body>

<h1>Lorem ipsum</h1>

<p>

Lorem ipsum dolor sit amet, consectetur

adipiscing elit. Nullam quis scelerisque

mauris. Curabitur aliquam ligula in erat

placerat finibus. Mauris leo neque,

malesuada et augue at, consectetur rhoncus

libero. Suspendisse vitae dictum dolor.

Vestibulum hendrerit iaculis ipsum, ac

ornare ligula. Vestibulum efficitur mattis

urna vitae ultrices. Nunc condimentum

blandit tellus ut mattis. Morbi eget

gravida leo. Mauris ornare lorem a mattis

ultricies. Nullam convallis tincidunt

nunc, eget rhoncus nulla tincidunt sed.

Nulla consequat tellus lectus, in porta

nulla facilisis eu. Donec bibendum nisi

felis, sit amet cursus nisl suscipit ut.

Pellentesque bibendum id libero at cursus.

Donec ac viverra tellus. Proin sed dolor

quis justo convallis auctor sit amet nec

orci. Orci varius natoque penatibus et
The special case of !important
magnis dis parturient montes, nascetur

ridiculus mus.

</p>

</body>

</html>

The special case of !important

magnis dis parturient montes, nascetur

ridiculus mus.

</p>

</body>

</html>

We are going to link to an external CSS file. One of the difficulties with styling web pages is handling differences between browsers. We are going to do this by adding a file to normalize our default styles. We will use the open source normalize.css for this. Download the file from https://packt.link/kBTXT. Add the file to a styles folder and link to it from the template.html web page.

We are going to add a style element to the head element of template.html. In the style element, we want to set some styles used across all pages. We want to do the following:

We want to set box-sizing to border-box for all elements using the universal selector (*).
We want to add a font family with the Arial, Helvetica, and sans-serif values and a font size of 16 px to the whole page.

We want to add the #eeeae4 background color for the whole page. To do this, we will add a div element wrapper with the pageWrapper ID, where we will set the background color and padding to 16 px, and a full-page class, where we will set the minimum height to 100 vh (100% of the viewport height).

We want to add an h1 element selector that sets margin to 0 and adds padding of 16 px to the bottom of the h1 element.

In this section, we have used CSS to add color and style to a web page. We have looked at the syntax of CSS and learned how we can use CSS selectors to apply style rules to specific parts of a web page. We have also learned a way to calculate the specificity of CSS rules and we have learned about CSS custom properties and how these can help make code more maintainable and understandable.

Conclusion: Mastering HTML and CSS

The journey through the fundamentals of HTML (HyperText Markup Language) and CSS (Cascading Style Sheets) is both exciting and indispensable for anyone venturing into the world of web development. As the cornerstone of the internet, these technologies continue to evolve, making them more powerful, user-friendly, and accessible than ever before. By mastering HTML and CSS, developers can create stunning, responsive, and engaging websites that cater to the diverse needs of modern users.

HTML: The Structure of the Web

HTML is the skeleton of every web page. It provides the structure and meaning to the content displayed in browsers. In 2025, advancements in HTML5 have solidified its role as the foundation for modern web applications. With semantic elements like <header>, <footer>, <article>, and <section>, HTML5 not only enhances accessibility but also improves SEO (Search Engine Optimization) by helping search engines better understand the context of content.

HTML's adaptability extends to multimedia, offering built-in support for audio (<audio>) and video (<video>) without relying on external plugins. Combined with attributes like controls, autoplay, and muted, developers can effortlessly integrate dynamic content into web pages.

Moreover, forms in HTML have been revolutionized. Attributes like required, placeholder, and pattern simplify data validation, while input types such as email, date, and range improve user interaction. These features contribute to a more intuitive and engaging experience for both developers and end-users.

CSS: Bringing Design to Life

CSS breathes life into the structure created by HTML. It controls the visual presentation, enabling developers to transform static pages into aesthetically pleasing and interactive interfaces. In 2025, CSS is more versatile than ever, with features like CSS Grid and Flexbox redefining layout design.

CSS Grid offers a two-dimensional system, making complex layouts like grids, carousels, and galleries easy to implement. Flexbox, on the other hand, excels in single-axis alignment, ensuring elements are distributed evenly and resized dynamically based on available space. Together, these tools empower developers to craft responsive designs that work seamlessly across devices.

Modern CSS also includes powerful selectors, pseudo-classes, and pseudo-elements that streamline styling. Variables (--variable-name) enhance code reusability, while features like media queries and container queries adapt designs to varying screen sizes, making mobile-first design an industry standard.

Additionally, CSS transitions, animations, and transforms have introduced a dynamic dimension to web pages. From hover effects to intricate animations, CSS allows developers to engage users through visually appealing interactions.

The Role of Frameworks and Preprocessors

Frameworks like Bootstrap and Foundation have made CSS more accessible, offering pre-designed components and responsive grid systems. Meanwhile, preprocessors such as Sass and LESS extend CSS's capabilities by introducing variables, nested rules, and mixins, simplifying complex projects. These tools enhance productivity, making them indispensable for professional web developers.

Accessibility and Best Practices

Building accessible websites is no longer optional; it is a legal and ethical imperative. By combining semantic HTML with CSS best practices, developers can create inclusive web experiences. Techniques like ARIA (Accessible Rich Internet Applications), proper color contrast ratios, and keyboard-friendly navigation ensure websites cater to users of all abilities.

Best practices also include writing clean, maintainable code. Using external stylesheets, adhering to naming conventions (like BEM methodology), and optimizing for performance (e.g., minimizing CSS files) contribute to efficient and scalable development.

HTML and CSS in Modern Web Development

In 2025, the synergy between HTML, CSS, and other technologies is stronger than ever. The integration of HTML and CSS with JavaScript powers frameworks like React, Vue, and Angular, enabling the development of highly interactive single-page applications (SPAs). Additionally, tools like Tailwind CSS, which prioritize utility-first design, have gained popularity for their flexibility and speed.

The rise of JAMstack (JavaScript, APIs, and Markup) further underscores the importance of mastering HTML and CSS. Static site generators like Gatsby and Next.js leverage these technologies to build lightning-fast websites. Meanwhile, headless CMS platforms provide the content flexibility required for modern applications.

The Future of HTML and CSS

Looking ahead, HTML and CSS will continue to adapt to emerging trends. As web browsers become more sophisticated, new features like sub grid support in CSS Grid and enhanced form capabilities in HTML will further streamline development. The ongoing focus on performance, security, and accessibility ensures that these technologies remain at the forefront of web innovation.

Final Thoughts

Mastering HTML and CSS is an investment in your future as a web developer. These technologies form the foundation of the digital world, influencing everything from personal blogs to enterprise-level applications. By understanding their principles, embracing best practices, and staying updated with advancements, you can unlock endless possibilities in the realm of web development.

Whether you're a beginner taking your first steps or an experienced developer refining your skills, HTML and CSS offer a wealth of opportunities to create, innovate, and make a lasting impact on the web. The knowledge gained today will empower you to shape the future of digital experiences, one line of code at a time.

In conclusion, HTML and CSS are more than just technologies; they are the art and science behind the web. As we move forward into 2025 and beyond, let your journey with HTML and CSS be a testament to the boundless potential of creativity and innovation in web development.

2. Structure and Layout

Introduction

The structure and layout of a webpage form the foundation of web design and development. This introduction to HTML and CSS explores how these two technologies work in tandem to create visually appealing, functional, and accessible web pages. By the end of this guide, you'll understand the roles of HTML (HyperText Markup Language) and CSS (Cascading Style Sheets) and how to effectively use them to design structured and well-laid-out web pages.

1. What is HTML?

HTML (HyperText Markup Language) is the backbone of any webpage. It provides the structure and content for web pages by using a system of elements and tags. These tags define how content like headings, paragraphs, images, and links are displayed in a browser.

Key Features of HTML:

Elements and Tags:

Tags like <h1> for headings, <p> for paragraphs, and <a> for links structure the content.
Elements are represented as opening (<tag>) and closing (</tag>).

Attributes:

Tags can have attributes to provide additional information.
Example: <a href="https://example.com">Visit Example</a> (the href attribute specifies the link destination).

Semantic HTML:

Introduces tags like <header>, <footer>, <article>, and <section> for meaningful page structure.

Multimedia Support:

HTML supports images (<img>), videos (<video>), and audio (<audio>).

Example:

```
<!DOCTYPE html>
<html lang="en">
<head>
  <title>Introduction to HTML</title>
</head>
<body>
  <header>
    <h1>Welcome to HTML and CSS</h1>
  </header>
  <section>
    <p>This is an example of HTML structure.</p>
```

```
   </section>
   <footer>
    <p>&copy; 2025 Web Design 101</p>
   </footer>
 </body>
</html>
```

2. What is CSS?

CSS (Cascading Style Sheets) is a styling language used to control the visual presentation of HTML elements. It defines how elements appear, including their color, size, spacing, and position.

Key Features of CSS:

Selectors and Properties:

Selectors target HTML elements, and properties define their styles.
Example: h1 { color: blue; }

Types of CSS:

Inline CSS: Applied directly within an HTML element using the style attribute.
Internal CSS: Defined within a <style> tag in the <head> section.
External CSS: Stored in a separate file with a .css extension.

Cascading and Inheritance:

Styles cascade from top to bottom, with the most specific styles overriding others.
Some styles are inherited by child elements (e.g., text color).

Responsive Design:

CSS allows developers to create layouts that adapt to different screen sizes using techniques like media queries.

Example:

```
/* External CSS */
body {
  font-family: Arial, sans-serif;
  line-height: 1.6;
  margin: 0;
  padding: 0;
}
h1 {
  color: darkblue;
  text-align: center;
}
p {
  color: gray;
}
```

3. The Role of Structure in Web Design

The structure of a webpage, defined by HTML, ensures that content is organized and accessible. A well-structured page:

Improves Accessibility:

Semantic HTML helps screen readers and assistive technologies interpret the page.

Enhances SEO:

Proper use of headings, alt attributes, and meta tags improves search engine rankings.

Provides a Clear Hierarchy:

Organizing content with headings, lists, and sections creates a logical flow.

Common Structural Tags:

<header>: Contains introductory content or navigation links.
<nav>: Defines navigation links.
<main>: Represents the main content of the document.
<aside>: Contains supplementary content, like sidebars.
<footer>: Defines footer content, such as copyright information.

4. The Role of Layout in Web Design

The layout, defined by CSS, determines how content is visually arranged. A well-designed layout:

Guides User Interaction:

Visual hierarchy directs users to important elements.

Improves Aesthetics:

Proper spacing, alignment, and color schemes enhance visual appeal.

Ensures Responsiveness:

Adaptive layouts ensure usability on various devices.

CSS Techniques for Layout:

Box Model:

Every HTML element is treated as a rectangular box with properties for content, padding, border, and margin.

Flexbox:

A layout model for creating responsive and flexible layouts.

Example:
.container {
  display: flex;
  justify-content: center;
  align-items: center;
}

Grid Layout:

A two-dimensional layout system for creating grid-based designs.

Example:
.grid {
  display: grid;
  grid-template-columns: repeat(3, 1fr);
  gap: 10px;
}

Media Queries:

Used for responsive design by applying styles based on screen size.

Example:
@media (max-width: 600px) {
  body {
    font-size: 14px;
  }
}

5. Building a Simple Webpage

Below is a demonstration of a basic webpage with HTML structure and CSS layout:

HTML:

```
<!DOCTYPE html>
<html lang="en">
<head>
  <meta charset="UTF-8">
  <meta name="viewport" content="width=device-width, initial-scale=1.0">
  <link rel="stylesheet" href="styles.css">
  <title>My First Webpage</title>
</head>
<body>
  <header>
    <h1>Welcome to My Website</h1>
    <nav>
      <ul>
        <li><a href="#home">Home</a></li>
```

```html
      <li><a href="#about">About</a></li>
      <li><a href="#contact">Contact</a></li>
    </ul>
  </nav>
</header>
<main>
  <section id="home">
    <h2>Home</h2>
    <p>This is the home section.</p>
  </section>
  <section id="about">
    <h2>About</h2>
    <p>This is the about section.</p>
  </section>
</main>
<footer>
  <p>&copy; 2025 My Website</p>
</footer>
</body>
</html>
```

CSS:

```css
body {
  font-family: Arial, sans-serif;
  margin: 0;
  padding: 0;
  line-height: 1.6;
}
header {
  background: #333;
  color: #fff;
  padding: 10px 0;
  text-align: center;
}
nav ul {
  list-style: none;
  padding: 0;
}
nav ul li {
  display: inline;
  margin: 0 10px;
}
nav ul li a {
  color: #fff;
  text-decoration: none;
}
main {
  padding: 20px;
}
footer {
```

```
    text-align: center;
    background: #333;
    color: #fff;
    padding: 10px 0;
}
```

In the previous chapter, we learned about the basics of HTML and CSS. In this chapter, we will consolidate this basic understanding and look at how web pages are structured with HTML and CSS. When creating web pages using HTML, it is imperative that you use the correct elements. This is because HTML is read by both humans and machines, and so the content of a web page should be associated with the most appropriate element. Additionally, any error in the code might be difficult to track if the code base is too large.

The HTML language offers a vast array of different tags that we can place at our disposal. In this chapter, we will focus on the structural elements that are used to divide the web page up into its key parts. You may be familiar with the concept of a page header or footer, and these would be examples of structural elements. We will be looking at these amongst many other HTML structural elements.

In this chapter, we will focus our attention on the **HTML5** version of the language, which is the most current version of HTML. HTML5 offers us additional tags that enable us to make our markup more meaningful. The developer experience is more enjoyable compared to writing **XHTML** as the HTML5 language is less strict with regard to syntax.

Web pages are typically styled using CSS. Once we have our web pages marked up correctly, we need to know how to style these into a range of layouts. CSS offers us a range of options for laying out our pages, but the three most common methods are **float**, **flex**, and **grid**-based. In this chapter, we will explore each of these techniques in turn.

Just knowing the various layout methods is not enough to style web pages. We will investigate the box model, which is foundational to understanding how HTML elements are styled. We will break this down into the individual layers – **content box**, **padding**, **border**, and **margin**. With this knowledge in hand, you will be free to develop a host of different web page layouts.

We will now take a look at the structural elements provided by HTML and examine what the key elements are one by one.

Structural Elements

HTML5 provides us with a variety of tags that we can use when dividing our page into different parts. When browsing the web, you would have noticed that web pages typically have a few common things to them. For example, a web page will typically have a logo and page navigation area at the top of the page. We would call this area of the page the **header**. You may also have noticed that the bottom of the page may include a list of links and copyright information. We would call this area the **footer**. The following diagram shows the representation of a few of the main elements of a web page:

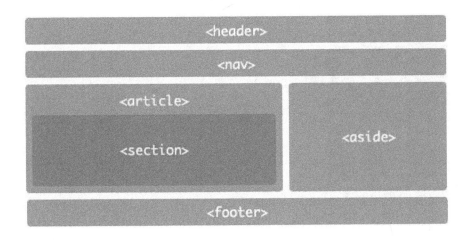

Figure: HTML5 page elements

In this topic, we will be looking at the following HTML5 page elements:

header
footer
section
article
nav
aside
div

The header Tag

The **header** tag is used to describe the header or top area of a web page. Typically, inside this tag, you would have the page heading, a logo, and, possibly, the page navigation. Prior to HTML5, you would use a **div** tag with a class name so that the header could be styled, and its intention was clear to developers. HTML5 improves on this by giving us a tag specifically for this very task. You will learn more about this improvement under the section. Now, examine the following codes that show the differences between the old and new way of writing the markup for the **header** area:

```
<!-- old way -->
<div class="header">
   ... heading, logo, nav goes here
</div>
<!-- new way -->
<header>
   ... heading, logo, nav goes here
<header>
```

Now, let's open the Packt website at https://www.packtpub.com/ to see how a header is represented in an actual website. In the following diagram, you can see that the header element is highlighted via a box, illustrating where a header element is typically placed on a web page:

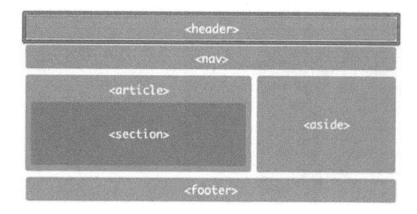

Figure: The header element

In the following figure, you can see that the header element is highlighted via a box. As this is an example taken from the Packt website, you will notice that it contains items such as the company logo, search bar, and the **Sign In** button:

Figure: The header element on the Packt site

The footer Tag

The **footer** tag is very similar to the **header** tag but is used at the bottom of a web page.
You would typically have the copyright information and website links inside the footer. Similarly, with the header tag in the previous version of HTML, you would use a **div** tag with a class name. Since the use of footers on web pages is so common, HTML5 provides a new tag solely for this purpose. The following codes show the differences between the old and new way of writing the markup for the **footer** area:

```
<!-- old way -->
<div class="footer">
  ... copyright, list of links go here
</div>
<!— new way -->
<footer>
  ... copyright, list of links go here
<footer>
```

In the following figure, you can see that the **footer** element is highlighted via a box, illustrating where a **footer** element is typically placed on a web page:

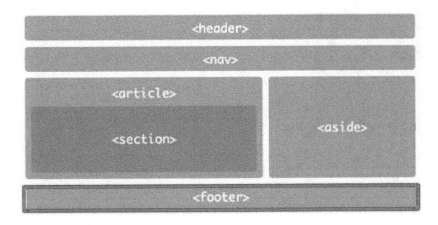

Figure: The footer element

In the following figure, you can see that the **footer** element is highlighted via a box. As this is an example taken from the Packt website, you will notice it contains items such as useful links and social media icons:

Figure: The footer element on Packt site

The section Tag

The **section** tag is different from the header and footer tags as it can be used in many different places on a web page. Some examples of when you would use a **section** tag could be for the main content area of a page or to group a list of related images together. You use this tag anytime you want to divide some of the markup into a logical section of the page. Again, prior to HTML5, you would most likely use a **div** tag with a class name to divide a section of the page. The following codes show the differences between the old and new way of writing the markup for the **section** area:

```
<!-- old way -->
<div class="main-content-section">
  ... main content
</div>
<!— new way -->
<section>
  ... main content
</section>
```

In the following figure, you can see that the section element is highlighted via a box, illustrating where a section element is typically placed on a web page:

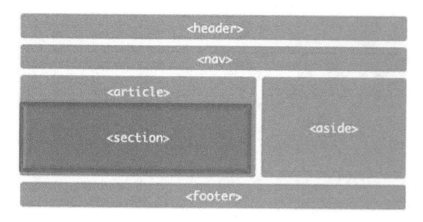

Figure: The section element

The article Tag

The **article** tag is used for the self-contained part of a web page. Some examples of an article could be an individual news article or blog post. You can have multiple articles on a page, but each must be self-contained and not dependent on any other context within the page. It is common to see the **article** tag used in conjunction with **section** tags to divide up an article into discrete sections. The following code shows this:

```
<article>
   <section>
    ...primary blog content
   </section>
   <section>
    ...secondary blog content
   </section>
</article>
```

In the following figure, you can see that the article element is highlighted via a box, illustrating where an article element is typically placed on a web page:

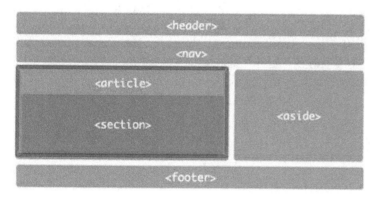

Figure: The article element

The nav Tag

Inside the navigation area, you will have a list of page links for the different pages of the website. Prior to HTML5, you would again use a **div** tag with a class name. The following codes show the differences between the old and new way of writing the markup for the navigation area:

```
<!-- old way -->
<div class="navigation">
   … list of links go here
</div>
<!-- new way -->
<navigation>
   … list of links go here
</navigation>
```

In the following figure, you can see that the **nav** element is highlighted via a box, illustrating where a **nav** element is typically placed on a web page:

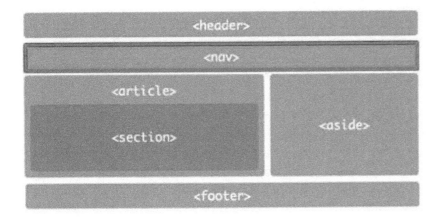

Figure: The nav element

In the following figure, you can see that the **nav** element is highlighted via a box. As this is an example taken from the Packt website, you will notice it contains a list of page links:

Figure: The nav element on the Packt site

The aside Tag

The **aside** tag is used to show content that is indirectly related to the main content of a document. You will typically see this tag used for sidebars or for showing notes relating to some content. Again, before the advent of HTML5, developers would use a **div** tag with a class name for this type of content. The following codes show the differences between the old and new way of writing the markup for the **aside** element:

```
<!-- old way -->
<div class="sidebar">
   … indirectly related content goes here
</div>
<!—new way -->
<aside>
   … indirectly related content goes here
</aside>
```

In the following figure, you can see that the aside element is highlighted via a box, illustrating where an aside element is typically placed on a web page:

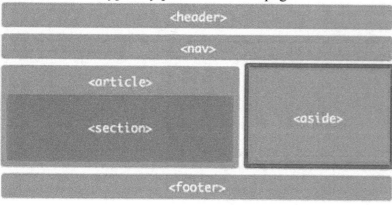

Figure: The aside element

The div Tag

The **div** tag is probably the most widely used tag on the World Wide Web. In fact, if you view the source code of your favourite website, most of the HTML elements you see will be **div** elements. This tag actually stands for division and is used to divide or group content together. Although HTML5 provides specialist elements for the most common types of page groups, you will still find many uses for using **div** tags. It might help to think of this element as a generic way to group the markup into logical parts. The following are a few example codes of how a **div** tag may be used:

<div class="sidebar">
 … indirectly related content goes here
</div>
<div class="navigation">
  <div class="navigation-inner">... navigation links go here</div>
</div>

That concludes our tour of the structural HTML elements that are important to us. We will now apply some of this theory with the help of an exercise.

A News Article Web Page

Now that we have an understanding of the structural elements provided by HTML5, let's put our newly acquired knowledge into practice by writing the structural HTML for a news article page. You can get a sense of what this type of page will look like by visiting a popular online news website.

Exercise: Marking up the Page

In this exercise, we will create the markup for our HTML5 page. Our aim will be to produce a page with output, similar to that of Figure without the <**section**> element in it.

Let's complete the exercise with the following steps:

Create a file named **news.html** in **VSCode**.
We will use the following starter HTML document, which contains some basic styling for our structural elements. Don't worry if you don't understand the CSS just yet; you will by the end of this book:

```
<!DOCTYPE html>
<html>
  <head>
    <title>News article page</title>
<style>    header,    nav,    article,    aside,    footer {    background: #659494;
border-radius: 5px;    color: white;    font-family: arial, san-serif;    font-size: 30px;
text-align: center;    padding: 30px;    margin-bottom: 20px;    }    header:before,
nav:before,    article:before,    aside:before,    footer:before {    content: '<';    }
header:after,    nav:after,    article:after,    aside:after, footer:after {    content: '>';    }
article {    float: left;    margin-right: 20px;    width: 60%;    }    aside {
float: left;
        width: calc(40% - 140px);    }    footer {    clear: both;    }
    </style>
  </head>
  <body>
    <!-- your code will go here -->
  </body>
</html>
```

First, let's add our first structural element, which is the **header** tag. We will place it in between the opening and closing body tags. In this example, we will just add some text as content but, when building a real web page, you would include things such as logos, search bars, and links:

```
<body>
  <header>header</header>
</body>
```

After our **header** tag comes the navigation area, which is used for including links to different pages of the website. Once again, we will just add some text for the content but, when building a real web page, you would include a list of links:

```
<body>
  <header>header</header>
  <nav>nav</nav>
</body>
```

For the main news article content, we will use an **article** tag. Once again, we will just add some text for the content but, when building a real web page, you would include the content of the articles:

```
<body>
  <header>header</header>
  <nav>nav</nav>
  <article>article</article>
</body>
```

To the right of the **article** tag, we have an **aside** tag, which will typically contain content such as advertising images or related content links:

```
<body>
  <header>header</header>
  <nav>nav</nav>
```

```
      <article>article</article>
      <aside>aside</aside>
</body>
```

Finally, we can finish off the markup for our web page by adding the **footer** tag at the bottom of the page. For now, we will just add some text as content but, in real life, you would include elements such as copyright information, and links to other pages:

```
<body>
      <header>header</header>
      <nav>nav</nav>
      <article>article</article>
      <aside>aside</aside>
      <footer>footer</footer>
</body>
```

If you now right-click on the filename in **VSCode** on the left-hand side of the screen and select **open in default browser**, you will see the following web page in your browser:

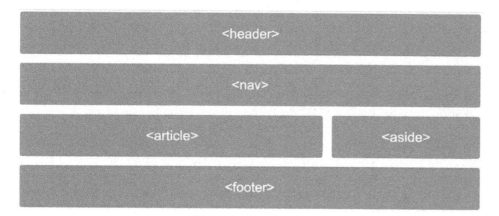

Figure: Output for the product page

If you look at this page in your browser, you may not be impressed with what you see, but you actually have the foundations in place for a web page.

Wireframes

When working on commercial projects, it is common for web page designs to be provided to web developers in the form of a wireframe. A wireframe is a low-fidelity design that provides enough information about a page for the developer to start coding. Usually, they will not include much visual design information and are focused on the main structure of a page. The following figure is an example of a wireframe for a new home page:

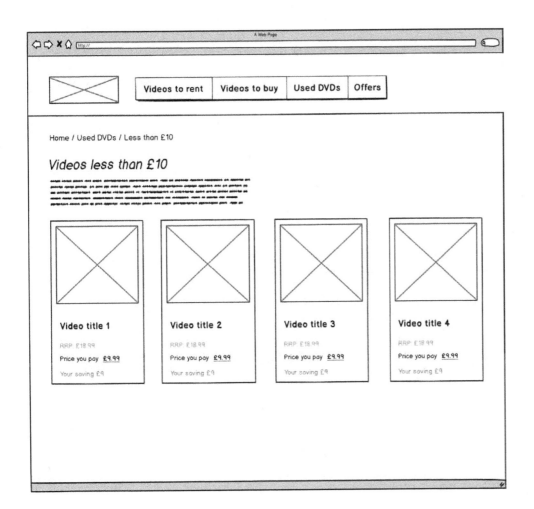

Figure: Example of a wireframe

Activity: Video Store Home Page

Suppose you are a frontend developer working for a tech start-up. You have been asked to build a home page for the online video store. You have been given the following wireframe from the UX designer:

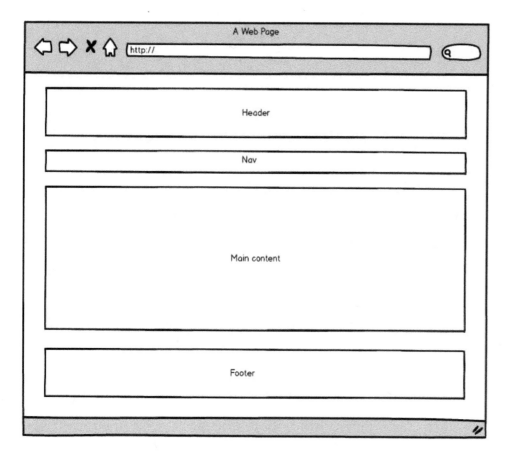

Figure: Wireframe as per the UX designer's expectation

Using your newly acquired HTML5 knowledge, you can start to convert the wireframe into working HTML code. At this stage, you should just be concerned with writing the structural HTML tags and shouldn't worry about content right now.

The aim will be to achieve a web page similar the following output screenshot:

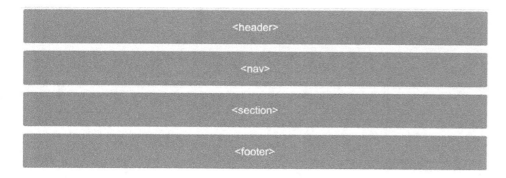

Figure: Expected output of video store home page

The steps are as follows:

Create a file named **home.html** in **VSCode**.
Use the following code as a page skeleton. Again, do not worry about not understanding the styling part of the code:

<!DOCTYPE html>

```html
<html>
  <head>
    <title>Video store home page</title>
    <style>      header,      nav,      section,      footer {      background: #659494;
border-radius: 5px;      color: white;      font-family: arial, san-serif;      font-size: 30px;
text-align: center;      padding: 30px;      margin-bottom: 20px;      }
      header:before,      nav:before,      section:before,      footer:before {
        content: '<';      }
      header:after,      nav:after,      section:after,      footer:after {      content: '>';      }
    </style>
  </head>
  <body>
<!-- your code will go here -->
  </body>
</html>
```

Start adding the HTML5 structural elements inside the **body** tag one by one.

Marking up the Page, we will just add the tag name for content such as **header** and **footer**.

If you now right-click on the filename in **VSCode** on the left-hand side of the screen and select **open in default browser**, you will see the web page in your browser.

Hopefully, you are now getting a feel for the process of putting basic web pages together. We will build on this knowledge in the coming exercises.

We are now ready to start making our web pages more realistic by learning some CSS page layout techniques.

CSS Page Layouts

CSS provides us with a range of possibilities for laying out web pages. We will be looking into the three most common techniques for laying out web pages. These are as follows:

float
flex
grid

Armed with this knowledge, combined with your knowledge of HTML structural tags, you will be able to code a range of web page layouts. The concepts learned in this part of the chapter will form the core of your frontend development skillset and you will use these techniques over and over throughout your career.

Video Store Product Page

In order to gain a solid understanding of how these three different approaches to layout work, we shall use a video store product listing page as a concrete example. We will work through solutions to the following design using the three most common layout techniques, one by one. For the examples that follow, we will only be concerned with the product section of the page:

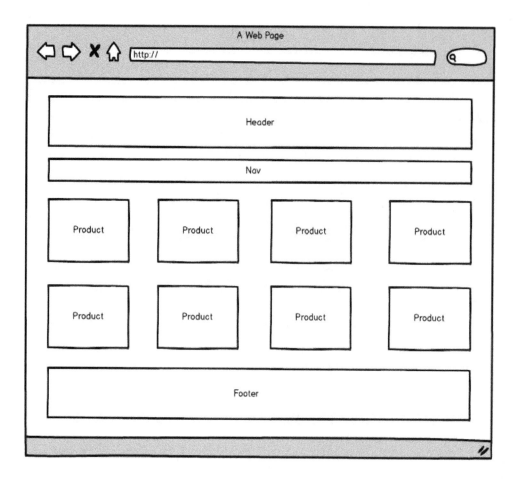

Figure: Product page wireframe

Float-Based Layouts

The **float**-based CSS layout technique is the oldest of the three. Whilst CSS provides us with improved techniques for layout, the **float**-based layout is still used today. Having a firm grasp of how **float**-based layouts work in practice will set you up for more advanced styling segments in this book.

The float Property

The CSS **float** property, when applied to an element, will place the element to either the left or right of its containing element. Let's examine a few examples of the most common values for this property.

To **float** elements to the right, you would use the **right** value, as shown in the following code:

float: right;

Whereas, to float elements to the left, you would use the **left** value, as shown in the following code:

float: left;

The **none** value isn't used as frequently but, with the following code, it can be handy if you wish to override either the left or right values:

float: none;

The width Property

When we apply the **float** property to elements, we typically will also want to give the element an explicit **width** value as well. We can either give a value in pixels or percentages. The following code shows the input for **width** in pixels, that is, by writing **px** after the value:
width: 100px;

Whereas the following code shows the input for **width** as a percentage, that is, by entering the **%** symbol after the value:
width: 25%;

Clearing Floated Elements

As the name suggests, floated elements do, in fact, appear to float in relation to the other non-floated elements on the page. A common issue with floated elements inside a container is illustrated in the following figure:

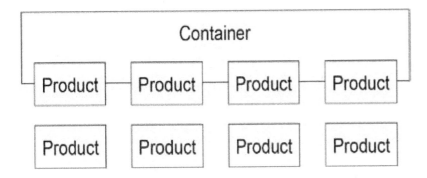

Figure: Floating elements' illustration

There are many solutions to this issue, but by far the easiest solution is to apply the following CSS to the containing element:

```
section {
  overflow: hidden;
}
```

With the preceding code added to the container, we will now have floated elements contained inside the wrapping element, as illustrated in the following figure:

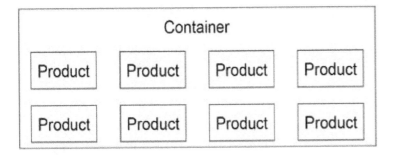

Figure: Cleared floats' illustration

The following example code shows how you could achieve the preceding layout using **float**:

```
<!-- HTML -->
<section>
  <div>product 1</div>
  <div>product 2</div>
  <div>product 3</div>
<div>product 4</div>
  <div>product 5</div>
  <div>product 6</div>
  <div>product 7</div>
  <div>product 8</div>
</section>
/* CSS */ section {
  overflow: hidden;
} div {
  float: left;   width: 25%;
}
```

Flex-Based Layouts

The **flex**-based CSS layout technique is a new and improved alternative to the **float**-based approach. With **flex**, we have much more flexibility and can easily achieve complex layouts with very little code. With **flex**, we no longer have to worry about clearing floating elements. We will now look into some of the key properties and values in order to let us build the product page layout using **flex**.

The flex Container

When developing **flex**-based layouts, there are two key concepts you must first understand. The first is the **flex** container, which is the element that contains the child elements. To activate a **flex** layout, we must first apply the following code to the container or parent element that holds the individual items:
display: flex;

We also have to choose how we want the container to handle the layout of the child elements. By default, all child elements will fit into one row. If we want the child elements to show on multiple rows, then we need to add the following code:
flex-wrap: wrap;

The flex Items

Now that we know how to set the **flex** container up, we can turn to the child elements.
The main issue of concern here is the need to specify the width of the child elements. To specify this, we need to add the following code:
flex-basis: 25%;

You can think of this as being equivalent to the width in our **float**-based example.
The following example code shows how you could achieve the product layout, as shown in Figure, using **flex**:

```
<!-- HTML -->
```

```
<section>
  <div>product 1</div>
  <div>product 2</div>
  <div>product 3</div>
  <div>product 4</div>
  <div>product 5</div>
  <div>product 6</div>
  <div>product 7</div>
  <div>product 8</div>
</section>
/* CSS */ section {   display: flex;
  flex-wrap: wrap;
} div {
  flex-basis: 25%;
}
```

Grid-Based Layouts

The **grid**-based CSS layout technique is the newest of the three different approaches we will be exploring. This new approach was introduced in order to simplify the page layout and offer developers even more flexibility vis-à-vis the previous two techniques. We will now look into some of the key properties and values to enable us to build the product page layout using a grid-based approach.

The grid Container

When developing **grid**-based layouts, there are two key concepts you must first understand. The first is the grid container, which is the element that contains the child elements. To activate a grid layout, we must first apply the following code to the parent element:
  display: grid;

Now that we have activated the container to use the **grid**-based layout, we need to specify the number, and sizes, of our columns in the grid. The following code would be used to have four equally spaced columns:
grid-template-columns: auto auto;

The grid Items

When we used **float** and **flex** layouts, we had to explicitly set the width of the child elements. With **grid**-based layouts, we no longer need to do this, at least for simple layouts.
We will now put our new-found knowledge into practice and build the product cards shown in Figure. We will use the grid layout technique since the product cards are actually within a **grid** layout, comprising four equally spaced columns.

Exercise: A grid-Based Layout

In this exercise, we will create our CSS page layout with the aim of producing a web page where six products are displayed as shown in the wireframe Figure.

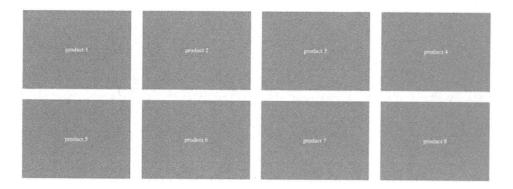

Figure: Expected output for the grid-based layout

Following are the steps to complete this exercise:

Let's begin with the following HTML skeleton and create a file called **grid.html** in **VSCode**. Don't worry if you do not understand the CSS used here; you will soon enough:

```
<!DOCTYPE html>
<html>
<head>
 <title>Grid based layout</title>
 <style type="text/css">   div {    background: #659494;    color: white;    text-align: center;
margin: 15px;    padding: 100px;    }
 </style>
</head>
<body>
</body>
</html>
```

Next, we will add the product items using **div** tags, which are placed inside a **section** tag. We will just add a product with a number inside each item, so we know what product each represents:

```
<body>
 <section>
  <div>product 1</div>
  <div>product 2</div>
  <div>product 3</div>
  <div>product 4</div>
  <div>product 5</div>
  <div>product 6</div>
  <div>product 7</div>
  <div>product 8</div>
 </section>
</body>
```

Now, let's add the following CSS in order to activate the **grid**-based layout. If you compare this to the other two techniques for laying out web pages, the code is very minimal:

```
section { display: grid;   grid-template-columns: auto auto auto auto; }
```

If you now right-click on the filename in **VSCode** on the left-hand side of the screen and select **open in default browser** you will see the web page in your browser repeat output for consistency.

If you now look at this page in your web browser, you should see a layout resembling the one shown in the screenshot.

We will now take a detour and look into some fundamental concepts of how CSS styles HTML elements.

The Box Model

So far, all the elements on our pages look almost identical because we have not learned how to adjust the size of each element. We are now ready to progress to more realistic page designs by introducing a foundational layout concept called the box model.

Try to picture each HTML element as a box made up of different layers. The different layers are the element's content box, padding, border, and margin. We will explore each of these layers one by one. The following figure illustrates how all aspects of the box model relate to one another. You can see that the margin is the outermost part, followed by the element's border and padding between the border and content area:

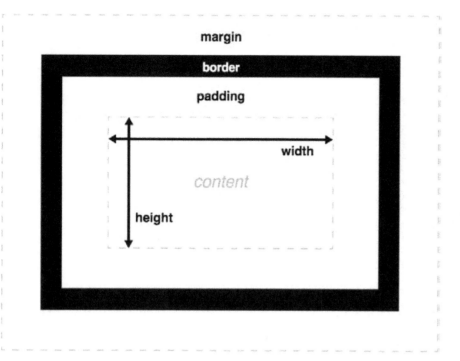

Figure: The box model

We will now look at each of the box model elements, in turn, starting with the innermost content box.

Content Box

The content box is the part of the element where the actual content lives. This is typically text but could contain other child elements or media elements such as images. The most important CSS properties for this layer are **width** and **height**. As a developer, you would typically give these values expressed in pixels or percentages. The following code shows some example values, followed by the corresponding output figure for these properties:

width: 200px; height: 100px;

In the following figure, we will see what the content area looks like after CSS is applied to the preceding code:

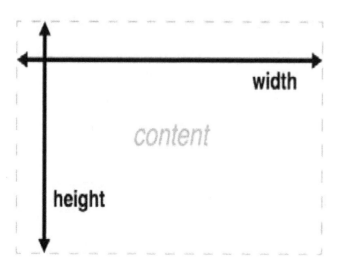

Figure: The content box

Next, we will work our way out to the next layer of the box model – padding.

The padding Property

The padding area is the layer that provides spacing between the content box and the border. The amount of spacing in this layer can be specified in all directions – top, right, bottom, and left. CSS provides a padding property where you can specify values for the amount of spacing in all directions. If you want to apply the same amount of **padding** in all directions, you can just give a single value. If you want to apply the same values for vertical and horizontal directions, you can specify two values. It also provides direction specific properties – **padding-top**, **padding-right**, **padding-bottom**, and **padding-left**. The following code shows a number of example values for these properties:

```
/* 50px of padding applied in all directions */ padding: 50px;
/* 50px of padding applied vertically and 0px applied horizontally */ padding: 50px 0;
/* 10px of padding applied to the top */ padding-top: 10px;
/* 10px of padding applied to the right */ padding-right: 10px;
/* 10px of padding applied to the bottom */ padding-bottom: 10px;
/* 10px of padding applied to the left */ padding-left: 10px;
```

The following figure illustrates what the **content** and **padding** areas would look like after CSS is applied to the following code:

width: 200px; height: 100px; padding: 25px;

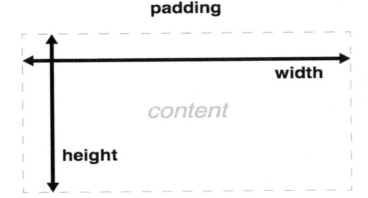

Figure: Padding

Now that we understand how the content and padding layers relate to one another, we will work our way out to the next layer of the box model – the border.

The border Property

The border area is the layer that sits between the end of the padding area and the beginning of the margin. By default, the border isn't visible; it can only be seen when you explicitly set a value that will allow you to see the border. Similar to the padding property, CSS provides a shorthand property called border, and also the direction specific properties – **border-top**, **border-right**, **border-bottom**, and **border-left**. All of these properties require three values to be provided; the **width** of the border, the **border** style, and finally, the color of the border. The following code shows some example values for these properties:

```
/* border styles applied in all directions */ border: 5px solid red;
/* border styles applied to the top */ border-top: 5px solid red;
/* border styles applied to the right */ border-right: 15px dotted green;
/* border styles applied to the bottom */
border-bottom: 10px dashed blue;
/* border styles applied to the left */ border-left: 10px double pink;
```

The following figure illustrates how the four different border styles would appear if applied to an element:

Figure: Border styles

The **content**, **padding**, and **border** layers is obtained with the following code:

width: 200px; height: 100px; padding: 25px; border: 10px solid black;

The following figure is the output for the preceding code:

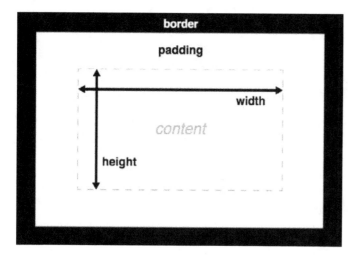

Figure: Border

Now that we understand how the content, **padding** and **margin** layers relate to one another, we will work our way out to the final layer of the box model – the **margin**.

The margin Property

The margin area is the layer that provides spacing between the edge of the border and out toward other elements on the page. The amount of spacing in this layer can be specified in all directions – top, right, bottom, and left. The CSS provides a margin property where you can specify values for the amount of spacing in all directions. It also provides direction-specific properties – **margin-top**, **margin-right**, **margin-bottom**, and **margin-left**. The following code shows a number of example values for these properties:
margin: 50px; margin: 50px 0; margin-top: 10px; margin-right: 10px; margin-bottom: 10px; margin-left: 10px;

The **content**, **padding**, **border**, and **margin** layers is obtained with the following code:
width: 200px; height: 100px; padding: 25px; border: 10px solid black; margin: 25px;

The following figure is the output for the preceding code:

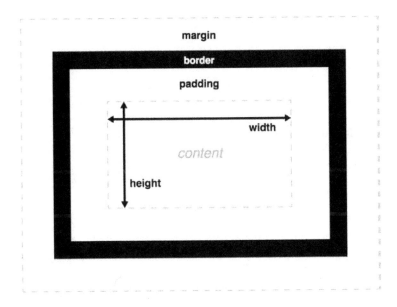

Figure: Margin

To get some practice looking at how different HTML elements make use of the box model, you can use the webtools inspector in your favourite browser. In Chrome, you can inspect an element and investigate how the box model is used for each element. If you inspect an element and then click the **Computed** tab on the right-hand side, you will see a detailed view. The following figure shows an example of an element from the Packt website revealing the values for properties from the box model:

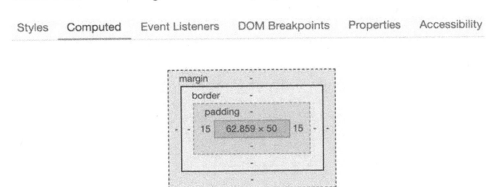

Figure: Chrome web tools box model inspection view

In the following exercise, we will play around with the different box model properties to get some practice with box model-related CSS properties.

Exercise: Experimenting with the Box Model

The aim of this exercise will be to create the three boxes as shown in the following output screenshot:

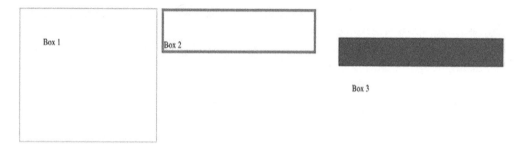

Figure: Expected boxes

The steps to complete the exercise are as follows:

1. First, let's add the following HTML skeleton to a file called **boxes.html** in **VSCode**:

```
<!DOCTYPE html>
<html>
<head>
  <title>Experimenting with the box model</title>
  <style type="text/css">
  </style>
</head>
<body>
  <div class="box-1">Box 1</div>
  <div class="box-2">Box 2</div>
  <div class="box-3">Box 3</div>
</body>
</html>
```

2. Now, let's add some CSS to the first box, observing the **width**, **height**, **padding**, and **border** properties we are adding. We will add the CSS in between the opening and closing style tags, as shown in the following code, to render the following figure:

```
<style type="text/css">
  .box-1 {   float: left;   width: 200px;   height: 200px;   padding: 50px;
    border: 1px solid red;
}
</style>
```

The following figure shows the output of the preceding code:

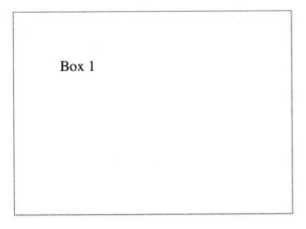

Figure: Output for box 1

3. Now, let's add the CSS to the second box in Figure, observing how the **width**, **height**, **padding**, and **border** properties differ from the first box. We are using percentage-based measurements for the width and height properties, as shown in the following code:

```
.box-2 {
float: left;    width: 20%;    height: 20%;    padding-top: 50px;    margin-left: 10px;    border: 5px solid
green;  }
```

The following figure shows the output of the preceding code:

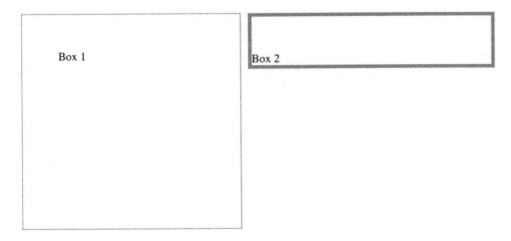

Figure: Output for boxes 1 and 2

4. Finally, let's add the CSS to the third box in Figure, observing how the **width**, **height**, **padding**, and **border** properties differ from the first and second boxes, as shown in the following code, to render the following figure:

```
.box-3 {    float: left;    width: 300px;    padding: 30px;    margin: 50px;
border-top: 50px solid blue;  }
```

The following figure shows the output of the preceding code:

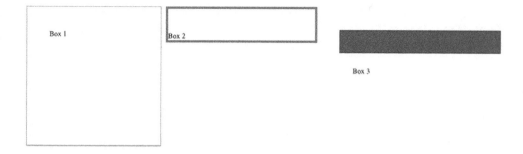

Figure: Output for boxes 1, 2, and 3

If you now right-click on the filename in **VSCode** on the left-hand side of the screen and select **open in default browser**, you will see the web page in your browser.

This should give you a sense of what's possible with the box model. Feel free to change the various different properties and experiment with different combinations.

Putting It All Together

We now know how to correctly markup a web page with the correct HTML5 structural tags. We also know how to use the three most popular CSS layout techniques. Finally, we have an understanding of how the box model works. We will now build the two complete web pages, combining all of the things we have learned so far in this chapter.

Exercise: Home Page Revisited

In this exercise, we will be using the wireframe in Figure for a home page design used in Activity, Video Store Home Page. We will build a version of this page, incorporating the concepts from the box model topic. Our aim will be to build a page as shown in the wireframe Figure:

The steps to complete this exercise are as follows:

Create a new file called **home.html** in **VSCode**.
Use the following HTML code as a start file. Again, don't worry if some of the CSS doesn't make sense to you. We will look into this part of the styling in more detail in Chapter, Text and Typography:

```
<!DOCTYPE html>
<html>
  <head>
    <title>Video store home page</title>
    <style>      header,      nav,      section,      footer {      background: #659494;
border-radius: 5px;      color: white;      font-family: arial, san-serif;      font-size: 30px;
text-align: center;      }      header:before,      nav:before,      section:before,      footer:before {
content: '<';
      }
header:after,      nav:after,      section:after,      footer:after {      content: '>';      }
    </style>
  </head>
  <body>
   <!-- your code goes here -->
  </body>
```

</html>

Now, let's add some styling for the structural elements. Notice how we have used what we have learned from The Box Model topic to include **border**, **padding**, and **margin** with our structural elements. We will use a border to visually define the outer edge of the element, along with some padding to add spacing between the text and the outer edge of the element and a bottom **margin** to provide vertical spacing between the elements. We will add this just before the closing style tag:

```
/* CSS code above */ header, nav, section, footer {   border: 1px solid gray;   padding: 50px;   margin-bottom: 25px;  }
</style>
```

If you now right-click on the filename in **VSCode** on the left-hand side of the screen and select **open in default browser**, you will see the web page in your browser as shown in the following figure:

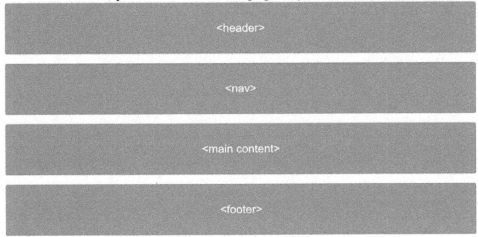

Figure: Output of home page

You should see a web page resembling the one shown in the home page wireframe.

Exercise: Video Store Product Page Revisited

In this exercise, we will be using the wireframe for a product page design as in Figure. We will build a more realistic version incorporating the box model. Our aim will be to build a page as shown in the wireframe.

The steps to complete the exercise are as follows:
Create a new file called **product.html** in **VSCode** with the following code:

```
<!DOCTYPE html>
<html>
<head>
  <title>Video store product page</title>
  <style>
  </style>
</head>
<body>
</body>
</html>
```

In order to add styling, add the following code in between the **style** tags:

```
header, nav, section, footer {    background: #659494;    border-radius: 5px;    color: white;    font-family: arial, san-serif;    font-size: 30px;    text-align: center;    }    header:before, nav:before, footer:before {    content: '<';    }    header:after, nav:after, footer:after {    content: '>';    }
```

We will now add the HTML for the page elements, which are **header**, **nav**, **section**, and **footer**. The product items will be **div** elements inside the **section** element, as shown in the following code:

```
<body>
 <header>header</header>
 <nav>nav</nav>
 <section>
  <div>product 1</div>
  <div>product 2</div>
  <div>product 3</div>
  <div>product 4</div>
  <div>product 5</div>
  <div>product 6</div>
  <div>product 7</div>
  <div>product 8</div>
 </section>
 <footer>footer</footer>
</body>
```

Now, let's add some styling for the structural elements. This is the same code as in the previous exercise. We will use a border to visually define the outer edge of the element, along with some padding to add spacing between the text and the outer edge of the element and a bottom margin to provide vertical spacing between elements. Again, we will add the CSS just before the closing **style** tag:

```
/* CSS code above */ header, nav, section, footer {   border: 1px solid gray;   padding: 20px;   margin-bottom: 25px; }
</style>
```

We will now need to add some styling for the product cards. We will use the **grid** layout technique, as this will allow our code to be as concise as possible:

```
/* CSS code above */ section {   display: grid;   grid-template-columns: auto auto auto auto; } section div {   border: 2px solid white;   padding: 30px;   margin: 10px; }
</style>
```

If you now right-click on the filename in **VSCode** on the left-hand side of the screen and select **open in default browser**, you will see the web page in your browser as shown in the following figure:

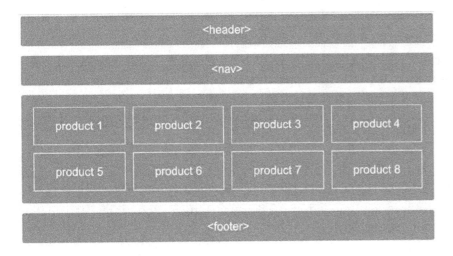

Figure: Output for the video store product page

You should now see a web page resembling the one shown in the product page wireframe.

Activity: Online Clothes Store Home Page

Suppose you are a freelance web designer/developer and have just landed a new client. For your first project, the client wants a web home page developed for their online clothes store.

Using the skills learned in this chapter, design and develop the home page layout for the new online store. The steps are as follows:

Produce a wireframe, either by hand or by using a graphics tool, for the new home page layout.
Create a file named **home.html** in **VSCode**.
Start writing the markup for the page.
Now, style the layout with CSS.

The following figure shows the expected output for this activity:

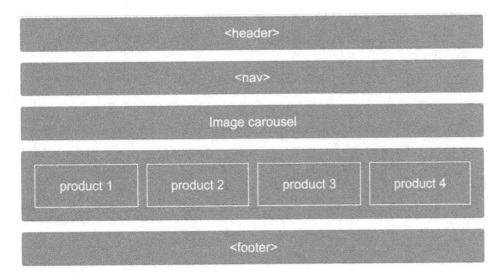

Figure: Expected output for the online clothes store home page

Conclusion:

The combination of HTML and CSS forms the bedrock of modern web development, allowing developers to create websites that are not only functional but also visually appealing and user-friendly. Understanding structure and layout is essential for crafting web pages that are accessible, maintainable, and responsive to various devices and screen sizes. Below is a detailed exploration of the key aspects and takeaways from mastering structure and layout with HTML and CSS in 2025.

1. The Importance of Structure in HTML

HTML (HyperText Markup Language) provides the foundation for every web page by defining its structure and content. A well-structured HTML document ensures:

Semantic Clarity: Using semantic elements like <header>, <nav>, <section>, <article>, and <footer> improves readability and accessibility. Semantic HTML enables screen readers and search engines to interpret the content better.
Scalability: Properly structured HTML facilitates collaboration among developers and ensures that future modifications are straightforward.
Best Practices: Following the correct HTML5 standards helps maintain consistency across browsers and devices.

Trends in HTML Structure:

Adoption of Web Components: Custom elements and shadow DOM are used extensively to create reusable, modular structures.
Accessibility (a11y): ARIA (Accessible Rich Internet Applications) roles and attributes are integrated with HTML elements to ensure inclusivity.
Dynamic Data Integration: JSON and APIs embedded within <template> tags are becoming standard practices for dynamic rendering.

2. CSS: The Art of Layout and Design

Cascading Style Sheets (CSS) empower developers to control the presentation of a web page, from colors and fonts to layouts and animations. Layout management is at the core of CSS, enabling sites to adapt seamlessly to diverse viewing environments.

Key Aspects of CSS Layout:

Box Model: Understanding padding, margins, borders, and content dimensions is fundamental for layout control.
Positioning: Relative, absolute, fixed, and sticky positioning allow precise placement of elements.
Display Types: Block, inline, inline-block, and CSS grid or flexbox displays provide the building blocks for layouts.

3. Modern Layout Techniques

CSS Grid:

CSS Grid has revolutionized web layouts by introducing a two-dimensional system. It enables developers to design complex, responsive layouts with minimal effort:

Grid-based systems allow the creation of rows and columns.
Named grid areas enhance readability and flexibility.
The repeat() function simplifies repetitive grid configurations.

Flexbox:

Flexbox excels at one-dimensional layouts, aligning items horizontally or vertically:
Perfect for centering elements or distributing space evenly.
The justify-content and align-items properties simplify alignment.

Innovations in Layout Techniques:

Subgrid Support: Subgrid functionality allows nested grid structures to align seamlessly with parent grids.
Container Queries: These allow styling based on an element's size rather than the viewport, making designs more adaptable.

4. Responsive Design: Adapting to Every Screen

In 2025, responsiveness is non-negotiable. With the proliferation of devices ranging from smartphones to 8K monitors, responsive design ensures usability across all platforms.

Core Techniques for Responsiveness:

Media Queries: Tailor styles for specific screen widths using @media.
Fluid Grids and Units: Use percentage-based widths, em, rem, or the clamp() function for scalable designs.
Flexible Images: Use max-width: 100% to ensure images fit within their containers.
Modern Frameworks: Frameworks like Tailwind CSS and Bootstrap offer pre-designed responsive utilities.

5. Advanced CSS Techniques for Structure and Layout

Variable Fonts:

Variable fonts enable flexible typography, reducing the need for multiple font files and enhancing performance.

CSS Custom Properties:

CSS variables (--property-name) simplify theming and allow dynamic style updates, particularly in conjunction with JavaScript.

Pseudo-elements and Pseudo-classes:

Utilize ::before, ::after, :nth-child(), and :not() for creative and efficient designs without additional markup.

6. Tools and Workflow Enhancements

Modern CSS Tools:

PostCSS: Automates repetitive tasks like auto prefixing and linting.
CSS-in-JS Libraries: Tools like Emotion and Styled Components integrate CSS with JavaScript frameworks.

Testing and Debugging:

Browser developer tools (e.g., Chrome DevTools) enable real-time layout debugging.
Lighthouse and web.dev tools evaluate layout performance and accessibility.

7. Accessibility and Inclusive Design

Accessible designs cater to users of all abilities:
Implement sufficient color contrast.
Ensure keyboard navigation is intuitive.
Use media features like prefers-color-scheme for dark mode support.

8. The Role of JavaScript in Enhancing Layouts

While HTML and CSS form the core, JavaScript is often used to enhance interactivity:
Dynamic class manipulation with frameworks like React or Vue.js.
Scroll animations and lazy loading for improved UX.

9. SEO and Performance Considerations

SEO Optimization:

Semantic HTML and proper meta tags (<meta> for descriptions, <title> for titles) are critical for search engine visibility.

Performance:

Efficient layouts rely on:
Minimized CSS files and critical CSS.
Content Delivery Networks (CDNs) for asset distribution.

10. Challenges and Solutions

Web development faces challenges like browser inconsistencies and maintaining backward compatibility.
The solution lies in:
Progressive enhancement strategies.
Feature detection using @supports.

Final Thoughts

Mastering structure and layout in HTML and CSS is more relevant than ever. As the web continues to evolve, so too must developers adapt, embracing new tools and practices while adhering to timeless principles of accessibility, responsiveness, and performance. By fully understanding the interplay of HTML and CSS and leveraging modern innovations, developers can build websites that stand the test of time, delivering exceptional user experiences in 2025 and beyond.

3. Cascading Style Sheets and Special Effects

Introduction

In the ever-evolving world of web development, Cascading Style Sheets (CSS) remain a cornerstone technology, enabling developers to create visually appealing and interactive web pages. Paired with HTML, CSS empowers designers to transform static structures into dynamic, engaging experiences. This guide explores the essentials of CSS and its role in crafting special effects, highlighting advancements and techniques to keep your designs modern and captivating.

1. What is CSS?

Cascading Style Sheets (CSS) is a stylesheet language used to define the presentation of a web document written in HTML. CSS allows developers to separate content from design, enabling cleaner, more maintainable code. It provides a powerful way to control the layout, colors, fonts, spacing, and overall aesthetics of a web page.

Key Features of CSS:

Cascading Rules: Styles can inherit from parent elements unless explicitly overridden.
Selector-based Styling: Targets specific elements or groups of elements in an HTML document.
Responsive Design: Enables adaptable layouts for different screen sizes and devices.
Cross-Browser Compatibility: Modern CSS ensures consistent appearance across web browsers.

2. Types of CSS

CSS can be applied to HTML documents in three main ways:
Inline CSS: Style is applied directly within an HTML tag using the style attribute.
Internal CSS: Defined within a <style> tag inside the <head> of an HTML document.
External CSS: Styles are written in a separate .css file linked to the HTML document using the <link> tag.

3. Structure of a CSS Rule

A CSS rule consists of selectors, properties, and values:

```
selector {
  property: value;
}
```

Selector: Identifies the HTML element(s) to style.
Property: Defines the style aspect (e.g., color, font-size).
Value: Specifies the property's appearance.

Example:

```
p {
  color: blue;
  font-size: 16px;
}
```

4. Cascading and Inheritance

CSS follows the **cascading** principle, resolving conflicts by:
Importance: Inline styles > internal styles > external styles.
Specificity: ID selectors > class selectors > element selectors.
Order: Later rules override earlier ones if they have the same specificity.

Inheritance:

Certain properties (e.g., text color, font) are inherited by child elements unless overridden.

5. Advanced CSS Techniques

a. CSS Variables

CSS variables enhance reusability and maintainability.

```
:root {
  --primary-color: #3498db;
}
button {
  background-color: var(--primary-color);
}
```

b. Flexbox and Grid

Modern layouts rely on Flexbox and CSS Grid for powerful, flexible designs:

Flexbox: One-dimensional layouts (row or column).
Grid: Two-dimensional layouts (rows and columns).

c. Media Queries

Media queries enable responsive design:

```
@media (max-width: 600px) {
  body {
    font-size: 14px;
  }
}
```

6. CSS for Special Effects

CSS can create stunning visual effects without the need for JavaScript.

a. Transitions

Transitions smooth changes between states:

```
button {
```

```
  transition: background-color 0.3s ease;
}
button:hover {
  background-color: #2ecc71;
}
```

b. Transformations

Transformations modify an element's appearance:

```
div {
  transform: rotate(45deg);
}
```

c. Animations

CSS animations bring static elements to life:

```
@keyframes slideIn {
  from {
    transform: translateX(-100%);
  }
  to {
    transform: translateX(0);
  }
}
div {
  animation: slideIn 1s ease-in-out;
}
```

d. Shadows

Add depth using shadows:

```
box-shadow: 5px 5px 15px rgba(0, 0, 0, 0.5);
```

7. Special Effects with CSS

a. Parallax Scrolling

Create a parallax effect by moving background images at a different speed than the foreground:

```
.parallax {
  background-image: url('background.jpg');
  background-attachment: fixed;
  background-size: cover;
}
```

b. Hover Effects
```
```

Enhance interactivity with hover effects:

```css
button:hover {
  transform: scale(1.1);
  background-color: #8e44ad;
}
```

c. Glassmorphism

A modern design trend:

```css
.glass {
  backdrop-filter: blur(10px);
  background: rgba(255, 255, 255, 0.2);
  border-radius: 10px;
}
```

d. CSS Masks and Clipping

Define element visibility:

```css
clip-path: polygon(50% 0%, 100% 100%, 0% 100%);
```

8. Combining CSS with HTML for Dynamic Effects

HTML structure lays the foundation for CSS-driven effects:

Html:

```html
<div class="card">
  <h1>Dynamic Card</h1>
  <p>Hover over this card for an effect.</p>
</div>
```

CSS:

```css
.card {
  border: 1px solid #ddd;
  padding: 20px;
  transition: transform 0.3s ease;
}
.card:hover {
  transform: translateY(-10px) scale(1.05);
}
```

9. Responsive Design and CSS Frameworks

a. Responsive Design

CSS enables designs that adapt to various devices. Techniques include:

Flexible grids
Relative units (%, em, rem)
Breakpoints using media queries

b. CSS Frameworks

Frameworks like Bootstrap and Tailwind CSS simplify responsive design and special effects:

Bootstrap: Predefined classes for grid layouts and components.
Tailwind CSS: Utility-first approach for rapid development.

10. Accessibility and Performance Optimization

a. Accessibility

Ensure CSS effects are accessible:

Use high-contrast colors.
Provide clear focus states for keyboard navigation.
Avoid relying solely on animations for conveying information.

b. Performance

Optimize CSS for faster loading:

Minify CSS files.
Combine multiple files into one.
Use a Content Delivery Network (CDN).

Let's begin,

Cascading Style Sheets (CSS) are used to define and customize the styles and layouts for your web pages. This means you can create style sheets to alter the design, layout, and responsiveness to different screen sizes on various devices from computers to smartphones.

CSS describes how HTML elements are to be displayed on screen and controls the layout of multiple web pages all at once. This is because the style sheets are stored in separate CSS files and are linked to the HTML document.

CSS solved a big problem. HTML was never originally intended to contain tags for formatting a web page and was created to describe the content of said web page. When more formatting attributes were added to the HTML 3.2 specification, it became a total nightmare for web developers to design and maintain websites. This is because fonts, formatting, layout, and color information were added to every single HTML tag on every page, so making changes and maintaining a website was a long and expensive process.

To solve this problem, the World Wide Web Consortium (W3C) created and introduced CSS. CSS removed the style formatting from the HTML page and allowed the developer to include the formatting and layout information in a separate file which could be included in all the other HTML pages that make up the website.

The word "cascading" means that styling rules flow down from several sources. This means that CSS has a hierarchy, and styles of a higher precedence will overwrite styles of a lower precedence. In other words, styles lower down the hierarchy have higher priority over those higher up. There are three methods you can use to include CSS styles in your HTML document.

First, you can include them inline using the style attribute within the opening tag:

```
<h1 style="color:blue; font-size:14px;"> Heading 1</h1>
```

You can embed the styles using the <style> element in the head section of a document:

```
<head>
   <style>
     H1 {color:blue; font-size:14px;"
     }
   </style>
</head>
```

You can include CSS styles saved in another file using the <link> element with the href attribute pointing to the CSS file:

```
<link rel="stylesheet" href="style.css">
```

External CSS Files

It is recommended that you add your CSS declarations to a separate text file and link that file into all the relevant HTML files. In this way, you have all your style declarations in one place and can change things easily.

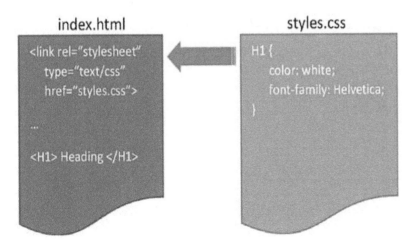

Figure: Linking a CSS File into an HTML Page

As we have seen in the previous chapter, we had to style each element every time we use it. These are known as inline styles and are very inefficient. What happens if we have a large website and we've styled every heading to be 20px, white, using the Helvetica font, and the client wants to change the color of the text or the font. We'd have to go through every instance and change it. Sounds like a nightmare to me.

A much better way is to define all the elements, tags, and so on using a style sheet. This is where CSS shows its true power. If the client came with the preceding request, and we used CSS style sheets, we would only have to change the declaration in the CSS, and every instance would change throughout the whole site. Create a text file with the .CSS file extension and make sure it's in the same directory as your HTML files.

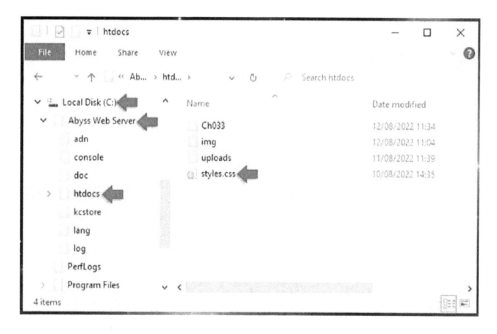

Figure: CSS Text File

Add this line in the <head> section of each HTML file that is to be styled using the declarations contained in the CSS file. Use the href attribute to point to the CSS file:

<link rel="stylesheet" type="text/css" href="styles.css">

CSS Syntax

Let's take a look at the basic syntax of a CSS rule. As you can see in Figure, the CSS rule consists of a selector and a declaration block.

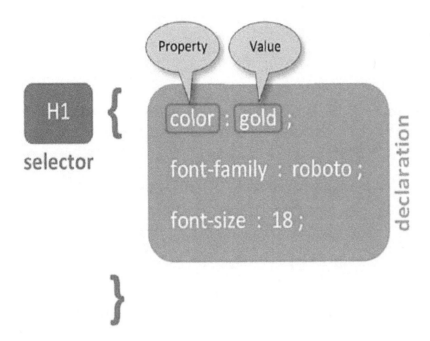

Figure: CSS Syntax

The selector points to the HTML or element you want to style. The declaration block starts with a curly brace and contains one or more style declarations separated by semicolons. Each declaration includes a CSS property name and a value, separated by a colon.

You can use these to configure the styles of the classes and selectors using various properties as you can see in Figure.

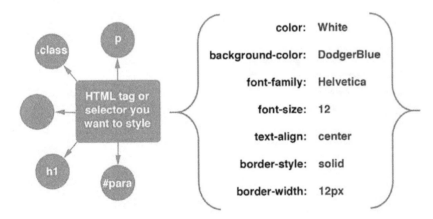

Figure: Styling Various CSS Selectors

Element Type Selector

This creates a general style for the declared element and is best used when all instances of that element are to be styled in the same way:

```
H1 {
color: white;
    font-family: Helvetica;
}
```

Here, all the H1 elements will be styled in a white Helvetica font.

Class Selector

A class selector is used to apply styles to a specific HTML element. You can name the class anything you want, and it must begin with a dot (or period). Use class selectors when you want to style multiple elements throughout the page or site with the same look or layout.

So, in this example, I'm creating a highlight style I can apply to various HTML elements such as headings <H1> and <H2> or a paragraph <p>:
.highlight {
background-color: yellow; }

In your HTML code, assign the **.highlight** class selector you defined in your CSS declarations using the class attribute in any HTML element. For example, if I wanted to highlight the heading on the <h2> tag, I'd use the class attribute and assign the class selector I defined earlier:

<h2 class = "highlight">
   The Home of the Roast
</h2>
Similarly, if I wanted to highlight the paragraph
<p class = "highlight">   Every day, our expert chefs...
</p>

Let's add this to our little web page. I've declared the **.highlight** class in the styles.css file. You can see it highlighted in Figure. I've applied the **.highlight** class selector to the <h2> HTML tag highlighted in the index. html file.

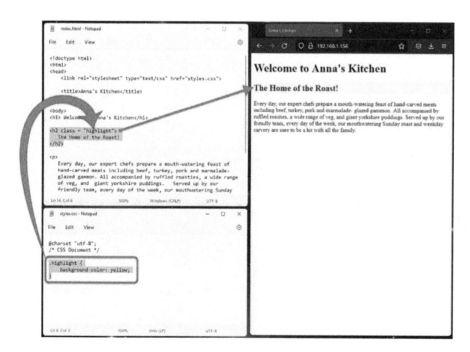

Figure: highlight Class **ID Selector**

The ID selector targets a single element and can only be used once per page.

ID selectors are defined in the CSS declarations using a hashtag # and should only be used when you have a single element on the page that will have that particular style or layout.

Here, we're going to set the background color of the footer to gold, and we want the footer to be 100 pixels high, the text aligned in the center, and the text aligned in the middle vertically:

```
#footer {
background-color : gold;    line-height : 50px;    text-align : center;    vertical-align : middle; }
```

You can now use the footer id in a div tag like this:

```
<div id= "footer"> </div>
```

Universal Selector

The universal selector matches every single element on the page. The universal selector is useful when you add a particular style in all the HTML elements within your web page:

```
* {   margin: 5;   padding: 5; }
```

Grouping Selectors

If you want to style more than one selector with the same styles, you can do this by grouping the selectors together.

For example, if I wanted to create a style where all my headings are in the center and are colored gold, instead of declaring them all individually as we see as follows:

```
h1 {    text-align: center;    color: gold; }
h2 {    text-align: center;    color: gold; }
h3 {    text-align: center;    color: gold; }
```

I can group all the selectors together followed by the declarations:
```
h1, h2, h3 {    text-align: center;    color: gold; }
```
This is much more efficient and allows you to declare the styles once.

Styling Text

If I wanted to style the H1 tag for my headings, I could write something like this in the styles.css file:

```
H1 {
font-color: yellow;
font-family: Roboto;
}
```

This would style all the H1 tags used subsequently in the HTML file.

If I wanted to style my subheadings <H2>, I can do the same. I want to change the font color to yellow with a Roboto font, but this time I want to make the text heavier or bolder. I can do this by adding the font-weight property:

```
H2 {
color: yellow;
font-family: Roboto;
font-weight: 400;
}
```

Let's take a look at what happens when we add the code to our website.

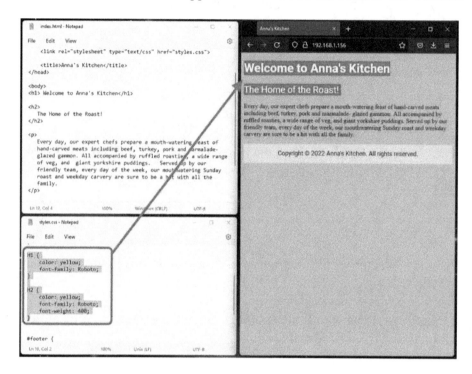

Figure: Adding Color to the Website

As you can see in Figure, the titles have changed font and color.

Figure: Changing Font Color

Try changing the font color and alignment in the styles.css file and see what happens.

Specifying Colors

You can specify colors using the following formats:

A Color keyword such as "red," "green," "blue," "transparent," "orange," etc.
A hex value such as "#000000", "#00A500", "#FFFFFF", etc.
An RGB value such as "rgb(255, 255, 0)"

Keyword

You can use a keyword for the color you want such as black, white, navy, silver, yellow, orange, dark orange, gold, and so on. See Appendix C for the full list. For example:

h1 {
color: orange;
}

Hex Value

A hex value represents colors using a six-digit code preceded by a hash character. The code is split into three two-digit hex numbers that represent the amount of red, green, and blue in varying intensities to create the color you want. The values are represented using the hexadecimal numbering scheme, not decimal.

See Appendix C for the full list.

hex	0	1	2	3	4	5	6	7	8	9	a	B	C	d
	e	F												
decimal	0	1	2	3	4	5	6	7	8	9	10	11	12	
	13	14	15											

So, for example, to create orange, we need full red, a bit of green, and no blue. FF in hex is 255 in decimal; A5 in hex is 165 in decimal. The hex code would be

red	green	Blue
FF	a5	00

We can use this hex code to represent the color we want:
h1 { color: #FFA500; }

RGB Value

You can specify a color using the rgb() function. This function accepts three values from 0 to 255, which specify the amount of red, green, and blue in varying intensities to create the color you want. So, to create orange, we need red mixed with a little bit of green but no blue.

red	green	Blue
255	165	0

h1 { color: rgb(255, 165, 0); }
See Appendix C for the full list of color codes.

Understanding Measurement Units

To control the size of certain objects such as fonts or images, the sizes are specified using various units. There are two types: absolute and relative.

Units that are absolute are the same size regardless of the parent element or window size. Table 4-1 shows some examples.

Table. Unit Meaning

Unit	Meaning
in	inch
mm	Millimeter
px	short for pixels and is usually used to measure the dimensions of an image
pt	short for points and is used to measure the size of a font

Units that are relative scale in relation to the parent element or window size depending on the unit used. Here are some examples:

Unit	Meaning
em	relative to the current font size of the element. if a font is 12pt, each em unit would be 12pt, so 2em would be 12 x 2 which is 24pt, similarly 1.5em would be 18pt
%	relative to the parent element or window size

Padding, Margins, and Borders

HTML elements can be considered as boxes. The CSS box model is essentially a box that wraps around every HTML element. Around the content are various layers; the first is padding, then the border, then the margin.

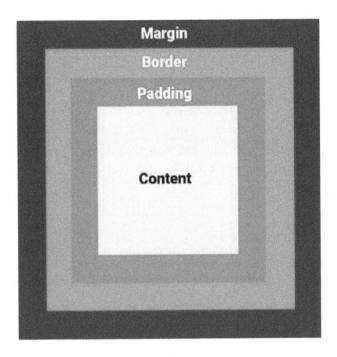

Figure: The Box Model

Let's take a look at the different parts. In Figure, we can see that,

The content of the box is where text and images appear.
The padding property is used to add space around the content, inside of the defined border.
The margin property is used to add space around the content, outside of the defined border.
The border-style property specifies what kind of border to display.

So, for example, let's add a style to our H1 heading:

.myClass {   padding: 10px;   border: solid 5px black;   margin: 20px; }

When we open the HTML page in the web browser, we will see something like Figure.

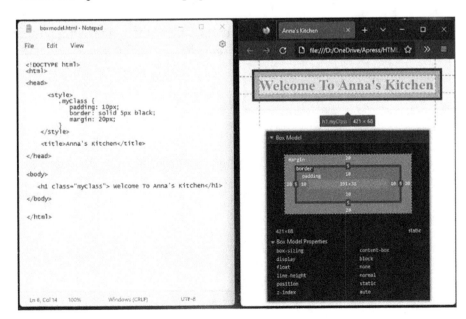

Figure: Boxes in Use

If you look in the web browser, you can see the box model around the heading. The dotted lines mark the edge of the content. Then we see 10px of padding, then a 5px thick black border, and 20px margin outside the border.

Layouts

In the previous section, the website we've been working on is very linear, meaning each section is just listed under the next. With style sheets, you're not just limited to restyling HTML tags, you can define layouts and sections.

Flexbox

Flexbox is a layout module designed for laying out content in one dimension (row or column, not both at the same time) and works best with items that have different sizes. Flexbox consists of **flex containers** (called the parent elements) that contain **flex items** (called the child elements).

Figure: Flexbox Container

The items in the flex container can be laid out in any direction and can "flex" their sizes which means the items can grow to fill unused space or shrink depending on the screen size.

We can create a container in our CSS code like this:
```
.flex-container {   display: flex;
}
```

The flex property in the display element sets how a flex item will grow or shrink to fit the space available in its container.

We can change the container direction to span rows or columns.

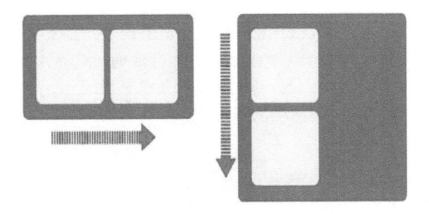

Figure: Flexbox Container Spanning Rows and Columns

If we want the items to be stacked side by side in rows.
This is the default.

Figure: Flexbox Container Spanning Rows

To do this, we use **flex-direction: rows**:

.flex-container {   display: flex;   **flex-direction: row; }**

If we want the items to be stacked on top of each other in columns,

Figure: Flexbox Container Spanning Columns

To do this, use **flex-direction: columns**:

.flex-container {   display: flex;   **flex-direction: column;** }

We can specify whether we want the items to wrap or not. Here, the items will wrap to the next row if the screen size is smaller.

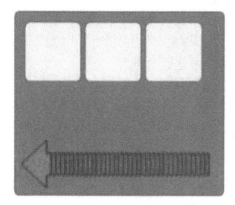

Figure: Flexbox Container Wrapping

In this example, we're going to wrap the contents, so we add **flex- wrap: wrap**:
.flex-container {   display: flex;   flex-direction: row;   **flex-wrap: wrap;** }

Now that we have created the container, we can add some items using the <div> element. In our HTML code, we can add
```
<div class="flex-container">
  <div> This is content inside item </div>
  <div> <img src="img/bluebox.png"> </div>
  <div> <img src="img/bluebox.png"> </div>
</div>
```

The order property specifies the order of the flex items:

```
<div class="flex-container">
  <div style="order: 3"> This is content inside item </div>
  <div style="order: 1"> <img src="img/bluebox.png"> </div>
  <div style="order: 2"> <img src="img/bluebox.png"> </div>
</div>
```

If we want to style the items inside the container, we can use the greater than ">" symbol:
```
.flex-container-name > child-item-name { ...
}
```

This symbol is used to select the element with a specific parent. Since each item in the flex-container is specified with a <div> element, these are the child items. So, the child-item-name we want is div, and it belongs to flex-container. Now let's change the background color to light gray, then add a margin and some padding to space out the items:

.flex-container > div {   background-color: #f1f1f1;   margin: 10px;   padding: 10px; }

In Figure, we have our HTML code open on the top left, with our CSS code open on the bottom left. On the right, we can see what it looks like in a web browser. What happens when you resize the width of the browser window?

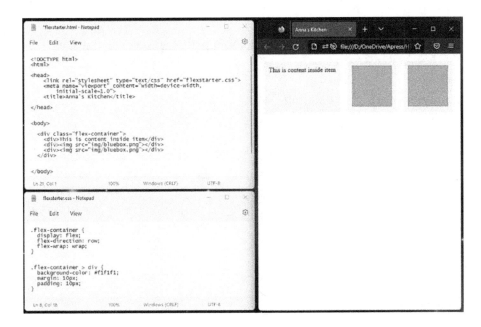

Figure: Resizing

Putting Flexbox into Practice

Let's create a layout for our website. Here, we want to create a header and a navigation bar along the top of the page; then underneath, we want to create the site content with a sidebar to the right – this is the only part we're using flexbox. Finally, we want to add a footer to the page.

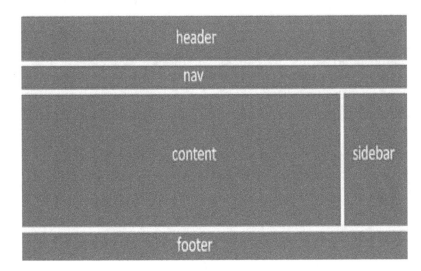

Figure: Website Layout

In the CSS code file, we can declare our header, navigation, and footer using simple CSS class selectors:

```
.header {  background: orange;  padding: 2em;  text-align: center; }
.nav {
  background: yellow;  padding: 1em;  text-align: center; }
.footer {  background: orange;  padding: 1em;
}
```

When we get to the content and sidebar, this is where we want to use flexbox. We can create our container:
.flex-container {   display: flex;   flex-direction: row; }

Then create the content and sidebar as child items of the container. Add some padding to space out the content, and set the background color of the sidebar to gray:
.flex-container > .content {   padding: 10px; }
.flex-container > .sidebar {   background-color: #f1f1f1;   padding: 10px;
}

Now in our HTML code file, we can add our header and nav bar using the <div> element. Just add the name of the selector defining the header using the "class" attribute in the opening <div> tag. Add the content to display between the opening and closing <div> tags:

```
<div class="header">
    <h1> Welcome To Anna's Kitchen</h1>
    <b> The Home of the Roast! </b>
</div>
```
Do the same for the nav bar:
```
<div class="nav">
    <a href="index.html"> Home </a> |
    <a href="menu.html"> Menu </a> |
    <a href="book.html"> Book a Table </a>
</div>
```

Next, we need to create our flexbox container to contain the content and sidebar. We can add the flex-container using the "class" attribute in the opening <div> tag:

```
<div class="flex-container">
```

Then inside the flex-container <div> element we declared earlier, we can add another <div> element with the content child item using the "class" attribute in the opening <div> tag:

```
<div class="content">
<p>
```
Every day, our expert chefs prepare a mouth-watering feast of hand-carved meats including <b> beef, turkey, pork and marmalade-glazed gammon.</b> All accompanied by ruffled roasties, a wide range of veg, and giant yorkshire puddings.   <i> Served up by our friendly team, every day of the week, our mouthwatering Sunday roast and weekday carvery are sure to be a hit with all the family.</i> </p>
```
    </div>
```

And do the same with the sidebar:

```
<div class="sidebar">
    <img src="img/menumap.png" width="220px" usemap="#foodmenu">
    <map name = "foodmenu">
      <area shape= "rect" coords = "0,0,220,202" href = "menu1.htm">
      <area shape= "rect" coords = "0,202,220,395" href = "menu2.htm">
      <area shape= "rect" coords = "0,395,220,596" href = "menu3.htm">
    </map>
```

</div>

Remember to close the **flex-container** with
</div>

We will see something like Figure.

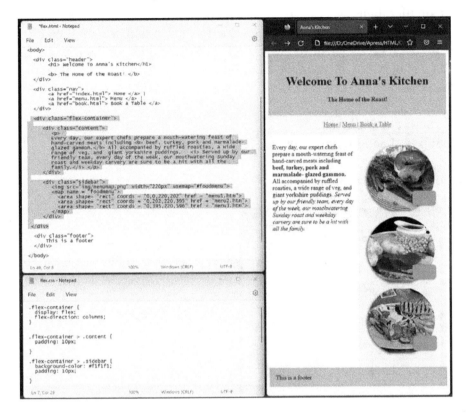

Figure: Flex Container

Notice that things don't wrap when we resize the window. To make things wrap, we need to add the flex attribute to the container:

.flex-container {   display: flex;   flex-direction: row;   **flex-wrap: wrap;** }
as well as to the children:
flex: flex-grow flex-shrink flex-basis;

flex-grow specifies how much the item will grow relative to the rest of the flexible items by a factor.
flex-grow: 0 means items won't grow.
flex- grow: 1 means items can grow larger than their flex-basis.
flex-shrink specifies how much the item will shrink relative to the rest of the flexible items.
flex-shrink: 1 means items can shrink smaller than their flex-basis.
flex-basis is the length of the item measured in "%", "px", or "em". You can also have values: "auto" or "inherit."

For example, if I add the following to the content item:
flex: 1 1 250px;

what does this mean?
flex-grow: 1 means items can grow larger than their flex-basis.

flex-shrink: 1 means items can shrink smaller than their flex-basis.

flex: 250px means once the first row gets to a point where there is not enough space to place another 250px item, a new flex line is created for the items. As the items can grow, they will expand larger than 250px in order to fill each row completely. If there is only one item on the final line, it will stretch to fill the entire line. So, we end up with this:

.flex-container > .content {   **flex: 1 1 250px;**   padding: 10px; }
.flex-container > .sidebar {   **flex: 1 1 50px;**   background-color: #f1f1f1;   padding: 10px; }

Let's take a look at what this looks like in a browser.

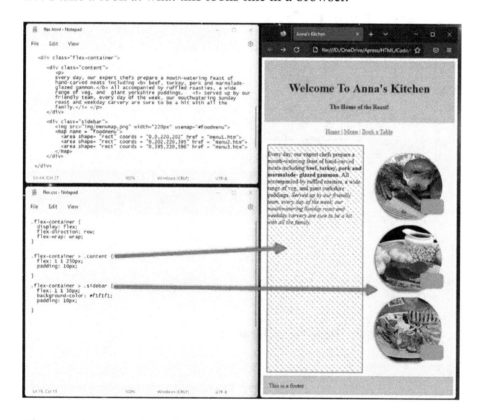

Figure: Flex Containers in the Browser

What happens when you resize the browser window? Notice how they stretch when we extend the width of the browser. Also, notice how the sidebar wraps when we reduce the width of the browser. It will wrap when the content gets to 250px.

Figure: The Sidebar Sized at 250px

Let's try it. Here, we've reduced the browser width and expanded the width to see what happens.

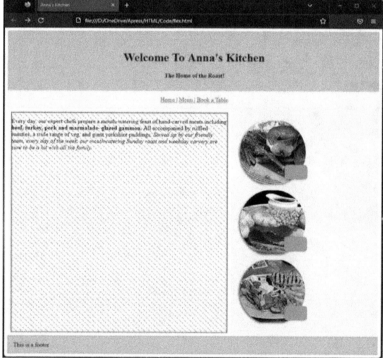

Figure: The Width Reduced and Expanded

Keep in mind that flexbox can only handle rows or columns, not both.

CSS Grid

A CSS grid layout is a two-dimensional grid-based layout system with rows and columns that is designed to make it easier to lay out web pages and enables a developer to align elements into columns and rows. A CSS grid is a perfect candidate for whole page layouts.

In Figure, the vertical lines are called columns, and the horizontal lines are called rows. The spaces between each column/row are called row gaps. Grid items such as images or text can be aligned along the rows and columns of the grid and are called grid items.

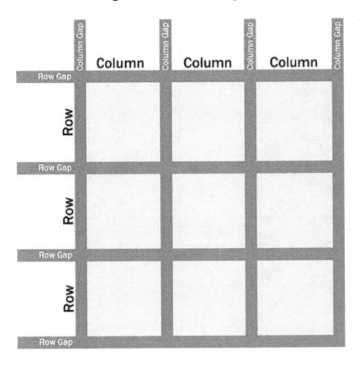

Figure: CSS Grid

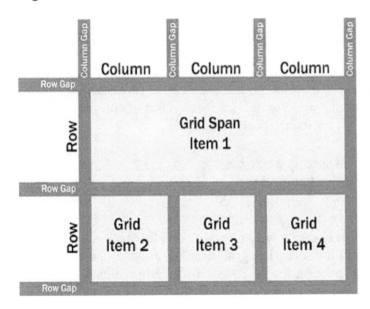

Figure: CSS Grid with Items

Putting CSS Grid into Practice

In this example, we want to lay out our website as follows. We want the width to span four columns. This means the header and the footer will span the full four columns. We also want the content to fill three columns (col 1, col 2, col 3). The sidebar will take up the last column (col 4). The site will also be split into three rows. The header on row 1, the content and sidebar on row 2, and the footer on row 3. We can see this layout in Figure.

Figure: CSS Grid Template

First, we need to create a grid container:
.container { **display:grid** }

Next, we need to specify how many rows and columns we are going to use. Looking at the template in Figure, we need four columns. The grid-template-columns property defines the number of columns in your grid layout. The "auto" attribute means the columns will be automatically sized.

You need to specify a size for each column. You can also specify a size here:
.container { display:grid   **grid-template-columns: auto auto auto auto;**
}

We now need to specify how many rows we want to use. Looking at Figure, we need three rows: one for the header, one for the content and sidebar, and another for the footer. The grid-template-rows property defines the number of rows in your grid layout. The "auto" attribute means the rows will be automatically sized. You need to specify a size for each row. You can also specify a size here:

.container {display:grid   grid-template-columns: auto auto auto auto;   **grid-template-rows: auto auto auto;** }

Now that we have created our container, we need to create the items. The first item is the header. Here, we've specified that we want the background of the header orange. Next, we want to state on which row/column the header starts:

grid-row-start: 1; grid-column-start: 1;

Here, we're starting on row 1, column 1, and the header ends before row 2, column 5. For this, we use the grid-row-end property. This defines how many rows an item will span or on which row line the item will end:

grid-row-end: 2; grid-column-end: 5; We end up with this:
.header {
background-color: orange; **grid-row-start: 1; grid-column-start: 1; grid-row-end: 2; grid-column-end: 5;** padding: 20px; text-align: center; }

Finally, we can add some padding to space out the contents of the header and align the text to the center. We can do the same for the footer. Here, the footer starts on row 3 and ends after column 4 (which is 5).

Again, we change the background color to orange and add some padding with the text aligned to the center:
.footer {
background-color: orange; grid-row-start: 3; grid-column-start: 1; grid-row-end: 4; grid-column-end: 5; padding: 20px; text-align: center; }

Now, for the content, this will start on row 2, but only span columns 1, 2, and 3 – so we end after 3 (which is 4). The sidebar will fill the last column:
.content { grid-row-start: 2; grid-column-start: 1; grid-row-end: 3; grid-column-end: 4; padding: 20px; }

For the sidebar, we want to start on row 2, but just fill the last column after the content, so we start on column 4 and end after column 4 (which is 5):
.sidebar {
background-color: lightgrey; grid-row-start: 2; grid-column-start: 4; grid-row-end: 3; grid-column-end: 5; }

Now we need to build the page using the grid containers in our HTML document. We do this with the <div> tag.

First, we add the container; remember we called the container layout- grid and it's specified as a class, so we add it using the class attribute to the opening <div> tag:
<div class="layout-grid">

Inside, we can add the elements. First is the header:
  <div class="header">
    <h1> Welcome To Anna's Kitchen</h1>
    <b> The Home of the Roast! </b> **</div>**
then the rest of the elements. Just add the contents to the elements between the two <div> tags:
  <div class="content">   ...
  </div>
  <div class="sidebar">   ...
  </div>
  <div class="footer">   ...
  </div>
</div>
Let's put it all together and see what it looks like Figure.

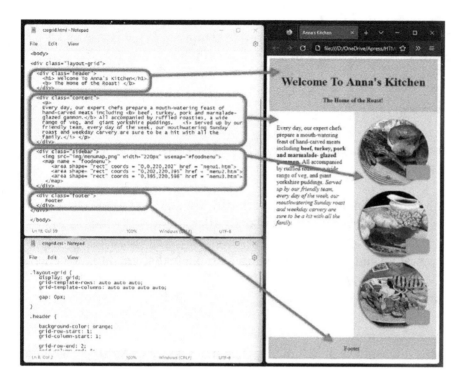

Figure: Elements Added

Responsive Grid Layouts

Responsive design is an approach to web design that allows your website content to adapt to different screen and window sizes used on a variety of different devices such as phones, tablets, and computers.
If we have a look at a simple website on a tablet, the screen looks OK and is sized correctly.

Figure: Web Design on a Tablet

Notice what happens when you resize the browser window on the PC. The layout starts to stretch and resize. You can see that the background image in the sidebar on the right no longer fits and is too small.

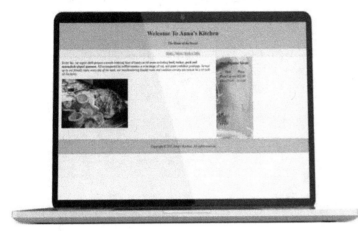

Figure: Web Design on a Laptop

Or if we view the website on a phone, the sidebar is hidden below the main text.

Figure: Web Design on a Phone

The layout changes depending on the screen size. Pages should be optimized for a variety of screen sizes, but how do we do this? These days, thanks to smartphones, tablets, laptops with different screen sizes, and PCs, many web pages are based on a responsive grid view. This means web pages based on a grid view are divided into columns.

A responsive grid view often has 12 columns and has a total width of 100%. This will shrink or expand as you resize the browser window.

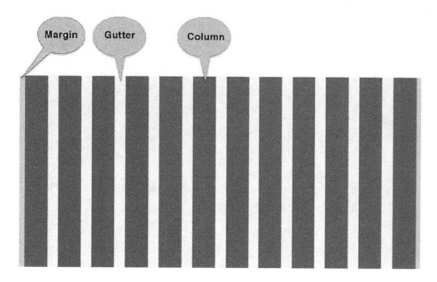

Figure: Responsive Grid View

Between each column, you'll find a gutter, and at either side of the grid, there is a margin.

To construct the grid view in CSS, first we calculate the percentage for one column:

100% / 12 **x 1** columns = 8.33%.
The next column would be 100% / 12 **x 2** = 16.66%.
The next column: 100% / 12 **x 3** = 25%.

And so on....
Next, we need to make one class for each of the 12 columns and the percentage sizes we calculated in the previous step:

.col-1 {width: 8.33%;}
.col-2 {width: 16.66%;}
.col-3 {width: 25%;}
.col-4 {width: 33.33%;}
.col-5 {width: 41.66%;}
.col-6 {width: 50%;}
.col-7 {width: 58.33%;}
.col-8 {width: 66.66%;}
.col-9 {width: 75%;}
.col-10 {width: 83.33%;}
.col-11 {width: 91.66%;}

.col-12 {width: 100%;}

This will create a grid layout like Figure.

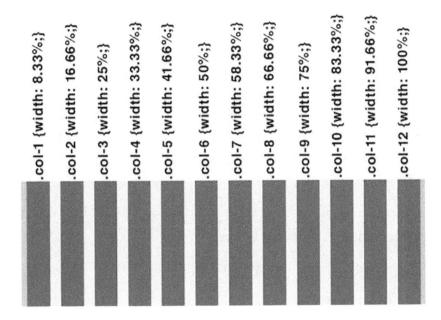

Figure: Responsive Grid View Showing Column Widths

Remember the CSS file we built in the previous section. Padding and borders should be included in the total width and height of the elements. To enforce this, we add the following to the top of the CSS file:
```
* {
  box-sizing: border-box;
}
```

We can add the column declarations to the bottom of the CSS file:

```
.col-1 {width: 8.33%;}
.col-2 {width: 16.66%;}
.col-3 {width: 25%;}
.col-4 {width: 33.33%;}
.col-5 {width: 41.66%;}
.col-6 {width: 50%;}
.col-7 {width: 58.33%;}
.col-8 {width: 66.66%;}
.col-9 {width: 75%;}
.col-10 {width: 83.33%;}
.col-11 {width: 91.66%;}
.col-12 {width: 100%;}
```

Now we can build the page using HTML. We can add the header and nav bar. These two sections will span 100% across the page:

```
<header>
   <h1> Welcome To Anna's Kitchen</h1>
   <b> The Home of the Roast! </b>
</header>
```

```
<nav>
  <a href="index.html"> Home </a> |
  <a href="menu.html"> Menu </a> |
  <a href="menu.html"> Book a Table </a>
</nav>
```

Next, let's add the content and sidebar. Now for this section, we want the content section to span eight columns across and the sidebar to span the remaining four columns:

```
<content class="col-8">
  <p>
  Every day, our expert chefs prepare a mouth-watering ... </p>
  <img src="img/carvery.jpg" width="365px">
</content>
```

You can see the main content will span eight columns as shown in Figure.

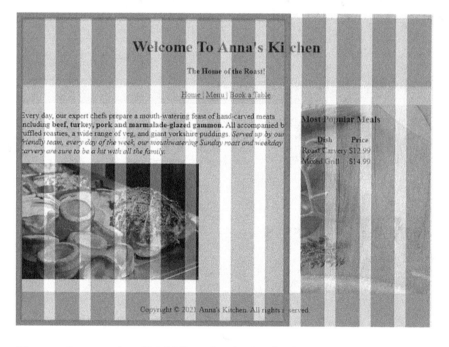

Figure: Responsive Grid View for the Main Content

After that, we can add the sidebar:

```
<sidebar class="col-4">
  <h3 align="center">Most Popular Meals</h3>
  <table align="center">
   <tr>
    <th>Dish</th>
    <th>Price</th>
   </tr>
   <tr>
    <td>Roast Carvery</td>
    <td>$12.99</td>
   </tr>
```

```
   <tr>
     <td>Mixed Grill</td>
     <td>$14.99</td>
   </tr>
</table>
</sidebar>
```

This spans four columns as we can see in Figure.

Figure: Responsive Grid View for the Sidebar

Now what happens when you resize the browser window? You'll see the content stretch to fill the screen.

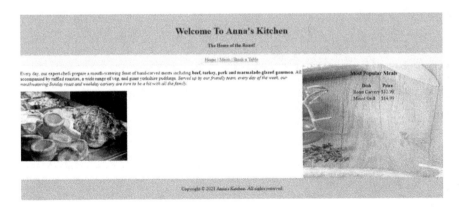

Figure: The Content Stretched to Fill the Screen

What happens when we view the site on a phone? The view on the phone, as seen in Figure, is a bit cramped and could do with some breakpoints to move the sidebar underneath.

Figure: A Cramped View on a Phone

To do this, we must understand what a viewport is. The viewport is the portion of the website that the user can see.

Figure: Viewport

A meta viewport tag gives the browser instructions on how to control the page's dimensions and scaling:

<meta name="viewport" content="width=device-width, initial- scale=1">
Using the meta viewport value, **width=device-width** instructs the page to match the screen's width in device-independent pixels. The **initial- scale=1.0** part sets the initial zoom level when the page is first loaded by the browser.

To provide the best experience, mobile browsers render the page at a desktop screen of about 767–980px in width and then scale the content by increasing font sizes and resizing the content to fit the screen.

Smart Phone	Tablet	Laptop
min-width: 767px	min-width: 768px max-width: 1023px	min-width: 1024px

Figure: The Website on Different Screen Sizes

Media queries make it possible to respond to a client browser with a customized display for certain viewport sizes. The @media rule includes a block of CSS properties only if a certain condition is true.

Going back to our CSS, we can style all column widths to span 100% of the width on smartphone devices with small screens. The following code selects any element that contains **"col-"** anywhere in the value of the class attribute:
[class*="col-"] {   width: 100%; }

This is known as a CSS attribute selector with the attribute we want to select enclosed in square brackets []. Here's the media query to deal with larger screens. The min-width media property specifies the minimum width of a specific device. So, the screen width needs to be 768px or greater. This would work well on larger tablets such as an iPad or a laptop.

```
@media only screen and (min-width: 768px) {
  .col-1 {width: 8.33%;}
  .col-2 {width: 16.66%;}
  .col-3 {width: 25%;}
  .col-4 {width: 33.33%;}
  .col-5 {width: 41.66%;}
  .col-6 {width: 50%;}
  .col-7 {width: 58.33%;}
  .col-8 {width: 66.66%;}
  .col-9 {width: 75%;}
  .col-10 {width: 83.33%;}
  .col-11 {width: 91.66%;}
```

```
    .col-12 {width: 100%;}
}
```

This creates a breakpoint when the browser window is 768px wide.

You can set your breakpoints using min-width and max-width properties. When should you use each one? Well, if you are designing your layout for small smartphone screens first, then use min-width breakpoints and work your way up. If you've designed the website for a desktop display first, and you want to adapt the layout for smaller screens, then use max- width and work your way down to the smallest screen.

Special Effects

Using HTML and CSS, you can add various effects to decorate your website. These include

Hover effects
Buttons
Rounded corners
Shadows
Gradients

These effects should be used sparingly as they can become irritating and distracting if used in abundance. However, effects can be useful to add emphasis to a section or object.

Text Effects

In this example, we are going to add a shadow effect to a heading. Using CSS, we can style the heading using the text-shadow property:

```
h1 {   text-shadow: 2px 2px 2px lightgrey; }
```

We can also change the text to white using the color property:

```
h1 {   color: white;   text-shadow: 2px 2px 2px lightgrey; }
```

Let's take a look at an example. Here, we've added a text-shadow property to the heading 1 selector as you can see in the about.css file.

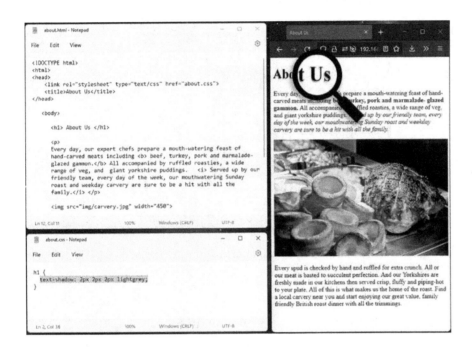

Figure: Text Shadow Property

In the web browser on the right in Figure, you can see the shadow around the heading.

Rounded Image Corners

We can style images. We can round the corners of the image. The amount of curve on the corner is called the border radius:

img {   border-radius: 10px; }

Let's take a look at an example. Here, we've added a border-radius property to the img selector as you can see in the about.css file in Figure.

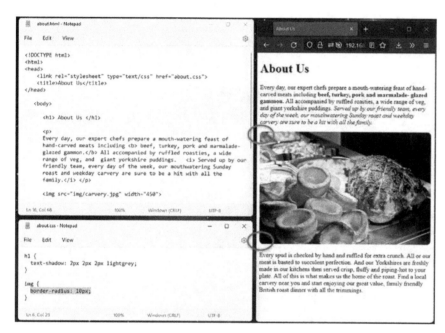

Figure: Rounded Corners

You can see the rounded corners of the photo in the browser window in Figure.

Buttons

We add styles to buttons. Here, we've created a button class selector. We've set the background color of the button to orange, the text to white, plus we've added rounded corners using the border-radius property.

We've also added a property to change the mouse pointer to a hand pointer using the cursor property:

.button {
background-color: orange;   color: white;   border: none;   border-radius: 4px;   padding: 15px 25px; cursor: pointer; }

Next, we've added a hover state for the button. Here, we've set the background color to green and the text to white whenever the mouse pointer hovers over the button:

.button:hover { background-color: green;   color: white; }

Finally, we add the class to the button in the HTML document:

```
<button class="button">Submit</button>
```

Let's take a look. At the bottom of the page in the web browser, you'll see the button change color and the cursor change to a hand pointer when you hover your mouse pointer over the button.

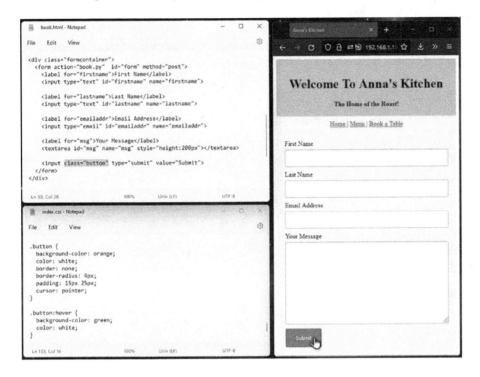

Figure: The Cursor Changes

Gradients

You can add gradients to your page. A gradient is a smooth transition between two or more specified colors.

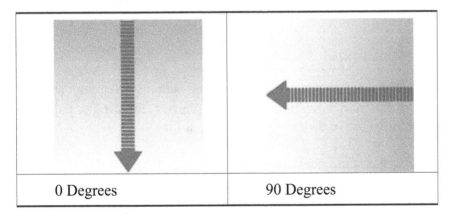

| 0 Degrees | 90 Degrees |

Figure: Gradients

Here, we've defined a linear gradient that goes from white to light gray down the page:

```
#gradient1 {
  background-image: linear-gradient(0deg, white, lightgrey); }
```

Now anything we want the gradient to span, we enclose in <div> tags: <div id="gradient1" style="text-align:center;"> ...

</div>

Let's take a look at an example. In Figure, we've defined a gradient ID selector. We've added a gradient spanning from light gray to white down the page (0 degrees).

We've also enclosed the text between the <div> tags, so we know where the gradient will start and where it will end.

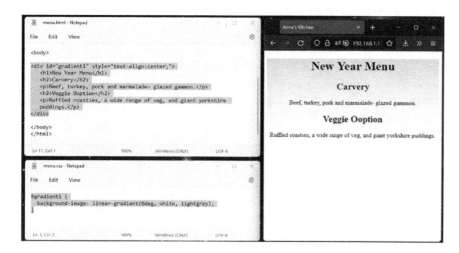

Figure: Gradients in Use

Conclusion: Cascading Style Sheets and Special Effects (HTML and CSS)

The evolution of web design is a testament to the synergy between form and function, and Cascading Style Sheets (CSS) have been pivotal in shaping this landscape. As we reach the culmination of our exploration of CSS and special effects, it's essential to reflect on their transformative impact on modern web development. This conclusion synthesizes the key learnings, highlights the practical applications, and envisions the future potential of CSS in web design.

The Power of CSS in Web Development

CSS, as a style language, separates content from presentation, enabling developers to craft visually appealing and responsive designs. It allows for the modularization of design elements, ensuring scalability and maintainability in web projects. By mastering CSS, developers unlock the ability to create:

Responsive Layouts: With techniques like Flexbox, Grid, and media queries, CSS ensures websites adapt seamlessly to various screen sizes and devices, enhancing user experiences.

Consistent Aesthetics: Centralized styling promotes uniformity across a website, maintaining brand identity while reducing redundancy in code.

Engaging User Interfaces: Modern CSS capabilities, such as animations, transitions, and transformations, empower developers to design dynamic and interactive experiences.

Accessibility and Usability: CSS tools, like custom properties and layout techniques, contribute to creating accessible web content, ensuring inclusivity for diverse user groups.

Mastering Special Effects

Special effects in CSS transcend mere aesthetics, adding depth and interactivity to web pages. They help capture user attention, convey messages effectively, and create memorable digital experiences. Here are key aspects of special effects:

1. Animations and Transitions

CSS animations and transitions breathe life into web elements. Subtle hover effects, loading animations, and scrolling transitions not only enhance usability but also communicate state changes intuitively. For example: Smooth button animations improve click ability.
Page-loading animations keep users engaged during content retrieval.

2. Transformations

CSS transformations enable the rotation, scaling, skewing, and translation of elements. These effects are crucial for modern web designs, allowing developers to create:

Eye-catching hero sections.
Interactive galleries and carousels.
3D effects that add depth to websites.

3. Parallax Scrolling

Parallax effects, achieved through CSS and JavaScript, create a sense of depth by moving background elements at different speeds relative to foreground content. This technique enhances storytelling and creates immersive user experiences.

4. Hover and Focus Effects

Hover and focus effects provide immediate visual feedback to users, improving navigation and usability. For instance:

Hover states on buttons guide user interactions.
Focus effects enhance accessibility for keyboard users.

5. Background Effects

Background gradients, patterns, and videos add visual richness to websites. CSS's gradient capabilities, combined with blending modes, enable unique and vibrant designs that resonate with modern aesthetics.

Challenges in CSS and Their Solutions

While CSS is a powerful tool, it comes with challenges that require strategic solutions:

Cross-Browser Compatibility CSS features may render differently across browsers. To address this:

Use vendor prefixes for experimental properties.
Test designs in multiple browsers.

Adopt progressive enhancement to ensure core functionality across all platforms.

Performance Optimization Excessive animations or large CSS files can impact page performance. Best practices include:

Minimizing CSS files through preprocessing and compression.
Optimizing animation performance with GPU-accelerated properties.
Leveraging lazy loading for non-critical resources.

Complexity Management As projects scale, managing CSS can become cumbersome. Developers can mitigate this by:

Using methodologies like BEM (Block Element Modifier) for structured CSS.
Adopting CSS preprocessors (e.g., Sass or Less) for reusable and maintainable code.
Embracing modern CSS-in-JS libraries in frameworks like React.

CSS in the Broader Context of Web Development

The advancements in CSS are complemented by its seamless integration with other web technologies:

HTML5 and Semantic Markup CSS works in harmony with HTML5's semantic elements, ensuring both visual and structural clarity. By targeting semantic tags (e.g., <header>, <section>, <article>), developers achieve both aesthetic and accessibility goals.

JavaScript and CSS Synergy JavaScript extends CSS's capabilities by enabling event-driven interactions and dynamic styling. Libraries like GSAP (GreenSock Animation Platform) and frameworks like Vue.js or React enhance CSS-based animations and special effects.

Web Performance Optimization CSS contributes to web performance when used strategically. Techniques such as critical CSS, asynchronous loading, and content delivery networks (CDNs) reduce render times and improve user experiences.

The Role of Tools and Frameworks

CSS frameworks and tools accelerate development while maintaining consistency and quality. Popular frameworks like Bootstrap, Tailwind CSS, and Foundation offer pre-designed components and utility-first approaches, empowering developers to:

Rapidly prototype designs.
Maintain responsive and consistent layouts.
Customize components for unique branding.

CSS tools like PostCSS, Autoprefixer, and PurgeCSS further optimize code by automating repetitive tasks, adding prefixes, and removing unused styles.

The Future of CSS

The trajectory of CSS is driven by innovation and user-centric design principles. Emerging features and trends promise to redefine the possibilities of web design:

Container Queries Building on the concept of media queries, container queries allow developers to style components based on the size of their containers rather than the viewport, enabling truly modular and reusable designs.

CSS Subgrid The CSS Grid layout revolutionized web design. The upcoming Subgrid feature enhances this capability, allowing for more precise alignment and nested layouts.

Web Animations API Integration While CSS handles many animations, the Web Animations API offers granular control and integration with JavaScript, enabling complex and highly interactive effects.

Native CSS Features for Dark Mode With the growing adoption of dark mode, CSS features like the prefers-color-scheme media query allow developers to adapt styles dynamically based on user preferences.

Advanced Typography Variable fonts and custom properties are shaping the future of web typography, allowing dynamic font adjustments for improved readability and performance.

Final Thoughts

In conclusion, CSS is not merely a tool for styling; it is the cornerstone of engaging and inclusive web design. Its adaptability, coupled with its integration with HTML and JavaScript, makes it an indispensable skill for modern developers. By mastering CSS, developers not only craft visually compelling websites but also contribute to a more accessible and efficient web.

As we look forward, the role of CSS in shaping digital experiences will only grow. The introduction of advanced features and frameworks will continue to push the boundaries of creativity and performance. For developers, staying updated with CSS trends and best practices is crucial to remain competitive in the dynamic field of web development.

Whether you are designing a minimalist portfolio, a complex e-commerce platform, or an immersive web application, CSS provides the tools to realize your vision. By embracing the power of CSS and special effects, you become not just a web designer but a creator of meaningful digital experiences. As the web evolves, so too will CSS, ensuring its place at the heart of innovative and impactful design.

4. Lists, Tables, Links, Forms, and Images

Introduction

HTML (HyperText Markup Language) and CSS (Cascading Style Sheets) form the backbone of web development. They enable developers to structure and style content on the web. This guide offers a comprehensive introduction to five essential HTML/CSS elements: Lists, Tables, Links, Forms, and Images.

1. Lists

Lists allow the grouping of related content in a structured manner. HTML provides three main types of lists:

1.1 Unordered Lists

Unordered lists () display items without a specific order, typically using bullet points.

HTML Example:

```
<ul>
  <li>Item 1</li>
  <li>Item 2</li>
  <li>Item 3</li>
</ul>
```

CSS Styling:

```
ul {
  list-style-type: square;
  padding-left: 20px;
}
li {
  font-family: Arial, sans-serif;
  color: #333;
}
```

1.2 Ordered Lists

Ordered lists () display items in a sequence, typically using numbers.

HTML Example:

```
<ol>
  <li>Step 1</li>
  <li>Step 2</li>
  <li>Step 3</li>
</ol>
```

CSS Styling:

```
ol {
  list-style-type: decimal;
  margin-left: 20px;
}
```

1.3 Definition Lists

Definition lists () present terms and their definitions.

HTML Example:

```
<dl>
  <dt>HTML</dt>
  <dd>A markup language for structuring web pages.</dd>
  <dt>CSS</dt>
  <dd>A stylesheet language for designing web pages.</dd>
</dl>
```

CSS Styling:

```
dl {
  margin: 20px 0;
}
dt {
  font-weight: bold;
}
dd {
  margin-left: 20px;
}
```

2. Tables

Tables organize data into rows and columns. While often replaced by more flexible layouts in CSS, tables remain valuable for tabular data representation.

2.1 Basic Table Structure

HTML Example:

```
<table>
  <tr>
    <th>Name</th>
    <th>Age</th>
    <th>City</th>
  </tr>
  <tr>
    <td>John</td>
    <td>25</td>
    <td>New York</td>
  </tr>
  <tr>
```

```
    <td>Jane</td>
    <td>30</td>
    <td>San Francisco</td>
  </tr>
</table>
```

2.2 CSS Styling for Tables

```
table {
  width: 100%;
  border-collapse: collapse;
}
th, td {
  border: 1px solid #ddd;
  padding: 8px;
  text-align: left;
}
th {
  background-color: #f4f4f4;
}
```

2.3 Advanced Features

Rowspan and Colspan: For merging cells across rows and columns.

Styling with nth-child:

```
tr:nth-child(even) {
  background-color: #f9f9f9;
}
```

3. Links

Links () connect web pages and resources, forming the web's backbone.

3.1 Basic Link Structure

HTML Example:

```
<a href="https://www.example.com">Visit Example</a>
```

3.2 Link Attributes

target="_blank": Opens the link in a new tab.
rel="nofollow": Prevents search engines from following the link.

Example:

```
<a href="https://www.example.com" target="_blank" rel="nofollow">Visit Example</a>
```

3.3 CSS Styling for Links

```
a {
  color: #007bff;
  text-decoration: none;
}
a:hover {
  color: #0056b3;
  text-decoration: underline;
}
```

4. Forms

Forms () collect user input.

4.1 Basic Form Structure

HTML Example:

```
<form action="/submit" method="post">
  <label for="name">Name:</label>
  <input type="text" id="name" name="name">

  <label for="email">Email:</label>
  <input type="email" id="email" name="email">

  <button type="submit">Submit</button>
</form>
```

4.2 CSS Styling for Forms

```
form {
  max-width: 400px;
  margin: 0 auto;
}
label {
  display: block;
  margin-bottom: 8px;
  font-weight: bold;
}
input {
  width: 100%;
  padding: 8px;
  margin-bottom: 16px;
  border: 1px solid #ccc;
  border-radius: 4px;
}
button {
  background-color: #007bff;
  color: white;
```

```
  padding: 10px 15px;
  border: none;
  border-radius: 4px;
  cursor: pointer;
}
button:hover {
  background-color: #0056b3;
}
```

4.3 Advanced Features

Validation:

```
<input type="text" required>
```

Styling Error States:

```
input:invalid {
  border-color: red;
}
```

5. Images

Images () enhance content visually.

5.1 Basic Image Inclusion

HTML Example:

```
<img src="image.jpg" alt="Descriptive Text">
```

5.2 Responsive Images

Use the width and height attributes in CSS for responsiveness.

Example:

```
img {
  max-width: 100%;
  height: auto;
}
```

5.3 Advanced Features

Lazy Loading:

```
<img src="image.jpg" alt="Descriptive Text" loading="lazy">
```

Background Images in CSS:

```
.image-container {
  background-image: url('background.jpg');
  background-size: cover;
  background-position: center;
}
```

Let's begin,

Traditionally, lists and tables are essential tools in print media for imposing structure on content. Their application in Web design is no different. They can also be combined with links, especially lists, to extend their application. This chapter discusses the HTML elements used to create them.

Learning Outcomes

After studying this chapter, you will know about HTML elements used to do the following:
Create different types of lists.
Describe the structure of tables and populate them with data. Define links to other parts of the same page, other pages within the same site, and external pages.

Lists

HTML allows you to create three different types of lists:

- **Unordered lists**, which are lists in which items begin with bullet points.
- **Ordered lists**, which are lists in which items start with numbers or alphabets and are in numeric or alphabetical order. Naturally, this is used only where the order of list items matters to meaning.
- **Definition lists**, which are lists made up of terms and the definitions for each of the terms.
The general principle that underlies how any of these lists is created is to first specify type of list and then the items of the list. Table lists the relevant elements.

TABLE

The List Elements

Element	Function
`<ul>...</ul>`	Defines an unordered list.
`<ol>...</ol>`	Defines an ordered type of list.
`<li>...</li>`	Defines a list item for an unordered or an ordered list.
`<dl>...</dl>`	Defines a definition list.
`<dt>...</dt>`	Defines a definition term for a definition list.
`<dd>...</dd>`	Defines a definition description for a definition term.

Figure demonstrates how the elements are used, and Figure shows the rendered result. It is useful to know that lists are indented by browsers by default, and all the elements are block-level elements. In addition, the list elements add space at the top and bottom by default and the size of the space is about the default font size used by the browser.

```
HTML
<h2>Unordered List</h2>
<ul>
   <li>First unordered list item</li>
   <li>Second unordered list item</li>
</ul>

<h2>Ordered List</h2>
<ol>
   <li>First ordered list item</li>
   <li>Second ordered list item</li>
</ol>

<h2>Definition List</h2>
<dl>
   <dt>The first term</dt>
     <dd>First term definition description</dd>
   <dt>The second term</dt>
     <dd>Second term definition description</dd>
</dl>
```

Figure: Example usage of all the list elements.

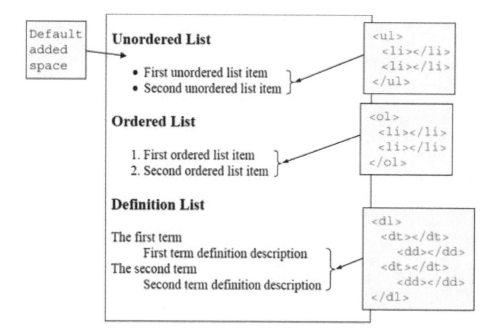

Common List Attributes

The <ol> element can take a number of attributes to influence numbering or lettering of the list items. The most commonly used attributes are the start attribute, which specifies the start value for numbering or lettering items, and the type attribute, which specifies the kind of marker to use for numbering or lettering, which must be 1, a, A, i, or I. Figure shows both attributes in use, and depicts the result. Note that the type attribute should be used only where the type of marker plays an important role, such as in legal documents, where items are referred to from elsewhere in a document by their number or letter; otherwise, the CSS list-style-type property, which is used to specify list-item markers, should be used, since specifying list-item markers is considered styling in Web design. List-item markers for the <ul> element can also be changed using this property. For example, it can be used to specify custom bullets points made from images.

```
HTML
<h3>Common list attributes</h3>
<h4>List 1 Part 1</h4>
<ol>
   <li>First ordered list item</li>
   <li>Second ordered list item</li>
   <li>Third ordered list item</li>
</ol>
<h4>List 1 Part 2</h4>
<ol start="4">
   <li>First ordered list item</li>
   <li>Second ordered list item</li>
   <li>Third ordered list item</li>
</ol>
<h4>A different list</h4>
<ol type="A">
   <li>First ordered list item</li>
   <li>Second ordered list item</li>
   <li>Third ordered list item</li>
</ol>
```

start="4" specifies to start numbering from "4"

type="A" specifies to order list by using uppercase Latin letters

Figure: Example usage of start and type attributes.

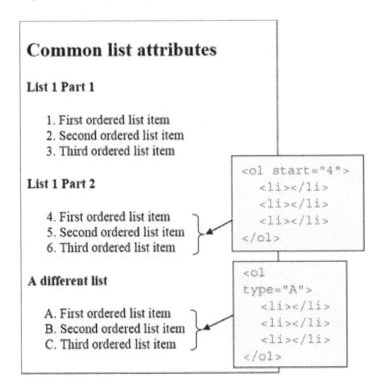

Figure: The rendered result

Nested Lists

Sometimes, it is necessary to create nested lists, which are lists that have lists as list items. To achieve this, a list element is simply placed in a list item element. Figure shows how this is done in the unordered and ordered lists, and Figure shows the result. Notice that in the nested ordered list, the type attribute is used to specify lowercase lettering. As mentioned earlier, if specifying marker type is just to order a list and the items are not to be referenced, then CSS should be used.

```
HTML
<h3>Nested Unordered List</h3>
<ul>
  <li>First item</li>
    <ul>
       <li>First item, first sub-item</li>
       <li>First item, second sub-item</li>
    </ul>
  </li>
  <li>Second item</li>
  <li>Third item</li>
</ul>

<h3>Nested Ordered List</h3>
<ol>
  <li>First item<//i>
    <ol type="a">
       <li>First item, first sub-item</li>
       <li>First item, second sub-item</li>
    </ol>
  </li>
  <li>Second item</li>
  <li>Third item</li>
</ol>
```

Figure: Example of nested unordered and order lists.

Nested Unordered List

- First item
  - First item, first sub-item
  - First item, second sub-item
- Second item
- Third item

Nested Ordered List

1. First item
   a. First item, first sub-item
   b. First item, second sub-item
2. Second item
3. Third item

Figure: The rendered result

Tables

Various types of information benefit from being presented by using a table. Tables are especially crucial for representing complex data, such as stock reports and time tables. The typical properties of a table are illustrated in Figure, all of which can be represented using HTML, except width, height, cell padding, cell spacing, and various other types of styling, which are defined by using CSS.

Figure: The typical properties of a table.

Table describes the HTML table elements used for defining the structural properties of a table.

TABLE

Some Commonly Used Table Elements

Element	Function
<table>...</table>	Creates a table.
<caption>...</caption>	Defines a table caption, which is like the title.
<th>...</th>	Defines a cell as a header for a group of column or row cells.
<tr>...</tr>	Defines a row in a table, and tr stands for table row.
<td>...</td>	Defines a cell in a table row of a table, and td stands for table data.
<colgroup>...</colgroup>	Defines a group of columns.
<col>	Defines a column and is usually in a <colgroup> element. Note that it is an empty element.
<thead>...</thead>	Defines a block of rows that define the head of the columns of a table.
<tbody>...</tbody>	Defines the set of rows that form the body for a table.
<tfoot>...</tfoot>	Defines a set of rows that summarize the columns of a table.

Basic Tables

<table>, <caption>, <th>, <tr>, and <td>

The table, caption, table heading, table row, and table data elements are common to almost any table, as they describe the essence of a table. For this reason, they are being discussed together. Figure shows how they are used, and Figure shows the table that is created.

As you should be able to see in the example, everything about a table goes between the opening and the closing tags of the <table> element and the contents of every row are placed inside the <tr> element. The contents can be table headings or table data, as well as information about the table, such as caption, included by using the <caption> element. Caption may be made strong or emphasized, using the <strong> or <em> element, and should not be wider than a table's width to avoid being clipped. The summary attribute is usually used to provide additional information about a table. Although browsers do not display the information, providing the information **improves accessibility**, because it is used by user agents that do not render HTML into visual information, such as screen readers, to adequately inform visually impaired users.

```
HTML
<h2>A basic table</h2>
<table summary="This table provides the inventory of fruits in
    stock">
 <caption>Fruits Inventory</caption>
 <tr>
   <td></td>
   <th>Item</th>
   <th>Bought</th>
   <th>Sold</th>
   <th>Balance</th>
 </tr>
 <tr>
   <td>1.</td><th>Apples</th><td>300</td><td>200</td><td>100</td>
 </tr>
 <tr><td>2.</td><th>Bananas</th><td>250</td><td>150</td>
     <td>100</td></tr>
 <tr><td>3.</td><th>Grapes</th><td>400</td><td>200</td>
     <td>200</td></tr>
</table>
```

Figure: Example usage of table elements.

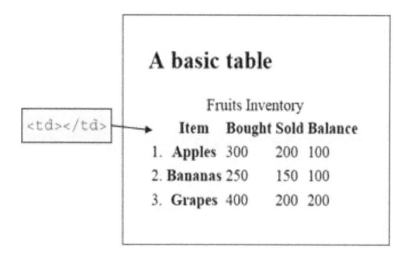

Figure: The rendered result with and without border.

Notice that even **when a cell is empty**, an empty <td> element is still used to represent it; otherwise, the table will not look properly when put together. Also notice that the contents of the <th> elements are displayed in bold. They are also displayed in the middle of the cell. Using the <th> element for headings (instead of using the <td> element and making the contents bold manually through CSS) is especially good practice, as user agents, such as screen readers, recognize the element and are therefore able to render it in the way that best communicates the contents of a table to the user. The element also enables pages to be indexed more effectively by search engines. In the example, there are both **row headers** (i.e., apples, bananas, and grapes) and **column headers** (i.e., item, bought, sold, and balance).

Columns' Grouping

As introduced in Table, the element used to group columns is the <colgroup> element. When used, it should be placed after caption but before any other table element. It can either contain <col> elements (each of which can represent one or more columns) or take the span attribute, but not both. The <col> element, too, may take the span attribute. The attribute specifies the number of consecutive columns spanned by an element. Figure shows how the <colgroup> and <col> elements are used together, and Figure shows how the <colgroup> element is used without the <col> element. Both produce the same result, shown in Figure.

In both examples, the span attribute specifies to group the next two columns and give the group a class name of "first_two", which is then used to make the group's background color gray by using CSS. The next < colgroup> or <col> element specifies to give the next column the class name of "next_col", which is used to make column's background color yellow. Note that the colors have been used here to only show the effects of the grouping elements.

```
HTML
<h3>Columns grouping</h3>
<table>
 <colgroup>
   <col span="2" class="first-two">
   <col class="next_col">
 </colgroup>
 <tr>
   <th>ID_No</th>
   <th>Name</th>
   <th>Age</th>
   <th>Height</th>
 </tr>
 <tr><td>10001</td><td>James Normal</td><td>28</td>
     <td>6ft 1in</td></tr>
 <tr><td>10002</td><td>Amanda Holmes</td><td>24</td>
     <td>5ft 6in</td></tr>
</table>
```

Figure: Example usage of the <colgroup> element with the <col> element.

```
HTML
<h3>Columns grouping</h3>
<table>
  <colgroup span="2" class="first_two"></colgroup>
  <colgroup class="next_col"></colgroup>
  <tr>
    <th>ID_No</th>
    <th>Name</th>
    <th>Age</th>
    <th>Height</th>
  </tr>
  <tr><td>10001</td><td>James Normal</td><td>28</td>
      <td>6ft 1in</td></tr>
  <tr><td>10002</td><td>Amanda Holmes</td><td>24</td>
      <td>5ft 6in</td></tr>
</table>
```

Figure: Example usage of the <colgroup> element without the <col> element.

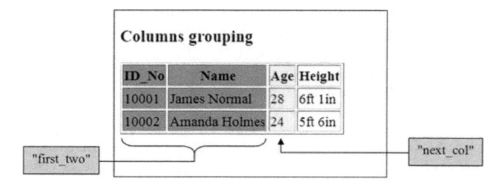

Figure: The result of Figures

Table Cells' Merging

<rowspan> and <colspan>

The merging of table cells is crucial in extending the application of tables beyond just using them to present basic information. In HTML, this is achieved with the rowspan and colspan attributes in the <th> and <td> elements. Figure shows how it is done, and Figure depicts the rendered result.

In the example, notice that the table has a border. This has been done by using CSS, and it is necessary to use it at this point to show the effects of rowspan and colspan, which otherwise will not have been apparent without a border. In the **first table row element**, the first rowspan attribute specifies that the cell should span one column (the default) and two rows; the colspan specifies that the cell should span one row (the default) and two columns.

Like the first, the second rowspan specifies to span one column and two rows. In the **second table row element**, the two <th> elements are used to put content in the second row of the table, which has only two columns, bearing in mind that the first cells of the first and fourth columns belong to the first row. The last two <tr> elements are used to fill the cells of the remaining rows, as normal.

```
HTML
<h3>Table cells merging<h3>
<table>
  <caption><em>Obesity statistics</em></caption>
  <tr>
    <td rowspan="2"></td>
    <th colspan="2">Average</th>
    <th rowspan="2">Obese <br> %</th>
  </tr>
  <tr>
    <th>Age</th>
    <th>Weight</th>
  </tr>
  <tr><th>Males</th><td>45</td><td>13st</td><td>41%</td></tr>
  <tr><th>Females</th><td>35</td><td>11st</td><td>33%</td></tr>
</table>
```

Figure: Example usage of rowspan and colspan attributes in cells merging.

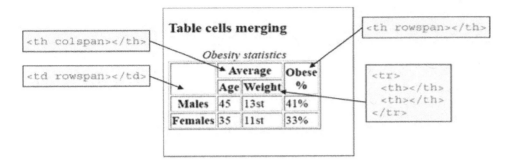

Figure: The result of Figure

CHALLENGE

Write the HTML code for the table below. You can again ignore the border. The centering of the content of the data cells is left as another

	Introduction to Web Design			
	Academic Session 2015/2016			
	No. of Years	Courses	Weeks	Project
Day	1	Mixed	13	Yes
Evening	2	Mixed		
Enjoy the unit!				

Long Tables

<thead>, <tbody>, and <tfoot>

Long tables can make it difficult to use a table and also make it inaccessible to users with disability who use assistive technologies, such screen readers. For example, when a table is longer than what can fit into one screen and scrolling is required, the header usually disappears, making it difficult to figure out what goes under which column. The elements intended to solve problems caused by long tables are <thead>, <tbody>, and <tfoot>. However, as of time of writing, the functionality of these elements is yet to be implemented enough in most browsers to fully realize the goals for which they have been designed.

The effects of the <thead>, <tbody>, and <tfoot> are not usually visible; therefore, the code in Figure will produce just an ordinary table, similar to the one in Figure. This is because these elements merely enable a table to be divided into header, body, and footer parts. It is recommended when the elements are used and a table is very long that the <tfoot> element is placed before the <tbody> element to enable the browser to render the footer before all rows of data are received, which can take time. When the elements are used, it is possible for users to scroll through the body of a table independently of the header and footer. With a long table, it may also be possible to have the header and the footer printed on every page of data, instead of just on the first and last pages, respectively.

```
HTML
<h3>Long table</h3>
<table>
  <caption><em>Fruits Inventory</em></caption>
  <thead>
    <tr>
      <td></td>
      <th>Item</th>
      <th>Bought</th>
      <th>Sold</th>
      <th>Balance</th>
    </tr>
  </thead>
  <tbody>
    <tr><td>1.</td><th>Apples</th><td>300</td><td>200</td>
        <td>100</td></tr>
    <tr><td>2.</td><th>Bananas</th><td>250</td><td>150</td>
        <td>100</td></tr>
    <tr><td>3.</td><th>Grapes</th><td>400</td><td>200</td>
        <td>200</td></tr>
    ...
  </tbody>
  <tfoot>
    <tr><td></td><td>Total</td><td>4050</td><td>5550</td>
        <td>4800</td></tr>
  </tfoot>
</table>
```

FIGURE Example usage of the <thead>, <tbody>, and <tfoot> elements.

Tables and Accessibility

Even when tables look well-structured to the eyes, assistive technologies can still interpret their contents inaccurately, causing problems for visually impaired users. For example, screen readers might read out their contents in the wrong order. This is especially likely when tables are complex, are simple but have unusual structure, or are created by using unusual practices. Providing information about the relationship between table cells is one of the ways in which the problem is minimized, and the attributes most commonly used to achieve this are scope, id, and headers. The scope attribute can be used by itself, while id and headers must be used together.

The scope Attribute and Accessibility

The scope attribute is used for defining the scope of a header (i.e., the cells that are affected by a header). It defines whether the header defined in the <th> element is for a row, column, or a group of rows or columns. Situations in which using it is recommended include when the header of a table is not in the first row or column and where a data cell that is marked up with the <td> element is used as a header. The attribute takes any of the four values: col, row, rowgroup, or colgroup.

Scope Function

Attribute Value

Col Means that the header applies to all the cells in the same row as the element. Row Means that the header applies to all the cells in the same column as the element. rowgroup Means that the header applies to all remaining cells in the row group to which header belongs, which are either to the left or to the right of the <th> element; however, it is to the right by default, since table directionality is left to right by default.

Different table directionality can be specified by the value of the dir attribute in the <table> element. It is a global attribute, whose value can be "ltr" (i.e., left to right, and the default), "rtl" (i.e., right to left), or "auto" (i.e., the browser decides, based on content). colgroup Means that the header applies to all remaining cells in the column group to which header belongs.

```
HTML
<h3>Long table</h3>
<table>
  <caption><em>Fruits Inventory</em></caption>
  <thead>
    <tr>
      <td></td>
      <th>Item</th>
      <th>Bought</th>
      <th>Sold</th>
      <th>Balance</th>
    </tr>
  </thead>
  <tbody>
    <tr><td>1.</td><th>Apples</th><td>300</td><td>200</td>
        <td>100</td></tr>
    <tr><td>2.</td><th>Bananas</th><td>250</td><td>150</td>
        <td>100</td></tr>
    <tr><td>3.</td><th>Grapes</th><td>400</td><td>200</td>
        <td>200</td></tr>
    ...
  </tbody>
  <tfoot>
    <tr><td></td><td>Total</td><td>4050</td><td>5550</td>
        <td>4800</td></tr>
  </tfoot>
</table>
```

Figure: Example usage of the scope attribute to aid accessibility

Notice that the code in the example is the same as that in Figure, except for the addition of the scope attribute to the cell of each row that is a header (but not in the first column) and the cells of the first row that are headers. Basically, as a general rule, all <th> elements and <td> elements that act as headers should have a scope attribute. The attribute does not affect the appearance of a table, so the code in the example produces the same result as in Figure.

The id and headers Attributes and Accessibility

As introduced in Chapter, the id attribute is a **global attribute** used to give a unique identity to an element. The headers attribute, on the other hand, is used to associate one or more header cells with a table cell. Its value must correspond to the id attribute of the <th> element with which it is associated. When multiple values are specified, the **values are spaceseparated**, each value again corresponding to the id attribute of the <th> element with which it is associated.

The technique is usually suitable for the situation when the use of the scope attribute is not enough to describe the relationships between table headers and data cells, such as when data cells are associated with more than one row and/or column header. Figure shows how the attributes are used together, and Figure shows the created table. Notice that as with the scope attribute, the id and headers attributes do not affect the display of a table.

Again, note that the border has been added by using CSS, and this has been done just to make the table clearer to see. In the **first table row element**, the <th> elements are given c, t, and e identities, respectively. In the **second table row element**, each <th> is given an id and is also associated with the corresponding <th> element defined in the first <tr>, using the headers attribute. In the **third table row element**, the headers attribute is used to associate each <td> element with the appropriate <th> element.

```
HTML
<h2>Accessibility, id and headers</h2>
<table>
 <tr>
  <th rowspan="2" id="c">Coursework</th>
  <th colspan="2" id="t">Tests</th>
  <th colspan="2" id="e">Exams</th>
 </tr>
 <tr>
  <th id="t1" headers="t">1</th>
  <th id="t2" headers="t">2</th>
  <th id="e1" headers="e">1</th>
  <th id="e2" headers="e">2</th>
 </tr>
 <tr>
  <td headers="c">20%</td>
  <td headers="t t1">10%</td>
  <td headers="t t2">10%</td>
  <td headers="e e1">30%</td>
  <td headers="e e2">30%</td>
 </tr>
</table>
```

Figure: Example usage of id and headers attributes to aid accessibility.

Figure: The rendered result of Figure

Links

Links, technically known as **hyperlinks**, are the very essence of the Web, because they are the feature that enables interconnection between pages and browsing, without which the Web would be non-existent. The common types of links are as follows:

Linking from a page to another website.
Linking from a page to another page on the same website.

Linking from a part of a page to another part on the same page.
Linking from a page to a specific part of a page on another website.
Linking from a page to an e-mail program to start a new message.

The element used to create all these types of links is the <a> element (known as **anchor element**). The element **defines an anchor** but not the hyperlink; the hyperlink reference attribute, href, and a value (which must be a URL) are required to do this, as shown in Figure. The content between the opening and the closing tags is what is turned into a hyperlink.

In the example, the text "Click here for BBC" is made a link, so that when it is clicked, the Web browser fetches the document "index.html" from the local hard disk cache, if a copy has been cached (saved), or requests it from the Web server at the location "http://www.bbc.co.uk" and displays it. By default, a new page replaces the current one in the browser window, unless the browser is instructed to display the new page in a new window, using the target attribute, which was introduced in Chapter.

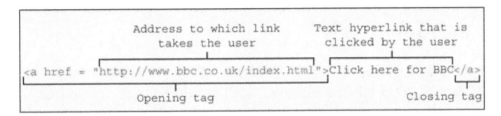

Figure: The structure of the HTML code for a hyperlink.

Linking to Another Website

When linking to a website, the link typically points to the home page (i.e., it is the URL of a website's root directory on a Web server that is typically specified); the URL of a specific document is not usually specified. When a link points to the root directory, the Web server usually serves the document **index.html** by default, which is the home page. Figure shows how this is done and depicts the result.

Where a link is inside text, as opposed to when used in a main menu, in order to enhance accessibility, **link text should be meaningful** enough to convey its purpose on its own and out of context. If this is not possible, any additional description providing the context for the link should be placed close to the link (e.g., in the same sentence or paragraph), such that it is easy for users to identify without moving focus from the link. A good example and a bad example are shown in the NOTE box that follows.

```
HTML
<h3>External links</h3>
<p>Popular links:</p>
  <ul>
    <li><a href="http://www.movies.com">Movies</a></li>
    <li><a href="http://www.fishing.com">Fishing</a></li>
    <li><a href="http://www.yogalessons.com">Yoga lessons</a></li>
    <li><a href="http://www.youtube.com">YouTube</a></li>
  </ul>
```

Figure: Example usage of the <a> element for external links.

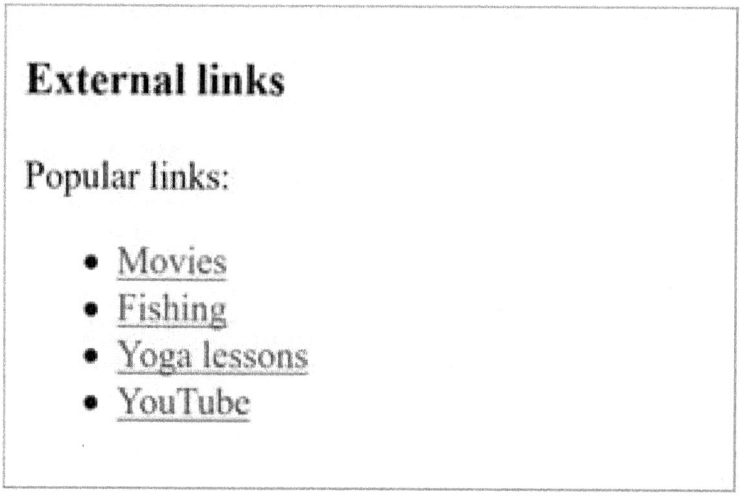

External links

Popular links:

- Movies
- Fishing
- Yoga lessons
- YouTube

Figure: The result of Figure.

NOTE: Examples of good and bad link texts

Good: "See the Information page to know more about…"
Not ideal: "To know more, click here to go to the Information page"
Poor: "Click here for more."

CHALLENGE

Create the menu links in Figure but without using the list elements to produce the following:

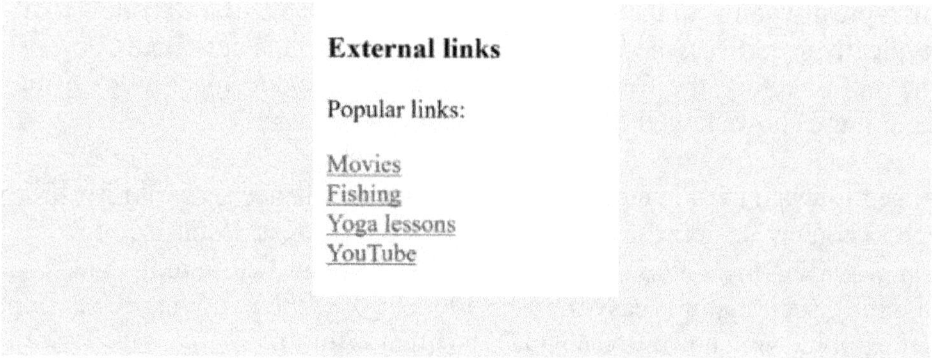

External links

Popular links:

Movies
Fishing
Yoga lessons
YouTube

Linking to Another Page on the Same Website

Linking a page to another page on the same website is similar to linking to another website, except that you do not need to specify an absolute address. Figure shows how it is done. Notice the relative addresses. It means that all the files are in the same directory (folder) as the page displaying the links. See Chapter for explanation of absolute and relative addresses. The main advantage of using relative addressing is that an entire site can be built on a local computer and then uploaded to a Web server for hosting, without having to make any adjustments after uploading, as long as the relationships between the locations of the pages are maintained.

```
HTML
<h3>Within-site links</h3>
<ul>
   <li><a href="index.html">Home</a></li>
   <li><a href="features.html">Features</a></li>
   <li><a href="support.html">Support</a></li>
   <li><a href="download.html">Download</a></li>
   <li><a href="about.html">About us</a></li>
   <li><a href="store.html">Store</a></li>
</ul>
```

Figure: Example usage of the <a> element for within-site links.

Linking to Another Part on the Same Page

Linking to another part of the same page is known as **within-page linking** and uses the same underlying principle as linking to a whole page, except that the points to which to link first have to be identified, after which the anchor element is used to link to them. The points are identified by using the id or name attribute.

Using the id Attribute

Figure shows how the id attribute is used to link within page, and shows the rendered result. The three sections to navigate to are identified as " instruction_video," "situation_video," and "scripted_video." The <a> element is then used to create links to the three sections from the menu at the top of the page, as well as to the start of the page from each section. Notice that the value of each href attribute starts with a # symbol, followed by the value of the id attribute of the element (i.e., section) to which to link. Using the # symbol alone for the value of the href attribute means to link to the start of the current page. An empty string (e.g., href="") or just href without any value can also be used.

```
HTML
<h2>Types of video style</h2>
Menu  <a href="#instruction_video">Instructional video</a><br>
       <a href="#situation_video">Situation video</a><br>
       <a href="#scripted_video">Scripted enactment</a><br><br>

       <h3 id="instruction_video">Instruction video</h3>
Part   <p>The main aim of this style is to share or deliver
          information. Examples of usage include in news
          broadcast and video documentary.</p>
       <p><a href="#">Top</a></p>

       <h3 id="situation_video">Situation video</h3>
Part   <p>In a situated video style, viewers are given the
          sense that they are watching an action from
          thecorner of the room.</p>
       <p><a href="#">Top</a></p>

       <h3 id="scripted_video">Scripted enactment</h3>
Part   <p>A video of this style is used for re-enacting a
          situation that is not practical to capture as it
          happens in real-life; or a situation that is made
          up.</p>
       <p><a href="#">Top</a></p>
```

Figure: Example usage of id attribute for within-page links.

Figure: The result in the browser.

Using the name Attribute

To use the name attribute to link within a page, you use the attribute with the <a> element to create anchors at the points to link to (i.e., the start of the page and the start of each of the three sections). Then, you use the <a> element again with the href attribute to create the necessary hyperlinks, again starting the href attribute's value with the # symbol, followed by the value of the name attribute of the <a> element (i.e., section) to which to link. This code is shown in Figure. Notice that no content is placed between the opening and closing tags of the <a> elements used to define the named anchor points to which to link. This is because it is not necessary.

```
HTML
<h2>Types of video style</h2>
<a href="#instruction_video">Instructional video</a><br>
<a href="#situation_video">Situation video</a><br/>
<a href="#scripted_video">Scripted enactment</a><br><br>

<p><a name="instruction_video"></a></p>
<h3>Instruction video</h3>
<p>The main aim of this style is to share or deliver
   information. Examples of usage include in news
   broadcast and video documentary.</p>
<p><a href="#">Top</a></p>

<p><a name="situation_video"></a></p>
<h3>Situation video</h3>
<p>In a situated video style, viewers are given the sense
   that they are watching an action from the corner of the
   room.</p>
<p><a href="#">Top</a></p>

<p><a name="scripted_video"></a></p>
<h3>Scripted enactment</h3>
<p>A video of this style is used for re-enacting a
   situation that is not practical to capture as it
   happens in real-life; or a situation that is made
   up.</p>
<p><a href="#">Top</a></p>
```

Menu { ... }

Part { ... }

Figure: Using the name attribute for the example in Figure.

Within-Page Links in Web Design

The use of within-page links is generally discouraged for various reasons. One, according to the NN Group, is that it **violates the mental model that users have of the way a hyperlink should behave**, and so, it can confuse them. This model is that a link leads to a new page that is displayed from start, and the Back button takes users to the previous page. However, the use of within-page links can be less confusing if it is made clear to users what to expect when they click them. One way in which this can be done is to have link description say where a link leads, for example, "for more, click to go to the relevant section." Also, there are situations where within page links are acceptable, such as when the sections of a page are summarized at the top of the page, with links leading directly to the sections. Examples of these types of situations include when presenting alphabetized lists, frequently asked questions (FAQs), and a page that has a table of contents at its start that leads to sections in the page, such as those shown in Figures.

NOTE: Accessibility application

The principle of linking from the top of a page to other parts of the page can be useful in making a page more accessible to screen reader users by including a "Jump to Main Content" link at the top of the page, so that it is one of the first things that screen reader users hear or users that use only keyboard encounter when using the tab key. The link enables users to skip long list of navigation menu and go directly to the main content. The link can also be hidden (made invisible), so that it does not interfere with the aesthetics of a design from the viewpoint of sighted users. This is done by using CSS, and how it is done is discussed under "Absolute positioning" in Chapter.

Linking to a Specific Part on Another Page

Linking to a specific part of a page on a website can be achieved with the same technique as used for linking to a specific part on the same page, as long as the part or section to be linked to on a page has a unique identification and it is known. All that is required is to add the identifier to the end of the link to the page. The URL can be relative or absolute. If the page in on the same website, then relative URL can be used, but if the page is on another website, it has to be absolute.

NOTE: Link to part of another page in design

Users should not be dumped in the middle of a new page without an indication of where they are. The part to which they are directed should have a clear heading that is visible, without the need to scroll up or down to see it. This can be done, for example, by using a named anchor above the header element that contains the heading, as shown in Figure.

Linking to an E-Mail Program

When a hyperlink points to an e-mail program, the user's e-mail program is opened with a new message addressed to the specified e-mail address. To achieve this, the <a> element is also used, except that the value of the href attribute starts with mail to: followed by the e-mail address to which you want the message to be sent. Figure shows how it is done, and depicts the result. When the link is clicked by the user, the default email client (program) on his or her computer is opened.

```
HTML
<h3>Email link</h3>
<p>Email me at:<a href="mailto:joe@example.com">
    joe@example.com</a><p>
<a href="mailto:customer@example.com">Email us</a>
```

Figure: Examples of how e-mail links are created.

Email link

Email me at: joe@example.com

Email us

Figure: The result in the browser.

Forms

On-line forms are an essential means of collecting information from users, and most websites require the completion of a form for one purpose or another. They are basically the screen version of traditional paper forms, and most of the features commonly used in paper forms translate well into screen forms. Like paper forms, they can be of any size, but they also incorporate other features, such as buttons, drop-down list, and buttons, and can be interacted with in various ways, including via mouse, digital pen, and touch. This chapter introduces the various elements used to build a Web form.

Form Element

Forms are used to collect information from users and vary widely in size and purpose. For example, it could contain just a single text field for the input of a search term to search the Web, two fields for taking the username and password to login to a site, or many types of inputs for collecting information about a user during registration. Every form, no matter how basic or complex, includes a button for the user to use to submit the form to the Web server for the processing of the entered information. The way the process works is illustrated in Figure.

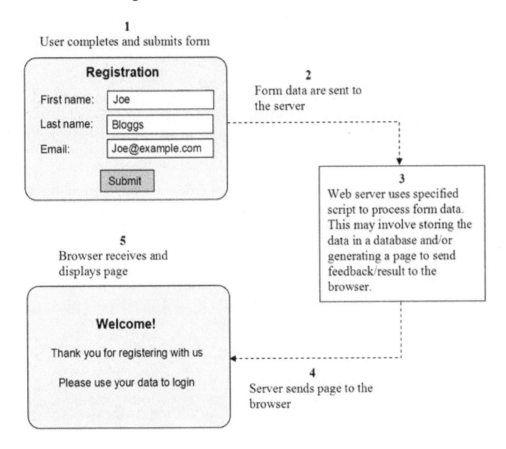

Figure: A basic illustration of how forms are handled.

The <form> element is the element that is used to hold all the various elements that are used to describe the features of a form. The elements used to collect input are known as **form controls**. A control must have a name. The information entered by the user is associated with this name, and both are sent by the browser to the Web server as a **name-value** pair. For example, in the illustration in Figure, if the names given to the controls are **fname, lname**, and **email**, respectively, then the name-value pairs sent would be **fname=Joe, lname=Bloggs**, and **email= joe@example.com**.

The <form> element allows these pairs to be sent to the Web server through the use of the action and method attributes. The action attribute allows you to specify the URL of the script to use by Web server to process the data, and the method attribute allows you to specify how the data should be packaged and sent to the Web server. The two possible methods are **GET** and **POST**, each of which is suitable for different situations.

With the **GET method**, the pairs are added to the end of the URL specified in the action attribute, separated by "?," with the pairs joined using "&."

Situations for which the GET method is well suited include when the amount of collected data is small and is going to be used for searching a database. It is not suitable for a lot of data, because it supports only 1024 characters. It should also not be used for sensitive information, because people can easily hack into it. It also does not support binary data, such as image files and Word documents.

With the **POST method**, the pairs are sent via what are called **HTTP headers**. The pairs are joined in the same way as in the GET method, that is, by using "&." The method is suitable for all the uses described above, for which the GET method is unsuitable. Figure shows how the action and method attributes are used with the <form> element.

In addition to the action and method attributes, the <form> element supports other attributes that are commonly used. Table lists them, starting with the two already mentioned.

```
HTML
<form method="post" action= "http://www.test.com/register.php">
  <!--Form control elements go here -->
</form>
```

Figure: Using the action and method attributes with the <form> element.

TABLE

Common Attributes Supported by the <form> Element

Form Element Attributes	Function
action	Specifies the URL of the script to use to process submitted form data.
method	Specifies the method to use to send submitted form data. Value can be get or post. Or, it can be dialog, when integrating the <form> element in the <dialog> element introduced in Chapter 3.
name	Specifies a unique name for a form.
enctype	Specifies how form data should be encoded and is applicable only to the POST method. Accepted values are application/x-www-form-urlencoded (the default), multipart/form-data (used for forms that contain files, binary data, and non-ASCII data, such as glyphs), and text/plain.
target	Specifies where to display the response to form submission. Acceptable values are _blank, _self, _parent, and _top, all of which were introduced in Chapter 2, under the <link> element.
accept-charset	Specifies the character encoding to use for submission. Accepts a space- or comma-separated list of character encodings.
novalidate	Specifies that form should not be validated and used with no value. The same result can be achieved using the formnovalidate attribute on a <button> or <input> element. These elements are discussed fully later in the chapter. The default is for a form to be validated.
autocomplete	Specifies whether or not browser should remember values entered previously by the user and use the best match to automatically complete an input or offer them as options as the user starts to complete the input. The values taken are on and off.

Form Controls

Forms can generally be boiled down to containing four categories of controls: those for **inputting text**, those for **making selections**, those for **uploading files**, and those for **starting an action**. Table lists the controls that can be used to achieve these goals, all of which are discussed in this section.

<input>

The <input> element is the most commonly used in forms, because it is used to display different types of controls. It is an inline element, which means that the <br> element or a block-level container element (e.g., <div> or <p>) must be used to go to a new line. It takes many attributes. The most important is the type attribute, as it specifies input type and the type of control interface that is displayed, which includes **text-input field**, **radio button**, **checkbox**, and **drop-down menu**. Other attributes specify the behaviour of these controls. Although there are many input types, their usage is based on the same principle, using the following format:

<input type="value">

Different sets of attributes are used with different input types. Some are mandatory, and others are optional. They will be introduced, as necessary, as the input types are presented.

TABLE

Form Controls and Elements Used with Them

Form Controls	Function
`<input>`	Defines a form control for user input.
`<button>...</button>`	Defines a button.
`<textarea>...</textarea>`	Defines a form control for multi-line user text input.
`<select>...</select>`	Used to create a drop-down list.
`<datalist>...</datalist>`	Used to create a drop-down list that suggests possible values from a range of values, based on what the user types in.
`<option>...</option>`	Defines an option in a select or datalist list.

Elements Used with Controls	Function
`<label>...</label>`	Used to associate a label with a control.
`<output>...<output>`	Used to display the result of a calculation or user action.
`<progress>...<progress>`	Used to display the completion progress of a task.
`<meter>...<meter>`	Used to display a level within a range.
`<optgroup>...</optgroup>`	Used to group options on a drop-down list.
`<fieldset>...</fieldset>`	Used to group controls. Also, it encloses them in a border.
`<legend>...</legend>`	Used to display a caption for the content of its parent `<fieldset>` element.
`<keygen>`	Although this element was introduced in HTML5, it has been deprecated and will no longer be supported by browsers, so its use is discouraged.

Input Types for Collecting Text

There are input types for collecting plain text as well as input types for collecting numeric data and formatted text, such as time and date, and most of them display an editable text-input field, into which the user can type. Some of them also have additional control features, such as increment decrement and/or drop-down menu buttons, to help user input. To better explain them here, they are presented in the categories of those used for plain text input, those for entering numbers, and those for entering time and date data.

Input Types for Collecting Plain Text

The input types introduced here are typically used to collect short text inputs from a user, such as personal details and search terms, which basically can consist of any character; however, you can also make them collect only certain types of characters and in a specific order. Table lists their names and functions.

All the input types in Table support the same set of attributes, except the **hidden-input type**, which supports only name and value. Table lists the attributes and their functions.

TABLE

Text-Input Type Values

Input Type	Function
text	Displays a single-line plain text box for text input.
password	Displays a single-line text box for text input and displays input as dots.
email	Displays a single-line text box.
url	Displays a single-line text box
tel	Displays a single-line text box
search	Displays a single-line text box.
hidden	Creates and hides an element from the user. Used to hold values for use by Web designer or developer.

TABLE

Attributes Supported by Input Types that Display Text Fields

Attribute	Function
name	Specifies a unique name for element.
value	Specifies the default value for element.
size	Specifies the length (in characters) of text-input field. Default is 20.
minlength	Specifies the minimum number of characters allowed in a text field.
maxlength	Specifies the maximum number of characters allowed in a text field.
pattern	Specifies an expression (a format) that user's input must match. When used, you should include a title attribute to describe the pattern.
placeholder	Gives an instruction or an example to user about what to enter in a text field.
readonly	Specifies whether or not users can edit a text field.
spellcheck	Specifies to check element's spelling and grammar. The values that it takes are true (which means to check), false (which means not to check), and default (which means to use a default value, such as the spellcheck value set for the parent element).
list	Specifies the id value on a <datalist> element with which to associate element.
required	Specifies that user must provide input for a control.
disabled	Specifies to disable a control, so that it is not responsive to user action.
autocomplete	Specifies whether or not browser should remember values entered previously by the user and use the best match to automatically complete a field or offer them as options as the user starts to complete the field. Typical values taken are on and off.
autofocus	Specifies to give input focus to a form control when a form loads.
autosave	Used to specify a unique category name for the search history saved by the browser for a **search-input type** field.
inputmode	Specifies which type of input mechanism (typically type of virtual keyboard) to display. It is used to display the type of keyboard that is most useful to the user for entering text into a control. It is especially useful for touch-screen devices, such as mobile phones. Values supported include verbatim, latin, latin-name, latin-prose, full-width-latin, kana, kana-name, katakana, numeric, tel, email, and url, each of which displays different type of keyboard.
multiple	Specifies whether the user is allowed to enter more than one value, and it can be specified by itself, without a value (instead of multiple="multiple"). It only applies to the **email-input type** (and **file-input type**, discussed later).

In the example, notice that all the input types have a similar format. The attributes used to perform the functions are described in Table. The **Username** and **Password** fields have been completed for the purpose of demonstration. The non-letter characters displayed in the **password-input type** field are automatic and for the purpose of preventing others from knowing what the user types. The required attribute ensures that a form is not allowed to submit until the user has completed the input for the element that has it. Notice that it does not have any value. The longhand is required= "required", which is unnecessary.

Since the attribute does not usually provide any visual cues until after a form has been submitted and the browser has prompted that a control must be completed, it can be useful to include some visual means of informing users of the controls that must be completed, so that they know beforehand. For example, the background or border of a field could be made with a different color from those of other controls. This is achieved using CSS, and how it is done is explained in Chapter.

```
HTML
<h3>Form text input</h3>
<form>
  <p>Please complete the form below:</p>
  <p>Username:<input type="text" name="uname" required></p>
  <p>Password:<input type="password" name="password" required></p>
  <p>Email:<input type="email" name="email"
        placeholder="e.g., joe@example.com" required></p>
  <p>Phone:<input type="tel" name="phone"></p>
  <p>Personal URL:<input type="url" name="url" size="25"
  maxlength="35"></p>
  <p>Search:<input type="search" name="term" value="bolts"></p>
  <p><input type="hidden" name="subject" value="registration"></p>
</form>
```

Figure: Example usage of plain text-input types.

Form text input

Please complete the form below:

Username: Joe12345

Password: •••••••

Email: e.g., joe@example.com

Phone:

Personal URL:

Search: bolts

Figure: Rendered result of Figure.

The use of the required attribute is a part of a process known as **form validation**, which involves checking a submitted form to ensure that all the required inputs have been completed and the inputs are of the correct type and/or format. It is an important process, because it ensures the integrity of submitted form data.

Traditionally, this was done using client-side JavaScript scripting. However, HTML now has attributes to help with the process. One of them is the required attribute. Another is the pattern attribute. Although the attribute is not used in the example, it can be useful for ensuring that users enter certain types of information, such as e-mail address, correctly. It is easy to specify. However, deriving the correct **regular expression** (also called **regex**) to specify can be difficult, because it involves mathematics.

```
HTML
<form>
  Enter product code (XXX999999):
  <input type="text" name="product" pattern="[A-Za-z]{3}[0-9]{6}"
    title="Three upper- or lower-case letters followed by six
    digits.">
</form>
```

Figure: Example usage of the pattern attribute.

The expression is used to verify that user input comprises three upper- or lowercase letters, followed by six digits. The content of the title attribute in the code is displayed when the cursor hovers over the text field. If the user enters an input whose format does not match the pattern, the browser immediately prompts him or her to re-input the data and also reminds him or her of the correct format. Using the attribute with email and password input types can be especially useful for ensuring that correct e-mail formats are inputted and that the passwords chosen by users are varied and complex and therefore difficult to guess by hackers.

To ensure password complexity, users are compelled to include a wide variety of combinations of lower- and uppercase letters, numbers, and characters. The explanation of how regular expressions are formulated is beyond the scope of this book. However, there are useful expressions on the Web. It is not important to understand how they work to be able to use them. You only need to know what they do.

Refer to Figure and notice the text in the **email field**, which is placed there with the placeholder attribute. It is temporary and disappears the moment the field receives focus or the user starts to type into it. Next, notice that the **Search text field** is filled with the word "bolts" by default. This is the effect of specifying the value attribute in the **search-input type**. In contrast, the **hidden-input type** does not display anything. It simply creates a **name-value pair**, "subject=registration," which is sent to the server when the form is submitted and used by the relevant script for decision making.

An example of how the input type is used is when the same script is used to process more than one form. Giving different hidden values to each form makes it possible for the script to identify which form has been submitted and process it accordingly. Finally, notice that the fields in the example are not vertically aligned. This is done using CSS and is dealt with in Chapter.

Input Types for Collecting Numbers

The input types for collecting numbers are number and range. As of time of writing, only some browsers support these input types. They include Firefox, Opera, and Chrome. Both input types support the same attributes as text-input types listed earlier in Table, except size, maxlength, pattern, and placeholder. Table lists the extra ones that they support.

Input Type: number

The **number-input type** displays a single line text field for the user to enter a number directly and also provides increment and decrement buttons, with which a number can be specified. Figure shows how it is used, and depicts the result. The min and max attributes specify the range of numbers allowed; the value attribute sets the initial number as 0; and the step attribute specifies that every click of the button should increase or decrease the value in the text field by 3.

TABLE

Attributes Supported by Input Types for Collecting Numbers **Attribute Function** min Specifies the minimum numeric value allowed. It can also be used for date value. max Specifies the maximum numeric value allowed. It can also be used for date value. step Specifies increment and decrement values when a control button is clicked.

```
HTML
<h3>Form number input</h3>
<form>
   <p>Please enter quantity required:</p>
   <input type="number" name="quantity" value="0" min="0" max="100"
     step="3">
</form>
```

Figure: Example usage of number-input control.

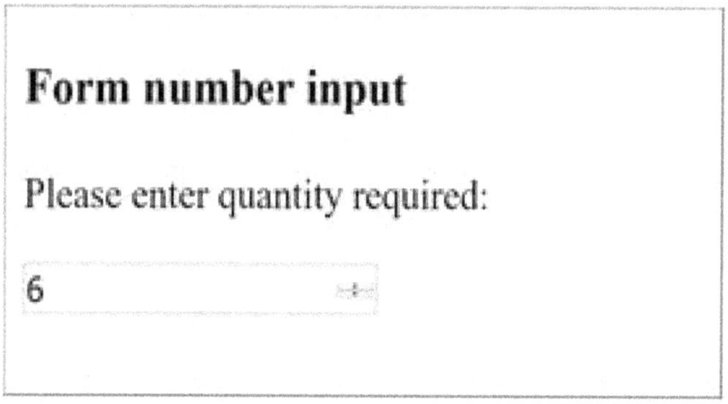

Form number input

Please enter quantity required:

6

Figure: Rendered result of Figure.

Input Type: range

The **range-input type** displays a slide control for inputting an integer (whole) number, as opposed to decimal number. Figure shows how it is used, and depicts the result. As in the previous example, the min and max attributes specify the range of numbers covered by the slide and the value attribute sets the initial number as 0.

The **disadvantage of the range-input type** is that it does not display any number. However, this functionality can be added using additional elements and attributes. Figure shows an example of how to do this, and depicts the result. The <output> element is responsible for displaying the numbers, and its initial content is set as 0. In the <input> element, the min and max attributes specify the range of numbers covered by the slide; the **value** attribute sets its initial number as 0; and the on-input form event attribute says that when an input is made (i.e., when the slide is moved), the value of the element bearing the name "quantity" should be replaced with the value of the one bearing the name "slide Input." A **form event attribute**, as you may recollect from Chapter, is an event generated by a form element when its state changes.

```
HTML
<h3>Form range input</h3>
<form>
  <p>Please enter quantity required:</p>
  <input type="range" name="quantity" value="0" min="0" max="100">
</form>
```

Figure: How the range-input type is used.

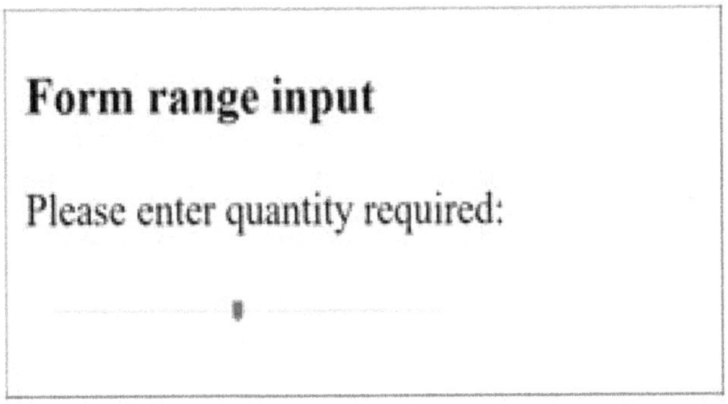

Form range input

Please enter quantity required:

Figure: Rendered result of Figure.

```
HTML
<h3>Form range input with values</h3>
<form>
  <p>Please use slide to enter quantity:</p>
  <output name="quantity">0</output>
  <input type="range" name="slideInput" min="0" max="100"
  value="0"oninput="quantity.value=slideInput.value">
</form>
```

Figure: Adding numbers display with the <output> element.

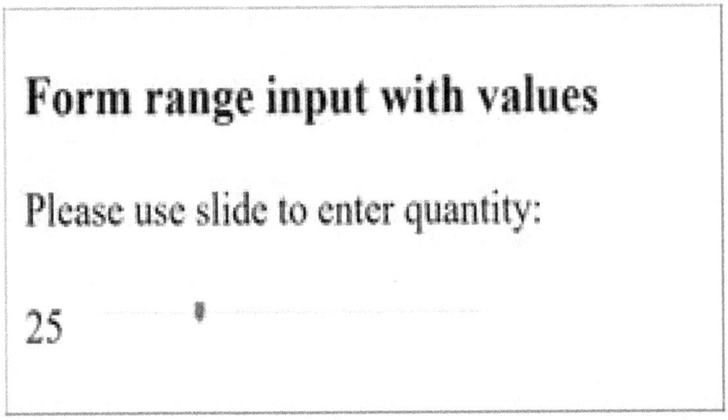

Form range input with values

Please use slide to enter quantity:

25

Figure: Rendered result of Figure.

In the previous example, the number displayed cannot be edited. However, it is possible to make it editable and also link it to the slide, so that the user can use either of the two to make an input. This can be done by **combining the range-input type with the number-input type**. Figure shows an example, and depicts the result. In the numbertype <input> element, the on-input attribute specifies that when the user enters a number in the box, the value of the range-input type should be replaced with that of the number-input type.

The reverse happens with the on-input attribute in the range-type <input> element when the slide is moved. All other attributes play the same roles, as described in the previous example.

```
HTML
<h3>Form range and number inputs</h3>
<form>
  <p>Please enter quantity in field or with slide:</p>
  <input type="number" name="numberInput" min="0" max="100"
   value="0" oninput="slideNumber.value=numberInput.value">
  <input type="range" name="slideNumber" min="0" max="100"
   value="0" oninput="numberInput.value=slideNumber.value">
</form>
```

Figure: Combining editable number field with the <output> element.

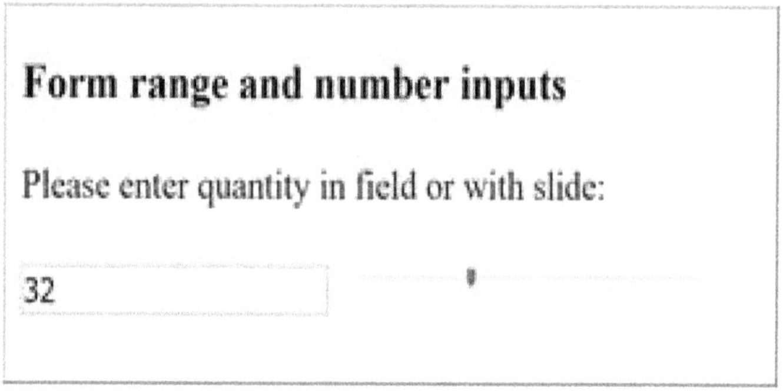

Form range and number inputs

Please enter quantity in field or with slide:

32

Figure: Rendered result of Figure.

Input Types for Collecting Time and Date

Like the number-input type, the category of input types for collecting time and date provides appropriately formatted text fields for users to make direct input and also provides additional button controls for choosing options. The relevant input types are time, date, datetime-local, month, and week. The input types support the same attributes as the **number-input types**, namely, min, max, and step. If the min or/and max attributes are specified, controls display only dates or times that satisfy the specified limits, and the increment or decrement button increments or decrements them only according to the specified step value when clicked.

Input Type: time

The **time-input type** displays a text box and a control for setting time. Figure shows how it is used, and Figure depicts the result. To use the control displayed, the user clicks the relevant time component and types in a value or uses the up and down arrows.

```
HTML
<h3>Form time input</h3>
<form>
  <p>Please enter time:<input type="time" name="time"></p>
</form>
```

Figure: Example usage of the time-input type.

Form time input

Please enter time: -- : -- --

Figure: Rendered result of Figure.

Input Type: date

The **date-input type** displays a single-line formatted text box and a drop-down calendar for setting date. The input format allowed by the text field depends on the date convention of the region of the world of the user. Figure shows how it is used, and depicts the result. To use the control displayed, the user, like with the **time-input type** control, clicks the relevant date component and types in a value or uses the up and down arrows. Various other arrows allow you to navigate to the required month and year.

```
HTML
<h3>Form date input</h3>
<form>
  <p>Please enter date:<input type="date" name="date"></p>
</form>
```

Figure: Example usage of the date-input type.

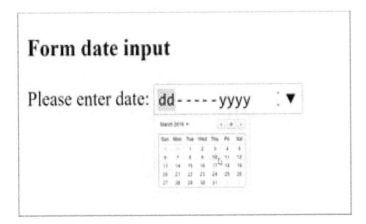

Form date input

Please enter date: dd - - - - - yyyy : ▼

Figure: Rendered result of Figure.

Input Type: datetime-local

The **datetime-local-input type** displays a text box and a date and time control for setting local date and time. Figure shows how it is used, and Figure depicts the result. The control displayed allows you to choose a date by clicking the downward arrow to display the calendar and then clicking a day on it. The time is entered by clicking the hour, minutes, or seconds component and by using the arrows to set the values. It is worth noting that HTML also specifies a **datetime-input type**, which is intended for setting global date and time, including time zone information. However, it is not, as of time of writing, supported by any major browser.

```
HTML
<h3>Form date and time input</h3>
<form>
  <p>Please enter date and time:</p>
  <p>Date and time:<input type="datetime-local"
    name="localdatetime"></p>
</form>
```

Figure: Example usage of the datetime-local-input type.

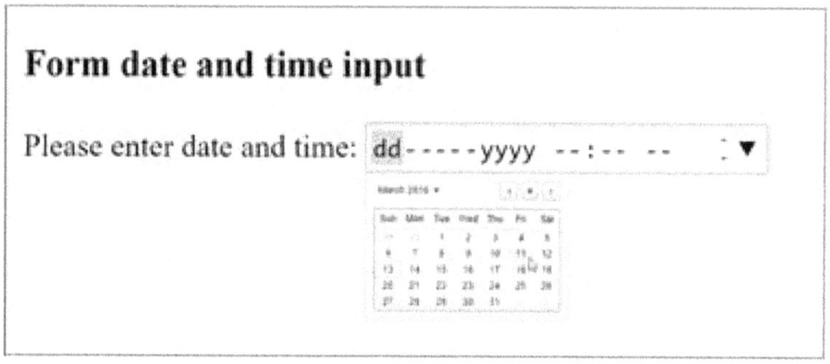

Figure: Rendered result of Figure

Input Type: month

The **month-input type** displays a formatted text box and a month-and-year control for setting month and year. Figure shows how it is used, and Figure depicts the result. The control allows you to choose a month by clicking the downward arrow to display a calendar and then clicking the next or previous arrow to navigate to the desired month. Alternatively, you could click the button that displays all the months, to choose one.

```
HTML
<h3>Form month input</h3>
<form>
  <p>Please enter month:<input type="month" name="month"></p>
</form>
```

Figure: Example usage of the month-input type.

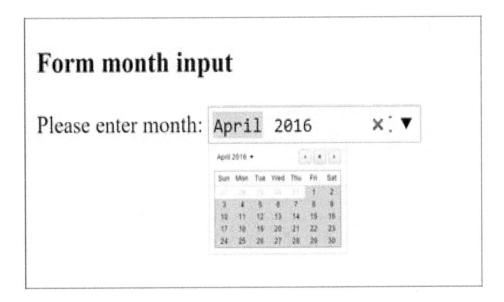

Figure: Rendered result of Figure.

Input Type: week

The **week-input type** displays a text box and a week-and-year control. Figure shows how it is used, and Figure depicts the result. The displayed control allows the user to choose the date by clicking the downward arrow to display a calendar. Different Web browsers display the control differently.

```
HTML
<h3>Form week input</h3>
<form>
  <p>Please enter week and year:<input type="week"
  name="week"></p>
</form>
```

Figure: Example usage of the week-input type.

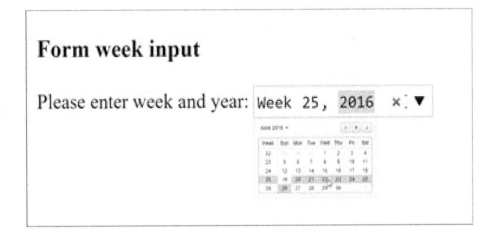

Figure: Rendered result of Figure.

Input Types for Offering Options

These input types allow you to provide users with options, from which they can choose. The two input types used for this are radio and checkbox. Table lists the attributes that they support.

Input Type: radio

The **radio-input type** displays a radio button and is used when you want users to choose only one from a set of options. Once a button is selected, it cannot be unselected by clicking it. It can only be unselected by clicking another button. This ensures that only one option can be chosen as answer to a question, and it is the values of the name and value attributes of the chosen option that are **used to create the name-value pair** that is sent to the server. This also means that radio buttons are not suitable when users are allowed to not choose an option.

In the example, notice that all the elements have the same name. This is because only one response is recognized for the question. It is worth noting that it may not always be a good idea to use the checked attribute, as it might cause some users to think that they have made a selection, even though they have not. This is because it is often easy to overlook things at a glance. In the case of the example, the consequence might be someone whose title is "Mrs" submitting the default response (i.e., "Mr"). Leaving all buttons unchecked makes it more unlikely that users will miss at a glance that they have not completed a question.

TABLE

Attributes for Radio Button and Checkbox

Attribute	Function
name	Specifies a unique name for element.
value	Specifies the default value for element.
form	Specifies the id value on the form with which to associate element.
disabled	Specifies to disable control, so that user cannot interact with it. It can be specified by itself, without a value (instead of disabled="disabled").
autofocus	Specifies that element should be given focus when page is loaded. It can be specified by itself, without a value (instead of autofocus="autofocus").
required	Specifies that element must be given an input.
checked	Specifies to select an <input> element by default.

```
HTML
<h3>Radio buttons</h3>
<form>
   Please choose one:<br>
   <input type="radio" name="salutation" value="Mr" checked>Mr
   <input type="radio" name="salutation" value="Mrs">Mrs
   <input type="radio" name="salutation" value="Miss">Miss
   <input type="radio" name="salutation" value="Ms">Ms
   <input type="radio" name="salutation" value="Dr">Dr
</form>
```

Figure: Example usage of the radio-input type.

Radio buttons

Please choose one:

• Mr ○ Mrs ○ Miss ○ Ms ○ Dr

Figure: Rendered result of Figure.

Input Type: checkbox

The checkbox-input type displays a checkbox that allows users to select or deselect it and is best for when you want users to be able to choose any number of options from a set of options per question. The values of only the checked checkboxes are sent to the server. The value of each checkbox is combined with the name to create a name-value pair for each option and sent to the server.

Notice that like with radio buttons, all the checkboxes for the question have the same value for the name attribute; however, more than one option can be selected. As long as the values of the value attributes are different, this is all right, since the **name-value pair** for each option will be different. From the viewpoint of the author who might write a script to process the form data, the common name identifies a question and the values of the value attributes identify the options associated with it. In addition, notice that there is space between each box and its label. This is because there is space in the code between each <input> element and its label.

```
HTML
<h3>Checkboxes</h3>
<form>
  Which of these do you commute with? </br>
  <input type="checkbox" name="commute"
   value="tube" checked> Tube
  <input type="checkbox" name="commute"
   value="train" checked> Train
  <input type="checkbox" name="commute" value="car"> Car
  <input type="checkbox" name="commute"
   value="motorcycle"> Motorcycle
  <input type="checkbox" name="commute"
   value="bicycle"> Bicycle
  <input type="checkbox" name="commute"
   value="walking" checked> Walking
</form>
```

Figure: Example usage of the checkbox-input type.

Checkboxes

Which of these do you commute with?
☑ Tube ☑ Train ☐ Car ☐ Motorcycle ☐ Bicycle ☑ Walking

Figure: Rendered result of Figure

Input Types for Starting an Action

These input types allow you to provide a push button that users can click or press to initiate an action. The action can be predetermined ones, such as the submission of a form, or it can be the execution of a script to perform a specific task. The relevant input types are submit, reset, button, image, file, and color.

Input Type: submit and reset

The submit-input and reset-input types are presented together, because they are typically used together. The **submit-input type** displays a push button, which when clicked or pressed makes the browser start the process of packaging and sending the information entered into a form by a user to the Web server. The input type supports usual attributes but also some that relate to forms and their submission. Indeed, the attributes perform similar functions as those listed earlier in Table for the <form> element. For example, the form action attribute does the same thing as the action attribute in Table lists them and their function.

TABLE

Attributes for Submit and Reset Buttons

Submit Attributes	Function
name	Specifies a unique name for element.
value	Specifies the default value for element.
disabled	Specifies to disable control, so that user cannot interact with it. It can be specified by itself, without a value (instead of disabled="disabled").
form	Specifies the id value of the <form> element with which to associate element. It allows you to place <input> elements anywhere within a document and not just within the <form> element.
autofocus	Specifies that element should be given input focus when page is loaded. It can be specified by itself, without a value (instead of autofocus="autofocus").
formaction	Specifies the URL for the script to use to process submitted form data, for example formaction=http://www.test.com/register.php. This is the same as using action="http://www.test.com/register.php" with the <form> element.
formmethod	Specifies the method to use to send form data to server, for example formaction="get". This is the same as using method="get" with the <form> element.
formnovalidate	Specifies that form is not to be validated, for example formnovalidate. This is the same as using novalidate with the <form> element.
formenctype	Specifies file encoding type, for example formenctype="text/plain". This is the same as using enctype="text/plain" with the <form> element.
formtarget	Specifies where to display the response to a form submission, for example formtarget="_blank". This is the same as using target="_blank" with the <form> element.

Like the submit-input type, the **reset-input type** displays a push button, but when clicked or pressed, it clears user's inputs and resets all the controls of a form to their default values. Unlike the submit-input type, it supports only the name, value, disabled, autofocus, and form attributes.

```
HTML
<h3>Form submit and reset buttons</h3>
<form>
  <input type="submit" value="Submit">
  <input type="reset" value="Cancel">
</form>
```

Figure: Example usage of submit- and reset-input types.

Input Type: image

The **image-input type** allows you to specify an image to be used as a submit button. It supports the same attributes as listed in Table for **submit**- and **reset**-input types, as well as the image-specific ones listed in Table.

TABLE

Attributes for Image Button **Attribute Function** src Specifies the URL of the image to use. width Specifies the width of image. height Specifies the height of image. alt Specifies the alternative text to use to describe image. It is essential for accessibility.

```
HTML
<h3>Form image button</h3>
<form>
    <p>Please enter login details:</p>
    <p>Username:<input type="text" name="uname" required></p>
    <p>Password:<input type="password"
    name="password" required></p>
    <input type="image" src="submit.png" width="148" height="32"
    alt="submit button">
</form>
```

Figure: Example usage of the image-input type.

Form image button

Please enter login details:

Username:

Password:

Figure: Rendered result of Figure

The actual size of the image used in the example was 200 × 50 pixels and was reduced to 148 × 30 pixels. It is **good practice to create an image that is as close as possible in size to the one required**. This is because the process of reduction can cause problems, such as making the text on the image too small to be legible. If the image specified is not found, a visual predetermined by the browser is displayed instead. This can be just text or a box with text in it.

Unfortunately, unlike the **submit**- and **reset**-input types that perform predetermined functions when activated, the image-input type needs to be told what to do when it is activated, and this is typically done using the onclick event attribute (which generates an event each time the element on which it is used is clicked) and the submit() JavaScript function (which submits a form when it is called). For example, adding onclick= "submit();" to the <input> element in Figure says to submit the form when the element (i.e., the image button) is clicked.

NOTE: Image button accessibility

To make an image accessible to the visually impaired, it is necessary to provide the text alternative that describes it. To make a functional image (i.e., an image used for a specific function, such as one used as a button or link), text alternative should describe its functionality instead of its appearance. More about image accessibility is discussed in Chapter.

Input Type: button

Like the reset-input and submit-input types, the **button-input type** displays a push button but with no predetermined behaviour. This means that like with the **image-input** type, you need to specify the function to perform when it is activated. Doing this again involves using the onclick event attribute and the **submit()** JavaScript function. The attributes that the input type supports are name, value, disabled, form, and autofocus. Figure shows how the input type is used, and Figure depicts the result.

The onclick attribute in the code specifies that when the <input> element is clicked to execute the JavaScript function called alert(), which displays the text between the quotes in an alert box. Different browsers display the box in different ways. Firefox was used in the example, in which when the "Show Message" button was clicked, the window changed to gray to indicate its current role as background and the box is displayed on top.

```
HTML
<h3>Form action button</h3>
<form>
  <input type="button" value="Show Message" onclick="alert
    ('This message is displayed using a JavaScript function.')">
</form>
```

Figure: Example usage of the button-input type.

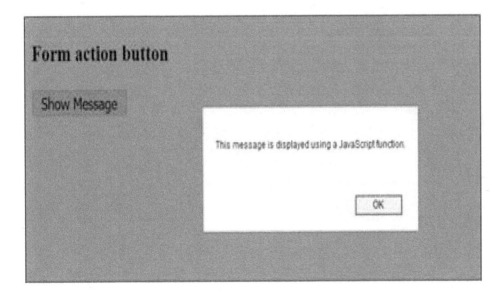

Figure: Rendered result of Figure.

Input Type: file

The **file-input type** displays a single-line text field and a browse button to allow users to select files for uploading. However, it does not provide a control for the actual uploading; this is done using the **submit-input type**, which you have already read earlier in this chapter. Any time a website allows you to browse and select a file on your computer for upload, it is likely that it is the input type that is being used. The attributes supported are listed in Table.

The control in the example is from Internet Explorer. Different browsers display different designs of control. In Firefox, Chrome, or Opera, the text field is usually not as clear to see as of time of writing. Clicking the field or the button of the control displays a dialog box, with which the user can navigate to the required file or files. The accept attribute specifies that the file types expected are **jpeg** and **png** image files, and the multiple attributes specifies that many files can be selected for upload. Typically, selecting multiple files involves first selecting one and then holding down the Shift, Control, or Command key while selecting others.

TABLE

Attributes for the File-Input Type

Attribute	Function
name	Specifies a unique name for element.
value	Specifies the default value for element.
disabled	Specifies to disable control, so that user cannot interact with it. It can be specified by itself, without a value (instead of disabled="disabled").
form	Specifies the id value of the <form> element with which to associate element. It allows <input> elements to be placed anywhere within a document and not just within the <form> element.
autofocus	Specifies that element should be given focus when page is loaded. It can be specified by itself, without a value (instead of autofocus="autofocus").
required	Specifies that element must be given an input in order form to be submitted. It can be specified by itself, without a value (instead of required="required").
multiple	Specifies whether the user is allowed to upload more than one file. It can be specified by itself, without a value (instead of multiple="multiple").
accept	Specifies the file types that are accepted.

```html
HTML
<h3>Form file upload control</h3>
<form>
  <p>Select file:</p>
  <input type="file" name="imagefile" accept="image/jpeg,
  image/png" multiple>
</form>
```

Figure: Example usage of the file-input type.

Form file upload control

Select file:

Browse...   No files selected.

Figure: Rendered result of Figure

Input Type: color

The **color-input type** allows you to display a color well (i.e., color picker), which allows a user to select a color for an element. Table lists the attributes that it supports. Figure shows how the input type is used, and Figure depicts the result.

TABLE

Attributes for Color-Input Type

Attribute	Function
name	Specifies a unique name for element.
value	Specifies the default value for element.
disabled	Specifies to disable control, so that user cannot interact with it. It can be specified by itself, without a value (instead of disabled="disabled").
form	Specifies the id value of the <form> element with which to associate element. It allows <input> elements to be placed anywhere within a document and not just within the <form> element.
autofocus	Specifies that element should be given input focus when page is loaded. It can be specified by itself, without a value (instead of autofocus="autofocus").
autocomplete	Specifies whether or not browser should remember values entered previously by the user and use the best match to automatically complete a field or offer them as options as the user starts to complete the field. The values taken are on and off.
list	Specifies the id value on a <datalist> element with which to associate element.

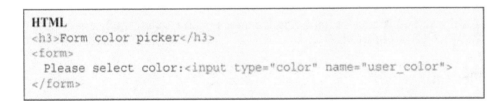

```
HTML
<h3>Form color picker</h3>
<form>
  Please select color:<input type="color" name="user_color">
</form>
```

Figure: Example usage of the color-input type.

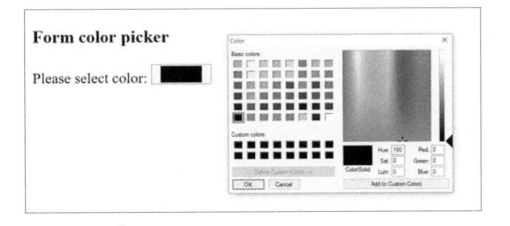

Figure: Rendered result of Figure.

Multipurpose Button

<button>...</button>

Like some of the action-button input types introduced earlier (i.e., submit, reset, and button), the <button> element is used to display a button. It is a multi-purpose element for creating buttons and is intended to give authors more flexibility and creative control over the appearance of buttons. For example, text can be easily combined with an image on a button to give it more meaning.

Notice the use of the <img> element and the associated attributes to add and size the green and red oval images. They have been used here to only- demonstrate the use of the <button> element and are discussed more fully in Chapter 6. The <button> element creates a **submit-type button** and displays its content on it, and the <img> element adds the image. The use of the alt attribute is important to make the button accessible, as it provides the text for the screen reader to read out. The sizes of the actual images were 24 × 24 pixels and created with transparent background in Photoshop.

TABLE Attributes for <button> Element

Attribute	Function
name	Specifies a unique name for element.
value	Specifies the default value for element.
disabled	Specifies to disable control, so that user cannot interact with it. It can be specified by itself, without a value (instead of disabled="disabled").
form	Specifies the id value of the <form> element with which to associate element.
type	Specifies type of button. Possible values include submit (which submits form data to server), reset (which resets controls to their initial values), and button (which allows behavior to be specified through scripts). If the attribute is not specified, the behavior of the button is set to submit.
autofocus	Specifies to give input focus to the button.
formaction	Specifies the URL for the script to use to process submitted form data, for example formaction=http://www.test.com/register.php. This is the same as using action="http://www.test.com/register.php" with the <form> element.
formenctype	Specifies file encoding type to use for form data, for example formenctype="text/plain". This is the same as using enctype="text/plain" with the <form> element.
formmethod	Specifies the method to use to send form data to server, for example formaction="get". This is the same as using method="get" with the <form> element.
formnovalidate	Specifies that form is not to be validated, for example formnovalidate. This is the same as using novalidate with the <form> element.
formtarget	Specifies where to display the response to a form submission, for example formtarget="_blank". This is the same as using target="_blank" with the <form> element.

```
HTML
<h3>Form button element</h3>
<form>
  <button type="submit"><img src="green_button.png"
  width="12" height="12">Start</button>
  <button type="submit"><img src="red_button.png"
  width="12" height="12">Stop</button>
</form>
```

Figure: Example usage of the <button> element.

Figure: Rendered result of Figure.

Multiple Lines Text Input

<textarea>...</textarea>

The <textarea> element allows you to display a control that allows users to enter multiple lines of plain text, as opposed to the single line allowed by the text-input types discussed earlier.

In the example, the dirname attribute is used only to explain how it works. It changes nothing, because it specifies the default directionality setting. It works as follows: when the form is submitted, its value, together with the directionality setting for the element, is sent as a name-value pair to the server. This means that the name-value pair sent for setting directionality is comment.dir=ltr. The directionality value "ltr" means left to right, which is the default. Directionality can be set using the dir attribute, a global attribute. The other value it takes is rlt (right to left).

TABLE Attributes for <textarea> Element

Attribute	Function
name	Specifies a unique name for element.
value	Specifies the default value for element.
maxlength	Specifies the maximum number of characters allowed in a text field.
minlength	Specifies the minimum number of characters allowed in a text field.
rows	Specifies the number of lines to show. Default is 2.
cols	Specifies the number of characters per line to show. Default is 20.
disabled	Specifies to disable control, so that user cannot interact with it. It can be specified by itself, without a value (instead of disabled="disabled").
form	Specifies the id value of the <form> element with which to associate element. It allows <input> elements to be placed anywhere within a document and not just within the <form> element.
autofocus	Specifies that element should be given focus when page is loaded. It can be specified by itself, without a value (instead of autofocus="autofocus").
autocomplete	Specifies whether or not browser should remember values entered previously by the user and use the best match to automatically complete a field or offer them as options as the user starts to complete the field. The values taken are on and off.
required	Specifies that element must have an input. It can be specified by itself, without a value (instead of required="required").
placeholder	Gives an instruction or an example to user about what to enter in a text field.
readonly	Specifies whether or not users can edit a text field.
spellcheck	Specifies to check element's spelling and grammar. The values that it takes are true (which means to check), false (which means not to check), and default (which means to use a default value, such as the spellcheck value set for the parent element).
wrap	Specifies whether or not inputted text should be wrapped when submitted. Its value can be soft (which means it is not to be wrapped) or hard (which means it is to be wrapped). If hard is specified, then the dirname attribute must be used to specify at which character to apply wrapping.
dirname	Specifies a name to be used to send directionality value of an element to the server. It is useful for extending accessibility to those who read and write from right to left.

```
HTML
<h3>Form textarea control</h3>
<form>
    <p>Please give us your comments below:</p>
    <textarea rows="5" cols="60" name="comments"
    dirname="comment.dir"></textarea>
</form>
```

Figure: Example usage of the <textarea> element.

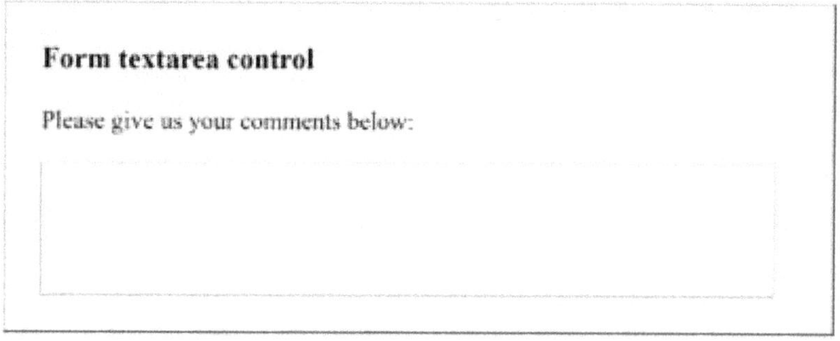

Form textarea control

Please give us your comments below:

Figure: Rendered result of Figure.

Drop-Down List

<select>...</select>

The <select> element is used to display a drop-down list, from which a user can choose one. Each item of the list is created using the <option> element, and the items are grouped using the <optgroup> element. Table lists the attributes supported by the <select> element. Table lists the attributes that the <option> element allows. Of the attributes, the <optgroup> element supports only the label and disabled. Figure shows how a drop-down list is created using these elements.

In the example, notice the nesting convention (indicated with the left brackets). It is important to get this right if the list is to work correctly. Figure 5.43 shows the drop-down list after the down arrow has been clicked to activate it. Notice that the values of the label attributes on the <optgroup> elements are automatically given emphasis. When the form is submitted, the value of the name attribute on the <select> element is attached to the value of the value attribute on the <option> element to create the name-value pair that is sent to the server.

TABLE

Attributes for <select> Element

Attribute	Function
name	Specifies a unique name for element.
size	Specifies the number of options to show. Default is 1.
multiple	Specifies to allow one or more options to be selected. It can be specified by itself, without a value (instead of multiple="multiple").
required	Specifies that element must be given an input. It can be specified by itself, without a value (instead of required="required").
autofocus	Specifies that element should be given focus when page is loaded. It can be specified by itself, without a value (instead of autofocus="autofocus").
disabled	Specifies to disable control, so that user cannot interact with it. It can be specified by itself, without a value (instead of disabled="disabled").
form	Specifies the id value on the form with which to associate element.

TABLE

Attributes for <option> Element **AttributeFunction** value Specifies a value for option. Label Specifies a label for option. Selected Specifies to select option by default. It can be specified by itself, without a value (instead of selected="selected").

Disabled Specifies to disable control, so that user cannot interact with it. It can be specified by itself, without a value (instead of disabled="disabled").

```
HTML
<h3>Form multiple select</h3>
<form>
  Please select your favorite movie:
  <select name="fav_movie">
    <optgroup label="Sci-Fi">
      <option value="startrek">Star Trek</option>
      <option value="starwars" selected>Star Wars</option>
    </optgroup>
    <optgroup label="Animation">
      <option value="shrek">Shrek</option>
      <option value="toystory">Toy Story</option>
    </optgroup>
  </select>
</form>
```

Figure: Example usage of the <select> element.

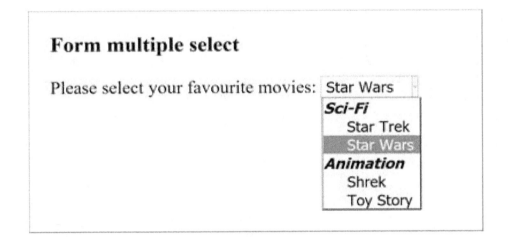

Figure: Using the multiple attribute with the <select> element.

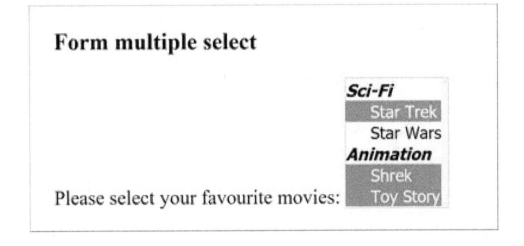

Figure: Rendered result of Figure

The <select> element also supports the selection of multiple options when the multiple attribute is used on it. The value of the size attribute can be set high to show many or all the options at once in order to make this easier. Figure shows the result of the same code in Figure but with the multiple attribute specified and the size attribute set to 6. Users can select more than one option by holding down a modifier key (e.g., Shift or Ctrl in Windows and Command or Option in Mac) while clicking the options. In the example, three options are selected. However, the use of **multiple select menus is not recommended** because of the difficulty in using them. For example, many people may not know how to use modifier keys. It may be better to use checkboxes where users are allowed to make multiple selections.

<datalist>...</datalist>

Like the <select> element, the <datalist> element creates a drop-down list, but it works in a different way. It works in combination with the text-type <input> and <option> elements, so that what is typed inside the text field determines the options displayed on the drop-down list. The element takes no special attributes; it takes only global ones, such as id.

In the example, when the user clicks, double clicks, or starts typing in the text-input field, the drop-down list is displayed, from which the user can choose one. If it is a long list and the desired item is not visible, then, as the user starts typing the desired word, the items are narrowed down to those that match the most to what is currently typed. However, for the element to work properly in this way, the value of the list attribute on the <input> element must match the value of the id attribute on the <datalist> element, which is "browsers" in this case.

```
HTML
<h3>Datalist</h3>
<form>
  Enter your favorite browser:
  <input type="text" name="favBrowser" list="browsers">
  <datalist id="browsers">
    <option value="Internet Explorer">
    <option value="Firefox">
    <option value="Chrome">
    <option value="Safari">
    <option value="Opera">
  </datalist>
</form>
```

Figure: Example usage of the <datalist> element.

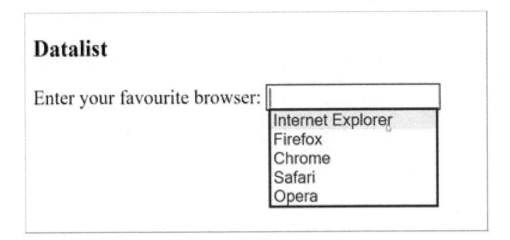

Datalist

Enter your favourite browser:

Internet Explorer
Firefox
Chrome
Safari
Opera

Figure: The result of Figure.

Showing Task Progress

<progress>...</progress>

The <progress> element allows you to display a control to show the progress of a task. The display is static and shows only a snapshot rather than a continuous display. In order to create a dynamic display, a script will have to be used to display snapshots at intervals. The specific attributes that it supports are value (which specifies the amount of task completed) and max (which specifies the total amount of task available to do).

```
HTML
<h3>Form progress element</h3>
<form>
  <p>Progress:<progress value="30" max="100"></p>
</form>
```

Figure: Example usage of the <progress> element.

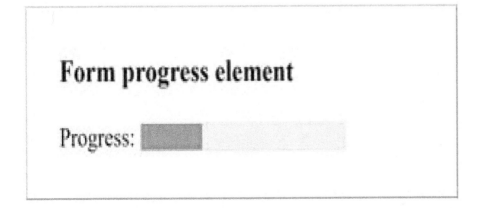

Form progress element

Progress:

Figure: Rendered result of Figure.

Displaying Measurement

<meter>...</meter>

The <meter> element is used to display a control that shows a gauge. Note that its function is different from that of the <progress> element and should be seen as displaying a measure of fullness, emptiness of capacity, speed, and so on.

TABLE

Attributes for <meter> Element

Attribute	Function
value	Specifies the measurement.
min	Specifies the lower limit of the range for the meter.
max	Specifies the upper limit of the range for the meter.
low	Specifies the point that marks the upper limit of the "low" part of the meter.
high	Specifies the point that marks the lower limit of the "high" part of the meter.
optimum	Specifies the optimum position for the meter.

```
HTML
<h3>Form meter element</h3>
<form>
   Voter turnout: <meter value=0.45></meter><span> 45%</span>
</form>
```

Figure: Example usage of the <meter> element.

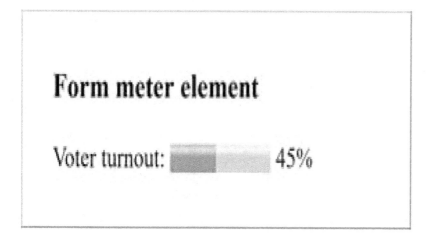

Figure: Rendered result of Figure.

Outputting Calculation Result

<output>...<output>

The <output> element is used to display the result of a calculation. However, the use of JavaScript is necessary to use it. To address this, HTML5 also includes the **valueAsNumber** property of JavaScript, which returns a string as a number and is relatively straightforward to use. Table lists the attributes supported by the element.

TABLE

Attributes for <output> Element **Attribute Function** Name Specifies the name for element. for Specifies in a space-separated list the id values of elements used in a calculation. form Specifies the id value on the form with which to associate element.

```
HTML
<h3>Form output element</h3>
<form oninput="sum.value = a.valueAsNumber + b.valueAsNumber">
  <p>Please enter date:</p>
  <input id="a" name="a" type="range" step="any"> +
  <input id="b" name="b" type="number" step="any"> =
  <output name="sum" for="a b"></output>
</form>
```

Figure: Example usage of the <output> element.

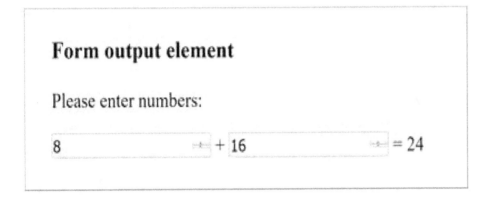

Figure: Rendered result of Figure.

The example shows two numbers being added together, as each is inputted by the user. The **number-input type** (discussed earlier) is used to collect each number, and the <output> element displays the content of the value of the name attribute (i.e., "sum"). The oninput event attribute on the <form> element takes care of the addition of the numbers and the placing of the result in "sum." The equation says to take the values stored in "a" and "b," use the valueAsNumber function to change each to a number, add the numbers together, and then make the result the value of the element named "sum." Notice the **dot convention**. This is the convention used in objectoriented programming to specify to access what is stored in a variable or apply a function to it.

Labeling Form Controls

<label>...<label>

In the examples shown so far, form controls have been labeled by simply placing text before them. However, this is limiting in various ways. For example, it makes it difficult to isolate them for styling, and since such labeling has no semantic meaning, it is not recognized by assistive technologies used by people with disabilities, making a form inaccessible to these users. The <label> element is designed to solve this problem and allows a label to be associated with a control. Table lists the attributes that it supports.
The <label> element can be used with or without the for attribute and can be wrapped around just the label of a form element or the label and the- element.

Notice that all the approaches produce the same type of labeling. In the code, numbers **1** and **2** show just the <label> element used, first to encapsulate the label and second to encapsulate both the label and the <input> element. Numbers **3** and **4** use the same principles but with the addition of the for and id attributes. This is known as the **label reference technique**, because the id attribute is used to associate the <input> element with the <label> element. Since an id is unique in a form, only one label can be associated with a form control. While all the four approaches are compatible with assistive technologies and are supported by HTML specification, number **3** is most commonly used, because it allows for the label to be styled separately and is consistent with how other types of controls are labeled.

TABLE

Attributes for <label> Element

Attribute	Function
for	Specifies the control with which to associate label.
Form	Specifies the form with which to associate label.

```
HTML
<h3>Form label element</h3>
<form>
  Please enter details:
  <p><label>Username:</label><input type="text"
     name="uname"></p>                           (1)
  <p><label>Password:<input type="password" name="password">
     </label></p>                                (2)
  <p><label for="email">Email:</label><input type="email"
     name="email" id="email"></p>                (3)
  <p><label for="phone">Phone:<input type="tel" name="phone" (4)
     id="phone"></label></p>
</form>
```

Figure: Example usage of the <label> element.

Form label element

Please enter details:

Username:

Password:

Email:

Phone:

Figure: Rendered result of Figure.

In some cases, the purpose of a form control may be clear enough, such that adding a label will create redundancy visually. An example is a text field that has a search button next to it. In such cases, although label is still added to make the control accessible to assistive technologies, it is made invisible by hiding it by using CSS. An alternative is to use the aria-label attribute, which provides a label to identify a form control to assistive technologies but does not provide the information visually. Although the title attribute can also be used for this, it is not supported by some screen readers and assistive technologies.

```
HTML
<h3>Form aria-label</h3>
<form>
  <input type="text" name="search" aria-label="Search">
  <button type="submit">Search</button>
</form>
```

Figure: Example usage of the aria-label attribute.

Figure: Rendered result of Figure.

Labeling and Accessibility

In addition to the point just made about labels and accessibility, there are other guidelines, especially regarding the placement of labels in relation to form controls. Although there are no strict rules, the best practice is to **follow popular placement convention**. This ensures that a form is not confusing to use and is accessible. For form controls that display text fields and select boxes, the convention is to place labels above them or to the left, depending on various factor. For example, visually impaired users and mobile phone users benefit from placing them above, because this reduces the width of a form and therefore the need for horizontal scrolling. For radio buttons and checkboxes, it is typical to place labels to the right.

Grouping Form Controls

<fieldset>...</fieldset>/<legend>...</legend>

The <fieldset> element groups together a set of controls and draws a border around them. The <legend> element adds caption to the border to describe the content of the group. While the <legend> element has no native attributes, the <fieldset> element takes the three attributes listed in Table 5.18. The **legend should be brief and descriptive**, especially because screen readers usually read it out for each control in the field set.

TABLE

Attributes for <fieldset> Element **AttributeFunction** name Specifies the name for element. Disabled Specifies to disable control, so that user cannot interact with it. It can be specified by itself, without a value (instead of disabled="disabled"). Form Specifies the id value on the <form> element with which to associate element.

```html
HTML
<h3>Form fieldset</h3>
<form>
  <p>Please complete the form below:</p>
  <fieldset>
    <legend>Personal Info</legend>
    <p><label for="uname">Username:</label><input type="text"
        name="uname" id="uname"></p>
    <p><label for="password">Password:</label>
        <input type="password" name="password" id="password"></p>
    <p><label for="email">Email:</label><input type="email"
        name="email" id="email"></p>
    <p><label for="phone">Phone:</label><input type="tel"
        name="phone" id="phone"></p>
  </fieldset>
</form>
```

Figure: Example usage of the <fieldset> element.

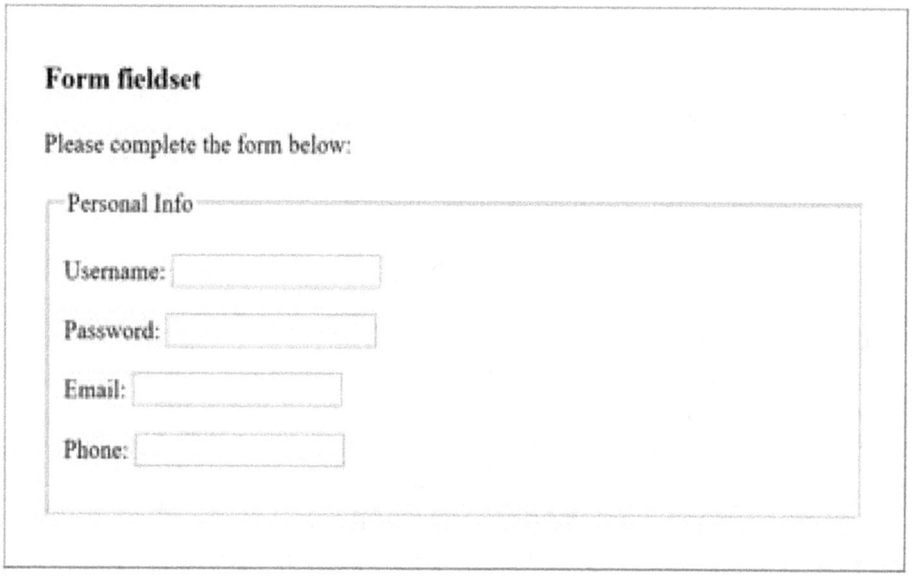

Form fieldset

Please complete the form below:

Personal Info

Username:

Password:

Email:

Phone:

Figure: Rendered result of Figure.

An Example Form

Some of the form controls introduced so far are brought together in Figure to produce an example of a typical form. Figure shows the result. Notice that the text input fields are not properly aligned vertically. In order for a form to look professional and be easy to use, these fields should be properly aligned. This is done using CSS, and how this is done is explained in Chapter.

```
HTML
<h3>Forms</h3>
<form>
  <p>Please complete the form below:</p>
  <fieldset>
    <legend>Personal Info</legend>
    <label for "fname">First name:</label><input type="text"
     name="fname" id="fname" required></label><br>
    <label for="lname">Last name:</label><input type="text"
     name="lname" id="lname"><br>
    <label for="email">Email:</label><input type="email" size="25"
     maxlength="35" name="email" id="email" placeholder=
     "e.g., joe@example.com"><br>
    <label for="url">Your personal URL (if any):</label>
     <input type="url" name="url" id="url"><br>
    <input type="radio" name="sex" value="male" id="sex1">
     <label for="sex1">Male</label>
    <input type="radio" name="sex" value="female" id="sex2">
     <label for="sex2">Female</label><br>
  </fieldset>
  <fieldset>
    <legend>Other Info</legend>
    Which of these do you own?<br>
    <input type="checkbox" name="car" id="own1">
     <label for="own1">Car</label>
    <input type="checkbox" name="bike" id="own2">
     <label for="own2">Bike</label>
    <br>
    <label for="fav_movie">Favorite Movie:</label>
    <select name="fav_movie" id="fav_movie">
      <optgroup label="Sci-Fi">
        <option value="startrek">Star Trek</option>
        <option value="starwars">Star Wars</option>
      </optgroup>
      <optgroup label="Animation">
        <option value="Shrek">Shrek</option>
        <option value="toystory">Toy Story</option>
      </optgroup>
    </select>
    <br>
    <label for="info">Extra info:</label><br>
    <textarea rows="4" cols="35" name="info" id="info">
     </textarea><br>
  </fieldset>
  <input type="submit" value="Submit">
  <input type="reset" value="Cancel"><br>
</form>
```

Figure: The <form> element and associated elements and attributes.

Forms

Please complete the form below:

Personal Info

First name: [ ]

Last name: [ ]

Email: [e.g., Joe@example.com]

Your personal URL (if any): [ ]

○ Male ○ Female

Other Info

Which of these do you own?

☐ Car ☐ Bike

Favourite Movie: [Star Trek ▼]

Extra info:

[ ]

[Submit] [Cancel]

Figure: The code in Figure rendered in a browser.

Form Design Guidelines

Forms should be aesthetically pleasing and easy to use in order to make interaction with them a good experience. The following are some guidelines on how these goals can be achieved:

• **Related fields should be grouped together** and arranged in a logical order, such as by enclosing them in a box or by using the same color, with each group having a meaningful title. The form itself should have a meaningful title.

• **Layout should be visually appealing,** with ample use of white space and properly aligned fields.

• The **size of fields should match or be longer than the size of data** to be entered, so that what users enter does not disappear into the left or right edges of the box, making it hard for them to follow what they are entering.

• **Only really important questions should be asked**; for example, asking for salutation is not always necessary.

• If possible, **each field should be validated immediately after it is completed** and correction should be requested, if necessary.

• **Users should be allowed to enter numbers**, such as phone and credit card numbers, in flexible formats, as requiring a strict format can create problems for some users, particularly the elderly.

• **Compulsory fields should be clearly marked**, such as with an asterisk, which may be in a contrasting color, typically red. However, too many compulsory fields can be discouraging, so fields should not be mandatory unless they are really necessary. Asking for users' addresses, for example, is likely to discourage them; e-mail is often adequate.

- **Keyboard focus should be set to the first field** when the form is displayed, as this minimizes total number of clicks. Also, if possible, when a field receives focus, information should be provided on the type of data required for the field.

- **It should be possible to change any entry at any point** before a form is submitted, and how to submit a form should be clearly indicated.

Images

Images have functions in almost everything we do that involves communication. Next to text, they are perhaps the most prevalent form of communicating content on the Web. Not only this, they have an indispensable role in the aesthetic appeal and the theme setting of Web pages. This chapter introduces the HTML elements used to add images, as well as design principles that guide effective use of images in Web design.

Adding Images with HTML

An image can be added to a Web page in two main ways. It can be embedded in the current page, or a link that points to its location can be provided. In the latter case, the image is usually displayed in a page by itself. Irrespective of whether an image is embedded or linked to, it can be used as an **image map**. This is an image that contains **hotspots** (clickable areas), which when clicked result in an event occurring, such as taking the user to a different destination to provide more information. Linking to an image is achieved using the <a> element, introduced in Chapter, and embedding one is achieved using the <img> element.

Traditionally, only one image source could be specified using the element, but by combining it with newer elements, such as <source> and <picture>, and with newer attributes, such as srcset and sizes, it is now possible to specify **multiple image sources**, from which the browser can choose the one that is best suited for a user situation, depending on the user's device screen pixel density, zoom level, and, possibly, other factors, such as network properties. If-conditions, known as **media conditions**, can also be used to help the browser determine which images to use and when to use them, as explained later. Multiple images that are provided to the browser to choose from are generally termed **responsive images**, and the technique is a response to the need to have images that are compatible with **responsive Web design**, discussed later in the Chapter.

TABLE

Elements for Incorporating Image in a Web Page

Element	Function
<img>	Embeds an image.
<source>	Used to specify multiple media sources. It represents nothing when used alone.
<picture>...<picture>	A container that allows multiple image sources to be specified, from which one is chosen to use with the contained <img> element.
<canvas>...</canvas>	Used to draw graphics by using scripting (typically JavaScript).
<svg>...</svg>	Used to embed an SVG element in HTML.
<map>...</map>	Defines an image map.
<area>...</area>	Defines a region inside an image map.

<img>, <source>, and <picture>

The <img>, <source>, and <picture> elements can be combined in different ways and used with various combinations of attributes to specify either a single image source or multiple image sources. The typically used attributes and their functions are listed in Table.

TABLE

Attributes Used with Elements Used to Embed Image

Attribute	Function
src	Specifies the URL of image resource. It is **obligatory**.
height	Specifies height of image in pixels (px).
width	Specifies width of image in pixels (px).
alt	Specifies **alternative text** (or **alt text**) description of image. This is the text that is displayed when image cannot be found, is not in a supported file format, or is not yet downloaded.
longdesc	Used to provide URL to a file that contains longer description about an image when short text alternative is not adequate. It is not supported by major browsers as of time of writing.
srcset	Used to specify images to use in different situations (e.g., for small screens and HD displays). It specifies a single **image URL**; a comma-separated list of strings, each string containing **an image URL** and an optional **width descriptor** that is the width of image, in pixels, followed by "w" (e.g., 640w); or a **pixel density descriptor** that is a positive floating number, followed by "x" (e.g., 1.5x). The **width descriptor** lets the browser intelligently select the best image, based on screen width, and the **pixel density descriptor** lets the browser select the best image, based on device pixel density. If no pixel density descriptor is specified, 1x is used. The attribute usually renders **fixed-size** images, except when used with the w descriptor.
sizes	Specifies a single **width descriptor** (e.g., sizes="150vw") or a single media-condition-width-descriptor pair (e.g., sizes="(max-width: 800px) 150vw"). It can also specify a comma-separated list of media-condition-width-descriptor pairs, with the **media condition** omitted in the last item (e.g., sizes="(max-width: 640px) 60vw, (max-width: 340px) 100vw, 50vw"). The last item is used as **fallback**. Although the vw (**viewport width**) unit is normally used, other length units (e.g., px) can also be used. The attribute is required when the srcset attribute is used with width descriptors.
media	Used to specify the condition under which an image source is used (e.g., media="(min-width: 600px)"). It is valid only in a <source> element that is a child of the <picture> element.
type	Specifies **MIME type** (or content type) of the specified image (e.g., type="image/jpeg").

Specifying a Single Image Source

Although responsive image technique is the future in Web design, if a page is not required to adjust to suit different user situations, then just specifying a single image source is adequate. Also, if a page is required to adjust but the images being used are vector-based images, such as **Scalable Vector Graphics** (SVG), a single source can be used. This is because vector-based images can scale to different sizes, as necessary, without depreciation in quality or a change in file size. A single image source can be specified using just the <img> element and the src attribute.

In the example, the src attribute specifies the image to embed (which is "yacht.jpg") and says that it is inside a folder named "images" that is inside the folder containing the HTML document. The alt and longdesc attributes perform the functions described in Table. Using the alt attribute also **contributes to accessibility**, because the text is what screen readers and other assistive technologies read out to visually impaired users. For this reason, it is important for alternative text to be an **accurate but concise description** of the content of the relevant image. It should not be a list of keywords (known as "**keyword stuffing**") designed to trick search engines, as this could get your website blacklisted (i.e., blocked by search engines). **For image used only for decoration, no description is required**, but the attribute should still be specified with nothing between the quotes (thus: alt=" ").

```
HTML
<h2>Image element</h2>
<img src="images/yacht.jpg" alt="A yacht race" title="A
 flotilla of yachts at the start of a racing regatta.
 "longdesc="yacht_race_desc.html" width="500" height="336">
```

Figure: Example usage of the <img> element.

Figure: Rendered result of Figure.

The title attribute, which is a **global attribute**, provides additional description for the image and is usually displayed when cursor hovers over an image, as shown in the rendered example. However, the attribute should not be used for essential information, since you cannot rely on everyone having access to it, because not every user uses a mouse and some browsers may not display it.

The width and height attributes specify the rendered size of the image. Rendered image size can also be specified using CSS. Both approaches have advantages and disadvantages. Most importantly, specifying size by using attributes enables faster download and more orderly rendering of a page. It also prevents layout from having to be reflowed multiple times as the page loads. This is because text usually downloads faster than images and the browser by default does not know the size of an image. The result of this is that when the attributes are not used, text finishes downloading, the browser displays it, and then moves it around to fit in the image when the image finishes downloading, resulting in an untidy rendering process.

In contrast, when the width and height attributes are specified and the browser encounters them, it reserves the right amount of space for the image and displays the text accordingly, so that when the image finishes downloading, it fits it in, without having to move the text significantly around. On the other hand, specifying size by using CSS allows for size to be controlled dynamically and also overrides whatever size is specified, using the width and height attributes.

Making an Image a Link, and Linking to an Image

Making an image clickable is an essential Web design practice and is done using the <a> element, which is the same element used to turn text into a hyperlink. The element and how the href attribute is used on it to create a link were discussed in Chapter.

In the example, notice that the entire <img> element, including all its attributes, is placed between the tags of the <a> element, just as is done to create text links. Also, notice that the cursor has changed shape to indicate that the image is clickable. Incidentally, the type of cursor shape to display can be specified using CSS. How this is done is shown in Chapter. The text link under the image links to the same image but displays it in a separate window when clicked. The first <br> element is used to place the link on a separate line, and the second to create an extra line. This is necessary, since <img> and <a> are inline elements and do not start on a new line.

```
HTML
<h2>Image link</h2>
<a href="http://www.w3c.org"><img src="images/yacht.jpg"
 width="500" height="336" alt="A yacht race image"
 title="A flotilla of yachts at the start of a racing
 regatta."></a>
<br><br>
<a href="images/yacht.jpg">A yacht race</a>
```

Figure: Using the <a> element to make an image a link and link to an image.

Figure: Rendered result of Figure.

Containing and Captioning Images Properly

Traditionally, the <img> element would be placed in the <p> or <div> element in order to be able to treat it as a self-contained unit. However, these elements are not semantically related to images. The <figure > container element, introduced in Chapter, was designed to address this. It allows images or a combination of media elements to be contained and treated as a separate unit. The <figcaption> element is intended to be used to add caption to the container.

```html
HTML
<figure>
  <h2>Containing images</h2>
  <img src="images/car_tunnel.jpg" width="500" height="336"
   alt="A car in a tunnel" title="A car driving through a
   traffic tunnel.">
  <figcaption>
     A car driving through a traffic tunnel.
  </figcaption>
</figure>
```

Figure: Example usage of <figure> and <figcaption>.

Containing images

A car driving through a traffic tunnel.

Figure: Rendered result of Figure.

Specifying Multiple Image Sources

In order to specify multiple image sources (i.e., **responsive images**), the <picture> and <source> elements need to be used with the <img> element, together with various combinations of the srcset, sizes, media, and type attributes. Situations in which it is necessary to use responsive images are known as **use cases**. More than one situation can occur together, in which case each situation is addressed. The commonly recognized use cases and how to specify responsive images for them are discussed here.

Specifying for Different Device Pixel Ratios

A device display screen is made up of many tiny dots called **pixels**. Device pixel ratio is the ratio of the number of these **physical screen pixels** to a **CSS pixel**, while CSS pixels are pixels used to specify lengths of elements in CSS. The difference between the two-pixel types is that the size of a device pixel is typically fixed, while that of a CSS pixel is variable and can be smaller or larger than a device pixel. For example, if an image that has a width of 200 px is zoomed in, it takes up more device pixels; however, the number of CSS pixels remain the same (i.e., 200) and the CSS pixels only expand as necessary.

High-resolution screens usually contain multiple device pixels per CSS pixel. Device screen pixels are explained further later in the chapter. Providing multiple images based on device pixel ratio is sometimes called **resolution switching** and is necessary in situations where different users might have different technology-based circumstances. For example:

Users' devices might have different physical screen sizes, usually measured diagonally.
Users might have screens with different pixel densities (i.e., pixels per inch).
Different zoom levels might be used.
Screen orientation might be different (e.g., landscape and portrait).

Network conditions (e.g., speed) might be different. This helps prevent the download of unnecessarily large images for slow systems.

To specify multiple images to deal with the above situations, the <img> element is used with the src and srcset attributes, along with the x descriptor. Figure shows how this is done.

```
HTML
<img src="images/yacht-400.jpg"
     srcset="images/yacht-600.jpg 1.5x,
             images/yacht-800.jpg 2x"
     alt="A yacht race"
     title="A flotilla of yachts at the start of a racing
            regatta."
     longdesc="yacht_race_desc.html"
     width="400" height="268">
```

Figure: Specifying responsive images for device-pixel-ratio use case.

In the example, the browser selects any of the image sources specified in the src- set attribute, using the specified pixel density descriptors (1.5x and 2x), also known as **display density descriptors**. Essentially, on displays with 1.5 device pixels per CSS pixel, the image with 1.5x pixel density is used, and on those with 2 device pixels per CSS pixel, the image with 2x pixel density is used. This means that browsers on devices with **high-PPI** (pixels per inch) screens select a high-resolution image (i.e., one with 1.5x or 2x) and other browsers select a normal (1x) image. Where no x descriptor is specified, it is assumed to be 1x.

If a browser does not support the srcset attribute, it uses the image source specified in the src attribute as fallback. Newer browsers that support srcset attribute usually use the source as one of the options and use it as if specified with a 1x descriptor. How x descriptors work in relation to image dimensions is that if the normal-resolution image is 400 x 268 and 1x, then the image specified with 1.5x should be 600 x 402 and the image with 2x should be 800 x 536. Notice that the naming of the image files matches the x descriptors' values. This is only good practice to avoid confusion and does not affect anything.

Specifying for Different Viewport Sizes

Providing multiple images for different viewport sizes is necessary in situations where different users might have devices that have different viewport widths. For example, a banner might be required to span the width of the viewport, whatever the size of the viewport, or an image might need to be sized to fit the width of differently sized columns. To specify responsive images to deal with these situations, the <img> element is used with the src, srcset, and sizes attributes, together with the w (width) descriptor. Figure shows how this is done.

In the example, the sizes attribute specifies that image should take up 100% of the width of the viewport. The srcset attribute provides the image sources from which to choose, along with their width descriptors (i.e., widths), and the src attribute specifies the fallback image when none of the options are suitable. The browser uses this information and various other factors to determine the best image source to select, and the selected image is displayed and scaled up or down to fit the full width of the viewport.

```
HTML
<img sizes="100vw"
    srcset="images/yacht-200.jpg 200w,
            images/yacht-400.jpg 400w,
            images/yacht-800.jpg 800w,
            images/yacht-1600.jpg 1600w"
    src="images/yacht-400.jpg"
         alt="A yacht race">
```

Figure: Specifying responsive images for viewport-size-based use case.

Specifying for Different Viewport Sizes Using Media Condition

Figure shows how **media condition** is used to specify the viewport widths at which different images should be used. These specified widths are called **image breakpoints** and are different from the **breakpoints for responsive layouts**.

In the example, the sizes attribute specifies that if the browser window's width is 480 CSS pixels or less to make image take up 100% of the viewport width; if it is not, but is 800 CSS pixels or less, to make image take up 70%; and if it is neither of the two (i.e., if it is wider than 800px), to make image take up a width equal to the value specified by the last item, which is 600px. When a media condition is true, the browser uses the associated rendered size (i.e., 100 or 70 vw) and the width descriptors in the srcset attribute to determine which image source to select. The selected image is then scaled up or down to occupy the specified percentage of the viewport. In basic terms, the code says that the wider the width of the browser, the less the percentage of it that should be taken up by the image.

```
HTML
<img sizes="(max-width: 480px) 100vw, (max-width: 800px) 70vw,
            600px"
    srcset="images/yacht-200.jpg 200w,
            images/yacht-400.jpg 400w,
            images/yacht-800.jpg 800w,
            images/yacht-1600.jpg 1600w"
    src="images/yacht-400.jpg"
    alt="A yacht race">
```

Figure: Specifying responsive images for viewport-size-based use case, using media condition.

Specifying for Different Image

Providing multiple images that have varying content is necessary in situations where different users might want to change the content or aspect ratio of an image to ensure that it is displayed in the best way, based on the size of a page or a screen. For example, the same image can be shown full size on large screens, showing everything contained in it, or it can be zoomed in and cropped on smaller screens to show only important parts. Providing multiple images for purposes such as these is known as **art direction**. To specify responsive images to solve such use case, the <picture> element and the <source> element, together with the media attribute, are used. Figure shows how this can be achieved.

```
HTML
<picture>
  <source media="(min-width: 720px)"
  srcset="images/yacht-fullshot.jpg">
  <source media="(min-width: 512px)"
  srcset="images/yacht-midshot.jpg">
  <img src="images/yacht-closeshot.jpg" alt="A yacht race">
</picture>
```

Figure: Specifying responsive images for image-content-based use case.

In the example, the browser selects the first <source> element and evaluates the condition in the media attribute. If it is true, it chooses the image source in the corresponding srcset attribute. If the condition is false, the browser goes to the next <source> element and does the same thing. If all the conditions in the <source> elements are false, the image source in the <img> element is used. This means that if the browser's width is 720 px or more, "images/yacht-fullshot .jpg" is selected; if the width is 512 px or more, "images/yacht-midshot.jp< " is selected; otherwise, "images/yacht-closeshot.jpg" is selected.

Notice that the dimensions of the images are not specified. They need to be specified, so that the browser can allocate space for the images before they are downloaded and so prevent multiple reflowing of layout during page rendering. To provide the dimensions, CSS properties and **CSS media queries (or media conditions)** are used, and how to do this is explained in Chapter 15. Also, to provide the dimensions for old browsers that do not support the <picture> element, the width and height attributes can also be used on the <img> element.

Specifying for Different Image and Device Pixel Ratios

It is possible to have situations where, in addition to solving for differences in image content, there is the need to solve for device pixel ratio. In such cases, images provided in different widths are also provided in different pixel densities.

The <source> element in the example says that if the browser window's width is 1024px or wider, to use one of the image sources in the srcset attribute used on it, based on the screen pixel density and other factors the browser deems relevant. This means that the high-resolution images (i.e., those with 2x and 3x) are used for high-resolution screens and the normal-resolution images are used for standard-resolution screens. If the width of the browser window is less than 1024 px, one of the image sources specified in the <img> element is used. Again, the high-resolution images are used for high-resolution screens and the normal-resolution images are used for standard-resolution screens.

```
HTML
<picture>
  <source media="(min-width: 1024px)"
        srcset="images/yacht-fullshot.jpg,
                images/yacht-fullshot-2x.jpg 2x,
                images/yacht-fullshot-3x.jpg 3x">
  <img src="images/yacht-closeshot.jpg" alt="A yacht race"
      srcset="images/yacht-closeshot-2x.jpg 2x,
              images/yacht-closeshot-3x.jpg 3x">
</picture>
```

Figure: Specifying responsive images for content and pixel ratio use case.

Specifying for Different Image File Formats

When the browsers of different users are likely to support different image file formats, it might be necessary to provide images in multiple file formats. You might, for example, want to offer a not-so-popular format that is smaller in file size and has better quality (in case a user's browser supports it) and a more popular format that has a poorer quality. This is done using the type attribute.

In the example, each srcset attribute specifies an image source and the type attribute specifies its MIME type. The browser goes through each <source> element and selects the first one that specifies an image whose format it supports. If it supports none of them, it selects the format specified in the <img> element. Notice how the <figure> and <figcaption> elements are used. They have the same effect as in when specifying a single image.

```
HTML
<figure>
  <picture>
    <source srcset="images/yacht.webp" type="image/webp">
    <source srcset="images/yacht.jxr" type="image/vnd.ms-photo">
    <source srcset="images/yacht.jp2" type="image/jp2">
    <img src="images/yacht.jpg" width="500"
      height="336" alt="A yacht race>"
  </picture>
  <figcaption>
      A yacht race in progress.
  </figcaption>
</figure>
```

Figure: Specifying responsive images for image-format-based use case.

<canvas>...</canvas>

The <canvas> element allows you to draw graphics on the fly. This enables the creation of dynamic images, such as the ones necessary in games, generation of graphs, and other images in real time. The attributes that it supports are width and height. Figure 6.13 shows how it is used. The example creates a canvas that is 150 x 150 pixels in size and has a unique identification of "oneCanvas." The fallback statement is displayed if a browser does not support the element. Note that because the element is just a container element, it does not display anything on its own, so the code does not display anything.

<svg>...</svg>

The <svg> element makes it possible to add to a Web page a type of image known as **vector image** (discussed more fully later in this chapter), which is created using coordinates. The element is useful for creating basic images on the fly but requires the understanding of a different type of markup language called SVG, which is beyond the scope of this book. In the example, the SVG <svg> element defines the image, the width and height attributes define the size, and the SVG <rect> elements define the rectangles and their sizes.

```
HTML
<body>
  <h3>Canvas element</h3>
  <canvas id="oneCanvas" width="150" height="150">
    Your user agent does not support the HTML5 canvas element.
  </canvas>
</body>
```

Figure: Example usage of the <canvas> element.

```
HTML
<body>
  <h2>SVG element</h2>
  <svg width="400" height="400">
    <rect x="30" y="10" width="250"
      height="250" rx="20"
      style="fill:#2111C0; stroke:#000000;
      stroke-width:2px;" />
    <rect x="90" y="70" width="250"
      height="250" rx="20"
      style="fill:#E10000; stroke:#000000;
      stroke-width:2px;" />
  </svg>
</body>
```
                                              ⎫ ┌─────────────────┐
                                              ⎬ │ Description   │
                                              ⎭ │ of rectangles   │
                                                 └─────────────────┘

Figure: Example usage of the <svg> element.

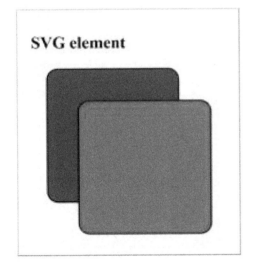

SVG element

Figure: The result of Figure

<map>...</map> and <area>...</area>

As mentioned earlier, the <map> and <area> elements are combined with the <img> element to create **image mapping**. To be able to use these elements to create image maps, they need to be combined with various attributes.

Image mapping has many applications. It is especially useful for providing information about different areas represented on a geographical map that would be impractical to put on the map. Essentially, an image map enables geometric areas placed on an image to be associated with hyperlinks. Creation of an image map involves the following:

Declaring and naming of map, using the <map> element with the name attribute.

Creating the hotspot regions, using the <area> element with the shape and coords attributes. The coordinates of shapes are typically difficult to work out. However, there are now various tools on the Web for doing this.

Attributes Used in Image Mapping

AttributeFunction name Specifies a unique name for element. Href Specifies the URL (address) of the destination of a link.
Shape Defines the type of shape to be created in an image map. coords Defines the x-y coordinates for the shape to be created.
Usemap Used with the <img> element to specify the name of the image map to use with an image to produce an image map.

A search for "image mapping" should reveal some of them. They allow an image to be uploaded and hotspots to be drawn on it, after which the x-y coordinates are generated, based on the top-left corner of the image being 0,0. Some also generate the image-map HTML code.

Linking of the hotspots to the desired destinations (files), using the href attribute.
Associating the map with an image containing areas and labels that correspond to the hotspots, using the usemap attribute. This, in principle, is like superimposing the hotspot shapes on the image.

Figure gives a rough illustration of the components of an image map, and Figure shows part of the code for implementing an image map.

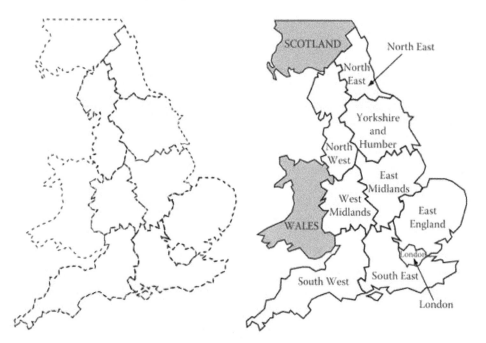

Figure: Map of hotspot shapes (left) and the image (right) with which it is combined to produce a clickable image.

```
HTML
<h3>Image map</h3>                           ┌──────── Creates hyperlink to London page
<map name="picture">                         │
   <area shape="poly" href="http://www.example.com/london.html" coords="422,
    562, 433, 565, 442, 559, 449, 554, 465, 555, 468, 567, 484, 564, 493, 573, 480,
    580, 496, 584, 483, 590, 475, 591, 471, 598, 468, 608, 461, 596, 454, 606, 443,
    592, 436, 601, 437, 587, 426, 582, 423, 569" alt="London">
   <area shape="poly" href="http://www.example.com/northeast.html" coords="304,
    11, 282, 34, 289, 49, 295, 59, 277, 74, 270, 72, 256, 96, 262, 111, 269, 111, 271,
    120, 262, 126, 266, 147, 277, 144, 284, 152, 280, 164, 284, 169, 281, 175, 293,
    187, 293, 197, 302, 191, 312, 196, 331, 183, 343, 191, 359, 195, 368, 187, 396,
    192, 401, 182, 375, 174, 369, 162, 356, 138, 357, 125, 344, 99, 346, 92, 338, 71,
    338, 51, 329, 35, 322, 39" alt="North East">
                              ┌──── Combines hotspots map with image
...                           │
</map>
<img src="england_regions.jpg" width="640" height="790" usemap="#picture"
alt="Regions of England">
```

Figure: Example usage of image-mapping elements.

In the example, the first <area> element creates a hotspot shape of the London region, which when clicked takes users to another page that provides information about the region. The second <area> element does the same for the Northeast region, and all the other regions (i.e., hotspot shapes) are created in the same way, all of which are enclosed within the <map> element. In the coords attributes, the first two numbers specify the x-y coordinates of the first point of the shape being created, and the next two numbers specify the x-y coordinates of the second point, and so on.

Document Embedding

In addition to allowing linking to other Web pages, HTML5 allows another Web page to be displayed inside a Web page and browsed independently. The element used for achieving this is the <iframe> element.

<iframe>...</iframe>

The <iframe> element is an inline element that allows content to be embedded in a page and interacted with by the user in various ways. Embedding content in this way is useful for embedding interactive applications, such as Google map.

TABLE

The HTML5 Attributes for the <iframe> Element

Attribute	Function
src	Specifies the URL for the page to be embedded.
width	Specifies the width of the frame.
height	Specifies the height of the frame.
name	Specifies a name for the frame.
seamless	Specifies that frame should be displayed in a way that makes it seem a part of the main page. For example, no scrollbars are shown. A value does not need to be specified; or "seamless" or "" may be specified (e.g., seamless="seamless" or seamless="").
sandbox	Specifies to disallow (or allow, if disallowed) certain features. The value may be empty (which means to apply all default restrictions, including disallowing plug-ins, form submission, scripts execution, links to other documents, and content to be treated as being from its original source), or the value may be a **space-separated list of keywords** that remove restrictions, including allow-forms, allow-scripts, allow-top-navigation, and allow-same-origin.
srcdoc	Specifies the content for the frame. If supported by the browser, it overrides what is specified in src. It is expected to be used with the seamless and sandbox attributes.

```
HTML
<body>
  <h3>iFrame Element</h3>
  <iframe width="400" height="300"
   src="https://www.google.com/maps/embed?
   pb=!1m18!1m12!1m3!1d158858.182370726!2d0.10159865000000001
   !3d51.52864165!2m3!1f0!2f0!3f0!3m2!1i1024!2i768!4f13.1!3m3
   !1m2!1s0x47d8a00baf21de75%3A0x52963a5addd52a99!2sLondon!5e0
   !3m2!1sen!2suk!4v1437373289145">
  <p>This browser does not support iframes<p>
  </iframe>
</body>
```

Figure: Example usage of the <iframe> element.

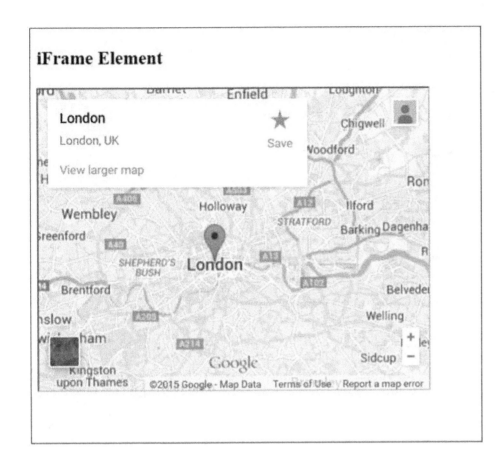

iFrame Element

Figure: The result of Figure

Obtaining the value for the src attribute required going to https://maps.google.co.uk and searching for London. Next, when the map for London was displayed, the three- line menu icon at the top-left corner of the map was clicked to display a drop-down list, from which "Share or embed map" was chosen. Next, in the dialog that appeared, the "Embed map" option was chosen and the code for embedding the map was copied and used, as shown in the example. Note that the code generated by the site, as of time of writing, has some attributes that are no longer supported by the <iframe> element and should therefore be removed.

Types of Images

Being aware of the makeup of the types of images used in Web design can be useful in understanding why they have the properties that determine how they are used. The images shown so far are known as **two-dimensional images** (2D images). They are 2D images because they are represented in only two dimensions, width and height. They are the most used images in Web design and fall into two categories, **bitmapped** and **vector** images.

Bitmapped Images

Bitmapped images, also known as **raster images**, are made up of tiny dots called **pixels**. In Web design, you might refer to these pixels as **CSS pixels**, as mentioned earlier. The image of the "H" in Figure gives an illustration. It is made up of both the white background and the "H," which are inseparable.

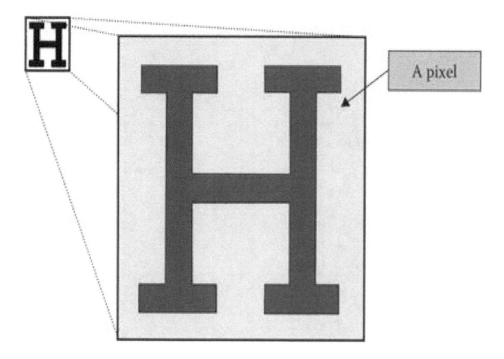

Figure: A graphical illustration of a bitmapped image.

Representing images in pixels inevitably produces properties that can be used to describe bitmapped images. These properties revolve around how many pixels are there in an image or specific area of it. They influence image quality and therefore have design implications. The three main properties are **image resolution, pixels per unit length**, and **color depth**.

Image Resolution

Image resolution describes how many pixels an image has, and it is specified in two ways. One is as pixel dimensions, and the other is as megapixels. **Pixel dimensions** are the width and height of an image in pixels. For example, 800 x 600 means that an image has width and height of 800 and 600 pixels, respectively. The term **megapixels**, on the other hand, describes the total number of pixels in an image and is expressed in megapixels. It is typically used for specifying the maximum resolution that a digital camera can produce and is the product of the width and the height of an image, in pixels.

For example, a black and white image with a pixel dimension of 800 x 600 is about 0.48 megapixels (i.e., 480,000 pixels). A higher image resolution produces a bigger image when displayed or printed. Figure shows an illustration. The design implication is that images that are too big for the screen, even when intended to be the only element on the screen or page; this often compels vertical and horizontal scrolling in order to view all parts of the image, essentially compromising user experience.

Pixel dimension should be determined when creating an image in order to prevent significant resizing later. Failing this, the usual practice is to, at least, create images of larger pixel dimensions than needed and then reduce and sharpen them in a graphics program, if necessary. Making small pixel dimensions bigger is much like trying to spread fewer than enough pixels over a larger area, which the computer responds to by, for example, creating "fake pixels," based on the values of original pixels, to make up for missing ones, resulting in a poorly defined image.

This technique of using "fake pixels," or pixels with estimated values, is known as **image interpolation**, and there are various ways of achieving it. Figure demonstrates the effects of image enlargement. The general practice is to not reduce size to the point where an image is so small that important details are no longer discernible or, in the case of enlargement, to gradually increase size (e.g., by 10% each time) to the point where an image starts getting blocky or blurry.

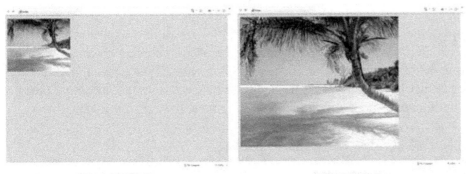

320 × 240 image   800 × 600 image

Figure: The same image with different pixel dimensions displayed in the same Web browser on a 1152 x 864 screen.

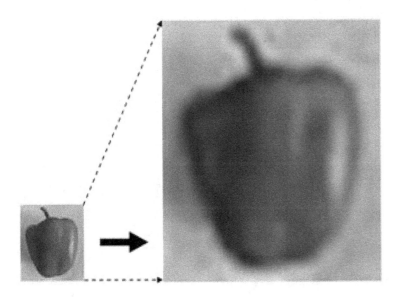

Figure: The effects of significant enlargement on image quality.

About Image Resizing

If images must be resized, then necessary things need to be done to preserve as much of the original characteristics as possible. There are a number of ways to achieve this. A graphics program, HTML, or CSS may be used to specify the desired size. The image may also be cropped. When an image is sized by specifying new dimensions, a possible byproduct that holds relevance in image display quality is **image aspect ratio** (IAR), which is the width of an image divided by its height, or the ratio of width to height.

The aspect ratio of an image is established from the starting width and height when the image is created, and width and height are specified in various ways, depending on how the image is created. For an image created with a graphics program, width and height are among the parameters specified for a new document. For a scanned image, they are the dimensions of the document that is scanned, but they may also be specified. For example, if the size of the document scanned or the dimensions set is 5 x 3 inch and scanning resolution is 300 pixels per inch (ppi), then the aspect ratio of the image created is:

= (width x resolution):(height x resolution) =

(5 x 300):(3 x 300) = 1500:300 = 5:3

The aspect ratio of an image must be retained; otherwise, distortion can occur, as shown in Figure.

In contrast, **when images are cropped**, there is no aspect ratio problem, because a new aspect ratio is created when an image is cropped, which means that cropping can also be used to change an image's aspect ratio. Image cropping is the trimming off of the edges of an image, and it is typically done in a graphics editor. The only issue with cropping is that it may adversely reduce the scope of an image, because some important details at the edges that complement the main elements in the image may be removed.

Original   Elongated   Squashed

Figure: An original image and images produced by resizing it incorrectly.

However, cropping could also be used deliberately for this purpose in order to remove unwanted details from an image and better focus on the important elements. In such a case, an image may first be enlarged and then cropped, or vice versa. Figure shows an example. Notice the difference in presence, focus, and aspect ratio.

Original image   Enlarged and cropped image

Figure: Enlarging and cropping an image to focus on a specific part.

Pixels per Unit Length

Pixels per unit length (or **pixel density**) describes the number of pixels per unit length and is also, confusingly enough, referred to as resolution in some context. In English speaking countries, the pixels per unit length most commonly used is **pixels per inch** (ppi), followed by **pixels per centimeters** (ppcm). Although it is a measure more commonly used to describe the quality of a display device, it is actually a more definite indicator of quality in bitmapped images than in pixel dimensions or megapixels. For example, if you are told that an image has a resolution of 72 ppi, this immediately conveys the sense of how densely packed pixels are in the image and therefore what quality to expect. On the other hand, if you are told that an image has a resolution of 398 x 265 pixels, or 0.10 megapixels, there is no indication of pixel density. In order for these values to make more sense in terms of quality, it would be necessary to know the physical dimensions of the image, so as to judge how densely packed the pixels are and therefore how much details are represented in the image.

Like aspect ratio, **the ppi value of an image is determined at the point of creation**. It affects the pixel dimensions of the image and the number of pixels that the image contains. For example, a 4 x 6 inch photograph scanned at 100 ppi will result in a bitmapped image that has a ppi value of 100, pixel dimensions of 400 x 600, and a total pixel number of 240,000 (i.e., 400 x 600). On the other hand, the same photograph scanned at 300 ppi will produce an image that has a 300 ppi value and a total pixel number of 2,160,000 (i.e., 1200 x 1800). The ppi specified when an image is created is usually saved with it. This is why it is sometimes referred to as **embedded resolution**. Generally, the choice of ppi depends on how an image will be outputted, since ppi affects image display and printing differently.

PPI and Displayed Image Quality

Incidentally, when an image is intended for display on a monitor screen, ppi affects quality only indirectly. This is because **monitors do not display images in pixels per inch** but based on pixel dimensions; that is, a 300 x 400 pixel image with 100 ppi, for example, is displayed on a standard-resolution screen with 300 pixels across and 400 pixels down. This means that no matter what ppi is used to create an image, it will not necessarily affect its display quality.

To demonstrate, a 5 x 4 inch document scanned at 72 ppi and 300 ppi will produce images with pixel dimensions of 360 x 288 (i.e., [72 x 5] x [72 x 4]) and 1500 x 1200, respectively, which will be different in size when displayed, as shown in Figure, in which the two images are displayed together in a Web browser. This basically means that when an image is displayed on the screen, ppi only affects the size at which it is displayed, not the quality. Naturally, zooming can then be used to increase or decrease the size of the image.

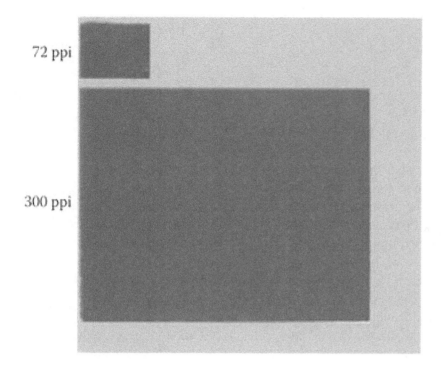

Figure: The relationship between the images of the same document scanned at 72 and 300 ppi.

So, what ppi should be used when creating images for Web design? Although computers and other devices used to access websites generally have ppi that is higher than 72 ppi, there is no logical reason to produce images intended for screen display at anything more than 72 ppi, since higher ppi will only result in larger files. However, it is a different matter when images are intended to be printed.

PPI and Printed Image Quality

In contrast to its effects on displayed images, ppi affects the quality of printed images directly. So, typically, what looks good on screen may not look good when printed. This is because printers generally print based on **dots per inch** (dpi) and also at a much higher resolution than computer monitors. Modern printers, for example, commonly have a resolution of 600 dpi and higher. This means that an image needs to be 600 ppi or more to ensure good quality when printed. If the resolution of an image is much lower than a printer's resolution (say a 72 ppi image is outputted on a 600 dpi printer), then the printed image will be either too small in size or not detailed enough to be considered good quality.

Generally, higher ppi values ensure better-quality printed images with finer details and subtler color transitions. The implication of this is that if images are intended to be printed, then it is important to ensure that they are produced using high enough ppi/dpi values. It is also important to know that a **low-quality (low-ppi) image cannot be improved by printing it at a higher dpi**. Increasing print resolution will only make pixels larger, resulting in pixelation. Likewise, once an image is created, increasing its ppi in a graphics program will not necessarily improve its quality. This means that where you want an image to be available both for screen viewing and printing, then separate versions should be provided.

Color Depth

To better understand the meaning of color depth, it is useful to know how color is produced on a device screen. A color display screen is made up of tiny dots called **pixels**, each of which can be made to produce any of many colors at a time by mixing three different colors in varying degrees. Each color component is represented with a number of bits, and **color depth** (also known as **bit depth** or **pixel depth**) is the total number of bits used to represent the three-color components. Color depth is also referred to as **bits per pixel (bpp)**, even **bytes per pixel (bpp)**, and it determines the number of distinct colors available to use for a pixel as well as the color quality of an image.

For example, 24-bit color depth (known as **true color**), which provides 16,777,216 colors theoretically produces better color quality than 8-bit color depth, which provides 256 colors. In theory, the higher the color depth, the more accurately the colors of an image can be represented, and therefore, the more realistically rich colors can be represented. Of course, the file size is also bigger. Figure shows the same photograph represented with different color depths. Notice the depreciation in color quality and the **posteriza- tion effect** (i.e., the banding of colors in different areas) as color depth drops to 4-bit and 1-bit. Although, in theory, 24-bit produces better quality than 8-bit, in reality, the difference is usually not visible.

Figure: An illustration of the effects of color depth.

Some technologies used for creating images, such as scanners, offer higher color depths than 24-bit, such as 32-bit and 48-bit, but these are unlikely to produce any discernable benefits, since humans are capable of differentiating only between about 10 million colors, most, if not all, of which are covered by 24-bit color depth. Also, humans are not very good at distinguishing between close variations of the same color, unless they are placed close to each other. However, higher color depths can be useful, because the extra bits can be used for other functions.

For example, in 32-bit color depth, 8 bits are used, each for the red, green, and blue color components (or **channels**) and the extra 8 bits for an **alpha channel** (or **transparency channel**). An alpha channel specifies which parts of an image should be transparent and by how much. Its value ranges from 0 to 255. When it is set to 0, the specified area of an image is fully transparent, and when set to 255, it is fully opaque. The channel is usually controlled with the **opacity** feature in graphics-editing programs and is usually specified as a value between 0% and 100% or between 0 and 1.0. The alpha channel has an important role in the production of images.

Vector Images

Unlike bitmapped images, vector images are not made up of pixels. Rather, they are made up of **geometric objects** (known as **geometric primitives**), such as points, lines, curves, and shapes, each of which can be defined in terms of a series of connecting points and/or mathematical expressions. A line, for example, is produced by connecting two points and a curve is produced by a mathematical equation. Figure shows an illustration of how an "H" might be represented.

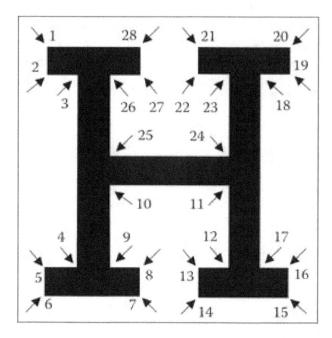

Figure: An illustration of the principle of vector graphic representation.

Looking at the figure, it is easy to imagine that a more complex vector graphic would comprise many more points, as shown in Figure. The figure shows a relatively complex vector graphic, which is actually one object created by connecting many points (**node points**).

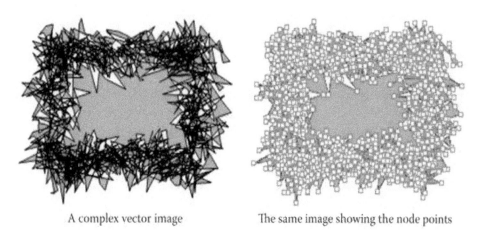

A complex vector image   The same image showing the node points

Figure: A demonstration of the makeup of a vector image.

Storing only the coordinates of the objects and a few other properties that make up vector images means that vector image files are **seldom large in size**, making the method an effective way of producing good-quality digital images that are small in size. Also, because they are stored as a series of coordinates, they can be scaled, translated, and deformed easily by simply manipulating the node points. This means that they are

very scalable (i.e., they can be enlarged without loss of image quality). Furthermore, their **quality is independent of display device resolution**, meaning that they can look good on displays of any resolution. Also, being small in size particularly makes vector images "Internet friendly," in that they download fast.

Some of the performance benefits of vector images are reduced by the fact that they still typically have to be saved in bitmapped file formats in order to use them on Web pages. An alternative to doing this is to save them in a vector-based format, such as SVG, mentioned earlier. SVG is both a vector graphics language and a file format, such that when a vector graphic is saved, it is also saved in the language, which a browser is then able to translate into a vector image and display. However, the use of SVG is not yet widespread, as of time of writing.

Another alternative to saving vector images as bitmapped is to save them in Flash file format, SWF, which is another vector-based format. However, a Web browser needs a plug-in in order to be able to display a vector graphic saved in the format. Furthermore, the popularity of the format has decreased, and this is unlikely to change, going into the future.

(a) (b)

Image File Formats and Image File Size

Irrespective of how images are created, be it via photography, scanning, or graphics programs, they are stored as image files in specific formats and there many image file formats. These formats provide different features and are suitable for different types of images. While some formats are designed to store all the data that make up an image, others are capable of making an image file size smaller. This is necessary because image file can be large, especially bitmapped image files. The technique of reducing file size in computing is known as **data compression**. Some formats are designed to reduce file size without affecting the quality of what the file produces. This is known as **lossless compression**.

Other formats are designed to allow the reduction of quality, if necessary. This is known as **lossy compression**. Image file formats combine both techniques in various ways to achieve their specific characteristics, and graphics production programs typically allow compression parameters to be set for any format that offers compression. Image file formats also offer other features, such as transparency, that make them suitable for different situations. Table lists some formats used on the Web, some of which are more commonly used than others.

Main Properties of the Image File Formats

Format	MIME type	Bitmap/ Vector	Lossless/ Lossy	Animation	Transparency
GIF (.gif)	image/gif	Bitmap	Both	Yes	Yes
JPEG (.jpeg, .jpg)	image/jpeg	Bitmap	Both	No	No
JPEG2000 (.jp2, .jpx)	imge/jp2	Bitmap	Both	Yes	Yes
JPEG XR (.jxr, .hdp, .wdp)	image/jxr, image/ vnd.ms-photo	Bitmap	Both	Yes	Yes
OpenEXR (.exr)	Image/x-exr	Bitmap	Both	Yes	Yes
PDF (.pdf)	application/pdf	Both	Both	Yes	Yes
PNG (.png)	image/png	Bitmap	Lossless	No	Yes
SVG (.svg)	image/svg+xml	Vector	None	Yes	Yes
SWF (.swf)	application/ x-shockwave-flash	Vector	Lossless	Yes	Yes
WebP (.webp)	image/webp	Bitmap	Both	Yes	Yes

Given that high-quality images produce very large files, it is often necessary to **balance file size against quality** when producing images for Web design, because large files can cause performance problems, such as long download time. It is no good, for example, if images are of very high quality and pages take frustratingly long times to display, as most users will probably not be prepared to wait. Similarly, it is no good to compress an image to the point that degradation is visible, as this might compromise the information being communicated and/or user experience. Figure shows the same image with different compression levels and their effect on quality and file size. Notice the visible degradation in 75% and 99% compressions.

Uncompressed: 165 K   50% Compression: 10.8 K

75% Compression: 3.4 K   99% Compression: 1.8 K

Figure: An illustration of the effects of compression on quality and file size.

To help with size-quality balancing, image production programs, such as Photoshop, typically provide information about the size of the file generated by an image and also how long it will take to transmit the file over a range of Internet connection speeds. However, while this information is readily available when using these programs, it can be useful to know how to calculate image file size and transmission time for when, for example, you are doing initial designing on paper and/ or have no access to a suitable program. After all, just because we have calculators does not mean that we should not know how to add, in case calculators are not available.

Calculating File Size Generated from Scanned Documents

An A4 (i.e., 8.5 x 11 inches) document scanned at 300 ppi and 24-bit color depth will generate an image file size of 25.25 MB. This can be calculated by multiplying the area of the document in square inches by the number of pixels per square inch to get the total number of pixels in the image, multiplying by the number of bits per pixel to get the total number of bits, and then dividing by 8 to get the number of bytes, thus: Document Image File Size = ((height width) × P P I 2 × color depth Using the formula for the above example gives:

File size = ((8.5 × 11) × (300 × 300) × 24) = 25 , 245 , 000 bytes = 25 , 245 , 000 / 1000 = 25 , 245 KB = 25 , 245 / 1000 = 25.25 MB

Calculating File Size Generated from Digital Camera

An image captured with a digital camera with pixel dimensions of 640 x 480 px at 24-bit color depth produces a file size of 0.92 MB. This is calculated by multiplying the total number of pixels by the number of bits per pixel to get the total number of bits and then dividing by 8 to get the number of bytes, thus: Document Image File Size = ((height × width) × PPI 2 × color depth) / 8 Image File Size = (pixel dimensions × color depth) / 8 Using the formula gives:

Image File Size = ((640 × 480) × 24) / 8 = 921 , 600 bytes = 921 , 600 / 1000 = 921.60 KB = 921.60 / 1000 = 0.92 MB

Calculating File Transmission Time

Given an Internet connection of 56.6 kilobits per second (kbps), a file that is 22.25 MB in size will take about 59 min to transmit. This can be calculated by dividing the size of the file by connection or transmission speed. Both must be in the same unit, such as bits, kilobits, bytes, and megabytes. The speed of 56.6 kbps is the slowest that people use to connect to the Internet. The following formula can be used to calculate transmission time:

Transmission Time = size of file / lowest transmission speed

Before using the formula, all values are converted to the same unit. In this case, file size is converted to the unit of the transmission speed, that is, **kilobits**. To do this, 25.25 MB is simply multiplied by 1000 twice to convert it to bytes, then multiplied by 8 to convert to bits, and then divided by 1000 to convert to kilobits. This is written as (25.25 x 1000 x 1000 x 8)/1000, which gives 202,000 kilobits. Using the formula gives: Transmission Time = 202, 000 kilobits / 56.6 kbps = 3568.91 s = (3568.91 / 60) min = 59.48 min

Guidelines for Effective Use of Images

The most useful function of images is their ability to instantly and effectively communicate either single or collective visual information. For example, when we look at a picture, most of the time, we immediately get an impression of what it is. Even when we cannot immediately figure out what the picture says, the time it takes to do this is often much less than the time it would have taken if the details of the picture were described in text. Graphics are also quite versatile in that they can be used to communicate various types of information. They can be used to **communicate reality or a concept**, to **create specific moods**, or to simply **beautify**. However, in order to achieve these goals, images need to be used correctly.

Decorative Images

The **use of graphics for decorative purposes should be minimized**, as they can place unnecessary burden on the download time of a page and are not appreciated by most users, anyway. Studies, for example, by the NN Group, which specializes in user experience, have shown that users generally pay attention to only those images that carry relevant information, such as photos of real people (not stock photos of models) and products, while ignoring decorative graphics. In particular, large graphics should not be used for decorative purposes, because whatever benefits they offer are likely outweighed by the performance problems that they are likely to cause.

The most common **decorative use of images is as background**. When an image is used for background, it should match the mood or context of a design; otherwise, it may create conflict and distraction. For example, a background image consisting of different-color balloons suits a page providing information about a party than one that is providing information about a funeral. Even when background image is relevant and complements a design theme, it should not be so overwhelming that it gets in the way of the content being delivered. This is unprofessional and particularly unacceptable in learning applications, given that focus is especially required during learning. To prevent background graphics from interfering with the content of a page, they should be subdued or toned down.

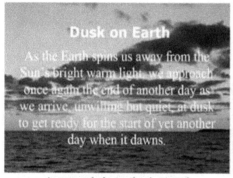

An overwhelming background   A subdued background

Figure: A demonstration of the effect of overwhelming background image and a possible solution.

Another common technique used to prevent background image from overwhelming content is to place the content in a plain color box on the background. However, this can look a bit messy, confusing, and distracting sometimes, especially when users have to scroll through the content. Also, the background can keep attracting the eyes from the periphery.

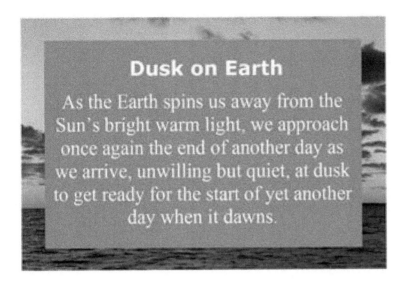

Figure: Preventing background from compromising legibility.

Large Images

The **automatic display of large images** should be avoided, even when they are relevant, because they can take too long to download and display completely. Instead, use thumbnails to introduce the images. If users then want to see the larger versions, they can click as required. For a thumbnail to be easy to be interpreted and therefore be effective for making a choice, it needs to contain useful information. However, this can sometimes be difficult to achieve, because neither of the two methods commonly used for creating thumbnails (i.e., scaling and cropping) produces completely satisfactory result.

Scaling produces the smaller version of an entire picture but may be too crowded to convey clear and useful meaning, while **cropping** produces a clearer and more detailed image but with too many useful parts cropped off. The recommended approach, called **relevance enhanced image reduction**, is to combine the two methods, so that the thumbnail is clear and also includes enough contexts to be meaningful. A more specific recommendation by Jakob Nielsen is that in order to produce a thumbnail that is 10% of the original image, the image is first cropped to 32% of its original size and then the result is scaled down to 32% of itself. So, assuming that the original image is 100 x 100 px, then cropping it to 32% gives 32 x 32 px (i.e., [32/100]*100 px), and scaling this down to 32% of itself gives an image that is roughly 10 x 10 px (i.e., [32/100]*32 px).

Images with Text

Where an image is used to support text or text is used to support an image, it is essential, especially in learning materials where comprehension is critical, that they are closely synchronized, so as to minimize the load on short-term memory. This prevents people from doing extra cognitive work to connect the two, as would be the case when they are far apart.

For example, the illustration on the left requires someone to look at a number on the image and then search out the matching item on the list underneath while holding the number in short-term memory, making it harder to construct the imagery that is vital for comprehension. However, the illustration on the right simply requires one glance, and because all the materials are together, constructing the imagery is easier.

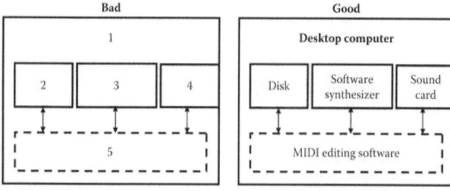

1. Desktop computer
2. Disk
3. Software synthesizer
4. Sound card
5. MIDI editing software

Figure: Two ways of using images with text.

When it is not feasible to place annotations on an image, connecting one element to the other directly, using something like a pointing line, as illustrated in Figure, can provide a reasonable compromise.

Figure: Another way of annotating an image.

Images and Captions

Caption should be provided with every image used to present content, either underneath it or in a body of text that is relevant to it, if used to complement a story. Figure shows part of the photo gallery of the website of a yearly tennis competition, in which this principle was not applied when the page was active. A series of images were simply presented, along with navigational aid that allowed linear or nonlinear navigation of the images. Although the images used as part of the background required no labeling, those used for content would have benefited from a brief description placed, for example, at the bottom. This would, no doubt, save those who did not know the player from wondering who she was and who she was playing at that moment.

Figure: Example of image being delivered without a description.

Acquiring Images for Use

There are various ways to acquire the graphics needed for a design, each of which has design situations for which it is most suitable. However, irrespective of the method used, the principle of having them in the right format, right pixel dimensions, and right resolution persists in order for them to be able to fit well into the intended design. The most common acquisition methods include stock images, graphics editors, photography, image scanning, and the use of coding.

Stock Images

For non-unique graphics requirements, stock images are a common option to consider. There are both free and commercial stock images of various categories and qualities available on the Web. Some are free for both private and commercial use, while license needs to be purchased to use some stock images commercially or for specific purposes. A license may be for unlimited use (as in the case of royalty-free stock images) or for just one-time use (as in the case of rights-managed stock images), or there might be other terms involved.

Graphics Editors

Vector graphics editors or bitmap graphics editors maybe used to create images. **Vector graphics editors** (drawing programs) allow the composition and editing of vector images, which can be saved in a variety of vector formats, such as SVG, EPS, PDF, VML, and WMF, or in bitmapped formats. They are better for line art or line drawing, which includes logos, sharp-edged illustrations (such as cartoons and clip arts), logos, technical illustrations, and diagrams. Drawing skill is of course necessary.

Popular programs used among professionals include Illustrator and CorelDraw. Popular free ones include Inkscape, and these are sufficient for beginners. **Bitmap graphics editors** (image editing programs) allow the painting and editing of pictures and save them as bitmap formats, such as GIF, JPEG, PNG, and TIFF. They are most suitable for retouching and manipulating photographs and creating photo-realistic images, which are typically images that are made up of many slightly different colors.

The most popular of these editors among professionals is Photoshop, which has a cheaper version called Photoshop Element. Free ones include GIMP and Raw Therapee. Online editors are also available.

Photography

This is an easier method of acquiring images than drawing or painting them, in that it mostly requires pointing a camera and capturing an image; however, taking some types of photographs requires expertise, in using both the right camera settings and techniques. There are two main types of cameras: point-and-shoot and digital single-lens reflex (DSLR) cameras. **Point-and-shoot** cameras are compact and easy to operate. Although mobile phone cameras are a type of point-and-shoot cameras, some may not produce images that are as good as dedicated point-and-shoot cameras, such as in lowlighting conditions. In contrast, **DSLR** cameras are larger and more complex to operate but take better pictures.

In addition to using the right settings and techniques, there is also the matter of using the right lighting setup to get the right mood. This usually involves using a combination of lights of different intensity placed at different angles and distances to the subject. The most common lighting scheme is **three-point lighting**. Naturally, shots from a camera can also be manipulated in graphics editors to correct imperfections or to create effects.

This is certainly necessary when producing **high-dynamic-range (HDR) images**. Production of HDR images typically involves combining differently exposed shots of the same scene (sometimes known as **bracketed photos**) and manipulating the properties of the resulting single image, such as color saturation, luminosity, contrast, and lighting. Bracketed photos are typically produced using **auto-exposure bracketing** (AEB) in cameras to capture three or more shots in sequence, using different exposures.

HDR images are images intended to be expressive and communicate something that is closer to what is seen in reality, such as the blurry yet sparkling points of light that the teary eyes see when looking at an illuminated high-contrast scene at night, something that a camera, for example, is not capable of capturing. They are used to create this type of realism, and more, including extreme and surreal visuals and typically high contrast and vibrancy.

Image Scanning

This is another easy way to acquire images; however, the images have to exist first in a physical form, whether on paper or on any other surfaces. Image scanners are typically hand-held or flatbed. **Hand-held scanners** are portable but more difficult to operate in that they are prone to shaking, which produces poor-quality images. **Flatbed scanners** are fixed, and using them requires simply laying an image on their glass surface and operating accordingly. Various image properties, such as scanning resolution (i.e., ppi) and contrast, can be set to ensure that the desired image quality is achieved. The use of 300 ppi is common for images intended for screen display.

Because standard image scanners do not produce good-quality images from **film negatives and slides**, these are scanned using a special type of scanner. They can be as easy to use as placing a negative in a carrier that they come with and feeding it into the scanner. Typical scanning resolution is much higher than that for normal scanning and ranges from 3000 to 4000 ppi.

Web Coding Languages

Web coding languages allow some types of graphics to be created procedurally and used in ways that are not possible with images created with non-procedural methods, in that the images are created dynamically. This means that images can be generated and changed in real time, making them suitable, for example, for generating graphics such as graphs, charts, and maps on the fly, based on, for example, continually changing data supplied by users. The most commonly used Web-specific languages are HTML, SVG, and JavaScript; however, general-purpose languages, such as C++, are also used. The main disadvantage of using coding languages to create images is that programming skill is required and the process can be time-consuming when complex images are involved.

Conclusion:

As we conclude our exploration of **lists, tables, links, forms, and images in HTML and CSS**, it is evident that these elements form the cornerstone of modern web design. They not only enable developers to structure content effectively but also create interactive and visually appealing experiences for users. Let's revisit and synthesize the key takeaways from each of these components and their transformative role in building user-centric web applications.

1. Lists: Organizing Content Efficiently

Lists are fundamental tools for presenting structured information. Whether it's an unordered list for bullet points, an ordered list for step-by-step instructions, or a description list for definitions, lists enhance readability and accessibility.

Key insights:

Use semantic HTML tags like <ul>, <ol>, and <dl> to convey meaning to both users and search engines. Leverage CSS to style lists, such as custom bullet points or numbered list formats, to align with the overall design language.
Interactive enhancements, like collapsible lists or animations, can improve user engagement.

Best practices:

Keep list items concise and focused.
Avoid deep nesting, as it can reduce clarity.
Ensure proper accessibility through ARIA roles and attributes.

2. Tables: Structuring Data Intuitively

Tables remain invaluable for displaying tabular data, such as reports, schedules, and comparisons. By combining semantic HTML with modern CSS, tables can transcend their traditional grid-like appearance and adapt to responsive designs.

Key insights:

Use <table>, <thead>, <tbody>, <tfoot>, <tr>, <th>, and <td> appropriately for clear structure.
Apply CSS to enhance aesthetics, such as zebra striping rows or highlighting columns.
Responsive design strategies, like converting tables to card layouts for smaller screens, ensure usability.

Best practices:

Keep tables simple and relevant to avoid overwhelming users.
Ensure accessibility with attributes like scope and aria-described by.

Test table designs across devices to maintain functionality and readability.

3. Links: Connecting the Web

Hyperlinks are the lifeblood of the internet, seamlessly connecting users to resources, pages, and functionality. The humble <a> tag has evolved into a powerful element for navigation and interaction.

Key insights:

Customize links with CSS for hover effects, color schemes, and transitions to guide user attention.
Ensure clear and descriptive link text for better usability and SEO.
Use attributes like target="_blank" judiciously to control how links open.

Best practices:

Avoid "click here" or vague link text; be specific.
Test links regularly to avoid broken connections.
Use appropriate link states (:hover, :focus, :visited) for an enhanced user experience.

4. Forms: Enabling User Interaction

Forms are the gateway to user interaction, enabling tasks like registrations, feedback submissions, and e-commerce transactions. Modern web development emphasizes both usability and security in form design.

Key insights:

Leverage semantic elements like <form>, <input>, <textarea>, <button>, and <label> for clear, accessible forms.
Use CSS to style form elements and provide feedback (e.g., validation error messages).
Integrate JavaScript for dynamic form behaviours, such as conditional fields or client-side validation.

Best practices:

Ensure forms are mobile-friendly and accessible.
Prioritize data privacy by using HTTPS and secure storage.
Provide real-time feedback to improve form completion rates.

5. Images: Elevating Visual Appeal

Images are essential for storytelling, branding, and enhancing user engagement. The right image, optimized for performance and accessibility, can make a lasting impact.

Key insights:

Use the <img> tag with appropriate alt attributes for descriptive content.
Optimize images for performance using modern formats like WebP and lazy loading techniques.
Employ CSS to control image placement, responsiveness, and effects like overlays or filters.

Best practices:

Use responsive techniques like srcset to serve appropriate images for different screen sizes.
Optimize images for SEO with descriptive filenames and alt text.
Balance aesthetics and loading speed to enhance user experience.

The Synergy of HTML and CSS

While each element plays a distinct role, their true power emerges when used together. HTML provides the structural backbone, while CSS offers limitless opportunities for creative expression. Together, they enable developers to craft experiences that are functional, engaging, and adaptable to user needs.

Emerging Trends and Tools

In 2025, advancements in web development continue to push the boundaries of what's possible with these foundational elements:

CSS Variables and Grid Layouts: Simplifying complex layouts and enabling dynamic designs.
Accessibility Standards: New tools and guidelines ensure inclusivity for all users.
Responsive Design: Growing importance with the proliferation of diverse devices.
Performance Optimization: Techniques like image compression and async loading for faster websites.

Building Accessible and Inclusive Web Designs

Accessibility is no longer optional; it is a core aspect of web design. Tools like ARIA roles, semantic HTML, and WCAG guidelines help ensure content is usable for all, including individuals with disabilities.

Final Thoughts

As web development evolves, so will the techniques and technologies be surrounding these elements. From AI-powered design tools to next-gen frameworks, the principles of lists, tables, links, forms, and images will remain central to creating meaningful digital experiences.

In conclusion, mastering these building blocks equips developers with the skills to create visually appealing, interactive, and accessible websites. By combining technical knowledge with creativity and user-centric design, you can harness the full potential of HTML and CSS to craft web experiences that stand the test of time.

5. The Box Model and Laying It All Out

Introduction

The following sections delve into key aspects of the box model and layout principles in HTML and CSS. This comprehensive guide will ensure you understand these fundamental concepts, allowing you to create well-structured, visually appealing web pages.

The Box Model

The CSS box model is the foundation of how elements are rendered on the web. It defines the structure of each HTML element as a rectangular box with properties like margins, borders, padding, and the content itself.

Inline vs. Block

Inline Elements: Inline elements, such as <span>, <a>, or <strong>, occupy only the width necessary for their content. They flow naturally with surrounding text and do not break onto a new line.

Block Elements: Block elements, like <div>, <p>, or <section>, start on a new line and occupy the entire width of their container. This behaviour makes them ideal for structuring the layout of a webpage.

Margins, Padding, and Borders

Margins: Margins create space between an element and its surrounding elements. They are transparent and can collapse when adjacent margins meet.

Padding: Padding is the space between an element's content and its border. Unlike margins, it is included inside the box and is visible when the background or border is styled.

Borders: Borders wrap around an element's padding and content, creating a visible boundary.

Floats

Floats allow elements to be taken out of the normal document flow and positioned to the left or right of their container. Commonly used for layouts before Flexbox and Grid, floats are still relevant for certain designs, like text wrapping around images.

A Little More About the Overflow Style

The overflow property controls how content behaves when it exceeds its container:

visible (default): Content spills out of the container.
hidden: Excess content is clipped.
scroll: Adds scrollbars for overflow.
auto: Adds scrollbars only if necessary.

Inline-Block

The inline-block display combines the behaviour of inline elements with block elements. It allows elements to sit side by side while still respecting their padding, margin, and border.

Margins for Boxes

Margins determine how far apart boxes are placed in the layout. They can be set individually (margin-top, margin-right, etc.) or collectively (margin shorthand). Negative margins pull elements closer together.

Padding... Not Just for Chairs

Padding is an essential part of spacing within a box. Proper use of padding enhances the readability and aesthetic appeal of a design.

Fun with Borders

Borders can be styled in various ways (solid, dashed, dotted, etc.) and customized using color, width, and rounding (border-radius). They are excellent for emphasizing sections or creating visual separation.

Laying It All Out

CSS layout techniques dictate the structure and responsiveness of web pages.

Layout Basics

Layouts define how elements are positioned on a page. Modern CSS offers tools like Flexbox, Grid, and media queries to build layouts that adapt seamlessly to different screen sizes.

Jekyll

Jekyll is a static site generator that simplifies building websites. It separates content from design, allowing developers to focus on the structure and aesthetics of their pages.

Layouts, Includes, and Pages (Oh My!)

Layouts: Define the overall structure of your site.
Includes: Reusable code snippets, like headers and footers, save time and ensure consistency.
Pages: Represent the individual views or sections of the site.

The Layout File

In Jekyll, the layout file acts as a template for multiple pages. By defining a single layout structure, you can maintain uniformity across all pages.

CSS File and Reset

CSS resets eliminate browser-specific styling inconsistencies. Tools like Normalize.css ensure a consistent baseline for styles across all browsers.

Includes Intro: Head and Header

Includes like <head> and <header> ensure that meta tags, styles, and navigation remain consistent across your website. These reusable snippets simplify updates.

Advanced Selectors

CSS advanced selectors provide granular control over styling:

Attribute selectors ([type="text"])
Pseudo-classes (:hover, :nth-child())
Pseudo-elements (::before, ::after)

Positioning

Positioning in CSS determines how elements are placed on the screen:

static (default): Normal document flow.
relative: Positioned relative to itself.
absolute: Positioned relative to the nearest positioned ancestor.
fixed: Positioned relative to the viewport, unaffected by scrolling.
sticky: A hybrid of relative and fixed positioning.

Fixed Header

A fixed header remains visible at the top of the viewport as users scroll. This feature is essential for persistent navigation.

A Footer, and Includes in Includes

Footers provide closure to a webpage and typically contain copyright information, links, or contact details. Using includes for footers ensures consistency across pages.

This comprehensive breakdown provides a detailed understanding of the box model and layout concepts. By mastering these principles, you'll be equipped to design and develop robust, visually appealing web pages.

Let's Begin,

In this chapter, we'll apply such sizing to one of the most important concepts in web design: the box model. When rendering HTML, the browser considers a page to be a collection of different boxes that contain content. Along with height and width, boxes can be styled to have borders (a line around the box), margins (the distance away from other boxes), and padding (empty space inside the box separating content from the border).

The CSS box model is the name for all the rules that determine how height, width, margin, padding, and borders are applied to elements. Elements of the box model can be quite confusing, with weird interactions between elements, counter-intuitive applications of styles, and ways of writing style values that can look strange at first glance. In this chapter, we'll take a tour through these different idiosyncrasies, learn a couple of methods for getting boxes to sit next to each other, and lay the necessary foundation for applying the box model.

Inline vs. Block

We'll begin our introduction to the box model by discussing the different effects of spacing and borders on inline vs. block elements. These two types of elements, behave differently in the context of the box model, so it's important to clarify the differences at the beginning.

Elements that are considered inline elements, like **span** or **a**, are only allowed to have margins and padding applied to the left and right (not top or bottom), and they won't accept a width or height set by CSS. None of these restrictions apply to block elements.

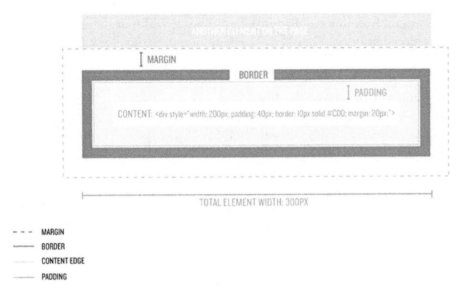

Figure: The default HTML box model.

Confusingly, some styles can cause an inline element to switch to be a block element. Floated elements become block elements and can suddenly have top and bottom margins or padding, plus active dimensions like height and width that were previously ignored. Changing an element's position on the page can also switch it from inline to block.

You don't have to rely on these quirks to change elements from inline to block, though—you can also directly force an element to change using CSS. There are actually a bunch of display property values that affect the way elements are drawn, with more being added all the time. In this tutorial, though, we are only going to consider five of the most important ones. Let's take a look!

display: none

The **display: none** style prevents the element from displaying on the page. For example, try updating the **.sociallink** class rules to include **display:none**, as shown.

Listing: Removing elements from the page.

.social-link {   **background**: rgba(150, 150, 150, 0.5);   **color: blue**;   **display: none**; }

When you save and refresh, you'll see that all those social links are now gone. This style is commonly used for hiding elements in interactive websites, especially when combined with JavaScript.

To restore the display of an element that has been hidden, all you need to do is set the **display** property to anything other than **none**, such as **initial** or **block**. (In Learn Enough JavaScript to Be Dangerous, we'll use this technique to make hidden elements appear with the click of the mouse.)

display: block

display: block forces an element to be a block element regardless of what it was before. If you don't set dimensions after changing an element to **display: block**, it will behave like any normal block element by taking up the entire width of its parent element.

As mentioned briefly above, inline elements (such as links and spans) can't have a width or height, but once you change the display property the dimensional styles get applied. To see how this works, let's first add a height to **.social-link**.

Listing: Adding dimensions to an inline element won't have an effect.

.social-link {   **background**: rgba(150, 150, 150, 0.5);   **color**: **blue**;   **height**: **36px**; }

When you save and refresh, you'll notice nothing changed—that's because the **.social-link**s are inline elements. Now add in the magical **display: block** and save.

Listing: Changing the display property allows the dimensional styles to apply.

.social-link {
 background: rgba(150, 150, 150, 0.5);   **color**: **blue**;   **display**: **block**;   **height**: 36px; }

Refresh your browser and you'll see that your social links are now 36px-tall block elements that stretch all the way across their parent elements.

display: inline **display: inline** turns a block element into an inline element (essentially the opposite of the **display: block** property). Any styles that don't apply to inline elements (such as width and height, top margins, and padding) will no longer be applied. In addition, the element will no longer be on its own line, but rather will flow with text like any other inline element.

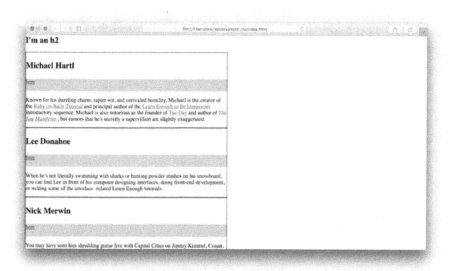

Figure: Look at those beautiful big gray rectangles.

display: inline-block

The **display: inline-block** property, which is a hybrid of **inline** and **block**, is a useful display setting, as it allows styling that normally works only on block elements— such as width and height, top margins, and padding—to be applied to a particular element. At the same time, it also lets the element as a whole act like an inline element. This means that text will still flow around it, and it will only take up as much horizontal space as it needs to contain the content (as opposed to the way that block elements stretch all the way across the page unless you give them a set width).

To see how this works, set the **.social-link**s to display as **inline-block** on your index page.

Listing: Setting the display of social links to **inline-block**.

.**social-link** { **background**: rgba(150, 150, 150, 0.5); **color: blue**; **display: inline-block**; **height**: 36px; }

When you save and refresh, you'll see that the links have the height style applied, but they are only as wide as the content.

Eventually, in Section, we are going to add in icons for the different social media websites, and we'll want these links to all have the same dimensions regardless of the content that is inside. To make sure that they are all exactly the same size, let's also add a width property to the social links.

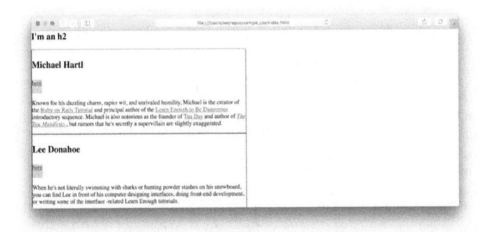

Figure: The links are now a combination of inline and block, stretching only as wide as the content.

Listing: The **inline-block** display lets you add a width to an inline element.

.**social-link** { **background**: rgba(150, 150, 150, 0.5); **color: blue**; **display: inline-block**; **height**: 36px; **width**: 36px; }

Your social links will now be nice little gray squares, like in Figure.

So, where do sites use this CSS style? The **inline-block** declaration is especially helpful when making site navigation, and when styling a group of elements so that they are side by side.

display: flex

display: flex is a powerful display property that forces all child elements to fill the entire parent element, and is highly customizable to allow for incredibly useful layout possibilities. The **flex** property is something that solves some of the most difficult long-running problems in page layouts.

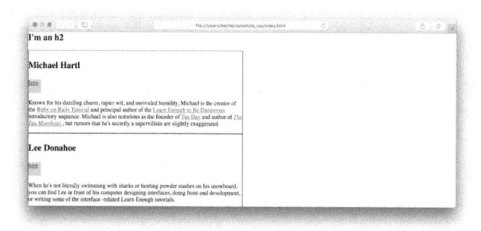

Figure: The links now have the same width and height.

We aren't going to play around with **display: flex** here because it really needs a whole chapter of its own to properly understand—a task we'll undertake.

Margins, Padding, and Borders

One of the most common places where developers interact with the box model is when adding margins, padding, and borders to elements on the page—the **margin** and **padding** properties control the space around or inside the elements, while the **border** property specifies the appearance of the boundary of the box. In this section, we'll take a first look at how these styles affect the box model (which includes some surprises), and then in Section we'll look in detail at how margin, padding, and border styles are used in practice. We'll begin by investigating padding and borders, which are different from margins in a key respect. In particular, if you specify the width of a block element, like a **div** or a **p**, and then apply a border or padding to it, the additional border or padding will go outside the content.

That means you can end up with an element that is bigger than the dimensions you specified. You'd think that if you said something should be 200px wide, it would always be 200px wide… but no, in the default state, CSS assumes that when you set a size for an element you are only talking about the content part of the element. This tends to generate a lot of confusion for people learning CSS, as they automatically assume that elements and their content are the same thing. Let's look at an example.

Suppose that you make a **div** and apply the following style:

width: 200px; padding: 40px; border: 10px solid #c00;

In this case, the entire element will end up being 300px wide on the page: 200px for the content, 40px each for the left and right padding, and 10px each for the left and right borders ($200 + 40 \times 2 + 10 \times 2 = $ **300px**).

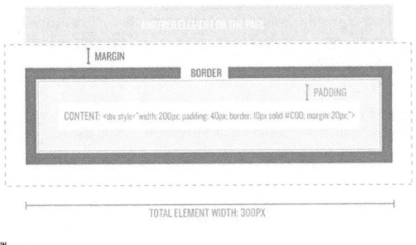

Figure: The default HTML box model again.

It is also possible to fix the total width of the content box, and force the border and padding to fit inside. The way to do this is with the **box-sizing** declaration. To see how this works, let's add some throwaway elements and styles to the page (which you can delete after seeing how this works).

Listing: Adding some test elements to the page to demonstrate box model properties.

```
<h2>I'm an h2</h2>
<div class="test-box">
  200px wide
</div>
<div class="test-box test-box-nosizing">
  200px wide + border + padding = 300px
</div>
<div class="test-box test-box-nosizing test-box-sizing">
  200px wide + border + padding + box-sizing: border-box = 200px
</div>
```

Then add the styles in Listing to the bottom of your style block (we'll be deleting these too).

Listing: Adding classes and styles for the test elements.

```
.test-box {   background: #9db6dd;   width: 200px; } .test-box-nosizing {   border: 10px solid #000;
padding: 40px;   } .test-box-sizing {    box-sizing: border-box;  }
</style>
```

When you save your work and refresh the browser, you'll see an assortment of boxes of different widths. Note how the **.test-box-sizing** class forces the div to be 200px wide in total. The **border-box** property caused the browser to draw the borders and padding inside the defined width.

Margin Weirdness

So, we've talked about how the box model can behave unexpectedly when it comes to borders and padding, but what about margins? Well, you would expect that, when two elements that both have margins are on the page next to each other, their margins would always apply. For example, if two elements both have **20px** of margin, you might expect that the elements would always end up being **20 + 20 = 40px** apart—but that isn't necessarily how it works.

A wise man (though not wise enough to exercise caution on the Ides of March) once said "experience is the teacher of all things", and in that spirit we will make changes to the page that let you see both examples shown in Figure.

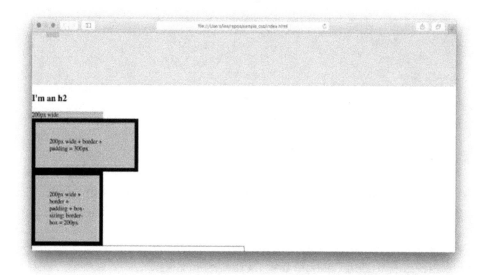

Figure: Different results even though all elements are set to 200px wide.

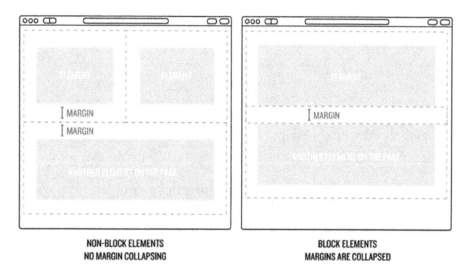

Figure: How the box model deals with margins between block and non-block elements.

We'll start by creating a situation where margins do behave in the intuitively expected manner.

Listing: Changing our test boxes to show expected margin behaviour.

```
.test-box {  background: #9db6dd;  display: inline-block;  margin: 50px;  width: 200px; } .test-box-nosizing {  border: 10px solid #000;  padding: 40px; } .test-box-sizing {  box-sizing: border-box;  display: block;  width: auto;
```

}

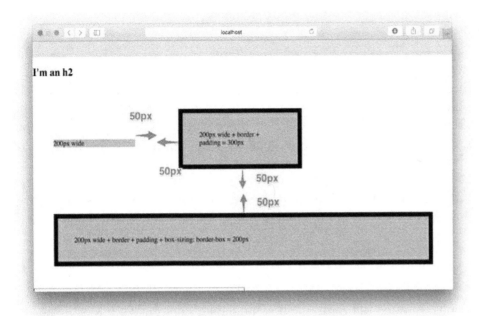

Figure: Trust us, they are all separated by the same distance.

Listing: Collapsing the margins.

```
.test-box {  background: #9db6dd;  margin: 50px; } .test-box-nosizing {  border: 10px solid #000;
padding: 40px; } .test-box-sizing {  box-sizing: border-box;
}
```

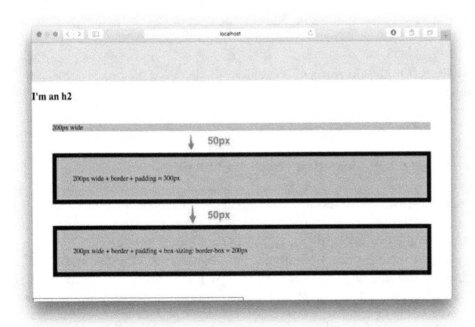

Figure: Less space now that the margins have collapsed.

The result is to magically collapse the margins: Now all the boxes are vertically separated by only 50px of margin, as shown in Figure.

The reason the first example worked as expected is that the first two elements weren't block elements, so the browser fully respected their set margins. Once they became block elements, though, the browser allowed for only one of the margins to apply.

The reason this exists goes all the way back to the bad old early days of HTML, when most websites used browser defaults for all elements (because there was no CSS). Some block elements (like paragraph ₚS) have default top and bottom margins to keep text away from other elements to enhance readability, and if there were no margin collapsing, then whenever you put two of these elements next to each other there would be too much space between them. So, at some point early on it was decided that when two block elements with margins follow each other, one of the top or bottom margins is canceled out.

In the next few sections, starting with Section, we'll be looking at how to put boxes side by side. If you are going to do the exercises, save the test blocks and styles; otherwise, you can delete the HTML and CSS styles from this section.

Floats

Now that we've seen some of the things to watch out for in the box model, let's start using it to style our sample site. When you are designing a site, you will often need different elements to sit next to each other on the page, and new developers often run into problems with how the box model affects their attempts to accomplish this. Perhaps unsurprisingly, there are a bunch of different ways to do this using CSS, and all have different positives and negatives. No single technique can be used across an entire site, so let's get started by learning about floating elements.

We used a property value called a **float** to move an image to the left side of a block of text. The idea is that when you set an element to float to the left or right (there is no **float: center**), all the inline content around it will flow around the floated element like water. Floated elements will always sit next to other floated elements on the same line, as long as there is horizontal room. If the elements are too wide, they will drop down to the next line.

Let's see this in action. We'll add **float: left** to the **.bio-box** class, and we'll also give the boxes some padding and a new (narrower) width.

Listing: The entire **index** page up to this point.

.bio-box { border: 1px solid black; float: left; font-size: 1rem; padding: 2%;

After you save your work and refresh the browser, the result should appear as in Figure.

Now all the boxes are in a row, but why is the last one spilling over to the next line?
It's because of the box model sizing issue from Section! The left and right borders, and the left and right padding got added onto the width of each **div**, making each one **25% + 1px border-left + 1px border-right + 2% paddingleft + 2% padding-right**, for a total size of **29% + 2px** of the page for each. Multiplied by 4, this gives **116% + 8px**, which is greater than 100%.

Let's fix this by adding the **box-sizing: border-box** style to the **div** to force the borders and padding inside the setwidth **div**.

Listing: Adding **border-box** to the bio boxes.

```
.bio-box { border: 1px solid black; box-sizing: border-box; float: left; font-size: 1rem; padding:
2%; width: 25%;
}
```

Now when you save and refresh, you'll have four boxes in a row that fill the page.

Clearing Floats

So, why might a developer not want to always use floating to get elements to line up side by side?
For one, there are only two options, **float: left** and **float: right**, but no **float: center**. That's annoying, but
manageable. The bigger problem is that the browser doesn't always know where to end the float. When you
float elements, you are telling the browser that you'd like the element to show up on the page in the place it
would naturally "float" to, but after that starting position, you want the rest of the page content to flow
around the floated element. This can disrupt the orderly box-like arrangement of elements, and create some
odd-looking layouts.

To see what we mean, add the paragraphs from Listing onto your test page below the closing **</div>** tag of
the **.bio-wrapper**.

Figure: Box sizing saves the day, and now our floated boxes fit.

Listing: Adding text to the page below the bios.

```
<div class="bio-wrapper">   .
  .

  .
</div>
<p>
```

Learn Enough to Be Dangerous is a leader in the movement to teach the   world <**em**>technical
sophistication</**em**>, which includes both "hard   skills" like coding, command lines, and version control,
and "soft   skills" like guessing keyboard shortcuts, googling error messages, and   knowing when to just
reboot the darn thing. </**p**>

```
<p>   We believe there are <strong>at least a billion people</strong> who can   benefit from learning
```
technical sophistication, probably more. To join   our movement, <**a**
href="https://learnenough.com/#email_list">sign up for our official   email list</**a**> now. </**p**>

```
<h3>Background</h3>
<p>

Learn Enough to Be Dangerous is an outgrowth of the
  <a href="https://www.railstutorial.org/">Ruby on Rails Tutorial</a> and the   <a
href="https://www.softcover.io/">Softcover publishing platform</a>.

This page is part of the sample site for
  <a href="https://learnenough.com/css-tutorial"><em>Learn Enough CSS and
Layout to Be Dangerous</em></a>, which teaches the basics of <strong>C</strong>ascading
<strong>S</strong>tyle   <strong>S</strong>heets, the language that allows web pages to be styled.
Other related tutorials can be found at   <a href="https://learnenough.com/">learnenough.com</a>.
</p>
```

When you save your work and refresh the page, you'll see that the floated elements have caused the text we just added to start under the rightmost float instead of starting on a new line.

In an ideal world, those paragraphs should stretch across the entire page since they are block elements. One way to get things back to the expected result would be to use the CSS **clear** rule, which is used to let the browser know to end floats. In this case, we could add **clear: left** to the first paragraph. You can try it by adding an inline style.

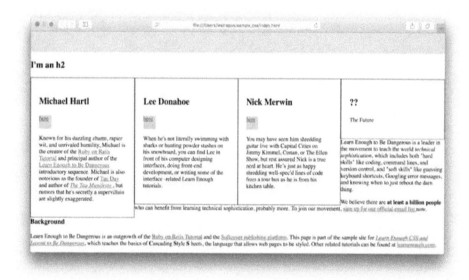

Figure: This is not what the doctor ordered.

Listing: A simple inline style to clear the float.

```
<p style="clear: left;">
```

This will force the paragraph onto a new line below the floated elements, and it will prevent any other element below it on the page from being altered by the float.

If the floating elements had been floated to the right using **float: right**, you would need to clear their float status with **clear: right**, or (if you just want to be extra careful) you can clear both types of floats using **clear: both**.

If you tried clearing the float with an inline style on your test page, you should remove the style from the p tag—just the mere sight of an inline style should make you feel queasy at this point (but they are handy at times for quickly testing styles).

Having to add a **clear** style directly onto any element (either inline or in the stylesheet) after floated elements is kind of a pain—especially on a dynamic site that might pull in snippets of code to build a page. You don't always know which elements will be following floats.

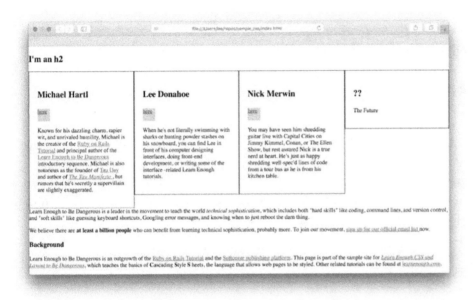

Figure: This works, but you don't want to have to manage clearing things on potentially every element.

A better way to clear floats is to apply a rule to clear everything inside a wrapper, such as the **.bio-wrapper** added in Listing. The idea is to arrange for the **.bio-wrapper** element, and everything in it, to act like a LEGO block that can safely be moved around without needing to worry about uncleared floats messing up a layout.

There are two methods to clear floats inside a wrapper: the **overflow** method and the **:after** "clearfix" method. We'll look at both of these methods here, and give more extensive coverage to the **overflow** property.

To see the **overflow** method in action, add the style from Listing to **.bio-wrapper**.

Listing: When **overflow** is set to **hidden**, floats are cleared.

```
/* BIO STYLES */ .bio-wrapper {  font-size: 24px;
```

```
overflow: hidden;
}
```

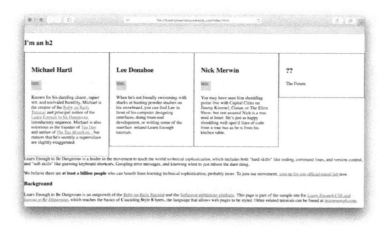

Figure: Same result, but self-contained instead of needing inline styling.

When you save and refresh, the paragraph of text will be safely below the floated elements with no inline styles, and no use of the **clear** property.

The problem with this method is that if you also need to set a height or width on the element that has **overflow: hidden** set, the content inside can get cut off. This happens most often with poorly built dropdown menus in a site navigation with floats that are cleared using the **overflow** method but where the header also had a set height. For example, Figure shows what Amazon.com's homepage dropdown menu would look like if they had mistakenly also set **overflow: hidden**.

Tricks like changing the live Amazon homepage can be accomplished by using a web inspector to edit a site's CSS dynamically in-browser, and then taking a screenshot of the result.

So, if you need to clear floats but also are worried about content being cut off because you absolutely, positively have to set a height on the wrapper element, you can use the **:after** method.
Let's see how it works. Remove **overflow: hidden** from the **.bio-wrapper** class, and add in the entire new declaration from Listing.

Figure: Changing the overflow on an element can hide parts that were supposed to stick out.

Listing: The more complicated **:after** method.

.bio-wrapper { **font-size**: 24px; } **.bio-wrapper**:after {   **visibility**: **hidden**;   **display**: **block**;   **font-size**: 0;   **content**: " ";   **clear**: **both**;   **height**: 0; }

There's a lot of new stuff in there, but don't worry about it for now. We'll discuss **:after** in more detail. The important thing for now is that **:after** creates a kind of imaginary element that comes at the end of the **bio-wrapper**—an imaginary element that we can add styles to! Setting **clear: both** on that element clears the floats and allows the content below to appear as intended. If you save the changes and refresh your browser, the text will still be cleared below the floated elements.

A Little More About the overflow Style

We used the **overflow** method to clear floats, but you may be wondering exactly why this method works… and also, what does **overflow** do in the first place?

The CSS **overflow** property tells the browser how to handle content inside a wrapper, if that wrapper has a set height or width. If the content in the wrapper doesn't fill the box, then **overflow** does nothing, but when there is more content than room to display that content, **overflow** comes into play. Because this property can be used to clear floats and control how content is displayed, it is worth exploring in detail.

The **overflow** style can be set to **visible**, which shows everything; **hidden**, which cuts content off at the boundaries of the wrapper; or **scroll**, which adds scrollbars to let you scroll up and down or left and right to see all the available content. You've seen this before if you've ever scrolled inside a box on a website without scrolling the entire page.

The Mozilla Developer Network page on the CSS overflow property includes a list of all the possible values.
overflow: hidden works for clearing floats because it makes the browser want to keep content contained entirely within the wrapper. If there is no set dimension on the wrapper, the browser just expands the boundaries of the wrapper to reach the end of the floated elements, and then lets the elements that follow display on the page normally.

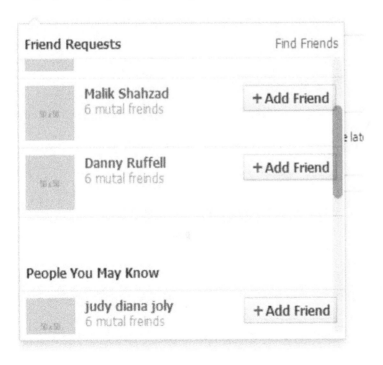

Figure: Scrolling within a box on a page without scrolling the page.

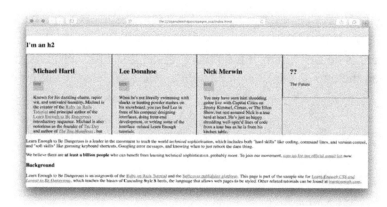

Figure: Some examples of overflow and containers.

Figure shows diagrams of some of the different possible overflow situations when containing floated elements, and why you have to be careful when adding a height to an element with **overflow** set to **hidden**. To see what happens with the different settings in practice, let's start with **overflow: hidden**, and also give the **.biowrapper** a background color and a height.

Listing: overflow set to **hidden** with a height set on the container.

.**bio-wrapper** {   **background-color**: #c0e0c3;   **font-size**: 24px;   **height**: **300px**;   **overflow**: **hidden**; }

Listing: overflow set to **visible** with a height set on the container.

.**bio-wrapper** {   **background-color**: #c0e0c3;   **font-size**: 24px;   **height**: 300px;
```
  overflc: visibl;
}
```

Figure: Setting **overflow** to **hidden** and adding a height cuts off the content.

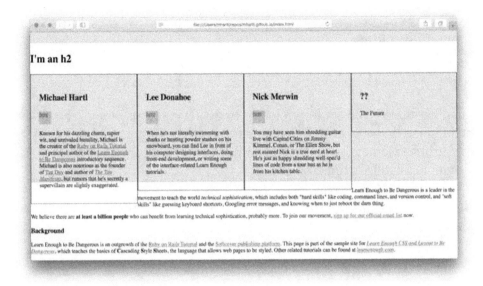

Figure: The content extends out of the green box due to **overflow: visible**.

You can see the content extending past the boundary of the **.bio-wrapper**.

Finally, let's try setting the value to **scroll**. An **overflow** set to **scroll** with a height set on the container will keep all the content inside the container, but you can scroll to see it.

Listing: Setting the **overflow** to **scroll**.

.bio-wrapper { **background-color**: #c0e0c3; **font-size**: 24px; **height**: 300px; **overflow**: **scroll**; }

Now the content is cut off, but if you put your cursor in the green box and scroll up or down with your mouse or trackpad, you'll be able to see the hidden content.

If you tried out these styles on your test page, set the **.bio-wrapper** back to the styles.

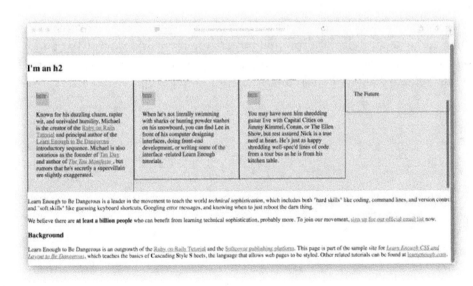

Figure: A scrollbar appears on the right just for the green box.

Listing: Returning the **.bio-wrapper** to **overflow: hidden**.

.bio-wrapper { **font-size**: 24px; **overflow**: **hidden**; }

Inline Block

The second way to get things next to other things is to set the elements to **display: inline-block**. This allows them to keep their block-style formatting (so they can have height and top/bottom margins and padding), while also letting us do things like control an element's position on a line of text by setting the style **textalign** on a wrapper to make everything align left, right, or center.

For this example, we are going to style the **li**s that contain the **.social-link**s inside the **.full-hero** at the top of the test page. Let's first give the unordered list tag **ul** a class called **.social-list**.

Listing: Adding a class name to the unordered list.

```
<ul class="social-list">
  <li>    <a href="https://example.com/"    class="social-link">Link</a>  </li>
  <li>    <a href="https://example.com/"    class="social-link">Link</a>  </li>
  <li>    <a href="https://example.com/"    class="social-link">Link</a>  </li>
</ul>
```

By default, the **li** tag produces block elements that each start on their own new line; list elements that are part of an unordered list also include a bullet point before each element's content. Why would we want to use such a list to display a person's social links?

Recall from Section that the result of a **li** tag depends on the parent list type. In particular, when wrapped inside the ordered list tag **ol**, the list elements get numbers instead of bullet points.

The answer is that we can unstyle the list (removing the bullet points, making it inline instead of block, etc.) and use it however we want! It has become a common practice to use the **ul** tag to contain sets of links for things like navigation, menus, etc., because it's the logical HTML element for grouping lists of things, which as designers gives us a nice structure to work with.

So, first let's unstyle that list, and then add a second declaration that targets the **li**s inside **.social-list** and switches them to **display: inline-block**. By the way, the right-angle bracket > on Line 12 in Listing is a more advanced selector called the child selector, and covered in more depth in Section.

Figure: Our **lis** are now in a row and have no bullet points.

Listing: Unstyling the list and making the **lis inline-block**.

/* SOCIAL LINKS */ .

. ..**social-list** {   **list-style**: **none**;   **padding**: 0; } .**social-list** > **li** {   **display**: **inline-block**; }

Hey, look at those elements all in a row!

Notice that there are little spaces between the elements in Figure. This is an annoyance that comes with using this technique, and it stems from the way that browsers treat **inline-block** elements as though they are just funky shaped words in a sentence. There are ways to get rid of that space, but we aren't going to get into those weeds here; instead, we are just going to ignore them since in our case it is nice to have a bit of space between elements. (For the record, when you use a float to get elements next to each other, there is no space between them at all.)

Box: Intro to Advanced Selectors

If you thought things weren't going to get any more complicated with selectors… you were wrong. We've barely scratched the surface! We are going to cover them more later in the tutorial, but for now we want to explain the child selector.

Take a look again at the style we declared in Listing:

.social-list > li {   display: inline-block; }

What this says is "select only lis that are direct children of the .social-list parent, and make them inline block." Remember that one of the goals when you are styling pages is to style only the things that need styling, without accidentally styling elements that will later need to be unstyled. When you use advanced selectors, you can better target your declaration.

For example, suppose we had a second nested unordered list in one of those lis, like this:

```
<ul class="social-list">
  <li>   <a href="https://example.com/"  class="social-link">Link</a>
  </li>
  <li>
   <a href="https://example.com/"       class="social-link">Link</a>
   <ul>
    <li>Item 1</li>
    <li>Item 2</li>
   </ul>
  </li>
  <li>
   <a href="https://example.com/"       class="social-link">Link</a>
  </li>
</ul>
```

In this case, the lis in the nested list would remain as block elements. This is because they are children of a plain ul element, and the CSS rule targets only children of a ul with class social-list. If you like, you can try out that example on your test page (and then delete it when you're done).

Figure: A simple **text-align: center** puts the boxes right in the middle.

Now let's center the links.

Listing: Centering the **inline-block** elements.

.social-list { **list-style**: **none**; **padding**: 0; **text-align**: **center**; }

You have no idea how hard what we did in Figure used to be before this **inline-block** technique was available. In the bad old early days of the Web, when we had to use tables for everything, it used to be a giant pain to get things to work right, but now it is as easy as we just saw. We can play around with aligning the links left or right, and everything will be nicely contained inside the ul without any need to clear floats.

Margins for Boxes

Now that we have a handle on arranging our boxes, let's look in detail at margin, padding, and borders. These styles allow developers to control the spacing between boxes (with **margin** in this section), the spacing inside boxes, and the size and look of the edges of boxes.

We'll start with the simplest kind of margin declaration, which we'll add to the **.bio-box**es at the bottom of the page, as shown in Listing.

Listing: Adding a margin declaration.

.bio-box { **border**: 1px solid black; **box-sizing**: **border-box**; **float**: left; **font-size**: 1rem; **margin**: 20px; **padding**: 2%; **width**: 25%; }

When you refresh the test page, you'll see that each one of the containers has moved away from everything else by **20px** in all directions.

The next question that you might be asking is, "Why are the boxes on two lines again? I thought we took care of that with **box-sizing: border-box**?"

The answer is that in the box model, margins always apply outside an element. So even though we've set the **boxsizing** style to **border-box**, the four **div**s at the bottom are now taking up 100% plus 8 * 20px, which is wider than 100%.

Figure: The boxes got some extra space, but broke onto two lines again.

So, how do we get everything to fit again? First, to make this easier we are going to switch to using the same units for each measurement (all percentages), and we are going to have to do a little bit of math. Let's first set the margins to be percentages, as shown in Listing.

Listing: Changing the margin from pixels to percent.

.bio-box { border: 1px solid black; box-sizing: border-box; float: left; font-size: 1rem; margin: 3%; padding: 2%;

```
  width: 25%;
}
```

Figure: Pretty good margin size.

Based on the result, this looks like a reasonable amount of spacing.

Now let's do the math. If we have a left and right margin of 3%, that means we need to reduce the size of each of the containers by 3% + 3% = 6% to get everything to fit. Because the original width was 25%, this means the new width should be 25% − 6% = 19%, as shown.

Listing: Changing the width to accommodate the margins.

.bio-box { **border**: 1px solid black; **box-sizing**: border-box; **float**: left; **font-size**: 1rem; **margin**: 3%; **padding**: 2%; **width**: 19%;
}

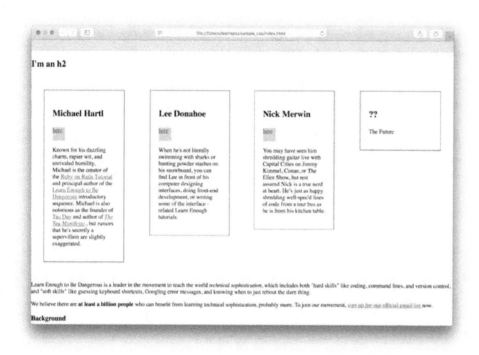

Figure: Everything fits again.

It fits again!

Now let's take a look at the actual style declaration to dig a little deeper into how it works. When we write **margin: 3%**, we are applying the margin in all directions around the box, which is the equivalent of applying these four styles all at once:

margin-top: 3%; margin-right: 3%; margin-bottom: 3%; margin-left: 3%;

The simple **margin** declaration that we used is a shorthand version that combines all the directions of the margin onto one line, and **margin: 3%** is the equivalent of writing this:

margin: 3% 3% 3% 3%;

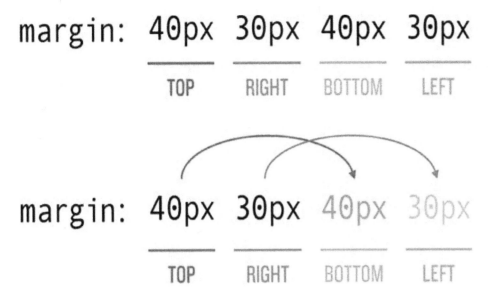

Figure: Think of the four values as going clockwise from the top.

As you may recall from Section, the order here is top, right, bottom, left, as illustrated in Figure.

What if you really only want the margin on certain sides of the **div**? For example, to set the top margin to **40px** and the left margin to **30px**, we could use the more specific declarations shown in Listing.

Listing: Changing the width to accommodate the margins.

.bio-box { border: 1px solid black; box-sizing: border-box; float: left; font-size: 1rem; margin-top: 40px; margin-left: 30px; padding: 2%; width: 19%; }

That will work just fine, but our code will start getting cluttered if we have to define every direction for every declaration that has a direction option. A better way to control where the margin goes is to use the single **margin** attribute and leverage the shorthand from Figure. To get margins of 40, 30, 40, and 30 pixels going around the **div** (clockwise from the top), we could style the **margin** like this:

margin: 40px 30px 40px 30px;

But guess what? As Figure shows, in addition to the shorthand **margin: 40px** (using a single number), it's possible to include only two values if your top and bottom values are the same, and your left and right values are also the same (but different from the top and bottom):

margin: 40px 30px;

This shorthand also works with just three values, like **margin: 20px 10px 40px**. This is missing the final value, which is the left margin, which will be filled in automatically from its opposite across the box (in this case, **10px**).

For our test page, let's set only a top margin of **40px** and a right and left margin of **1%**, and also increase the size of each container back to **23%** so that the entire row fills the available space.

Listing: Adding the margin declaration.

.bio-box { border: 1px solid black; box-sizing: border-box; float: left; font-size: 1rem; margin: 40px 1% 0; padding: 2%; width: 23%; }

After saving your work and refreshing the browser, you'll see that the **div** with the link has now moved down **40px** from the content above and 1% from the sides of the browser and from the other containers.

Looks great!

If you noticed that the margin between the boxes is different from the ends, that's because it's being doubled (due to the same margin on the left and right). We'll tackle this sort of issue with an advanced selector solution later in Section.

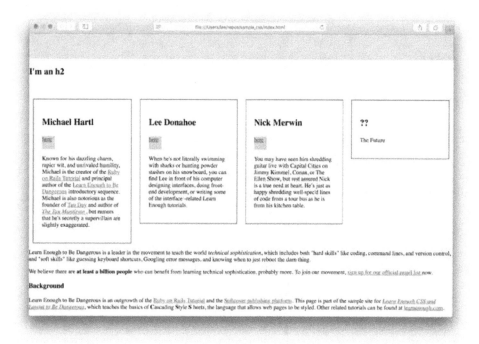

Figure: Much nicer spacing.

An Exception: margin: auto

You might be getting used to this by now, but of course there is another oddity that you should be aware of:

margin: auto.
If you have a block element, like a **div**, **p**, or **ul**, that has a width set by a style, you can make the browser center that element horizontally within its parent container by setting the left and right margins to **auto**.

The **margin: auto** trick does nothing for the top and bottom margins, though. Vertical centering is a much tougher nut to crack. We'll take a look at it starting, and we'll introduce an even more powerful method called flexbox in Section.

To see **margin: auto** in action, let's change the styling for the **.bio-wrapper** to give it a **max-width**, and then set the margin to **auto**. **max-width** is a CSS style that lets an element adapt its width to fit a space (up to a specified value); there's also a **min-width** that does the opposite. Both are helpful when designing sites that are intended to look good on both mobile and desktop platforms, since on the smaller screen you want content to fill the browser, but on a big screen that could look sloppy.

Listing: Applying **margin: auto.**

.**bio-wrapper** { **font-size**: 24px; **margin**: **auto**; **max-width**: **960px**; **overflow**: **hidden**; }

Save and refresh, and watch the box magically center.

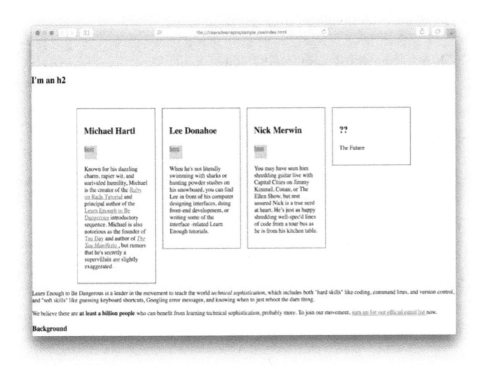

Figure: It's boxes… in the middle of the page!

Yet Another Exception: Negative Margins

Guess what? You can also make margins negative for elements. This draws the element up and out of the normal place it occupies on the page and overlays it on content that normally it wouldn't be able to affect. To see this in action, let's first add some images to the **.bio-box**es. Place an image above the **h3**s in each **.bio-box**.

Listing: Adding an image to each **.bio-box.**

```
<div class="bio-box">  <img src="https://placekitten.com/g/400/400">  <h3>Michael Hartl</h3>  .
   .
   .
</div>
<div class="bio-box">  <img src="https://placekitten.com/g/400/400">  <h3>Lee Donahoe</h3>  .
   .
   .
</div>
<div class="bio-box">  <img src="https://placekitten.com/g/400/400">  <h3>Nick Merwin</h3>  .
   .
   .
```

```
</div>
<div class="bio-box">  <img src="https://placekitten.com/g/400/400">
  <h3>??</h3>  .

        .

        .
</div>
```

And then add a little bit of CSS to resize the images.

Listing: A style to control the size of the images that we added.

```
/* BIO STYLES */ .
    .
. .bio-box img {  width: 100%; } .
    .
    .
```

With that, the images nicely fill up the space.

Now we'll add a negative top margin to the **.bio-box h3**s, as well as some extra styling for the text.

Listing: A negative margin moves an element out of its natural position.

```
.bio-box h3 {  color: #fff;  font-size: 1.5em;  margin: -40px 0 1em;  text-align: center; }
```

Our new styles have pulled the header text out of its normal place and instead have drawn it on top of the images.

Negative margins might seem like an odd property to allow, but they are actually useful from time to time. Negative margins also allow us to extend some content up and out of a box and overlap that content into a space where it normally wouldn't be able to be positioned, all while maintaining its properties as a normal block-level element.

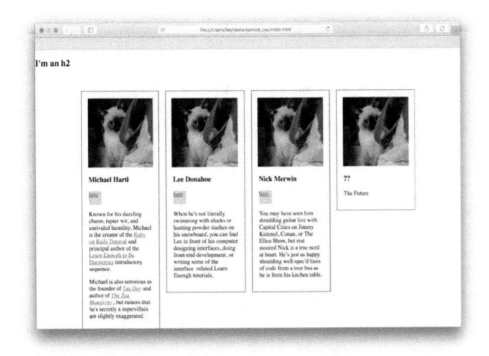

Figure: Your **.bio-boxes** should now look a little fluffier.

Padding... Not Just for Chairs

As we saw at the beginning of Section, padding is similar to margins, except instead of pushing away things that are outside the element, it pushes the content inside an element away from the edges of the element. This is ideal when you want to have a box containing text have a background color or a border but you don't want the text ending up smashed against the edge of the container.

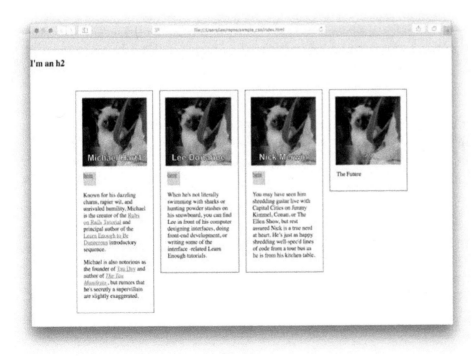

Figure: Negative margins move elements outside their natural position on the page.

Padding values are declared using the same syntax as for margins, including the shorthand from Figure. Let's try it out and remove only the top padding from our **.bio-box**es by changing the styling to match Listing.

Listing: The padding value shorthand works just like the margin shorthand.

.bio-box { **border**: 1px solid black; **box-sizing**: border-box; **float**: left; **font-size**: 1rem; **margin**: 40px 1% 0; **padding**: 0 2% 2%; **width**: 23%;
}

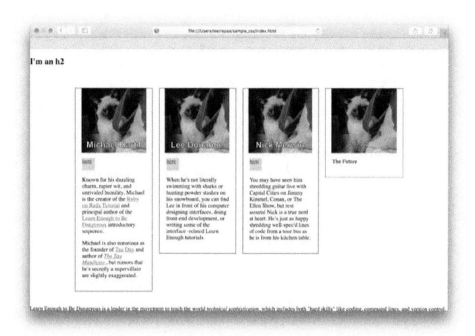

Figure: Hey, look, no top padding.

Padding is one of the easier CSS properties to understand, as it doesn't have a whole lot of weird exceptions.

Fun with Borders

You might have wondered about the **border: 1px solid black** style that has been on the **div**s this whole time. As you might have guessed, this style declaration is also a shorthand similar to margin and padding, but slightly different in that it is three totally different style declarations condensed into one (instead of just different directions, as with margin and padding).[7] The most common usage is to apply a border to all sides of an element, like this:

I did not guess this. —Michael
border: 1px solid black;

This is actually a condensed version of the following rules:

border-width: 1px; border-style: solid; border-color: black;

All of those styles behave like the margin and padding in that they are directional shorthand that applies styling to the top, right, bottom, and left, like this:

border-width: 1px 1px 1px 1px; border-style: solid solid solid solid; border-color: black black black black;
Note that the **border-style** declaration isn't a number, but rather can take on the following values: **none, hidden, dotted, dashed, solid, double, groove, ridge, inset,** and **outset**.

You might ask, "Well, that is all well and good, but what if I don't want all sides of a border to be the same?" The shorthand doesn't seem to cover that. What would the most efficient way be to make a 1px border that is colored black on three sides, but is red on one side (let's say the bottom side)? One way to achieve this look would be to separately declare all the different sub-declarations of the shorthand, like this:

border-width: 1px; border-style: solid; border-color: black black red;

Or you could do it in a more condensed way and take advantage of the fact that rules that come after a similar declaration take precedence.

Listing: Styling a border to have different colors on different sides.

.bio-box { **border**: **1px solid black**; **border-color**: **black black red**; **box-sizing**: **border-box**; **float**: **left**; **font-size**: 1**rem**; **margin**: 40**px** 1**%** 0; **padding**: 0 2**%** 2**%**; **width**: 23**%**; }

Listing sets a border around the entire element and then changes the color of one of the sides. The second declaration doesn't overwrite the entire border declaration; instead, it has an effect only on the part that pertains to border color. So by starting with a more generic style and then adding another style that changes some specific element, you can often accomplish a lot of work in just a couple lines of CSS.

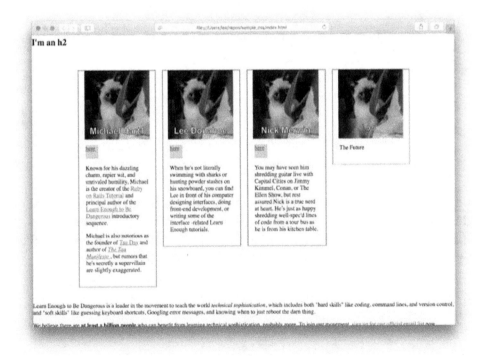

Figure: Now the bottom border is red.

Before moving on, let's remove the red border, and revert the padding change from Listing. The result should look like Listing.

Listing: Reverting a couple of **.bio-box** styles.

```
.bio-box {
  border: 1px solid black;  box-sizing: border-box;  float: left;  font-size: 1rem;  margin: 40px 1% 0;
padding: 2%;  width: 23%; }
```

Border Radius

The border can also have a radius set, which creates a box with rounded corners. To see how this works, add the CSS in Listing to the styles targeting the social links on the test page.

Listing: Adding a **border-radius** to an object to make rounded corners.

```
.social-link {  background: rgba(150, 150, 150, 0.5);  border-radius: 10px;  color: blue;  display: inline-block;  height: 36px;  width: 36px; }
```

The box should now have nicely rounded corners!

Figure: Rounded corners on the social links.

Making Circles

Want to see how to make circles using just HTML and CSS? The trick is to give the elements a set width and height, and then make the **border-radius** big enough to make the border larger than the width of the element, while also making sure the height and width of the element are equal (so that the "box" is a perfect square). Let's bump up the **border-radius** from Listing, and also give the **lis** in the **.social-list** a little margin.

Listing: A very large value for **border-radius** makes a circle.

```
/* SOCIAL STYLES */ .social-link {  background: rgba(150, 150, 150, 0.5);
border-radius: 99px;  .
  .
    .
} .social-list {  list-style: none;  padding: 0;  text-align: center; }
.social-list > li {  display: inline-block;
margin: 0 0.5em; }
```

Look at those circles!

The links look a little weird with all that text, though, so let's change the text in the links in the hero and in the **.biobox**es to the more compact values "Fb", "Tw", and "Gh" The result appears in Listing.

Listing: Making the text a little shorter for the social links.

```
<ul class="social-list">
  <li>    <a href="https://example.com/" class="social-link">Fb</a>
  </li>
  <li>    <a href="https://example.com/" class="social-link">Tw</a>
  </li>
  <li>    <a href="https://example.com/" class="social-link">Gh</a>
  </li>
</ul> .

.
. <a href="https://twitter.com/mhartl" class="social-link">Tw</a> .
. . <a href="https://twitter.com/leedonahoe" class="social-link">Tw</a> .
. .
<a href="https://twitter.com/nickmerwin" class="social-link">Tw</a>
```

Save and refresh, and your links should look like Figure.

Hmm… it still looks a little odd with the text up at the top, and down at the bottom of the page the text isn't even centered in the circle (in the **.full-hero** container it is inheriting a **text-align: center** style). Let's clean up the look and make sure that it stays the same regardless of usage.

Figure: Rounded boxes have become circles!

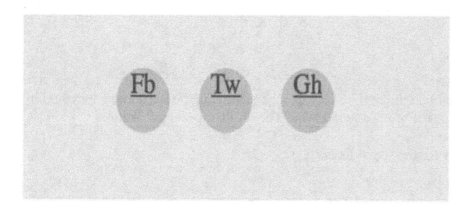

Figure: A little better.

We are going to add padding, and you may recall from Section that we'll need to add in a **box-sizing: borderbox** so that we make sure the padding doesn't change the dimensions of the element:

box-sizing: border-box; padding-top: 0.85em;

Let's also change the color of the text, change the font, make it bold, align it to the center, and remove the underline with a new style called **text-decoration** (set to **none** to remove the default underline for links):

color: #fff; font-family: helvetica, arial, sans;
font-weight: bold;
text-align: center; text-decoration: none;

Finally, we'll set the font size using an **em** value (so that its size makes sense in the local context), add equal height and width, and set the line height, which we'll talk about more in a moment:
font-size: 1em; height: 2.5em; line-height: 1; width: 2.5em;

The equal height and width make the element a square, so that it will be a circle when **border-radius** is applied.

Listing: Changes to almost all the properties of the social links.

.social-link {   background: rgba(150, 150, 150, 0.5);
border-radius: 99px;   box-sizing: border-box;
color: #fff;   display: inline-block;   font-family: helvetica, arial, sans;
font-size: 1rem;   font-weight: bold;   height: 2.5em;   line-height: 1;
padding-top: 0.85em;   text-align: center;   text-decoration: none;
vertical-align: middle;   width: 2.5em; }

Those fully rounded and styled links look pretty great!

Of all the new styles that we used, the most potentially confusing ones are probably **font-family** and **verticalalign**.

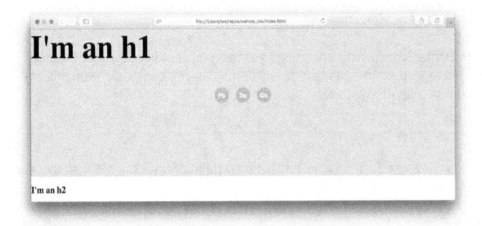

Figure: Muuuuch better.

Looking back at Listing, you might think that **vertical-align** is something that can position elements in the middle of other elements, but in reality, it has an effect only on objects that are inline, or inline block, and it centers them only in relation to the line of text that they appear on.

The **font-family** change in Listing involves defining what is called a font stack, which is just a list of font options that the browser should try to use:
font-family: helvetica, arial, sans;

Sometimes fonts can't be loaded from the Internet, or aren't available on a user's computer, so you start with the specific font you want as the first font, and then add the names of alternate fonts (separated by commas). Different computers have different fonts installed by default, and users can also add their own.

For instance, Apple computers have a classic font called Helvetica (by "classic" we mean that it was designed in 1957 and there's even a documentary about it). Windows has a knockoff of Helvetica called Arial (and designers hate it). To see what the two look like in comparison.

Font comparison chart from "Arial vs. Helvetica, Can You Spot the Difference?"

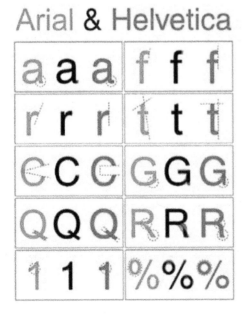

Figure: Arial is considered a cheap knockoff of Helvetica, and you probably shouldn't use it.

To find out which common fonts are available on which operating systems, you should consult a resource like CSS Font Stack. It is also possible to load your own custom fonts onto a user's computer, which is a great way to add to the unique visual branding of your site.

Line Height

As seen briefly in Listing, another aspect of text design is the line height, which defines the space above and below text and other inline elements. Any text on your site that is multiline should have the line height increased to make reading easier. An ideal amount would be around 140% to 170%, depending on the font. The **line-height** property works like **em** in that **1** equal **100%**, but there's no associated unit as with **em**, **px**, etc. For example, to arrange for the **.bio-copy** to have a line height equal to 150% of the base font size, we can set the **lineheight** to **1.5**.

Figure: The result of increasing the line height.

Listing: Changing the line height for the **.bio-copy**.

.**bio-copy** { **font-size**: 1**em**; line-height: 1.5; }

The spacing between lines is now increased, which in some contexts can make the copy easier to read.

Listing: The current index page.

```
<!DOCTYPE html>
<html>
 <head>
  <title>Test Page: Don't Panic</title>
  <meta charset="utf-8">
<style>      /* GLOBAL STYLES */
html, body {      margin: 0;      padding: 0;      }
```

```css
h1 {        font-size: 7vw;        margin-top: 0;        }
a {        color: #f00;        }
/* HERO STYLES */
.full-hero {
background-color: #c7dbfc;
height: 50vh;
}
/* SOCIAL STYLES */
.social-link {
background: rgba(150, 150, 150, 0.5);
border-radius: 99px;
box-sizing: border-box;
color: #fff;
display: inline-block;
font-family: Helvetica, arial, sans;
font-size: 1rem;
font-weight: bold;
height: 2.5em;        line-height: 1;
padding-top: 0.85em;
text-align: center;        text-decoration: none;
vertical-align: middle;        width: 2.5em;        }
.social-list {        list-style: none;
padding: text-align: center;
}
.social-list > li {
display: inline-block;
margin: 0 0.5em;
}
/* BIO STYLES */
.bio-wrapper {
font-size: 24px;        margin: auto;
max-width: 960px;        overflow: hidden;
}
.bio-box {
border: 1px solid black;
border-color: black black red;
box-sizing: border-box;        float: left;
font-size: 1rem;        margin: 40px 1% 0;
padding: 0 2% 2%;        width: 23%;        }
.bio-box h3 {
color: #fff;        font-size: 1.5em;
margin: -40px 0 1em;        text-align: center;
}
.bio-box img {        width: 100%;        }
.bio-copy {        font-size: 1em;        line-height: 1.5;        }
.bio-copy a {        color: green;        }
</style>
  </head>
  <body>
    <div class="full-hero hero-home">
      <h1>I'm an h1</h1>
```

```html
<ul class="social-list">
 <li>
  <a href="https://example.com/" class="social-link">Fb</a>
 </li>
 <li>
  <a href="https://example.com/" class="social-link">Tw</a>
 </li>
 <li>
  <a href="https://example.com/" class="social-link">Gh</a>
 </li>
 </ul>
</div>
<h2>I'm an h2</h2>
<div class="bio-wrapper">
 <div class="bio-box"><img src="https://placekitten.com/g/400/400">
<h3>Michael Hartl</h3>
  <a href="https://twitter.com/mhartl" class="social-link">Tw</a>
  <div class="bio-copy">
   <p>

Known for his dazzling charm, rapier wit, and unrivaled humility, Michael is the creator of the
<a href="https://www.railstutorial.org/">Ruby on Rails Tutorial</a> and principal author of the
<a href="https://learnenough.com/"> Learn Enough to Be Dangerous</a> introductory sequence.
   </p>
   <p>

Michael is also notorious as the founder of <a href="http://tauday.com/">Tau Day</a> and author of
<a href="http://tauday.com/tau-manifesto"><em>The Tau Manifesto</em></a>, but rumors that he's
secretly a supervillain are slightly exaggerated.

</p>
  </div>
 </div>
 <div class="bio-box">
  <img src="https://placekitten.com/g/400/400">
  <h3>Lee Donahoe</h3>
  <a href="https://twitter.com/leedonahoe" class="social-link">Tw</a>
  <div class="bio-copy">
   <p>

When he's not literally swimming with sharks or hunting powder stashes on his snowboard, you can find
Lee in front of his computer designing interfaces, doing front-end development, or writing some of the
interface-related Learn Enough tutorials.

</p>
  </div>
 </div>
 <div class="bio-box">
  <img src="https://placekitten.com/g/400/400">
  <h3>Nick Merwin</h3>
```

```
<a href="https://twitter.com/nickmerwin" class="social-link">Tw</a>
<div class="bio-copy">
 <p>
```

You may have seen him shredding guitar live with Capital Cities on Jimmy Kimmel, Conan, or The Ellen Show, but rest assured Nick is a true nerd at heart. He's just as happy shredding well-spec'd lines of code from a tour bus as he is from his kitchen table.

```
</p>
    </div>
   </div>
   <div class="bio-box">
    <img src="https://placekitten.com/g/400/400">
    <h3>??</h3>
    <p>
     The Future
    </p>
   </div>
  </div>
```

`<p>` Learn Enough to Be Dangerous is a leader in the movement to teach the world `<em>`technical sophistication`</em>`, which includes both "hard skills" like coding, command lines, and version control, and "soft skills" like guessing keyboard shortcuts, googling error messages, and knowing when to just reboot the darn thing. `</p><p>` We believe there are `<strong>`at least a billion people`</strong>` who can benefit from learning technical sophistication, probably more. To join our movement, `<a href="https://learnenough.com/#email_list">`sign up for our official email list`</a>` now. `</p>`

```
    <h3>Background</h3>
    <p>
```

Learn Enough to Be Dangerous is an outgrowth of the `<a href="https://www.railstutorial.org/">`Ruby on Rails Tutorial`</a>` and the `<a href="https://www.softcover.io/">`Softcover publishing platform`</a>`. This page is part of the sample site for `<a href="https://learnenough.com/css-tutorial"><em>`Learn Enough CSS and Layout to Be Dangerous`</em></a>`, which teaches the basics of `<strong>`C`</strong>`ascading `<strong>`S`</strong>`tyle`<strong>`S`</strong>`heets, the language that allows web pages to be styled.

Other related tutorials can be found at `<a href="https://learnenough.com/">`learnenough.com`</a>`.

```
    </p>
  </body>
</html>
```

Laying It All Out

Now that we've got a good base of CSS knowledge, it's time to learn how to put everything together into a real website. This chapter and the next is where we really kick things into high gear, with material you're unlikely to see in any other CSS tutorial. To get started, our first step will be to transform our previous work into a more manageable set of templates and page layouts that can be easily reused and updated (in accordance with the DRY principle.

Along the way, we'll add more styling as a way to learn more complex aspects of CSS, while refining our design to be more suitable for use as a personal or business website. The result will be a professional-grade example that shows a variety of aspects of modern site design.

Layout Basics

There are an infinite number of ways that you can design content layouts for the Web, but over the years certain conventions have become common to many sites, as shown in Figure. These may include elements like a header that contains site navigation and a logo (which typically links to the homepage); a hero section paragraph-style content with optional asides; and a page footer containing repetition of some elements from the header as well as things like links to About or Contact pages, privacy policy, etc. These commonalities are the result of years of trial and error, and by incorporating such familiar elements into our site we help new visitors orient themselves and find what they're looking for.

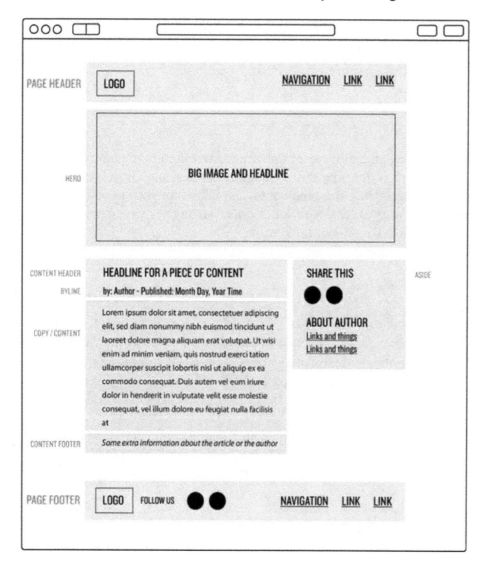

Figure: Elements of a typical web page.

One thing you may notice from Figure is that many elements, such as the header and footer, are the same (or nearly the same) on every page of our site. If we made each page by hand, that would make our markup ridiculously repetitive—if we wanted to make a change, updating all those pages would be a nightmare. This is an issue we faced repeatedly in Part I, where we simply copied and pasted common elements like navigation links onto every individual page. We promised to teach you how to use a templating system to solve this problem. In this section, we'll fulfill this promises by installing and using the Jekyll static site generator to eliminate duplication in our layout.

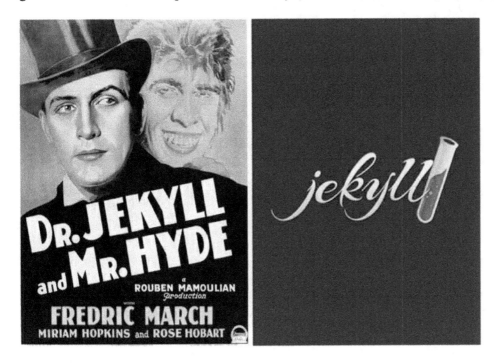

Figure: Not Jekyll and Hyde… rather, Jekyll the static site generator! (Poster image courtesy of BFA/Alamy Stock Photo.)

Jekyll

In addition to supporting templates, Jekyll also includes a bunch of other useful features:

Write content in Markdown (the lightweight markup format we first discussed in Chapter of Learn Enough Developer Tools to Be Dangerous) in your text editor of choice.
Write and preview your content on your site locally in your dev environment.
Publish changes via Git (which also gives you an automatic off-site backup).
Host your site for free on GitHub Pages.
No database management.

By using Jekyll, we managed to avoid the complexity that comes with most CMSes (databases, server configuration) and instead were able to focus on things like optimizing the UI and providing a better user experience. To work in this environment, the most a front-end engineer had to learn was the Liquid template language that Jekyll uses, and boy is that simple.

Installing and Running Jekyll

Jekyll is written in the Ruby programming language, and is distributed as a Ruby gem, or self-contained package of Ruby code. As a result, installing Jekyll is easy once you have a properly configured Ruby development environment.

If your system is not already configured as a dev environment, you should consult Learn Enough Dev Environment to Be Dangerous at this time. This step might prove challenging, especially if you decide to configure your native system, but in the long run the effort is well worth the reward.

Once you've got a working dev environment, you can install Jekyll using Bundler, a manager for Ruby gems. We can install Bundler using the **gem** command, which comes with Ruby:

$ gem install bundler -v 2.2.17
Next, we need to create a so-called **Gemfile** to specify the Jekyll gem:
$ touch Gemfile
Then use a text editor to fill the **Gemfile** with the contents shown.

Listing: Adding the Jekyll gem.

source 'https://rubygems.org' gem 'jekyll', '4.2.1'

Finally, we can install the jekyll gem using **bundle install** (with a little extra code to ensure that we're using the right version of Bundler):

$ bundle _2.2.17_ install

Although Jekyll is designed to work with a system of templates, in fact it can work with a single file, such as our current **index.html**. To see how it works, we can run the Jekyll server in our project directory (using **bundle exec** to ensure that the right version of Jekyll gets run):

$ bundle _2.2.17_ exec jekyll serve

If you're working on a native system or a virtual machine (as opposed to a cloud IDE), at this point the Jekyll app should be available at the URL http://localhost:4000, where localhost is the address of the local computer and 4000 is the port number. The result should look something like Figure.

Figure: No more URL pointing to a file—you're running on a server now!

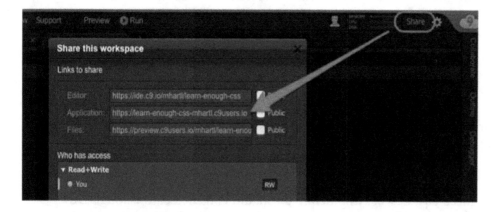

Figure: Sharing the URL on the cloud IDE.

If you're using the cloud IDE suggested in Learn Enough Dev Environment to Be Dangerous, you'll have to pass options for the port number and host IP number when running the **jekyll** command:

```
$ bundle _2.2.17_ exec jekyll serve --port $PORT --host $IP
```

Here **$PORT** and **$IP** should be typed in literally; they are environment variables provided by the cloud IDE to make the development site accessible on an external URL. Once the server is running, you can visit it by selecting Share and then clicking on the server URL. The result, apart from the browser URL, should be the same as for the local system. (For simplicity, in what follows we sometimes refer to localhost:4000, but users of the cloud IDE should use their personal URL instead. Mutatis mutandis.)

After starting the Jekyll server, you should find a new folder in your project called **_site** (with a leading underscore):

```
$ ls
_site index.html
```

This folder contains the output from the Jekyll server as it builds your site from the source files (currently just **index.html**).

The **_site** directory and all its contents are generated by Jekyll every time a file is saved, and if you were to make any changes in the **_site** folder they will be automatically overwritten. As a result, you should never make changes in any of the **_site** files themselves—they would only be overwritten by Jekyll. There's nothing more frustrating than accidentally working on updates in an automatically generated folder, only to have your changes overwritten by an uncaring static site generator.

Image courtesy of mangostar/123RF.

NOOOOOOOOOO!!!!!!!

Figure: TFW changes accidentally made in generated files get overwritten.

Because all its content is generated by Jekyll, it's a good idea to ignore the **_site** directory by adding it to your **.gitignore** file, and there's a Bundler configuration directory called **.bundle** that should also be ignored:

```
$ echo _site/ >> .gitignore
$ echo .bundle >> .gitignore
$ git add .gitignore
$ git commit -m "Ignore the generated site and Bundler directories"
```

You should also add the **Gemfile** (and the associated auto-generated **Gemfile.lock** file) to the repository:

```
$ git add -A
$ git commit -m "Add a Gemfile"
```

Layouts, Includes, and Pages (Oh My!)

One of the most powerful features of Jekyll is its ability to factor different parts of a website into reusable pieces. To accomplish this, Jekyll uses a system of folders and conventional names for files, along with a mini-language called Liquid. Originally developed by Tobi Lütke, cofounder of online store powerhouse Shopify, Liquid is a system for adding content to a site using what are in effect simple computer programs.

Tobi is also an alumnus of the Rails core team.

Files inside a Jekyll project can be static, meaning that they do not get processed by the Jekyll engine, or they can be dynamic and get constructed with Jekyll magic. (The site is still static because it consists of static files on the server, even if those files are generated dynamically by Jekyll. In other words, the files don't change once they've been generated by Jekyll, so the results are the same for every visitor of the site.) There are four main types of magic objects/files that the Jekyll engine can use in an automated way to build your site:

Layouts/layout templates
Includes
Pages/page templates
Posts

We'll discuss each of these in abstract terms for reference, but their exact uses won't become clear until we see some concrete examples starting in Section.

Layouts/Layout Templates

Anything in the special **_layouts** directory can have Jekyll magic, meaning those files get read by the engine looking for Liquid tags and other Jekyll formatting.

One of the key parts of many Jekyll pages is frontmatter, which is metadata at the top of an HTML file (in YAML format) that identifies the kind of layout to be used, a page-specific title, etc. A fairly complicated example might look like this, where the frontmatter is everything between the two triple-dashes ---:

```
<a href="#">link or two</a> ---
<div>
  <p>Lorem ipsum dolor sit paragraph.</p>
<div>
```

In a simpler but still common example, the frontmatter identifies only the page layout template to be used when rendering the page:

```
--layout: default ---
<div>
  <p>Lorem ipsum dolor sit paragraph. </p>
<div>
```

We'll see the effects of this sort of code starting in Section.

If there is no frontmatter in a layout file, then it is a true layout, and it needs to have a full HTML page structure. If there is frontmatter, then the file is a layout template that can be built into other layouts, and it doesn't need to have a full HTML page structure.

Layouts are often the most base-level objects, defining a standard page with a **DOCTYPE**, **html**/**head**/**body** tags, **meta** tags, stylesheet links, JavaScript, etc., and they usually pull in includes like a site header or site footer. You often need only one default layout for a site, but you can also use layout templates for things like blogs.

Layouts have the special ability to load content, like posts, using a generic Liquid tag that looks like this: **{{ content }}**. We'll see a short example of this in an exercise, and we'll apply it to our full site.

Includes

Files in the **_includes** folder can have Jekyll magic even though they don't need frontmatter, and these files are always intended to be built into something else. Includes tend to be little snippets of a site that get repeated on many pages, such as the header and footer or a standard set of social media links. Includes will be covered in Section.

Pages/Page Templates

Any other HTML file in the project directory is a page. If there is no frontmatter in the file it is a static page, and Jekyll magic will not work (Liquid tags go unprocessed). If a page has frontmatter, though, it will need to specify a layout, and then all the Jekyll magic will be available. We'll cover pages more in Chapter.

Posts, and Post-Type Files

Posts are self-contained pieces of content, such as blog posts or product details, that are saved as files in the **_posts** directory. Some forms of content (like blog posts) are typically organized by date, while others (like product descriptions) are organized based on other attributes into collections.

The Layout File

Let's start playing around with a Jekyll layout by adapting our site into the framework. The end result of this section will be a page that looks exactly like the current **index.html**, but which is created in a way that will give us greater power and flexibility down the road. This includes getting a first taste of templates and frontmatter.

This isn't how you would normally go about creating a site if you were starting from scratch. Layout files are usually pretty bare-bones, and a more common development process is to create a spartan layout using the command **jekyll new** and then start doing the real work in the pages and includes. In our case, though, we've already done a lot of work in our single **index.html** file; using it as our initial layout means that, as we learn about different aspects of Jekyll, we can pull the parts we need out of the layout, thereby showing how a whole site can be sliced up and reassembled.

As we explained in Section, the Jekyll convention for layouts is to place these files in a directory called **_layouts** (with a leading underscore), which you should create in the root directory of your application (**repos/<username>.github.io**):

$ mkdir _layouts

Any HTML file in the **_layouts** directory can serve as a layout, so to get started we'll copy the existing **index.html** into the layouts directory to create a default layout:

$ cp index.html _layouts/default.html

At this point, your project files should look something like Figure.

To get our site back up and visible, replace the entire contents of **index.html** with the code shown.

Listing: The site index with Jekyll frontmatter.

layout: default ---

As mentioned in Section, the content is known as the Jekyll front-matter, and by adding it to the **index.html** file we've turned a static page into a Jekyll page template.

The frontmatter is the secret sauce that lets Jekyll know that it needs to read through an HTML page to see if it should process any of the content. By specifying **layout: default**, we've arranged for Jekyll to use **default.html** as the page layout. Because **default.html** is currently a fully self-contained page, the result of visiting http://localhost:4000 is to render our entire test page. In other words, Jekyll just takes the contents of **default.html** and inserts it into **index.html**.

Figure: Your files and directories should look like this.

As mentioned in Section, this sort of transformation, where we change the underlying code without changing the result, is known as refactoring. It may seem like we've done nothing, but we'll see in Section how this new structure lets us slice and dice our website into reusable pieces.

CSS File and Reset

Now that we've refactored our test page into a layout (**default.html**) and a page template (**index.html**), we're going to start the process of breaking our monolithic HTML/CSS file into its component parts. The first step is to create a standalone CSS file with a reset that eliminates troublesome browser defaults for margins, padding, etc. Then we'll pull all the CSS out of the test site's **style** block and put it into the same external file.

To get started, create a new folder in the project directory called **css**, and then create a new file in that directory called **main.css**, either using the terminal like in Listing, or by just adding the folders and files in your text editor.

Listing: Creating a new CSS folder and blank document in the terminal.

You have to name your directory exactly **css**, because Jekyll automatically looks for CSS files in that location, but you can use whatever filename makes you happy for the actual CSS file.

No self-respecting and properly perfectionist developer wants to leave the appearance of important elements up to the browser makers, so we'll apply a full CSS reset to create a blank slate for our designs. Recall that we created a mini-version of a CSS reset, where we reset the margin and padding for **html** and **body** tags. Now it's time to upgrade our site to use an industrial-strength reset. The resulting CSS may look intimidating, but don't worry—we're putting it in Listing precisely so that you can copy and paste it without having to understand the details.

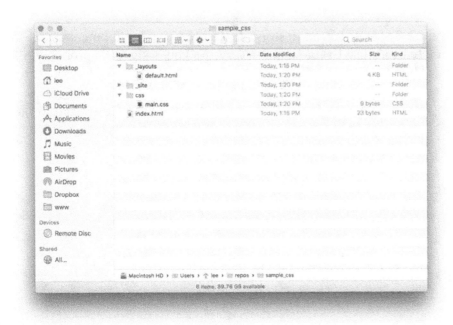

Figure: The new **css** folder and **main.css** file.

Listing: A standard CSS reset.

```css
html, body, div, span, applet, object, iframe, h1, h2, h3, h4, h5, h6, p, blockquote, pre, a, abbr,
acronym, address, big, cite, code, del, dfn, em, img, ins, kbd, q, s, samp, small, strike, strong, sub, sup,
tt, var, b, u, i, center, dl, dt, dd, ol, ul, li, fieldset, form, label, legend, table, caption, tbody, tfoot,
thead, tr, th, td, article, aside, canvas, details, embed, figure, figcaption, footer, header, hgroup, menu,
nav, output, ruby, section, summary, time, mark, audio, video {  margin: 0;  padding: 0;  border: 0;
font: inherit;  vertical-align: baseline; } /* HTML5 display-role reset for older browsers */ article, aside,
details, figcaption, figure, footer, header, hgroup, menu, nav, section {  display: block; } body {
 line-height: 1; } blockquote, q {  quotes: none; } blockquote:before, blockquote:after, q:before, q:after
{  content: '';  content: none; } table {
border-collapse: collapse;  border-spacing: 0; } strong, b {  font-weight: bold; } em, i {  font-style:
italic; } a img {  border: none; }
/* END RESET*/
```

Note that the CSS in Listing doesn't need to be wrapped with the **style** tags the way the styles in the HTML file did; as we'll see in Listing, the browser understands from the link that everything inside the file is CSS. We see in Listing that most of the standard HTML elements get some sort of styling applied to them. The big block of selectors at the top is pretty much every HTML element in the spec forced to have margin and padding set to zero, a border of zero, and told to inherit font styles. This might seem a little extreme to target every element, but when we are making a custom website there is no reason to leave browser defaults for things like margin, padding, and border in place—otherwise, we could end up having to undo styling all over our stylesheet. It's better to undo a lot of stuff right off the bat, and then only add positive styling later on.

Figure: Reset rules aren't set in stone… or any other kind of tablet. (Etching image courtesy of World Archive/Alamy Stock Photo; tablet graphic courtesy of Oleksiy Mark/Shutterstock)

Also, don't think that the above reset styling is something set in stone. If later in your development career you find yourself adding the same styling to every (say) **table** tag on every site you design, it's probably best just to add that to your reset. As usual, the DRY principle applies.

With the reset added, we're now in a position to move the custom CSS style developed so far in the tutorial into **main.css**. This involves first opening **default.html** and cutting all the CSS inside the **style** tag, leaving the tag empty.

Listing: The default layout with CSS cut out.

```html
<!DOCTYPE html>
<html>
 <head>
  <title>Test Page: Don't Panic</title>
  <meta charset="utf-8">
  <style>
  </style>
 </head>
 <body>  .
```

.

.

```
  </body>
</html>
```

Next, paste the CSS into **main.css** (possibly using something like Shift-Command-V, which pastes at the proper indentation level), and then delete the mini-reset that targeted only **html, body** that we added before since it is now redundant.

Listing: The entire CSS file up to this point.

html, body, div, span, applet, object, iframe, h1, h2, h3, h4, h5, h6, p, blockquote, pre, a, abbr, acronym, address, big, cite, code, del, dfn, em, img, ins, kbd, q, s, samp, small, strike, strong, sub, sup, tt, var, b, u, i, center, dl, dt, dd, ol, ul, li, fieldset, form, label, legend, table, caption, tbody, tfoot, thead, tr, th, td, article, aside, canvas, details, embed, figure, figcaption, footer, header, hgroup, menu, nav, output, ruby, section, summary, time, mark, audio, video { margin: 0; padding: 0; border: 0; font: inherit; vertical-align: baseline; } /* HTML5 display-role reset for older browsers */ **article, aside, details, figcaption, figure, footer, header, hgroup, menu, nav, section { display: block; } body { line-height: 1; } blockquote, q { quotes: none; } blockquote:before, blockquote:after, q:before, q:after { content: ''; content: none; } table { border-collapse: collapse; border-spacing: 0; } strong, b { font-weight: bold; } em, i { font-style: italic; } a img { border: none; }**
/* END RESET*/
/* GLOBAL STYLES */ **h1 { font-size: 7vw; margin-top: 0; } a { color: #f00; }**
/* HERO STYLES */ **.full-hero { background-color: #c7dbfc; height: 50vh;
}**
/* SOCIAL STYLES */ **.social-link { background: rgba(150, 150, 150, 0.5); border-radius: 99px; box-sizing: border-box; color: #fff; display: inline-block; font-family: helvetica, arial, sans; fontsize: 1rem; font-weight: bold; height: 2.5em; line-height: 1; padding-top: 0.85em; text-align: center; text-decoration: none; vertical-align: middle; width: 2.5em; } .social-list { list-style: none; padding: 0; text-align: center; } .social-list > li { display: inline-block; margin: 0 0.5em; }**
/* BIO STYLES */ **.bio-wrapper { font-size: 24px; margin: auto; max-width: 960px; overflow: hidden; } .bio-box { border: 1px solid black; box-sizing: border-box; float: left; font-size: 1rem; margin: 40px 1% 0; padding: 2%; width: 23%; } .bio-box h3 { color: #fff; font-size: 1.5em; margin: -40px 0 1em; text-align: center;
} .bio-box img { width: 100%; } .bio-copy { font-size: 1em; line-height: 1.5; } .bio-copy a { color: green; }**

As you can verify by refreshing the browser, the page is now completely unstyled.

To restore the styling, all we need to do is tell the layout page about **main.css**. The way to do this is to replace the **style** tags in the **head** section with a link to our stylesheet.

Figure: It's been a long time since our site was this naked and unstyled.

Listing: Using a **link** tag to load **main.css**.

```
<!DOCTYPE html>
<html>
  <head>
    <title>Test Page: Don't panic</title>
    <meta charset="utf-8">    <link rel="stylesheet" href="/css/main.css">
  </head>
```

The **link** tag in Listing tells the browser that it will be loading a stylesheet (**rel** is short for "relationship"), and then specifies a URL (in this case an absolute one that looks at the site's root directory by starting the URL with a forward slash) that leads to the file.

Recall from Section that paths can be either relative (local to the computer serving the file), or absolute (accessed by a full URL). For example, the path **css/main.css** is relative, while **/css/main.css** is absolute. It's important to understand that using the **link** tag to load an external stylesheet has nothing to do with Jekyll; this general technique works even on hand-built web-sites that don't use any site builder. The stylesheet doesn't actually need to be local, either—theoretically, it can be anywhere on the Internet—but for our purposes we want to use a local file so that it's easy to make changes.

Now when you refresh the browser the styles should be properly applied, and the page will pretty much look how it did before our refactoring, although there will be some places where things don't look right because of the CSS reset.

Before moving on, let's make a few minor changes to prove that we know how to update styles via the CSS file. Ever since we started with this page, the fonts have looked a little… old-school. Let's add in a general style to the page **body** that will cascade down to every element on the page and change all body text to a nice, clean, sans-serif font.

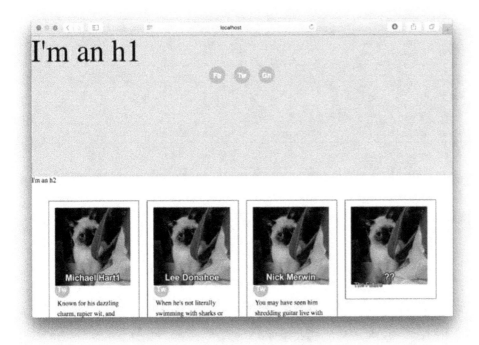

Figure: Same old page, with some minor oddities.

Listing: A good spot for this would be in the "Global Styles" section of the CSS file.

/* GLOBAL STYLES */ **body** {   **font-family**: helvetica, arial, sans; }

When you save your work and refresh the browser, everything should still look the way it did before, but with all new fonts across the page.

Finally, in order to avoid the overlap between the bio box and social links, we'll change the CSS for the latter to be **display: block** with a margin.

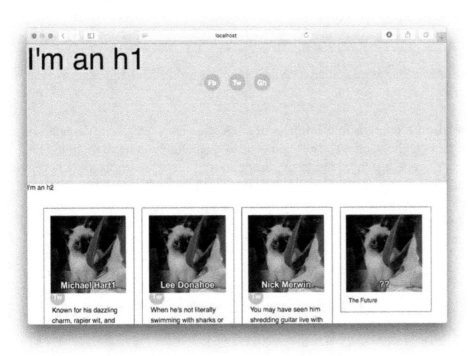

Figure: Same old page, all-new fonts.

Listing: Fixing up the social link spacing.

.bio-box img { **width**: 100%; } **.bio-box .social-link** { **display: block; margin: 2em 0 1em;** } **.bio-copy** { **font-size**: 1em; }

The result appears in Figure.

Figure: Better spacing for the social links.

Includes Intro: Head and Header

Now that we've factored the CSS into a separate file (and added a CSS reset), it's time to start slicing up the default page into reusable pieces. Jekyll provides includes to help us with this important task. (Note: In this context, the word "include" is used as a noun, which is not standard English but is standard in the world of static site generators. This usage also changes the pronunciation; the verb form is "in-CLUDE", but the noun form is "IN-clude".)

This distinction exists in many other English words, such as AT-tri-bute (noun)/at-TRI-bute (verb) and CON-flict (noun)/con-FLICT (verb).

Includes are supposed to be the smallest/most reusable snippets of site code. They are usually loaded into either layouts or templates, but in fact can be used anywhere on a site—you can even have included call other includes. Since these snippets of code are intended to get dropped into the site almost anywhere, you should always try to make sure that any includes you create have code that is portable and self-contained.

Image courtesy of vivid pixels/123RF.

LET'S PUT SOME
INCLUDES IN YOUR INCLUDES

SO YOU CAN INCLUDE
WHILE YOU INCLUDE!

Figure: You can put includes in includes, so you include have includes.

Jekyll includes are located in a dedicated folder called **_includes** (as with **_lay-outs**, the underscore is important). Go ahead and create that folder now, together with a new file called **head.html**.

Listing: Creating the includes folder and adding in a new file.

At this point, your project folder should look something like Figure.
As you might have guessed, we're going to use **head.html** to hold the **head** tag and its contents. The way to do this is first to cut that content out of **default.html**, and then paste it into **head.html** (possibly using Shift-Command-V to paste with the proper indentation), as shown in Listing.

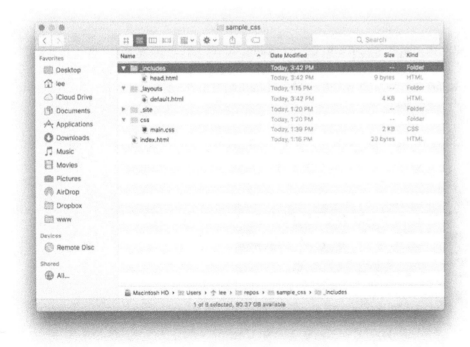

Figure: The project directory with added includes.

Listing: Moving **head** to its own file.

```
<head>
  <title>Test Page: Don't Panic</title>
  <meta charset="utf-8">
  <link rel="stylesheet" href="/css/main.css">
</head>
```

To include the contents of **head.html** back into the **default.html** layout, we'll use our first example of the Liquid language mentioned in Section, which looks like this:

```
{% include head.html %}
```

Here **include** is a Liquid command to include the file in question (in this case, **head.html**). The special syntax **{% ... %}** tells Jekyll to replace the contents of that line with the result of evaluating the code inside. Because Jekyll automatically knows to look in the **_includes** directory, the result will be to insert the contents of **head.html**.

Replacing the original **head** section with the corresponding Liquid snippet gives the code.

Listing: Including the site head using Liquid.

```
<!DOCTYPE html>
<html>
  {% include head.html %}
  <body>
```

After making these changes, you should refresh your browser to confirm that the page still works.

Page Header: Up Top!

At the top of a typical web page, you will usually find some sort of site-level navigation that takes users from page to page on the site, and also includes site branding. This section is often referred to as the site header (not to be confused with the **head** tag, which is the HTML header). Implementing such a header site-wide is a perfect application of Jekyll includes.

To get started, let's add a new Liquid tag to **header.html** (which we'll create in a moment) at the top of the **default.html** file.

Figure: Some site headers from popular websites.

Listing: Including the header HTML.

```
<!DOCTYPE html>
<html>
  {% include head.html %}
  <body>
    {% include header.html %}
    <div class="full-hero hero-home">
      <h1>I'm an h1</h1>
      <ul class="social-list">
```

Next, create a new blank document in the **_includes** folder called **header.html**:

You can of course use your text editor to create the file rather than using **touch**.
$ touch _includes/header.html

The header itself will use two semantic elements (i.e., elements that have meaning): **header** to contain the header and **nav** for the navigation links, which are organized as an unordered list **ul**.

We'll also use the classes" header" and" header-**nav**" to make it easier to apply styles across a range of browsers. The resulting code appears in Listing.

Listing: The basic structure of our site header.

```
<header class="header">
  <nav>
    <ul class="header-nav">
      <li><a href="/">Home</a></li>
      <li><a href="#">Nav 1</a></li>
      <li><a href="#">Nav 2</a></li>
      <li><a href="#">Nav 3</a></li>
    </ul>
  </nav>
  <a href="/" class="header-logo">Logo</a>
</header>
```

Save and refresh your browser and now you'll see your new site header.

Figure: Our not-very-attractive header.

Navigation and Children

Now, let's style that ugly header!
The end goal for our design is to create a traditional sort of header, with a logo on the left-hand side that will send users back to the homepage, and site navigation at the top right. As a final step, we'll change the position of the header so that it will sit on top of content below it.

The first thing that we are going to do is move the navigation to the right and put the ᴜs into a horizontal row by changing their display property to **inline-block**. The result, which we suggest inserting immediately after the global styles.

Listing: Adding header styles.

```
/* HEADER STYLES */ .header-nav {   float: right; } .header-nav > li {   display: inline-block; }
```

Note in Listing that we've used the more advanced child selector > to target the. That is to make sure that if we wanted to put a second level of links into the menu, only the direct children would be **inline-block**.

After saving and refreshing, you'll see that the menu has moved.

You might have wondered why the logo is below the navigational list in Listing even though it comes first when viewing the header from left to right. The reason is that we knew all along that we were going to float the navigation to the right side of the screen, and if the logo appeared before the navigation in the HTML order then the menu would start at the bottom of the logo. This is because even a floating element respects the line height and position of normal block or inline elements that come before it, which in this case would lead to unwanted space around the logo. You can check this yourself by switching the positions of the logo and nav links; you'll see that the menu starts lower as a result.

Figure: Navigation moved to the right and all in a line.

Figure: Switching the logo to come first adds unwanted space.

Now let's add in some padding on the list items and make those links a little more stylish. We are going to add some padding to move the navigation away from the edges of the page:
padding: 5.5vh 60px 0 0;

We are also going to give each ⅼⅰ in the navigation a bit of left margin so that it isn't bumping right up against its neighbour:

margin-left: 1em;

For the links themselves, we'll change the color and the size, make the font bold so that it is easier to read, get rid of the default link underlines (as is done in about 99% of site headers), and also automatically transform the text to be uppercase:

color: #000; font-size: 0.8rem; font-weight: bold; text-decoration: none; text-transform: uppercase;
Here we've used **#000** instead of **black**; it's important to learn how to use these two interchangeably. After adding the appropriate selectors, the styling changes look like Listing.

Listing: Styling the navigational links.

```
.header-nav {
  float: right;
```

padding: 5.5vh 60px 0 0; } **.header-nav > li** { **display**: **inline-block**; **margin-left**: 1em; } **.header-nav a** { **color**: #000; **font-size**: 0.8rem; **font-weight**: **bold**; **text-decoration**: **none**; **text-transform**: **uppercase**; }

Your page navigation should now look like Figure.

So how did we come up with those exact styles? The values came from just adding a couple of styling rules, and then tweaking the numbers until things looked good. Design isn't always a systematic process—often you just need to make changes and then play around with the numbers until you get something you like. When designing websites, there tends to be an extended period of experimentation, so don't worry if it takes you time to get things right when you work on your own!

Figure: Navigational links are now a bit more stylish.

Advanced Selectors

In order to add an extra bit of polish to the site header, we are going to introduce a few more advanced CSS selectors, and then we'll continue to add in more styling for the rest of our page. These advanced selectors include pseudo-classes, first-child/last-child, and siblings.

Pseudo-Classes

It's always nice to have links do something when a user rolls over them, especially since we removed the underlines from the links in Listing. Those underlines on links are called design affordances, and they are there to give users the suggestion that something will happen if they move the cursor to the link and click. Some people may argue that all links on a site should have some affordance that clearly marks them as something clickable, either with underlines or by making them look like buttons (HOLY WAR!!!). At this point in time, though, the design convention of putting plain-text links that don't have underlines (or some other special style) in a header is something that most Internet users are now accustomed to. You just know that the things at the top of the page are clickable.

Without underlines or other immediately visible affordances, though, it is important to show users a response to rolling over the link with their cursor. You really want people to know that they are interacting with an element that does something after they perform an action.

All HTML links have a set of what are called pseudo-classes that allow developers to style different interactions with the link:

:hover: Styles what happens when a user rolls over the link (applies to any element, not just links)
:active: Styles what happens when a user clicks the link
:visited: Styles what the link should look like if a user has already visited the linked page

The way to add a pseudo-class to a style declaration is by combining the element or class name with the pseudo class, like this:

.header-nav a:hover { **color**: #ed6e2f; }

This use of the **:hover** pseudo-class arranges to change the color of the link when the user's mouse hovers over it. (For now we've just picked a random orange color that will stand out nicely against the blue background.)

We'll add a second change as well, which is to make the logo partially transparent on hover using the **opacity** property. The combined result appears in Listing.

Listing: Adding hover states to the navigational links.

.header-nav a:hover, **.header-nav a**:active { **color**: #ed6e2f; }
.header-logo:hover, **.header-logo**:active { **opacity**: 0.5; }

Note that we've added the same styling to the **:active** pseudo-class in order to give mobile users feedback as well.

Save your styles and refresh, and now the nav links will turn orange on rollover, and the logo will turn 50% transparent.

There are a bunch of other very useful pseudo-classes that are regularly used in designing layouts. We'll talk about some of these throughout the rest of this section, and we'll see further examples in Section.

Siblings

Let's look at two additional advanced selectors, and then after seeing how they work, we'll use one to add another little style detail to our site navigation. CSS supports two sibling selectors, both of which are written like the child selector > when making a declaration:

The adjacent sibling +: Selects a single element only if it is right next to the primary element in the declaration. For example, **h2 + p** selects a **p** tag only if it is immediately preceded by an **h2** tag.
The general sibling ~: Selects all elements of the type in the declaration if they follow the primary element.

For example, **h2 ~ p** applies to all **p** tags preceded by an **h2** tag.

Let's hop out of working on the header for a second to create an example to use with the sibling selectors. In your **default.html** file, replace the **h2** tag with the HTML from Listing.

Listing: Replacing the **h2** and adding some text.

<h2>THE FOUNDERS</h2>
<p> Learn Enough to Be Dangerous was founded in 2015 by Michael Hartl, Lee Donahoe, and Nick Merwin. We believe that the kind of technical sophistication taught by   the Learn Enough tutorials can benefit at least a billion people, and probably more. </p>

`<p>`Test paragraph`</p>`

We can target the paragraph that directly follows the h2 with the style shown in Listing.

Listing: Adding an adjacent sibling selector.

h2 + p { font-size: 0.8em; **font-style: italic; margin: 1em auto 0; max-width: 70%; text-align**: center; }**

Notice that only the first paragraph is styled.

Listing: The general selector targets all elements that come after a specified element.

h2 ~ p { font-size: 0.8em; **font-style: italic; margin: 1em auto 0; max-width: 70%; text-align**: center; }**

You may also have noticed from Figure that the **p**s in the **.bio-box**es below aren't styled. That is because the sibling selectors don't pass styles to elements that are wrapped inside any other elements. They only work on elements inside the same parent.

Figure: Only the **p** immediately after the **h2** is styled.

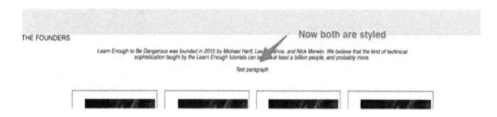

Figure: All **p** tags after the **h2** are now styled the same.

Looking back to the header, we can use a sibling selector in the site header navigation to target all the **li**s after the first **li**, and add in a little extra styling to help visually separate the links using the styles in Listing. You might have seen something like this online: a little vertical line between navigational links to help separate them from other links in a list. Let's use a sibling selector to add some divider lines.

Listing: Using the general sibling selector to add styling to the header navigation.

.header-nav > li { display: inline-block; margin-left: 1em; } .header-nav > li ~ li { border-left: 1px solid rgba(0, 0, 0, 0.3); padding-left: 1em; }

The rule **.header-nav > li ~ li** in Listing says to apply the subsequent rules to all **li** elements next to an initial **li** inside an element with class **".header-nav"**— in other words, every **li** in the menu after the first one. This way, the divider lines appear before every menu item except the first.

Now that the navigation is fairly spiffy, let's turn our attention to the logo, which will give us a chance to learn a little bit about CSS positioning.

Figure: Menu divider lines.

Positioning

In this section, we are going to take a look at how positioning works in CSS, focusing on the site logo, and then we'll finish off the header design. CSS positioning can be a little tricky, and honestly there are people who work with CSS all the time who regularly get confused trying to get positioning to work right. So if this section seems long and loaded with examples, just bear with us and work through it all—you'll find that understanding CSS positioning is an essential skill.

When you style an element's position, there are two basic possibilities:

Have the browser draw the element in its natural position in the normal flow of content on the page. Remove the target from the flow of content and display it in a different place using directional styles—left, right, top, and bottom—and an additional dimension, the so-called **z-index**.

When an element is moved around out of its natural position with directional styles, it doesn't affect other elements in the document—it either covers them up or is hidden behind them. It becomes like a ship cast adrift, torn free from its mooring on the page.

While it might be self-explanatory to move something left or right, or to change its top or bottom position, you might not be familiar with the idea of a **z-index**. The **z-index** property (which can be any nonnegative number, 0 by default) determines whether an element is displayed above or below other elements, as in farther "into" the screen or farther "out" toward the viewer. It's an element's 3D position.

You can think of this like looking down at a big stack of papers—the higher the **z-index** number is, the higher up the stack toward you the element is. A **z-index** of **0** would be the bottommost piece of paper. We'll see a concrete example of the **z-index** in Section.

In order to change those directional styles, we first need to alter an element's **position** property. The **position** style in CSS can be given five different values (though one of them isn't really used). We'll start with one of the most common one, static.

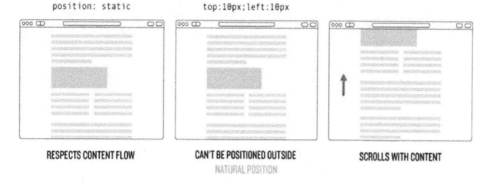

position: static   top:10px;left:10px

RESPECTS CONTENT FLOW   CAN'T BE POSITIONED OUTSIDE   SCROLLS WITH CONTENT
                              NATURAL POSITION

Figure: How **position: static** affects elements.

- **position: static**
This is the default positioning of elements in the flow of content.
An element that has no position style set, or has **position: static**, will ignore directional styles like left, right, top, and bottom.

- **position: absolute**
Positions the element at a specific place by taking it out of the document flow, either within a parent wrapper that has a **position:** value other than **static**, or (if there is no parent) a specific place in the browser window. It is still a part of the page content, which means when you scroll the page, it moves with the content.

Also lets you define a **z-index** property.

Because the element is removed from the document flow, the width or height is determined either by shrinking to the content inside, or by setting dimensions in CSS. It behaves kind of like an element set to **inline-block**.

Causes any float that is set on the object to be ignored, so if you have both styles on an element you might as well delete the float.

- **position: relative**
This is like static in that it respects the element's starting position in the flow of content, but it also allows directional styles to be applied that nudge the element away from the boundary with other elements.

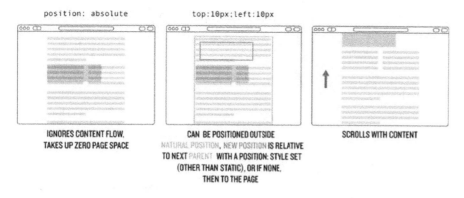

position: absolute   top:10px;left:10px

IGNORES CONTENT FLOW,   CAN BE POSITIONED OUTSIDE   SCROLLS WITH CONTENT
TAKES UP ZERO PAGE SPACE NATURAL POSITION, NEW POSITION IS RELATIVE
                          TO NEXT PARENT WITH A POSITION: STYLE SET
                          (OTHER THAN STATIC), OR IF NONE,
                          THEN TO THE PAGE

Figure: How **position: absolute** affects elements.

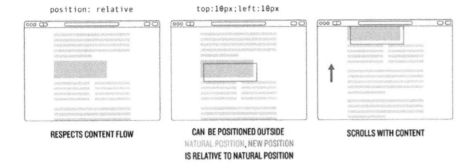

Figure: How **position: relative** affects elements.

It allows absolutely positioned items to be contained within, as though the relatively positioned element were a separate canvas. In other words, if an absolutely positioned element is inside a relatively positioned element, a style of **top: 0** would cause the absolutely positioned element to be drawn at the top of the relatively positioned element rather than at the top of the page.

Also allows you to change the **z-index** of the element.

• **position: fixed**
Positions the element at a specific place within the browser window totally separate from the page content. When you scroll the page, it won't move.

Let's you set **z-index**.

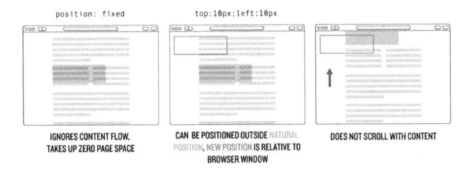

Figure: How **position: fixed** affects elements.

Has the same need to have dimensions set as **position: absolute**; otherwise, it will be the size of the content inside.
Also causes floats to be ignored.

• **position: inherit**
– This is not very common, so we aren't going to discuss it other than to say it makes the element inherit the position from its parent.

Let's play around with some examples. First, let's add in some styles for the header to better see the boundaries and to give it dimensions.

Listing: Added styles for the **.header** class.

```
/* HEADER STYLES */ .header {   background-color: #aaa;   height: 300px;   width: 100%; }
```

Let's now absolutely position the **.header-logo** and set it to **50px** from the bottom.

Figure: The parent container has no position style set.

Listing: Adding an initial **position: absolute** to the logo.

.**header-nav** > li:first-child **a**:hover {   **color**: #fff; } .**header-logo** {   **bottom: 50px**;   **position**: **absolute**; }

Now save and refresh… where did the logo go?

The logo link ended up way at the bottom because the parent element that wraps the **.header-logo** doesn't have any **position** style applied. Also, if you scroll the page up and down you'll notice that the **.header-logo** still moves with the page. Let's constrain the logo to stay within the header by adding a position property.

Figure: The absolutely positioned **.header-logo**.

Listing: Setting a position other than static on the wrapper.

.header { **background-color**: #aaa; **height**: 300px; **position**: **relative**; **width**: **100%**; }

With the **position** rule in Listing, the **.header-logo** will now be **50px** from the bottom of the gray header box, and any positions that we give to **.header-logo** will be determined based on the boundaries of the **.header** container. The way that the position is based off of the boundaries of the parent is what we meant when we said that setting a parent wrapper to **position: relative** made it like a separate canvas—everything inside that is absolutely positioned takes its place based on the dimensions of the parent.

Note here that when an element is absolutely positioned, the directional styles don't add or subtract distance— setting **bottom: 50px** doesn't move it toward the bottom, but rather sets the position **50px** from the bottom. So **right: 50px** puts the element **50px** from the right edge.

Negative positions work as well, and as long as the overflow of the parent wrapper isn't set to **hidden**, the absolutely positioned element will get placed outside the boundaries of the parent.

Listing: Trying out negative positioning on our object.

.header-logo { **bottom**: **-50px**; **position**: **absolute**; **right**: **50px**; }

After adding that style and refreshing your browser, the logo should be in a position similar to what is shown in Figure.

Figure: Positioning the logo on the right-hand side.

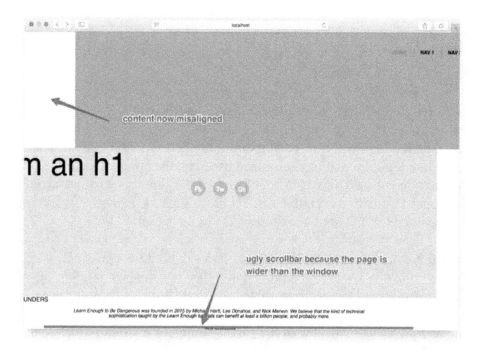

Figure: This sort of thing looks sloppy.

You might be asking, "Well, what happens if I set both a top and bottom, or a left and right?" The answer is that, for whatever reasons, the top and left properties will take priority and the bottom and right will be ignored.

Another thing to consider is when you set a position property, you are manipulating elements and messing around with the natural page flow, which means that it is possible to cause misalignments. So if you add **left: 200px** to the **.header**, the width of the element (which is 100%) isn't recalculated. Instead, the entire **.header** box is pushed over by 200px, and your browser window will have horizontal scrollbars and look broken.

You have to be careful!

While we are still just playing around in the positioning sandbox, we should take a look at ways to deal with a situation that comes up anytime positioning in CSS is discussed: How do you center an absolutely positioned object horizontally and vertically in a way that allows the object to be any size… and allows the wrapper to be any size?

Let's first look at an old method where the object that we are centering has a set height and width—centering this is easy. Give the logo a width and height, remove the old positioning, and change the background to better see the object.

Listing: Adding height and width dimensions to the logo.

.header-logo { **background-color**: #000; **height**: **110px**; **position**: **absolute**; **width**: **110px**; }

Now let's center it.

You might think that centering the element would be as simple as giving the **.header-logo** class a style of **left: 50%** and **top: 50%**—that should put it in the middle, both horizontally and vertically, right?

Listing: Positioning the **.header-logo** in the center?

.header-logo { **background-color**: #000; **height**: 110px; **left: 50%**; **position**: **absolute**; **top**: **50%**; **width**: 110px; }

Well, no, the reason this didn't work is that when the browser positions an object, it calculates the distance using the same-named edge—so when you apply **top: 50%**, it moves the top edge (not the center point) of **.header-logo** 50% away from the top of **.header**; similarly, applying **left: 50%** tells the browser to move the left edge 50% away from the left of **.header**. The result is that the object we are trying to position is off-centre by half of its width and height.

How do we solve this and get our object in the actual center? The older method mentioned above was to use a negative margin to move the object up and left. This only works if you know the size of the object, though, since trying to use something like a percentage would move the object based on the size of the parent (recall from Section that percentage values are based on the size of the parent object). Since the height and width of the box are **110px**, half of that is **55px**.

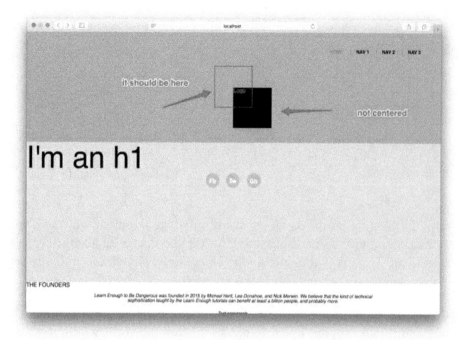

Figure: The red box in the expected position if centered vertically and horizontally.

Listing: Adding in the negative margins to position the black box in the right spot.

.**header-logo** {   **background-color**: #000;   **height**: 110**px**;   **left**: 50%;   margin: **-55px 0 0 -55px**; **position**: **absolute**;   **top**: 50%;

```
  width 110px;
}
```

Figure: Negative margins worked!

That works just fine, but you'd always be limiting yourself to centering only objects with fixed dimensions.

If you wanted to make a slightly bigger (or smaller) centered object, you'd have to recalculate sizes and margins, and then make changes to your CSS. That's too much work, and it wouldn't work at all with dynamically sized elements. Thankfully there is a better, relatively new CSS style called **transform** that can help. The **transform** property allows developers to do all sorts of amazing things like move objects around, rotate them, and simulate three-dimensional movement.

The upside for centering objects is that this new style calculates all these movements based on the object itself. So if we move it 50% to the left using **transform**, the browser looks at the object's width, and then moves it to the left 50% of its own width, not the width of the parent.

The actual style declaration looks like this: **transform: translate(x, y)**— where **x** is replaced by the distance along the x-axis (left is negative, right is positive), and the same for the y-axis (up is negative, down is positive). So, to move our object left and up half its width and height, we'd add the **transform** style like you.

Listing: Moving an object using **transform**.

```
.header-logo {  background-color: #000;  height: 110px;  left: 50%;  position: absolute;  top: 50%;
transform: translate(-50%, -50%);  width: 110px; }
```

Now when you save your work and refresh the browser you'll have a black box in the center of the gray header. It doesn't matter what dimensions you give for either the **.header-logo** or **.header**—you'll always have a vertically and horizontally centered object. To try it out, delete the height and width that we gave the **.header-logo**.

When you save and refresh your browser, the now-smaller box will still be centered vertically and horizontally.

A Real Logo

All right, enough positioning playtime. Let's get back to making this site look good by putting an actual logo in that **.header-logo**. In your project directory, add a new folder called **images**:

$ mkdir images

Now let's put the image into the **header.html**.

Figure: No matter what size the object is, it stays right in the center.

Listing: Replacing the word logo with a logo image.

```
<header class="header">
 <nav>
  <ul class="header-nav">
   <li><a href="/">Home</a></li>
   <li><a href="#">Nav 1</a></li>
   <li><a href="#">Nav 2</a></li>
   <li><a href="#">Nav 3</a></li>
  </ul>
 </nav>
 <a href="/" class="header-logo">
  <img src="/images/logo.png" alt="Learn Enough">
 </a>
</header>
```

Now we are going to make a whole lot of changes to whip this part of the site into shape. As in Section, we aren't going to go through and give a reason why each value is the exact number we chose. Styling a section of a site is a non-linear process at times, and you'll likely need to experiment a lot.

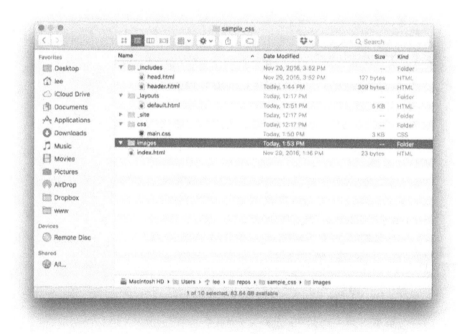

Figure: New images folder in your project directory.

First, we are going to make the header background color black and any text in the header white as follows:

```
.header {   background-color: #000;   color: #fff; }
```

That's also going to require that we change the color of the links, as well as the rollover color for the first-child link in the navigation:

```
.header-nav > li:first-child a:hover {   color: #fff;
```

}

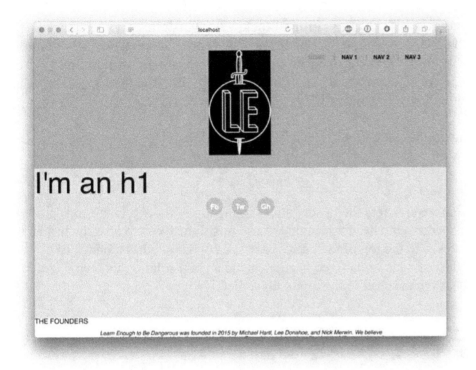

Figure: The initial (sub-optimal) logo placed on the page.

We'll also need to change the background color of our little divider lines so that it is partially transparent white instead of partially transparent black:

border-left: 1px solid rgba(255, 255, 255, 0.3);

Then we are going to move the **.header-logo** into the top left, and shrink the image a bit:

.header-logo { background-color: #000; box-sizing: border-box; display: block; height: 10vh; padding-top: 10px; position: relative; text-align: center; width: 10vh; } .header-logo img { width: 4.3vh; }

We chose **10vh** for the size of the link, and for the image we set the width to be 4.3% of the height of the container (**4.3vh**). We got those values after playing around with different numbers, and settling on this size for a balance of readability while not taking up too much space.

You'll notice that most of the sizing styles are on the link that wraps the image and not on the image itself. The reason we did that was so that if there is a problem downloading the image, or a delay, there is still a nice, big clickable link in the header.

Putting everything together gives us Listing, which includes all the styling for the site header so far.

Listing: Changing up the styling for the header and logo.

/* HEADER STYLES */ **.header** { **background-color**: #000; **color**: #fff; } **.header-logo** { **background-color**: #000; **box-sizing**: **border-box**; **display**: **block**; **height**: 10vh; **padding-top**: 10px; **position**: relative; **text-align**: **center**; **width**: 10vh; }

.header-logo:hover, .header-logo:active { background-color: #ed6e2f; } .header-logo img { width: 4.3vh; } .header-nav { float: right;
 padding: 5.5vh 60px 0 0; } .header-nav > li { display: inline-block; margin-left: 1em; } .header-nav > li ~ li { border-left: 1px solid rgba(255, 255, 255, 0.3); padding-left: 1em; } .header-nav a { color: #fff; font-size: 0.8rem; font-weight: bold; text-decoration: none; text-transform: uppercase; } .header-nav a:hover, .header-nav a:active { color: #ed6e2f; } .header-nav > li:first-child a { color: #ed6e2f; } .header-nav > li:first-child a:hover { color: #fff; }

Save and refresh, and your header should look like Figure. That logo's lookin' sharp!

Fixed Header

You may have noticed the recent design trend where the header sticks to the top of the screen as you scroll down the page. This is called a fixed header—the header is styled to use **position: fixed** to take the header entirely out of the page content and stick it to the top of the user's browser. If your site has a bunch of different sections that your users need to navigate to, a fixed header can be a good solution to keep them from getting annoyed that they always have to scroll to the top to do something new.

Figure: The header, now styled.

The way to implement a fixed header is to change the positioning of the header to **fixed** while specifying a **z-index** for the header. Recall from the beginning of Section that the **z-index** determines whether an element is drawn in front of or behind other elements. We'll want to give our header a large value for **z-index**, which will force the browser to draw the element above other elements (i.e., closer to the user using our stack-of-paper analogy).

The styles to change the positioning value and set a **z-index** are shown in Listing.

Listing: Fixing the header's position means that content will now scroll under it.

.header { background-color: #000; color: #fff; position: fixed; width: 100%; z-index: 20; }

When you check the work in your browser, you'll find that the header is now pinned to the top of the screen, and when you scroll, all the content will scroll underneath.

The resulting black bar at the top looks cool, but what if we were to put a border around the entire page? It could look interesting to have a dark area around the whole site to frame the content. We can arrange for this with the styling shown in Listing.

Listing: Just for fun, let's put a border around the entire site.

```
/* GLOBAL STYLES */ html {
  box-shadow: 0 0 0 30px #000 inset;   padding: 0 30px; }
```

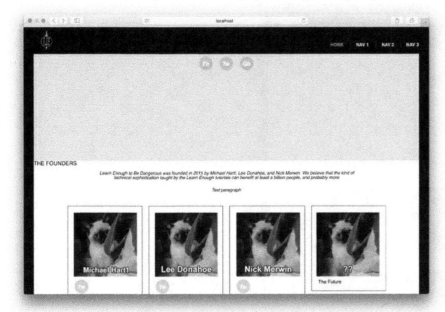

Listing introduces the **box-shadow** style, which is a relatively new CSS style that lets you add drop shadows to HTML elements, and the declaration that we added is a shorthand for **box-shadow: x-axis y-axis blur size color inset**. We aren't going to go any deeper into it, but if you want to play around with box shadows there are a number of sites that let you fiddle with the settings, such as CSSmatic box shadow.

After saving and refreshing, you might have noticed that the logo in the header now looks a little off since it isn't right up in the corner anymore. This is because we increased the padding on the entire site by **30px** for the black border. Let's use a negative value (**-30px**) on the positioning to get it back in place.

Listing: Using a negative value to move the logo back into place.

.header-logo {   **background-color**: #000;   **box-sizing**: **border-box**;   **display**: **block**;   **height**: 10vh;   **left**: -30px;   **padding-top**: 10px;   **position**: **relative**;   **text-align**: **center**;   **width**: 10vh; }
The fixed final header should now look like Figure.

One thing you might have noticed is that after adding fixed positioning to the header, the big h^1 text in the hero is covered. We'll tackle this issue in Section.

Now that we've got the header squared away, let's turn our attention to the other end of the site.

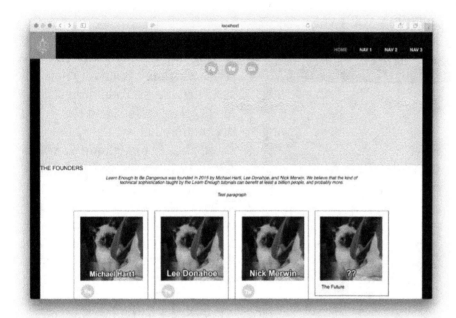

Figure: A completed page header.

A Footer, and Includes in Includes

After creating and styling a site header, a natural next step is to style the page footer. This is the navigational/informational section that can be found at the bottom of a site.

Often, the footer is a partial replication of the navigational elements from the header (just styled in a slightly different way), but many sites add to that a bunch of other content—everything from store locations and hours to additional content links.

Since the footer is found at the end of the page and contains ancillary information, you don't really need to worry about space (there's plenty of room at the bottom!). What we mean by that is that you can think of the footer as extra space, where users aren't required to see everything there. Many sites, such as Amazon, have a lot of content in a giant footer at the bottom of the page.

We'll start by creating a new **footer.html** file inside the **_includes** folder:

$ touch _includes/footer.html

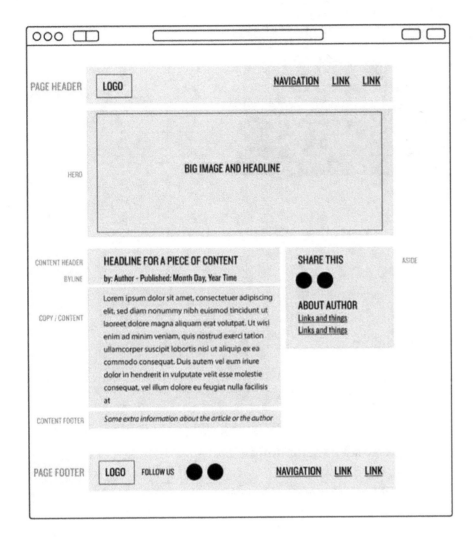

Figure: A refresher on the elements of a typical web page, including a page footer.

Next, we'll add some HTML. We're going to wrap the footer in another HTML5 semantic tag, the **footer** tag. As with the **header** tag, this is a semantic element that works just like a standard **div**, but gives automated site readers (such as web spiders and screen readers for the visually impaired) a better idea of what the purpose is of the content inside. We are also going to add in a logo link similar to the one in the header.

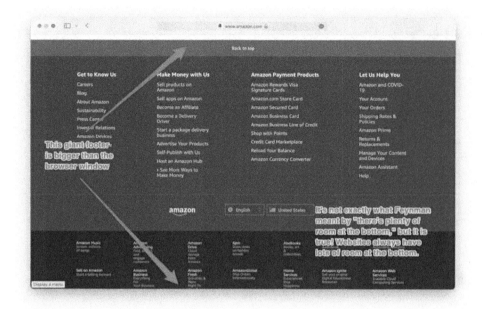

Figure: A giant footer.

Listing: Adding in the basic footer structure.

```
<footer class="footer">
  <a class="footer-logo" href="/">
    <img src="/images/logo.png" alt="Learn Enough"/>
  </a>
  <h3>Learn Enough <span>to Be Dangerous</span></h3>
</footer>
```

To include the footer in the default layout, we'll follow the model from Listing and use Liquid to insert the contents of **footer.html** just before the closing **body** tag in **default.html**.

Listing: Add in the Liquid tag to the default layout.

```
  </p>
    {% include footer.html %}
  </body>
</html>
```

Now let's add some styling as well. We'll give the footer a black background, like the header, and we'll give it some padding. We'll make sure that the content inside is easy to read by using **vh** units, which causes our padding to take up a large portion of the screen:

background-color: #000; padding: 10vh 0 15vh;

We'll also constrain the size of the logo so that it isn't a giant image, and style the **h3** and the span that is inside it (just to add a little design detail to give some of the text a different color). All together the footer styling looks like Listing.

Listing: The initial styles for the footer.

```
/* FOOTER STYLES */ .footer {   background-color: #000;   padding: 10vh 0 15vh;   text-align: center;
} .footer-logo img {   width: 50px; } .footer h3 {   color: #fff;   padding-top: 1.5em;   text-transform:
uppercase; } .footer h3 span {   color: #aaa; }
```

```
/* HERO STYLES */
```

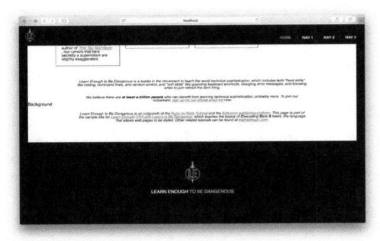

Figure: The first stab at the footer is looking pretty good.

Save and refresh, and the result should appear as in Figure. And it looks... not too bad!

But let's make it a little more useful and also add in the navigational links from the header. You could just copy and paste the HTML from the header, but if you added a new page you'd have to edit your navigation in two spots... we hope the mere suggestion of that is making your programmer's itch flare up again. Since those nav links are always going to be the same in both the header and the footer, we can create a new include to include in includes (thereby fulfilling the promise from Figure—it wasn't (just) a joke!).

We don't want to take the outer **ul** from Listing since it has a **header-nav** class applied to it (well, you could add that in the include, then unstyle all the header styles, and then restyle to fit the footer—but that would be a lot of unnecessary work). So, the content of our new include will just be the lis and the links—in other words, the content that definitely needs to be repeated.

To eliminate repetition in the links, let's create a new file in the **_includes** directory and name it **nav-links.html**:

$ touch _includes/nav-links.html

Then cut the **lis** and links out of the **.header-nav** and paste them into the new include.

Listing: We've cut and pasted in the **lis** and links.

```
<li><a href="/">Home</a></li>
<li><a href="">Nav 1</a></li>
<li><a href="">Nav 2</a></li>
<li><a href="">Nav 3</a></li>
```

We can replace the links in the header file with a Liquid tag, as shown in Listing.

Listing: Updating the header with an include and a second class.

```
<ul class="header-nav nav-links">   {% include nav-links.html %}
</ul>
```

Note that we've also added a **.nav-links** class in Listing so we can add styling to the links that will be shared between the header and footer. Before, we were targeting and styling the links using the class **.header-nav**, but now that the links are going to be in multiple places, that isn't a good name to use to target the styling common to both the header and the footer.

Now that we've factored the nav links into a separate include, let's add them to the navigation section in the footer.

In order to allow footer-specific styling, we'll also add a **footer-nav** class (in analogy with the header's **header-nav** class), as well as the general **nav-links** class added in Listing. The result appears in Listing.

Listing: The new Liquid tag to load the links in the footer.

```
<footer class="footer">
  <a class="footer-logo" href="/">
    <img src="/images/logo.png" alt="Learn Enough"/>
  </a>
  <nav>
    <ul class="footer-nav nav-links">        {% include nav-links.html %}
    </ul>
  </nav>
  <h3>Learn Enough <span>to Be Dangerous</span></h3>
</footer>
```

Now let's add some styling. First, we should move some of the styles that before were defined on **.header-nav a** over to **.nav-links a**, and change the class that is targeting the **:hover** and **:active** states from **.header-nav** to **.navlink**, as in Listing.

Listing: Moving link styling into a new **.nav-links** class.

```
.header-nav a {   color: #fff; } .nav-links a {   font-size: 0.8rem;   font-weight: bold;   text-decoration: none;   text-transform: uppercase; }
.nav-links a:hover, .nav-links a:active {   color: #ed6e2f; }
```

Again, the idea is that we want navigational links to look similar between the header and footer, and then for any changes that are specific to one location or the other by targeting the links using either the **.header-nav** or the **.footer-nav** class.

Finally, we'll add footer-specific styles, as shown in Listing.

Listing: New styling for footer navigation and links.

```
.footer-nav li {   display: inline-block;   margin: 2em 1em 0; }
.footer-nav a {
```

```
    color: #ccc;
}
```

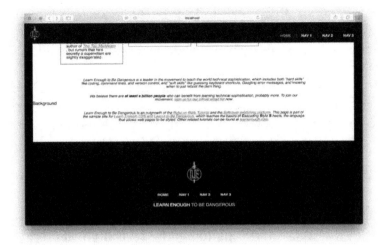

Figure: Styled header and footer with nav links from an include.

When you save and refresh, you'll have a nice header and footer, both pulling their navigational links from the same place.

If you want to double-check and sync up all your styles, Listing has the current state of the CSS declarations for the site.

Listing: The full header and footer styles.

html, body, div, span, applet, object, iframe, h1, h2, h3, h4, h5, h6, p, blockquote, pre, a, abbr, acronym, address, big, cite, code, del, dfn, em, img, ins, kbd, q, s, samp, small, strike, strong, sub, sup, tt, var, b, u, i, center, dl, dt, dd, ol, ul, li, fieldset, form, label, legend, table, caption, tbody, tfoot, thead, tr, th, td, article, aside, canvas, details, embed, figure, figcaption, footer, header, hgroup, menu, nav, output, ruby, section, summary, time, mark, audio, video { margin: 0; padding: 0; border: 0; **font: inherit;**
vertical-align: baseline;
} /* HTML5 display-role reset for older browsers */ **article, aside, details, figcaption, figure, footer, header, hgroup, menu, nav, section {** display: block; **} body {** line-height: 1; **} blockquote, q {** **quotes: none; } blockquote:before, blockquote:after, q:before, q:after {** content: ''; content: none; **}** **table {** border-collapse: collapse; border-spacing: 0; **} strong, b {** font-weight: bold; **} em, i {** font-**style: italic; } a img {** border: none; **}**
/* END RESET*/
/* GLOBAL STYLES */ **html {**
  box-shadow: 0 0 0 30px #000 inset; padding: 0 30px; **} body {** font-family: helvetica, arial, sans; **} h1** **{** font-size: 7vw; margin-top: 0; **} a {** color: #f00; **} h2 ~ p {** font-size: 0.8em; font-style: italic; margin: 1em auto 0; max-width: 70%; text-align: center; **}**
/* HEADER STYLES */ **.header {** background-color: #000; color: #fff; position: fixed; width: 100%; z-index: 20; **} .header-logo {** background-color: #000; box-sizing: border-box; display: **block;**
height: 10vh; left: -30px; padding-top: 10px; position: relative; text-align: center; width: 10vh; **}** **.header-logo:hover, .header-logo:active {** background-color: #ed6e2f; **} .header-logo img {** width: 4.3vh; **} .header-nav {** float: right; padding: 5.5vh 60px 0 0; **} .header-nav > li {** display: inline-**block; margin-left: 1em; } .header-nav > li ~ li {** border-left: 1px solid rgba(255, 255, 255, 0.3);

padding-left: 1em; } .header-nav a {   color: #fff; } .nav-links a {   font-size: 0.8rem;   font-weight: bold;   text-decoration: none;   text-transform: uppercase; }
.nav-links a:hover, .nav-links a:active {   color: #ed6e2f; } .header-nav > li:first-child a {   color: #ed6e2f; } .header-nav > li:first-child a:hover {   color: #fff; }
/* FOOTER STYLES */ .footer {   background-color: #000;   padding: 10vh 0 15vh;   text-align: center; } .footer-logo img {   width: 50px; } .footer h3 {   color: #fff;   padding-top: 1.5em;   text-transform: uppercase; } .footer h3 span {   color: #aaa; } .footer-nav li {   display: inline-block;   margin: 2em 1em 0; }
.footer-nav a {
color: #ccc;
}
/* HERO STYLES */ .full-hero {   background-color: #c7dbfc;   height: 50vh; }
/* SOCIAL STYLES */ .social-list {   list-style: none;   padding: 0;   text-align: center; } .social-link {   background: rgba(150, 150, 150, 0.5);   border-radius: 99px;   box-sizing: border-box;   color: #fff;   display: inline-block;   font-family: helvetica, arial, sans;   font-size: 1rem;   font-weight: bold;   height: 2.5em;   line-height: 1;   padding-top: 0.85em;   text-align: center;   text-decoration: none;   vertical-align: middle;   width: 2.5em; } .social-list > li {   display: inline-block;   margin: 0 0.5em; }
/* BIO STYLES */ .bio-wrapper {   font-size: 24px;   margin: auto;   max-width: 960px;   overflow: hidden; } .bio-box {   border: 1px solid black;   box-sizing: border-box;   float: left;   font-size: 1rem;   margin: 40px 1% 0;   padding: 2%;   width: 23%; } .bio-box h3 {   color: #fff;   font-size: 1.5em;   margin: -40px 0 1em;   text-align: center; } .bio-box img {   width: 100%; } .bio-box .social-link {   display: block;   margin: 2em 0 1em; } .bio-copy {   font-size: 1em;
} .bio-copy a {   color: green; }

Finally, in case you haven't been doing your own Git commits and deploys, now would be a good time to do one:

$ git add -A
$ git commit -m "Finish initial layout"

You'll discover that GitHub Pages is fully Jekyll-aware, and automatically generates and displays the site based on the contents of the repository—free static site hosting!

Conclusion:

Understanding the intricacies of the **CSS box model** and layout strategies is foundational to web development. These concepts govern how elements behave, interact, and appear on a webpage. As web design continues to evolve, these principles remain a cornerstone for creating professional, user-friendly interfaces. Let's revisit and contextualize the key topics covered while offering insights into their practical applications and forward-looking importance.

The Box Model: A Cornerstone of CSS

The box model is the lens through which every HTML element is styled and structured. By manipulating its components—**content, padding, border, and margin**—developers can fine-tune spacing, alignment, and element boundaries.

Inline vs. Block: Recognizing the behaviour of inline and block elements is crucial for structuring content. Inline elements integrate seamlessly into text flows, while block elements define distinct sections of the layout. This distinction allows developers to organize content hierarchically, ensuring clarity and accessibility.

Padding and Margins: Beyond aesthetics, proper padding and margins influence usability. For example, adequate padding enhances readability by preventing text from crowding borders, while strategic margins establish logical visual separation between sections.

Borders: More than just decoration, borders can emphasize key elements like buttons or alerts, drawing user attention where it's needed most.

The box model equips developers with the tools to create visually appealing and functional designs, adaptable to varying content and user needs.

Floats and Overflow: Legacy and Modern Relevance

While the introduction of **Flexbox** and **CSS Grid** has revolutionized layouts, floats remain a vital technique in specific use cases. They are especially relevant in scenarios such as:

Wrapping text around images.

Implementing lightweight layouts when advanced techniques are unnecessary.

The **overflow** property complements floats, allowing developers to control how content behaves when it exceeds its container. These properties, when combined, provide flexibility in content organization.

Inline-Block and Advanced Box Techniques

The inline-block display bridges the gap between inline and block elements, offering more layout options while maintaining predictable flow. Meanwhile, mastering advanced box techniques like negative margins, border-radius, and background styling opens up creative possibilities. These skills enable developers to craft unique interfaces that stand out in a competitive digital landscape.

Laying It All Out: The Power of CSS Layouts

CSS layouts transform static content into dynamic, responsive web pages. Modern techniques like **Flexbox** and **Grid** have simplified complex layouts, making them accessible to developers at all levels.

Jekyll and Dynamic Site Management

For static site generators like Jekyll, layout principles extend beyond CSS. By separating content, design, and functionality, developers can create scalable, maintainable sites. Features like:

Reusable Layouts: Ensure consistent structure across pages.
Includes: Save time by centralizing frequently used components like headers and footers.
Jekyll's integration with modern CSS frameworks makes it a robust choice for building blogs, portfolios, and small business sites.

CSS Resets and Advanced Selectors: Control and Consistency

CSS resets provide a clean slate, ensuring cross-browser compatibility. Combined with **advanced selectors**, developers can apply precise styling rules to achieve polished designs:

Attribute Selectors: Enable dynamic styling based on HTML attributes.
Pseudo-Classes and Elements: Add interactivity and design elements like hover effects or decorative elements.

These tools allow for creative freedom while maintaining consistent behaviour across devices and browsers.

Positioning and Fixed Elements: Enhancing User Experience

Positioning strategies like absolute, fixed, and sticky unlock advanced layout capabilities. For example:

Fixed Headers: Keep navigation accessible during scrolling, enhancing usability on content-heavy pages.
Sticky Elements: Provide dynamic behaviour, like keeping a sidebar in view until a certain scroll threshold. These techniques elevate user experience, especially on mobile devices, where space and interaction are constrained.

Footers and Consistency with Includes

Footers often serve as the anchor of a webpage, containing critical links, copyright information, or contact details. By using **includes**, developers can maintain uniformity across all pages, ensuring users have a seamless experience navigating the site.

Practical Applications and Best Practices

To effectively apply these concepts, consider the following practices:

Start with a Solid Foundation: Use CSS resets to create a uniform starting point.
Plan Layouts Thoughtfully: Define the structure before applying styles to prevent rework.
Prioritize Responsiveness: Use media queries and CSS Grid to adapt designs for various screen sizes.
Optimize Performance: Minimize reflows and repaints by grouping layout and style changes.
Focus on Accessibility: Ensure that elements are visually distinct and keyboard navigable.

The Future of Layouts: What Lies Ahead?

CSS is an ever-evolving language, with new features and methodologies continually emerging. Developers should stay informed about:

Subgrid: Expanding the capabilities of CSS Grid for nested layouts.
Container Queries: A game-changer for responsive design, allowing styles to adapt based on parent container sizes.
Custom Properties: Enhancing reusability and maintainability of styles.
These advancements promise to simplify workflows and enable more creative freedom in web design.

Final Thoughts

The journey through the box model and layout principles in HTML/CSS 2025 underscores their pivotal role in web development. By mastering these techniques, developers gain the ability to create visually appealing, user-friendly, and responsive designs. From basic spacing adjustments to advanced layout strategies, these skills empower developers to craft experiences that delight users and stand the test of time. As CSS continues to evolve, embracing its future-ready features will ensure developers remain at the forefront of modern web design.

This conclusion encapsulates the importance of the discussed topics while inspiring developers to continue learning and experimenting with CSS layouts.

6. CSS Selectors and Tools

Introduction

CSS Selectors: The Basics

CSS selectors are at the heart of styling HTML elements. They define the rules for targeting specific elements in a document, allowing developers to apply styles precisely. The basic selectors include:

Element Selector

The element selector targets all HTML elements of a specific type. For example:

```
h1 {
  color: blue;
}
```
This rule will style all <h1> elements in the document with a blue color.

ID Selector

The ID selector targets a single, unique element identified by its id attribute. IDs should be unique within a document. Syntax uses the # symbol:

```
#header {
  background-color: gray;
}
```
This applies a gray background to the element with id="header".

Class Selector

The class selector targets all elements with a specific class attribute. Multiple elements can share a class. The syntax uses a . symbol:

```
.card {
  border: 1px solid black;
  padding: 10px;
}
```
This applies the styles to all elements with class="card".

Introduction to Chrome Inspector

The Chrome Inspector (also known as DevTools) is an essential tool for developers working with CSS and HTML. It allows you to:

Google Chrome Inspection Basics

Open DevTools:

Right-click on any web page element and select **Inspect**.

Use Ctrl + Shift + I (Windows/Linux) or Cmd + Option + I (Mac).

Inspect Elements:

Hover over elements in the Elements pane to see their dimensions, margins, padding, and borders.
Click an element to view its CSS rules, styles, and computed properties in the Styles tab.

Live Editing:

Modify HTML or CSS directly in the DevTools to preview changes in real time.
Use the Console to experiment with JavaScript and dynamically manipulate styles.

Debugging Tools:

Use the **Sources** tab to debug JavaScript and CSS.
Identify performance bottlenecks with the **Performance** tab.

More Advanced Selectors

Advanced selectors provide greater flexibility and power when targeting elements.

Asterisk Selector

The asterisk * selector targets all elements:

```
* {
  margin: 0;
  padding: 0;
}
```
This resets margins and padding for all elements in the document.

Descendant Selector

The descendant selector targets elements nested within a parent element:

```
div p {
  font-size: 16px;
}
```
This applies the rule to all <p> elements inside <div> elements.

Adjacent Sibling Selector

The adjacent sibling selector (+) targets an element that is immediately preceded by another element:

```
h1 + p {
  font-style: italic;
}
```
This styles a <p> element only if it directly follows an <h1>.

Attribute Selector

Attribute selectors target elements based on their attributes:

```css
a[href] {
  text-decoration: none;
}
```

This removes the underline from all links with an href attribute.

Nth-of-Type Selector

The nth-of-type selector targets specific elements based on their index:

```css
li:nth-of-type(2) {
  color: red;
}
```

This makes the second <li> element in each list red.

Specificity and the Cascade

Understanding specificity and the cascade is critical to mastering CSS. Specificity determines which rules are applied when multiple selectors target the same element, while the cascade resolves conflicts between rules.

Inheritance

Certain CSS properties, such as color and font-family, are inherited by default. For example:

```css
body {
  font-family: Arial, sans-serif;
  color: black;
}
```

All text within the body inherits these styles unless overridden.

Specificity

Specificity is calculated based on the types of selectors:

Inline styles (e.g., style="color: red;") have the highest specificity.
ID selectors (e.g., #header) are more specific than class selectors.
Class, attribute, and pseudo-class selectors (e.g., .card, [href], :hover) have medium specificity.
Element selectors (e.g., p, h1) are the least specific.

Example:
```css
/* Less specific */
p {
  color: green;
}
```

```
/* More specific */
.card p {
  color: blue;
}
```

In this case, <p> elements within .card will be blue.

Assignment

When multiple rules have the same specificity, the rule that appears later in the stylesheet takes precedence:

```
h1 {
  color: red;
}
h1 {
  color: blue;
}
```

Here, <h1> elements will be blue.

By mastering these concepts and tools, developers can create precise, maintainable, and efficient CSS for any project. Pairing selectors with the Chrome Inspector ensures accuracy and speeds up the development process.

Let's begin,

Element, Id & Class

```
selector {
  property: value;
}
```

We are going to be focusing on three CSS selectors; element, Id, and class. There are also more options for selecting elements we are going to learn, we will see the different selectors that we can make use of, and build a simple to-do list together.

Make a new file, save the file as todolist.HTML, and then lay the HTML structure, on the <title> tag name it "todo list" inside the <body> tag type <h1> element and then insert also "todo list" there, followed by a <ul> and <li> but in each <li> type some text and a little checkbox.

If you still remember how to do checkbox, it is input type equals checkbox, and then you have your text which is **"Purchase Gold"**, then duplicate the <li> and rename it as **"Buy Groceries"** and the third one as **"Get This Guide"**

```
<> todolist.html  ✕

C: > Users > Unlimited > Documents > HTML > <> todolist.html > ⊘ html
  1    <!DOCTYPE html>
  2    <html>
  3    <head>
  4        <title>Todo List</title>
  5    </head>
  6    <body>
  7    <h1>Todo List</h1>
  8    <ul>
  9        <li>
 10            <input type="checkbox">
 11            Purchase Gold
 12        </li>
 13        <li>
 14            <input type="checkbox">
 15            Buy Groceries
 16        </li>
 17        <li>
 18            <input type="checkbox">
 19            Get This Guide
 20        </li>
 21    </ul>
 22    </body>
 23    </html>
```

So, if you open the above HTML file in your browser, you are going to see a blank and not styled version of your list item.

The next thing is to connect a stylesheet. To do that, connect the non-existing stylesheet and create the stylesheet. Some people would call this an error-driven development, where we write something that we know won't work which is the link of the uncreated stylesheet, and then we make it work afterward. Name it **todo.css** in-between your <head> tag

```
<head>
    <title>Todo List</title>
    <link href="todo.css" type="text/css" rel="stylesheet">
</head>
```

Create the "todo.css" file, make sure both documents are saved in the same folder. And just to make sure that it is connected, do something like body background orange

```
<> todolist.html ●      # todo.css   ✕

C: > Users > Unlimited > Documents > HTML > # todo.css > ❖ body
  1    body {
  2    |     background: ▢ orange;      ⬅
  3    }
```

If you refresh your browser, you will get the orange background as a sign that your stylesheet is properly connected with your HTML file

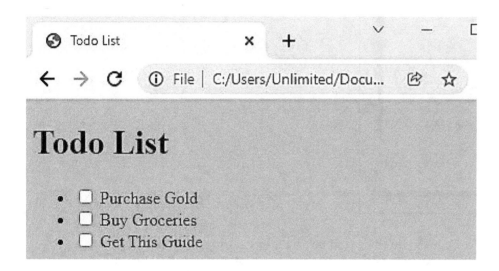

Element Selector

Element selector is the type of tags as you can specify <div> or <p> or <body> and then it will select all corresponding elements in all instances that match

```
<div>
    <p>You say yes</p>
    <p>I say no</p>
</div>

<div>
    <p>You say goodbye</p>
    <p>I say hello </p>
</div>
```

```
div{
    background: purple;
}

p {
    color: yellow;
}
```

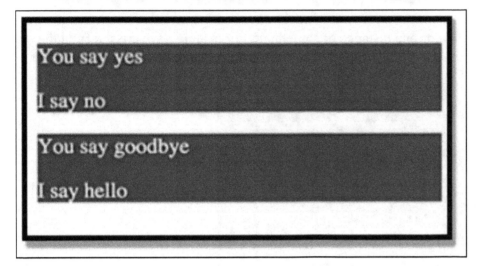

In the above instance, we have two <div> and each <div> has two <p>, so set all div's to background purple, to get two purple divs. Likewise, set all paragraphs tag to be color yellow, to get four yellow paragraphs.

Back to our **todo list**, select the <body>, do the same for all <li> and give them a border of 2px solid red

```
<> todolist.html          # todo.css    X

C: > Users > Unlimited > Documents > HTML > # todo.css > ↳ li
1     li {
2     |     border: 2px solid ▢red;
3     }
```

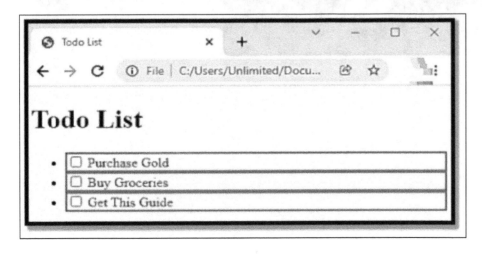

Id Selector

Next, single out one <li> or one <h1> or one instance of something. For example, we are selecting the third <li> and turning it yellow by altering the HTML slightly and then using a hook that we include into our HTML tag, in our CSS we refer back to it and turn it yellow.

```
<div>
   <p>You say yes</p>
   <p>I say no</p>
</div>

<div>
   <p>You say goodbye</p>
   <p id="special">I say hello </p>
</div>
```

The first step is to add a hook which is called Id, and the Id works in such a way that you can add it as an attribute to any element Id equals, and then in quotes, any name that you want. You can refer to that later by writing hash sign and then the name of the Id and that will select the one element that matches that Id name

```
div{
   background: purple;
}

#special {
   color: yellow;
}
```

In return below is the outcome.

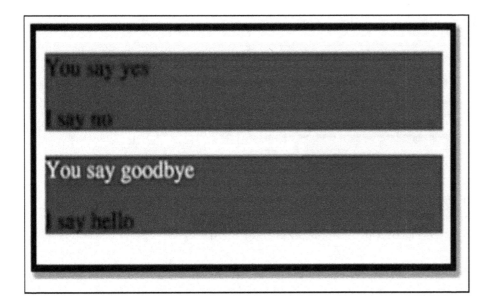

So back to our **"to-do list"**, let's apply the same to our **"to-do list"**. Let's say that we want **"get this guide"** <li> list item to look slightly different, what you can type within or inside the opening tag of the <li> at the front and type the name of Id to be given to it like unique (this can be any name at all).

It is a way to target one individual element and one note about an Id, it can only appear on a page one time, trying to duplicate it on other tags becomes invalid HTML. So, it is always supposed to be a one time on a page, it is purely used to fetch a single element out, you can, however, have multiple Id's on a page as long as they don't appear more than once. let's go with the unique Id and give it a background-color

```
<li id="unique">   ⬅
    <input type="checkbox">
    Get This Guide
</li>
```

Go to your CSS file and write unique, start the styling Id with a hashtag, followed by the name of the Id which is linked to an element, in our case, it is our <li> that has the name "unique".

This informs CSS that you mean the Id, simply write a CSS inside the **#unique** curly brace inside it, do a background color, and make it yellow. Save the file.

```
5    #unique {
6        background-color: ■ yellow;
7    }
```

Refresh your browser, as you can see, only the specified <li> which is the last <li> **"get this guide"** receive the effect as declared. As you can see the stated <li> has taken the declared effect of the yellow background

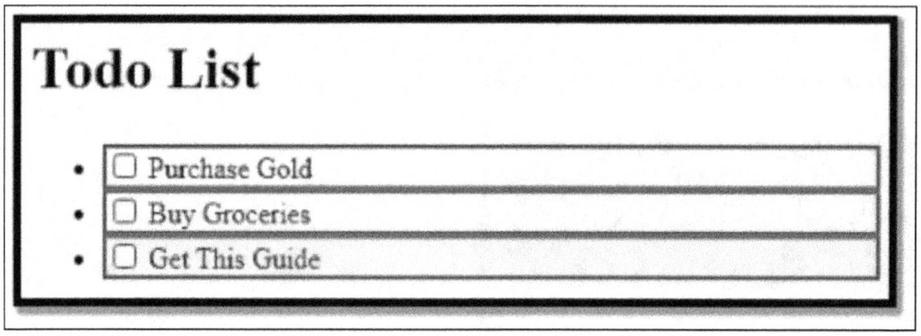

Todo List

- ☐ Purchase Gold
- ☐ Buy Groceries
- ☐ Get This Guide

There are a few things I want to point out, the first is that the element code for the border is still working which turns all <li> and gives them a red border including the Id selector that we applied yellow background into, and then we are adding on top of that border by including a yellow background only to the last <li> base on the hook that we added and called in Id inside our HTML <li>.

To sum up, an Id as a way to single out an element, you can only use an Id once per page but we can have as many Id as we want on a page, Id's are great to single out an individual element but oftentimes we want to have multiple elements that look similar but we don't want all <li> for instance.

Class Selector

To style half of the <li> one way and half of them another way, we could use a class to achieve that. Class works like an Id, except it is called a class and we can apply it to any number of an element on a page. As you can see below, we are applying a class called the "highlight" to the first paragraph and the third paragraph

```html
<div>
   <p class="highlight">You say yes</p>
   <p>I say no</p>
</div>

<div>
   <p class="highlight">You say goodbye</p>
   <p>I say hello </p>
</div>
```

And then we refer to it in our CSS with a dot instead of a hash sign. So, again to contrast that from the previous selected Id, use the "hash sign" to select but in the class selector we use "dot sign", otherwise they work the same way

```css
div{
   background: purple;
}


.highlight {
   background: yellow;
}
```

As you can see, our duplicated class appears effectively in the applied area

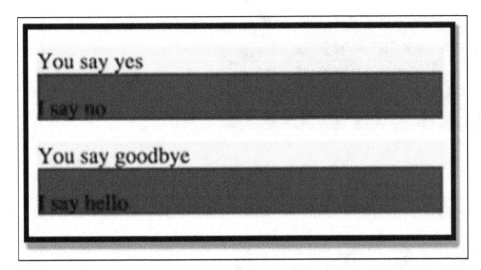

Now, let's apply the same example to our **"to-do list"** as a way of practicalizing it. Add a class into your HTML, this time, we are using the first two <li> left to practicalize this by strikethrough, so there will be a lint through the text, so when we look at "purchase gold" and **"buy groceries"** there should be a strike through going through the text.

Remember that the third <li> won't be included since it has an Id attribute. On the first two <li> add a class and this time, the class element will be named as "settled", save it

```
10        <li class="settled">  ⬅
11            <input type="checkbox">
12            Purchase Gold
13        </li>
14        <li class="settled">  ⬅
15            <input type="checkbox">
16            Buy Groceries
17        </li>
18        <li id="unique">
19            <input type="checkbox">
20            Get This Guide
21        </li>
```

If you refresh the browser and nothing happens, that's because you don't have any style yet on the first two elements. Go to CSS and write dot followed by the name of the class which is settled inside curly brace and pass the style inside. Introduce a new style of colored text-decoration, and text-decoration is a way to add a line through but there are a few things that you can do, you can add an underline, you can add a wavy underline, line-through, and then overlined which is a line through except it is placed on the top

```
.settled {
    text-decoration: line-through;
}
```

Refresh your browser and see the result.

One quick note on the HTML file, since the first two items have been strikethrough, you can also decide to make the checkbox ticked whenever the page load or the browser refreshes

```
<li class="settled">
    <input type="checkbox" checked>
    Purchase Gold
</li>
<li class="settled">
    <input type="checkbox" checked>
    Buy Groceries
</li>
<li id="unique">
    <input type="checkbox">
    Get This Guide
</li>
```

The line through or strikethrough items have been ticked, the checked effect is not from CSS but it is important just to know that you can do that.

We have the element selector to select all of a given element all <li>, <div>, <p>, etc. We have the Id selector which will select the one element with the matching Id and we always need to use a hash sign or symbol. And then lastly, we have the class selector which is very similar to the Id selector except that we select the class name as many times as we want on a given page, unlike an Id which is only once.

Introduction To Chrome Inspector

Google Chrome Inspection

In this section, we are going to be highlighting some of the developer tools that Google Chrome gives us to work with HTML and CSS. For easy understanding, we are going to use our **"todo list"**

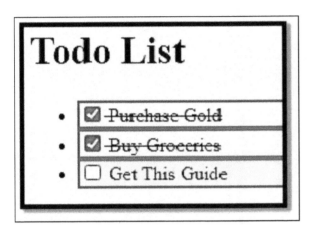

Highlight two things, first, **"view page source"** just like we did with the HTML, right-click on any page, let us make use of our **"todo list".** Once you right-click on the webpage, multiple options will be shown, select **"view page source"**

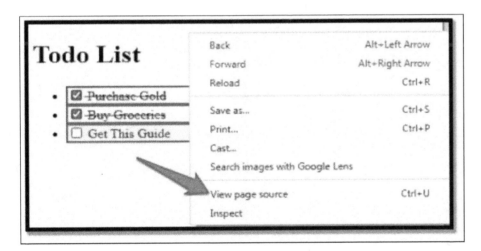

"View page source" will redirect you to the HTML codes as shown below.

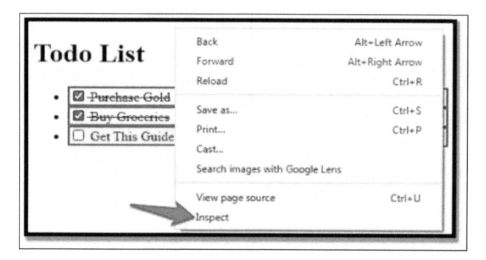

```
Line wrap □
 1  <!DOCTYPE html>
 2  <html>
 3  <head>
 4      <title>Todo List</title>
 5      <link href="todo.css" type="text/css" rel="stylesheet">
 6  </head>
 7  <body>
 8   <h1>Todo List</h1>
 9   <ul>
10      <li class="settled">
11          <input type="checkbox" checked>
12          Purchase Gold
13      </li>
14      <li class="settled">
15          <input type="checkbox" checked>
16          Buy Groceries
17      </li>
18      <li id="unique">
19          <input type="checkbox">
20          Get This Guide
21      </li>
22   </ul>
23  </body>
24  </html>
```

We can't change the codes but you can right-click on inspect element

To launch the element inspector, to get a new view. You will learn about all of these soon. For now, we are just starting at this **element's tab**. So, what this is, it is actually a nice interactive representation of all of HTML elements, we have our **<doctype>, <HTML>, <head>, <title>, <body>,** and so on

You will notice some things if you hover over these elements. For example, hover on h1 from the **elements tab** it will highlight the **"todo list"** which is inside your h1 tag, and also a little box indicating the hovering element which is <h1> element that was hovered on.

As long as you keep on collapsing the little arrow icon, more embedded elements will be shown

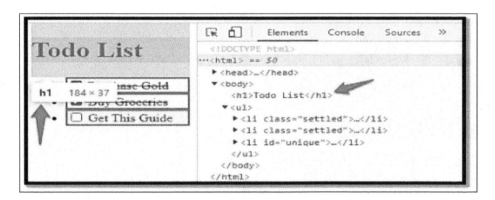

What you should focus on is the CSS style tab below the elements tab, it can be located at the bottom of any angle of the browser the mean thing is to locate it.

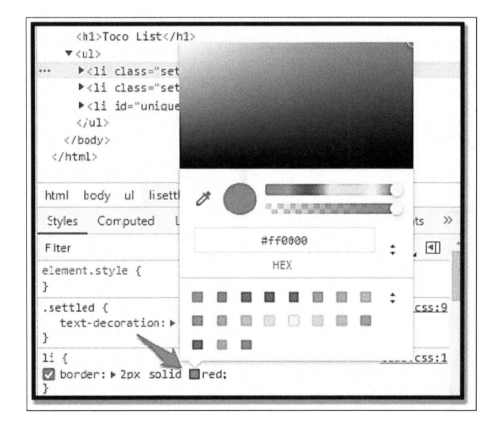

```
    ▶ <li class="settled">...</li> == $0
    ▶ <li class="settled">...</li>
    ▶ <li id="unique">...</li>
   </ul>
  </body>
 </html>
```

html   body   ul   li.settled

| Styles | Computed | Layout | Event Listeners | DOM Breakpoints | » |

Filter   :hov   .cls   +   ◁

```
element.style {
}
```

.settled {   todo.css:9
    text-decoration: ▶ line-through;
}

li {   todo.css:1
    border: ▶ 2px solid ■red;
}

li {   user agent stylesheet

Note: Any area you click on the styles for that selected element, it will be shown to you for inspiration, if need be, and temporary changes can be made, if need be, as said earlier, this is just to debug.

We can click on any tags or elements for adjustment which will be effective in as much that the page is not refreshed or reloaded, as you can see, the color of a border was selected which popup multiple colors selections

```
    <h1>Toco List</h1>
  ▼ <ul>
    ▶ <li class="set
    ▶ <li class="set
    ▶ <li id="unique
   </ul>
  </body>
 </html>
```

html   body   ul   li settl

| Styles | Computed | L | ts   »

Filter   ◁

```
element.style {
}
```

.settled {   css:9
    text-decoration: ▶
}

li {   css:1
☑ border: ▶ 2px solid ■red;
}

#ff0000
HEX

Don't forget that the changes don't change the original file at all, this is only in the browser as soon as you refresh this page or close the window the changes go away.

So, this is useful in two different ways, first is to work on your code or page and test things out and see what happens when you change any elements, and the other useful thing is looking at someone else code.

In summary, we just want to demonstrate that you can open inspector in google chrome, and you can view HTML and CSS, and not only can you view it but you can manipulate it. You can interact with it; you can try changing things and you can do that on your site or you can do that on anyone else site. And so, it is useful when you want to replicate somebody's design where you want to replicate an effect.

More Advanced Selectors

In this section, we are going to discuss other ways of selecting elements aside from the three main ones that we have seen so far. And just to recap those three are the element selector, the class selector, and the Id selector. Element selector will look like **<li>, <div>, <p>,** etc. And class will look like **.unique, .img, .table,** etc. While Id selector will look like **#unique, #img, # table, etc.** And whatever we put inside will target an Id or a class or all elements of a type.

In this chapter, we will be focusing on five of them which. To begin, create an HTML file name **demo.HTML** as shown below.

```
        <link rel='stylesheet' type='text/css' href='selectors.css'>
    </head>
    <body>
    <h1>Selector Demo</h1>
    <a href="https://www.google.com">Click Me For Google</a>
        <ul>
            <li>Apples</li>
            <li>Oranges</li>
            <li>Bananas</li>
        </ul>

    <h4>Popular Sites</h4>
        <ul>
            <li>Carrots</li>
            <li>Peas</li>
            <li>Asparagus</li>
        </ul>

    <h4>Popular Sites</h4>
        <ul>
            <li>
                <a href="https://www.google.com">Google</a>
            </li>
            <li>
                <a href="https://www.facebook.com">Facebook</a>
            </li>
            <li>
                <a href="https://www.amazon.com">Amazon</a>
            </li>
        </ul>
    </body>
```

Here is the reflection of the above codes. this is some basic HTML where we have <h1> as **"selector demo"** below it is a link tag that goes to google followed by a URL with three <li> tags, then we have an

<h4> as **"popular sites"** with another <ul> with three <li>, and then another <h4> with three <li> and each has a link element, the first one also goes to **"Google",** the second one goes to **"Facebook"** and the last one goes to **"Amazon"**

Asterisk selector

So, we have a simple hypertext markup and then we have a stylesheet included called selectors.css, in here, fill out your CSS, and the very first one we are going to discuss is called the asterisk selector, it will select everything on the page. This is not something you should do often, but it looks like this

And then whatever you do, it will apply to every single element. Let's make use of border as an example, border 1px solid light grey

```
C: > Users > Unlimited > Documents > HTML > # selectors.css > ❖ *
1 ∨ * {
2        border: 1px solid ■ lightgray;
3    }
```

And you can see, every single element on the page, the body, h1, h4, every link, ul, li, all get a border around it. This isn't something you need to do a lot but you will see it occasionally.

Descendant Selector

The next one is the descendant's selector and this one you will use and see all the time, the descendant selector takes two or more tag names or two or more selectors and chains them together.

For example, if we want to select all of the anchor <a> tags that are inside of an <li> only the anchor <a> tag inside of an <li> not the anchor <a> tag outside of an <li>. We are going to be selecting all the anchor tag that are descendants of an <li>.

To do that, the syntax looks like <li> space then an anchor <a> tag

This will select everything that is a <a> tag inside of an <li> and you can keep going with this if you had more to also rewrite the above-illustrated code like the one below. Every anchor tag that is inside of a <li> is

also inside of a <ul> which is what we have in our HTML but that is redundant in our case

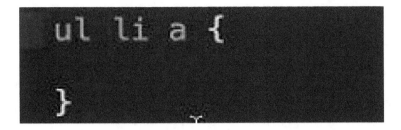

And we could also say every anchor tag or everything the class **".hello"** inside of a <li> but we don't have any markup that matches that

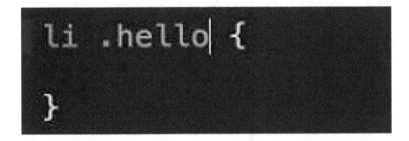

Every anchor tag inside of an <li>, and let just give it a color of red, then save it

```
4
5    li a{
6    |    color: ■red;
7    }
```

As you can see, once you refresh your browser or reload it, the effect will automatically take place, those three anchor tags are now red while the one outside of <li> is unchanged.

Adjacent selector

The adjacent selector allows you to select elements that come after other elements which are not nested inside like a <li> nested inside a <ul>, it allows us to select a sibling.

Let's select all <ul> that come after an <h4> and we mean the same level not indented not inside the <h4> but directly after just as a sibling on the same level of an <h4>, so that is called the adjacent selector and it

looks like this

```
h4 + ul {

}
```

Without the plus sign, this would be all our <ul> inside a <h4> but with a plus sign, it indicates that we are calling a separate selector together not nested. Let's see our it works, we are going to be adding a border 4px solid red, and we should see these, the two <ul> after all the <h4> elements that are adjacent, they come after the <h4> on the same level having a red border

Attributes

The attribute selector is a way to select elements based on any attribute, in our case we are going to do a selection **href** attribute, we are going to check it out by turning all the links to Google where **href** is google.com, and also going to make them one color but you could also use this to select all images of a particular source or all inputs of a particular type like all checkboxes or all password field or something similar.

For the syntax, type anchor tag and then square braces, and inside type the attribute that we are looking for as shown in the illustration below, **href** equals google.com which will select every anchor tag

```
a[href="http://www.google.com"] {

}
```

Give it a color, let's give it a background blue

```
13    a[href="https://www.google.com"] {
14        background-color: ■yellow;
15    }
```

As you can see, the two links that are carrying Google URL has been identified with a yellow background color but the other two links don't go to Google, they go to Facebook and Amazon so they are unchanged

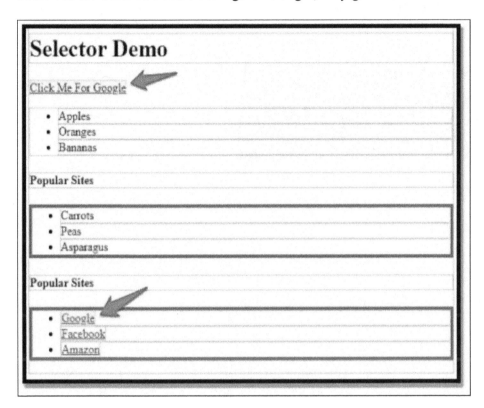

You will see attribute selector a lot or will have an input type that equals text if you want it to style all text input differently, or if you want it to style all checkboxes one way because all inputs even though there are so many different inputs color, to color inputs and file pickers, password, email, submit button, etc. They are all input tags. Simply selecting by input is going to give you all different types of inputs.

```
input[type="text"] {
    background: blue;
}
```

```
input[type="checkbox"] {
    background: blue;
}
```

Nth of type

Nth of type take a number like three or five, and then it selects every end of a specific element, so if you want to select every 5th <div>, or every second <li>, or the tenth paragraph on a page, you can use nth of type.

In this case, if you want to select the final <ul> and do something to the final URL and the third one. Let's say you want to give it a different border or different background, select <ul> colon followed by the nth of type bracket inside the parenthesis, enter a number like three, then type background, and give it obvious background like light green

```
17    ul:nth-of-type(3) {
18    |      background-color:  lightgreen;
19    }
```

Only the third <ul> turned light green.

This is useful if you want to select something down the page.

Specificity And the Cascade

In this section, we will be discussing inheritance and specificity.

Inheritance

We have a simple HTML file below that has a single <ul> with four <li> inside, and we are going to write our style in a <style> tag, we will be working with internal CSS but it is always better to do this in an external stylesheet

```
1    <!DOCTYPE html>
2    <html>
3    <head>
4    |      <title>Specificity</title>
5    </head>
6    <body>
7    <ul>
8          <li>John</li>
9          <li>Paul</li>
10         <li>George</li>
11         <li>Ringo</li>
12    </ul>
13    </body>
14    </html>
```

So, we are going to style the <ul> and give it a color of purple

```
1    <!DOCTYPE html>
2    <html>
3    <head>
4        <title>Specificity</title>
5        <style type="text/css">
6            ul {
7                color: ☐purple;
8            }
9        </style>
10   </head>
11   <body>
12   <ul>
13       <li>John</li>
14       <li>Paul</li>
15       <li>George</li>
16       <li>Ringo</li>
17   </ul>
18   </body>
19   </html>
```

And when we do that, you will see that when we refresh the <li> become purple. So, what happened there? You know that we styled the <ul> and the <li> was indirectly changed and it inherited that color from the parent element

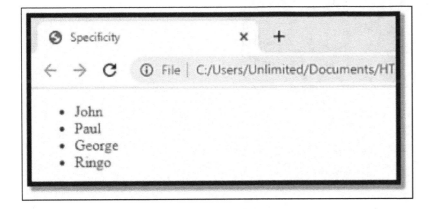

Another example of that is by adding a paragraph above the <ul> that means it is not inside the <ul> tag

```
1    <body>
2    <p>Hello World!!!</p>
3    <ul>
4        <li>John</li>
5        <li>Paul</li>
6        <li>George</li>
7        <li>Ringo</li>
```

The <p> tag turns out to be black which is text default color on a browser

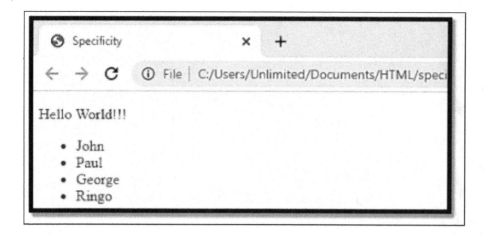

Let's clear all our internal stylesheet codes and type body curly brace color red semicolon

```
1    <!DOCTYPE html>
2    <html>
3    <head>
4        <title>Specificity</title>
5        <style type="text/css">
6            body {
7                color: ■red;
8            }
9        </style>
10   </head>
```

As you can see, everything is now red

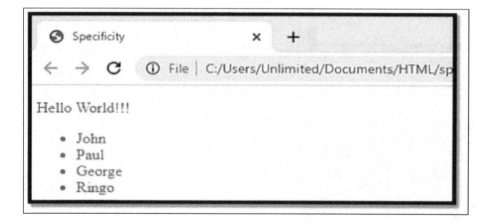

So, this is demonstrating the concept of inheritance, where if we set a property on a parent element, it can also affect a child element. So, if you want it to make all paragraphs <p> and list items <li> red. You don't have to set paragraphs <p> and turn them red, and then select list item <li> and turn them red. Just select the body, which will take effect on all the elements. So, the next thing that you are going to be shown is what happens if you specify paragraph <p> tag and style it green

```
1   <!DOCTYPE html>
2   <html>
3   <head>
4       <title>Specificity</title>
5       <style type="text/css">
6           body {
7               color: red;
8           }
9           p {
10              color: green;
11          }
12      </style>
```

If you refresh, you will see of course that the paragraph turned green

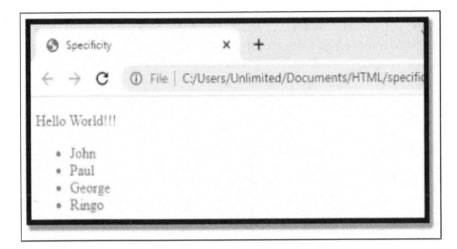

Likewise, if you want the <ul> to turn blue and also the <li> inside the <ul> because they inherit from that.

```
1   <!DOCTYPE html>
2   <html>
3   <head>
4       <title>Specificity</title>
5       <style type="text/css">
6           body {
7               color: red;
8           }
9           p {
10              color: green;
11          }
12          ul {
13              color: blue;
14          }
15      </style>
```

What is happening here is demonstrating the idea of specificity in CSS. As you can see, the blue of <ul> has overridden the body color of green. So, you have multiple styles that could be impacting this same <li>, it could be red, and which start as green, and then returning it blue because they're supposed to be green

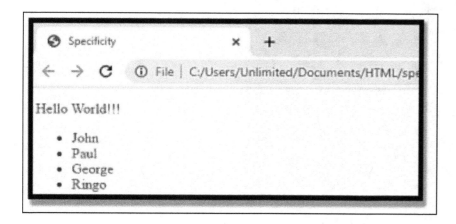

If you proceed and inspect one of these elements, you will notice that <ul> is inherited which tells us that the blue color is "inherited from <ul>" And if you scroll down a bit, you will see an inheritance from <body> the color is red but it is crossed out which means it is not being applied at all, and instead, the blue style is being applied.

This shows us this red style coming from the <body> tag is attempting to be applied or it is targeting the <ul> element that we have selected but it is crossed off which means it is not being applied

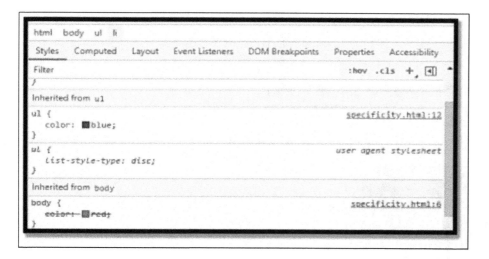

Specificity

Specificity is this idea in CSS that we can have multiple styles targeting one element.

The <li> is being turned red or it is being targeted by the <body> styling which is red, also being targeted by the <ul> styling which turns everything in the <ul> to be blue. And so, CSS has to decide which one wins. And in this case, whatever style is closest to the element or whichever one is more specific and so what that means is that the <body> is very general, it is everything, and the <ul> is more specific which is going to win out. But this is just a simple case.

Add in more selectors that are <li> color to be orange

```
li {
    color: ■orange;
}
```

And as you would expect it makes all <li> orange color

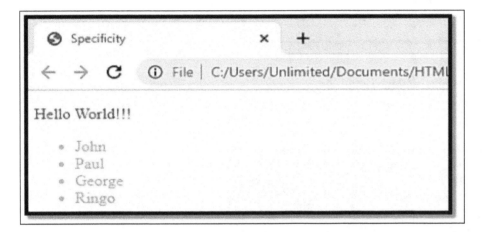

And if we highlight one of the orange elements and right-click to inspect it

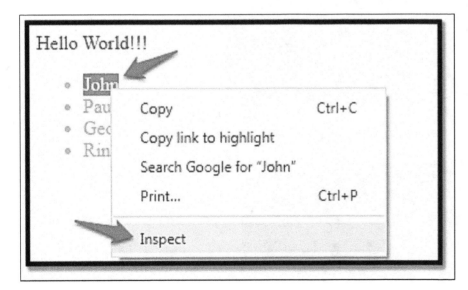

It has been turned red by the <body> but that is crossed off, it has turned blue by the <ul> selector, and then it turned orange by the <li> selector and that one wins out because it is the closest element to the text.

```
li {                                                    specificity.html:15
    color: ■orange;
}
li {                                                    user agent stylesheet
    display: list-item;
    text-align: -webkit-match-parent;
}
Inherited from ul
ul {                                                    specificity.html:12
    color: ■blue;
}
ul {                                                    user agent stylesheet
    list-style-type: disc;
}
Inherited from body
body {                                                  specificity.html:6
    color: ■red;
}
```

These are all simple cases where it is pretty clear which one wins. Let's introduce something on top of the two of the <li>, let style the first <li> and the last <li> an inline styling by passing a class into it called "highlight"

```
<body>
<p>Hello World!!!</p>
<ul>
    <li class="highlight">John</li>
    <li>Paul</li>
    <li>George</li>
    <li class="highlight">Ringo</li>
</ul>
</body>
```

Style the class in the internal stylesheet, give it a color of green, and save it

```
.highlight {
    color: □purple;
}
```

Refresh your browser, as you can see that the highlight class wins and it turned purple because of that highlight class.

This is showing us something where a <li> styling is directly targeting all <li> making them orange, and then **"class selector"** is also directly targeting a few <li> that have the class attribute of purple, and in the battlefield of overriding selectors class wins out because a class declaration is closer than element declaration

There are actually very specific rules for how this works and we are going to show it to you in just a second but before that, we just want to add one more example so let's say we also give one of the class elements an Id element called "special"

```
<p>Hello World!!!</p>
<ul>
    <li id="special" class="highlight">John</li>
    <li>Paul</li>
    <li>George</li>
```

We will target that Id element called "special", give it a color of **"hot pink"** and save it

```
#special {
    color: ■hotpink;
}
```

And then refresh or reload your browser, you will see that Id element wins out

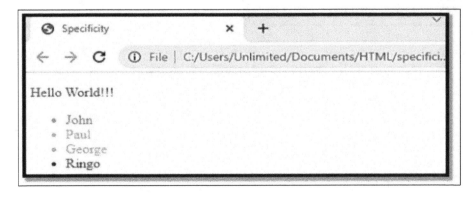

And one more time, if you highlight the pink text and inspect it

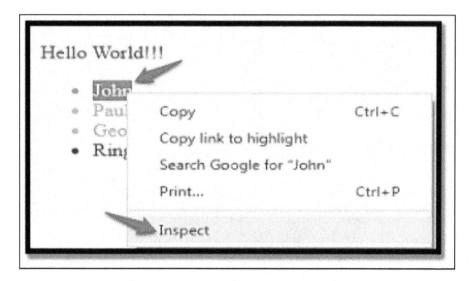

You will see that you have a style from the <body> that is not applied, one from the <ul> that is inherited but not applied

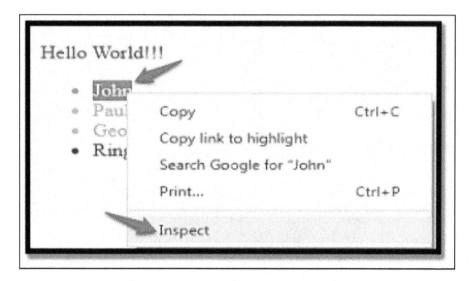

Another one from the <li> that is not applied, one from the **class** that is not applied, and then one from the **Id special** that is applied. So, in this case, the Id wins because it is the closest to styling

```
#special {
    color: ▇hotpink;
}

.highlight {
    color:  ▇purple;
}

li {
    color:  ▢orange;
}
```

As mentioned earlier there are very specific rules as to how this works. How is specificity calculated? When CSS sees that there are 3 or 4 different colors that this <li> could be targeting, how does it know which one to pick, and the way that it does, it runs the calculation so it assigns a numeric value to each of those selectors.

So, it is going to assign a numeric value to the <ul>, and then to <li>, and then to **".highlight",** and then to **"#special".** And as we know the Id named **"special wins out"** is not necessary because of the order of arrangement but because of the closeness to the <li>

```
body {
    color: ▇red;
}
p {
    color: ▇green;
}
ul {
    color: ▢blue;
}
li {
    color: ▢orange;
}
.highlight {
    color: ▢purple;
}
#special {
    color: ▇hotpink;
}
```

Assignment

In this exercise, you will cover everything that we have discussed as far as CSS selectors, you will not build any sort of complete cohesive website. This one is more of a traditional exercise with a bunch of problems very short problems. There is a material link where you can have access to download the HTML and CSS file both the exercise and the solution.

And below is the preview of the CSS file, it is empty aside from a bunch of comments and these comments give you instructions for what you need to do.

The first line of text is the most important line **"style the HTML elements according to the following instructions, and do not alter the existing HTML to do this right. Only the CSS should be worked upon."**

```
1    /* Style the HTML elements according to the following instructions.
2    DO NOT ALTER THE EXISTING HTML TO DO THIS.  WRITE ONLY CSS!
3
4    /* Give the <body> element a background of #bdc3c7*/
5
6
7    /* Make the <h1> element #9b59b6*/
8
9
10   /* Make all <h2> elements orange */
11
12
13   /* Make all <li> elements blue(pick your own hexadecimal blue)*/
14
15
16   /*Change the background on every paragraph to be yellow*/
```

Conclusion: Mastering CSS Selectors and Beyond

The journey through CSS selectors is fundamental to building well-structured, visually engaging, and highly functional web applications. By understanding the core concepts—element, ID, and class selectors—and progressing to more advanced techniques, we gain a powerful toolkit for crafting precise and efficient stylesheets. Let's summarize and reflect on the key takeaways from this exploration.

Revisiting the Basics

The foundation of CSS lies in its ability to target HTML elements for styling. The three basic selectors form the bedrock of this capability:

Element Selector: Targets elements based on their tag name, offering a straightforward method to apply styles globally to specific types of elements. For example:

```
p {
    font-size: 16px;
}
```

This selector is ideal for setting default styles for common elements like headings, paragraphs, and divs.

ID Selector: Provides a unique way to style a single element using its id attribute. IDs should be unique within a document, ensuring precise targeting:

```
#header {
   background-color: #f4f4f4;
}
```

Class Selector: Offers flexibility by allowing multiple elements to share the same styling through a class attribute:

```
.button {
   color: white;
   background-color: blue;
}
```

Classes are reusable, making them ideal for modular and scalable design systems.

Exploring Advanced Selectors

Moving beyond the basics, advanced selectors enable intricate and dynamic styling possibilities. These include:

Asterisk Selector: Targets all elements universally. While powerful, its usage should be limited to avoid performance issues and unintended side effects.

```
* {
   margin: 0;
   padding: 0;
}
```

Descendant Selector: Selects elements nested within others, enabling context-specific styling.

```
div p {
   line-height: 1.5;
}
```

Adjacent Selector: Targets an element immediately following a specified sibling.

```
h1 + p {
   margin-top: 10px;
}
```

Attribute Selector: Styles elements based on attributes and their values, unlocking advanced customizations.

```
input[type="text"] {
   border: 1px solid #ccc;
}
```

Nth-of-Type Selector: Provides granular control over targeting specific child elements based on their position.

```
tr:nth-of-type(odd) {
    background-color: #f9f9f9;
}
```

These selectors, when combined, enable developers to write concise and effective CSS, significantly enhancing both maintainability and scalability.

Chrome Inspector: A Developer's Ally

Modern web development heavily relies on tools like the Chrome Inspector, which provides real-time insights into how CSS selectors and rules are applied. By using the Inspector, developers can:

Debug issues in styling by analyzing the CSS applied to elements.
Experiment with changes directly in the browser, previewing updates before implementing them in the stylesheet.
Understand specificity and inheritance through detailed breakdowns of applied rules.
This tool is invaluable for refining designs, improving performance, and identifying conflicts in CSS.

Specificity, Cascade, and Inheritance

Understanding how CSS rules are prioritized ensures consistent and predictable styling outcomes:

Specificity: Determines which CSS rule takes precedence. A higher specificity score wins:

Inline styles: Highest specificity.
ID selectors: Higher than class selectors.
Class selectors: Higher than element selectors.

Cascade: Resolves conflicts when multiple rules apply to the same element. The order of rules and specificity plays a critical role.

Inheritance: Certain CSS properties are inherited by default (e.g., color, font-family), while others require explicit declaration (e.g., border, margin). Developers can force inheritance using the inherit value.
By mastering these principles, developers can create stylesheets that are not only effective but also easy to manage.

Building Efficient and Maintainable CSS

Here are some best practices for writing CSS:

Organize Your Styles: Structure your CSS logically—grouping related rules and following a consistent naming convention like BEM (Block-Element-Modifier).

Use Comments: Annotate your code for clarity, especially in large projects.

Avoid Overusing IDs: While powerful, IDs can lead to overly specific and rigid styles. Prefer class selectors for reusability.

Minimize Universal Selectors: Use universal selectors sparingly to avoid performance hits.

Leverage Variables: CSS variables improve consistency and make updates easier:

```
:root {
    --primary-color: #3498db;
}
.button {
    background-color: var(--primary-color);
}
```

Test Across Browsers: Ensure cross-browser compatibility by testing styles in different environments.

CSS in Modern Development

CSS has evolved significantly, with tools like preprocessors (SASS, LESS) and methodologies (Atomic CSS, Tailwind CSS) offering advanced capabilities. Modern CSS focuses on:

Responsive Design: Using media queries and flexible layouts to adapt to various screen sizes.

```
@media (max-width: 768px) {
    .container {
        flex-direction: column;
    }
}
```

Performance Optimization: Minimizing CSS files through techniques like minification, tree-shaking, and critical CSS extraction.

Dynamic Styling: With CSS-in-JS and frameworks like React and Vue, CSS is increasingly integrated into JavaScript workflows.

Final Thoughts

CSS selectors are the cornerstone of styling web applications, providing the means to craft beautiful, accessible, and performant designs. By mastering the basics, exploring advanced techniques, and understanding the nuances of specificity and inheritance, developers can create stylesheets that are both elegant and robust. Coupled with tools like Chrome Inspector and modern best practices, CSS becomes a powerful ally in delivering exceptional user experiences.

As you continue your journey, remember that CSS is not just a language for styling; it's a canvas for creativity, a tool for accessibility, and a cornerstone of the web's visual identity. Embrace its intricacies, experiment boldly, and strive for designs that delight users and stand the test of time.

7. Styling Solutions with CSS, Testing, and Sass/SCSS

Introduction

CSS (Cascading Style Sheets) is an integral part of modern web development, enabling developers to style and present HTML content effectively. In this section, we explore foundational concepts of styling with CSS, advanced techniques for testing and organizing CSS code, and the powerful tools offered by CSS preprocessors like Sass and SCSS.

1. Styling with CSS

1.1 Basics of CSS

CSS provides the structure for styling elements in an HTML document. It allows developers to control layout, typography, colors, spacing, and more, using a variety of selectors and properties.

CSS Syntax: CSS rules are written in a structure that consists of a selector and declaration block.

```
selector {
    property: value;
}
```

Selectors:

Element Selector: Targets HTML tags.

```
p {
    color: blue;
}
```

Class Selector: Targets elements with a specific class attribute.

```
.highlight {
    background-color: yellow;
}
```

ID Selector: Targets a single element with a specific ID.

```
#unique-header {
    font-size: 24px;
}
```

Attribute Selector: Targets elements based on attributes.

```
input[type="text"] {
    border: 1px solid gray;
```

}

1.2 Advanced Styling Techniques

Box Model: Understand the content, padding, border, and margin layers for element spacing and layout.
Flexbox and Grid Layouts: Powerful tools for creating responsive designs.

```css
.container {
    display: flex;
    justify-content: center;
    align-items: center;
}
```

Pseudo-classes and Pseudo-elements: Style dynamic states or specific parts of an element.

```css
a:hover {
    text-decoration: underline;
}
```

Variables: Introduced in CSS3, variables enable reusable, maintainable code.

```css
:root {
    --primary-color: #3498db;
}
body {
    color: var(--primary-color);
}
```

2. Testing and Organizing CSS

As CSS projects grow, organizing and maintaining style sheets become critical. Testing ensures that the styles behave as expected across browsers and devices.

2.1 Organizing CSS

Modular CSS: Split styles into smaller, reusable files and import them into a main file.

```css
/* base.css */
body {
    font-family: Arial, sans-serif;
}

/* main.css */
@import 'base.css';
header {
    background-color: #333;
    color: #fff;
}
```

Naming Conventions: Use consistent naming systems like BEM (Block-Element-Modifier).

```
.block__element--modifier {
   color: red;
}
```

Reset and Normalize: Include CSS resets or normalize.css to handle cross-browser inconsistencies.

2.2 Testing CSS

Cross-Browser Compatibility: Test styles on multiple browsers (Chrome, Firefox, Safari, Edge) to ensure consistent rendering.

Responsive Design Testing: Use tools like browser developer tools and frameworks like Bootstrap to test responsiveness.

Automated Testing: Tools like **Percy** and **BackstopJS** enable visual regression testing for style changes.
Linting: Use CSS linters like Stylelint to enforce coding standards.

```
npm install stylelint --save-dev
```

2.3 Debugging CSS

Browser Developer Tools: Inspect and modify styles in real-time.

CSS Validation Services: Tools like the W3C CSS Validator can check for syntax errors and adherence to standards.

3. The CSS Preprocessor: Sass and SCSS

CSS preprocessors like Sass (Syntactically Awesome Stylesheets) and SCSS (a newer syntax for Sass) extend CSS by introducing programming-like features, making stylesheets more maintainable and dynamic.

3.1 What is Sass/SCSS?

Sass is a CSS preprocessor that introduces features like variables, nested rules, mixins, and functions. SCSS (Sassy CSS) is a superset of CSS3 and fully compatible with it, offering a more CSS-like syntax.

3.2 Features of Sass/SCSS

Variables: Store reusable values like colors, fonts, and dimensions.

```
$primary-color: #3498db;
body {
   background-color: $primary-color;
}
```

Nesting: Organize styles hierarchically for better readability.

```
nav {
   ul {
```

```scss
    list-style: none;
    li {
        display: inline-block;
    }
  }
}
```

Mixins: Reusable blocks of styles.

```scss
@mixin flex-center {
    display: flex;
    justify-content: center;
    align-items: center;
}
.box {
    @include flex-center;
}
```

Inheritance: Share styles between selectors using the @extend directive.

```scss
.button {
    padding: 10px 20px;
    border-radius: 5px;
}
.primary-button {
    @extend .button;
    background-color: blue;
    color: white;
}
```

Functions: Perform calculations and logic.

```scss
@function calculate-rem($size) {
    @return $size / 16 * 1rem;
}
h1 {
    font-size: calculate-rem(32px);
}
```

3.3 Advantages of Using Sass/SCSS

Improved readability and maintainability of stylesheets.
Reusability through mixins and functions.
Easy theming and dynamic styling with variables.
Minification and optimization through the compilation process.

3.4 Setting Up Sass/SCSS

Install Sass using npm or a package manager.
npm install -g sass

Compile SCSS to CSS.
sass style.scss style.css

3.5 Organizing SCSS Projects

Follow the **7-1 Pattern**: Split files into directories like base, components, layout, and utilities, with one main file for importing.

```scss
// main.scss
@import 'base/reset';
@import 'layout/grid';
@import 'components/buttons';
```

3.6 Example SCSS Workflow

SCSS File (style.scss):

```scss
$primary-color: #3498db;

@mixin border-radius($radius) {
    border-radius: $radius;
}

.button {
    background-color: $primary-color;
    color: #fff;
    @include border-radius(5px);
    &:hover {
        background-color: darken($primary-color, 10%);
    }
}
```

Compiled CSS:

```css
.button {
    background-color: #3498db;
    color: #fff;
    border-radius: 5px;
}
.button:hover {
    background-color: #2c80b9;
}
```

4. Modern Trends in Styling with CSS and Sass/SCSS

4.1 CSS Frameworks and Libraries

Frameworks like Tailwind CSS and libraries like Bootstrap streamline styling with pre-defined classes.

4.2 CSS-in-JS

Modern frameworks like React support styling within JavaScript using libraries like styled-components.

4.3 Dynamic and Custom Styling

With CSS variables and Sass, developers can create themes and dynamic styles effortlessly.

4.4 Component-based Styling

CSS Modules and SCSS support encapsulated, component-specific styles.

Let's begin,

Styling with CSS

Welcome to the pleasure dome! Now that you've familiarized yourself with the important basics of CSS, such as selectors, the box model, positioning, and layout, you can turn your attention in this chapter to things such as website design—or, more simply—the CSS elements you can use to make websites more beautiful.

The main focus is clearly on working with text at first, as text is usually the most important thing on most websites. In addition, you may want to design elements such as lists or tables with CSS. Likewise, I'll briefly describe the design of images and graphics with CSS. You'll also learn newer options such as moving and rotating or animating elements using CSS. At the end of the chapter, I'll briefly describe how you can design HTML forms.

Designing Texts with CSS

The purpose of most websites on the internet is to convey information. Usually, the flow of information on websites consists of text, images, and videos. The most important type of information flow on the web is text. CSS provides an impressive amount of CSS features for this purpose, which you can use to design or customize texts for websites. I'll describe these CSS features in more detail in the following sections.

Selecting Fonts via "font-family"

You can use the CSS feature font-family to select the font for the text within an element. As the value for this CSS feature, you can pass the name of the font you want to use to format the text within the HTML element, for example:

body { font-family: Arial; }

This sets the font between <body> and </body> to Arial.

A prerequisite for the corresponding font to be used for display is that it must be installed on the local system of a visitor to the website. In the case of the Arial font, this is probably pretty much the case. Nevertheless, you can specify several alternatives separated by commas—called a font stack. Here's an example:

body { font-family: Arial, Verdana, sans-serif; }

In this case, the Arial font is used between the HTML elements <body> and </body>. If the visitor doesn't have this font installed on his system, the web browser can use Verdana as an alternate font. If that font also isn't available on their system, you instruct the web browser to select any sans-serif font on the system and use it to display the text.

The list can be as long as you want, and the web browser will use the first font installed on the system. Fonts that contain a space in their name must be specified between quotation marks (e.g., "Courier New").

If No Suitable Font Is Available

If no specified font from font-family is available on the system, the default font of the web browser will be used.

Overview of Generic Fonts

To be on the safe side, it's recommended to specify a generic font (or font class) in a list of different fonts at the end. There are five different generic fonts listed in Table. In Figure, you can see the different font classes printed for better distinction.

Font Class	Meaning	Known Examples
serif	In serif fonts, you'll find small fine lines or tick marks at the end of the letter stroke across the base direction.	Times Times New Roman Georgia Bookman
sansserif	These are sans-serif fonts where the end of the stroke is straight.	Arial Verdana Helvetica Lucida
monospace	These are fonts with a fixed width, where all letters have the same width.	Courier Courier New Andale Mono Fixed
cursive	The name is somewhat confusing because these are fonts that are meant to give the impression of a cursive script.	Comic Sans MS Florence Parkavenue Monotype Corsiva
fantasy	These are often decorative ornamental fonts that can be used for creative purposes and are less suitable for entire passages of text.	Impact Haettenschweiler Oldtown Brushstroke

Table Various Generic Font Classes

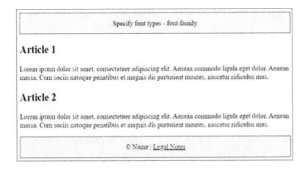

serif **sans-serif**

monospace

cursive **fantasy**

Figure: The Five Different Generic Fonts: "serif", "sans-serif", "monospace", "cursive", and "fantasy"

Of course, you could simply specify just a generic font such as a sans-serif:

body { font-family: sans-serif; }
However, it can't be predicted with certainty which sans-serif font will then be used to display text.

Inheritance of Fonts

Fonts are inherited by the subordinate elements as long as no custom font has been written in the subordinate elements. Often, therefore, a font is defined for <body> that applies to the entire document, for example:

body { font-family: Arial, Verdana, Helvetica, sans-serif; }

In Figure, you can see an HTML document /examples/chapter/index. html without font family for the body element, while in Figure, there's one with the CSS feature font-family for the body element.

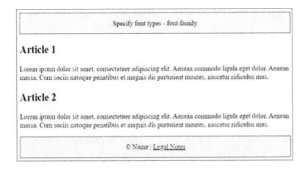

Figure: An HTML Document with the Default Font of the Web Browser

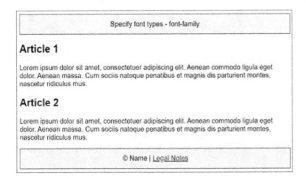

Figure: The Same Document Again, but Now with the CSS Feature "font-family": Sans-Serif Font (Here,

Arial) Was Used I've slightly extended this example for demonstration purposes:

```css
body { font-family: Arial, Verdana, Helvetica, sans-serif; }
.footer, .header { background-color: papayawhip;     border: 1px solid black;
padding: 2% 2%;
text-align: center;     font-family: cursive; }
.article { font-family: Georgia, Times, serif; } ...
```

Listing /examples/chapter/css/style.css

We first use the body type selector to specify a sans-serif font such as Arial, Verdana, Helvetica, or even a generic font for the entire document. This font is used as the default font if no other font is specified for an element. Then, for the footer and header elements, we let the system select a cursive type with the generic font class cursive, so the result here will probably look different on different computers. For the text in the article elements themselves, we use a serif font such as Georgia, Times, or any other serif font available on the system. The results are displayed in Figure.

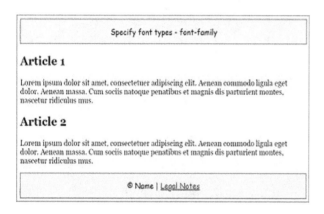

Figure: Multiple Different Fonts in Use

Number of Different Fonts

In practice, you should keep the number of different fonts on a web page rather low. Too many fonts won't necessarily make a website look better. A good guideline should be to use no more than three or four fonts. However, this also depends on the type of website.

Benefits and Drawbacks of "font-family"

The drawback of using font-family to select the font is that a font must be installed on the visitor's computer. So, you're quite limited in the choice of fonts. Mostly common fonts such as Times, Times New Roman, Georgia, Helvetica, Arial, or Verdana are used.

The use of font-family does have one advantage: you don't have to worry about font licenses because you don't share the font.

Analyzing Fonts in Firefox

At this point, I'd like to discuss the **Fonts** tab, which you can find in the Developer Tools in the Firefox web browser. In addition to the default settings of the web browser, you can also use it to determine the fonts of other websites if you particularly like one of them. You can also make adjustments to the font size, line height, character spacing, or stroke width here to see in the browser what it would look like with different settings. The matching values will then be displayed inline in the HTML element.

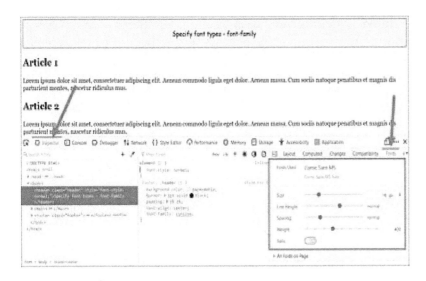

Figure: You Can Analyze and Change the Font Used on a Web Page in Firefox, Which Makes the Effects Visible in the Browser Window

Providing Fonts via Web Fonts: "@font-face"

@font-face allows you to use fonts that aren't installed on visitors' computers. To do this, you just need to specify a path from where the font can be downloaded.

To add fonts to a website using the @font-face rule, you need the following: **font-family**

Specify the name of the font. You can then pass this name as a value for the font-family feature. **src**

Set the path or link to the font file. You can also provide different versions of the font. **format**

Specify the file format in which the font is available.

Here's a theoretical example of how you can include such a downloadable font for a website:

@font-face {   font-family: 'A font name';   src: url('path/to/my/font.ttf') format('truetype'); }

Again, you can use these web fonts in CSS via the CSS feature font-family:

body { font-family: 'A font name', Times, Georgia, serif; }

As a fallback solution, you can specify a list of alternate fonts if the font (here, 'A font name') couldn't be downloaded and used.

Longer Loading Time

Logically, adding additional resources to your website, as you did here with the web fonts, also means that the loading time will increase. In addition, you often have no control over fonts that are hosted and made available on another server.

Different File Formats for Web Fonts

The different file formats for the fonts seem a bit exotic at first. Not everyone is familiar with font file abbreviations such as EOT (Embedded Open Type; format('eot')), WOFF (Web Open Font Format; format('woff')), TTF (TrueType; format('truetype')), OTF (Open Type; format('opentype')), and SVG (SVG

Fonts; format('svg')).

Meanwhile, the WOFF format standardized by the W3C seems to be gaining more and more acceptance. WOFF is a compressed TIFF format with additional information such as the origin or license of the font and is supported by the latest web browsers. The oldest of the formats, EOT, on the other hand, was used by the older Internet Explorer up to version 8. Other older web browsers, on the other hand, used the TTF or OTF formats. The SVG format is popular for displaying on the iPhone or iPad, but it's also used by Safari.

However, you can do without SVG now because iPhone and iPad also support the WOFF format. To provide the widest possible support for the downloadable font, you can provide the fonts in multiple formats.

In practice, this is how you reach almost all web browsers to provide a font in a particular file format:

```
@font-face {    font-family: 'A font name';    src: url('path/to/font.eot'); /*IE9*/    src:
url('path/to/font.eot#iefix') format('eot'), /*IE5-8*/       url('path/to/font.woff') format('woff'),
url('path/to/font.ttf') format('truetype'),       url('path/to/font.svg#svgFN') format('svg');
}
```

This way, you can include different formats for different web browsers. If a web browser doesn't support a certain format, it chooses the next possible font format. You could do without TrueType and SVG altogether in this example nowadays. The first EOT file is used for the old Internet Explorer 9. The hash **(#)**, in turn, is a browser switch for even older Internet Explorer versions prior to version 9. At this point, the web browser in question stops reading. All other web browsers, however, read their preferred font format.

Having Fonts Converted to Different Formats

When you've found a font that you want to use, you often don't have all the necessary formats such as EOT, WOFF, TTF, or SVG ready. For this purpose, the Font Squirrel website offers a free service: you can upload a font file and have it converted to all other formats. Then you download the different formats, and the CSS rule with @font-face is included in an extra CSS file. However, after embedding web fonts, you should always test the rendering quality in different web browsers because the quality can differ significantly between web browsers when rendering.

In addition, you can use the font-style, font-weight, and font-stretch features in the @font-face rule, which is very useful when the font exists in different files, for example:

```
@font-face {  font-family: 'A font name';  src: url('path/to/my/font.eot');  src: url('path/to/my/font.eot#iefix')
format('eot'),       url('path/to/my/font.woff') format('woff'),       url('path/to/my/font.ttf') format('truetype'),
url('path/to/my/font.svg#svgFN') format('svg'); }
@font-face {  font-family: 'A font name';  src: url('path/to/my/font-it.eot');  src: url('path/to/my/font-
it.eot#iefix') format('eot'),       url('path/to/my/font-it.woff') format('woff'),       url('path/to/my/font-it.ttf')
format('truetype'),       url('path/to/my/font-it.svg#svgFN') format('svg');    font-style: italic;
}
```

This allows you to use the italic font for styling purposes in addition to the regular version of the font, for example:
```
... p { font-family: 'A font name', Times, Georgia, serif; } .it { font-style: italic; }
<p>Regular version of the embedded font</p>
<p class="it">Cursive version of the embedded font</p>.
```

Embedding Royalty-Free Fonts by Google into the Website

The easiest way might be to use a font from Google Fonts and embed it into the website. However, "easy" doesn't mean it's "not complicated" but rather refers to ease of getting the necessary licenses. If you use fonts from the web for a custom project, you really need to be sure that you have the permission to do so from the font's developer. Even a "free" font doesn't always mean that it's free for all purposes.

On the upper-left side of the Google Fonts website, you'll see a magnifying glass icon to search with some filters to find the font you need. For the category (**Categories**), you select the type of font (**Serif**, **Sans Serif**, **Display**, **Handwriting**, or **Monospace**). You can filter out other properties using **Font properties** with the thickness or font width. Then, you can select the desired fonts via the preview.

Once you've clicked on a font, you can specify the **styles**. Useful styles are regular, italic, and bold. Click **+ Select this style** to add a font style. The selected styles will be displayed in the **Review** tab on the right.

Figure: Fonts on https://fonts.google.com

Figure: I've Chosen the Roboto Font with a Regular, Italic, and Bold Font Style

Once you're done with the selection, take a look at the **Review** tab on the right side where you'll find the code to embed the font on your website under the text **Use on the web**. You can choose between a link element, an @import rule, or a JavaScript. Copy and paste the code to your website.

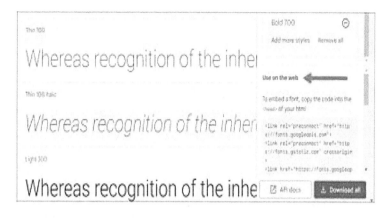

Figure: A <link> Element or an "@import" Statement Enables You to Add the Code to the Website via Copy and Paste.

In the following example, the Roboto font from Google Fonts was embedded and used via @import:
@import url('https://fonts.googleapis.com/css2?family=Roboto:ital,wght@0,400;0,700;1,400&display=swap');
body {   **font-family: 'Roboto', sans-serif;**
}

Listing /examples/chapter/css/style.css

You can see the result with the HTML document /examples/chapter/index. html in Figure.

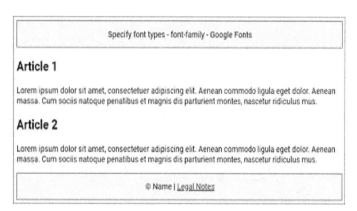

Figure: Here, the Roboto Font from Google Fonts Was Downloaded and Embedded

Google Fonts and the GDPR

If you offer fonts from a Google server on your website, you may feel insecure about the General Data Protection Regulation (GDPR) because data gets transferred between your website visitors and Google. If you want to be on the safe side, you can also offer Google Fonts "locally" in your own web space. For this purpose, you'll find the google-web fonts-helper tool to pack up and download the appropriate font formats.

Pros and Cons of "@font-face"

The advantage of @font-face is certainly that it allows you to finally use fonts that aren't installed on the computers of your website visitors. However, this font needs to be downloaded beforehand, which might slow down the loading of the website a bit. In addition, here you need to know the license of the font used and whether the distribution of the font is allowed or not. If you want to be absolutely sure in this regard, you need to either create your own fonts or use @font-face via a free or commercial service. In that case, the service takes care of the licensing arrangements with the font manufacturer.

Using Icons via Icon Fonts

Adding graphics to the website is basically no big deal anymore. However, it gets somewhat more complicated if you want to insert an icon in the middle of a text. And that's particularly difficult when you want the icon to look equally good on any device, from a small screen such as a smartphone to a screen with an extremely high resolution. Sure, you could make the icon responsive as a graphic and scale it accordingly, but it won't necessarily make the result more attractive (blurry or pixelated). On the other hand, you could also provide multiple versions of the graphic, and SVG as a graphic format still comes to mind as a possible workaround.

However, you can save this effort right away and just use icon fonts instead. The icon fonts name already suggests what it's about, and those who have a lot to do with word processing might know fonts such as Wingdings from Microsoft, which use icons. You only need to include the corresponding icon fonts via @font-face. This makes it possible to treat these icons like an ordinary font. For example, you can adjust the appropriate size with the CSS feature font-size.

There are several providers of attractive icon fonts. Here we'll introduce and use one of the arguably more popular icon fonts, Font Awesome. A list of other popular icon fonts can be found at the end of the section. To download icon fonts, you need to create an account at fontawesome.com. However, it is also possible to use the icon fonts via a CDN server. For more details, please refer to the fontawesome.com website.

If you've downloaded and unpacked Font Awesome, you'll also find other embedding options in the package, such as for the CSS preprocessor Less, for example. For our purposes, the contents of the css and webfonts folders, which are located below the webfonts-with-css folder, are sufficient for now. The css folder contains all the necessary CSS statements, while you can find the font icons in webfonts. Both folders were copied to the directory of the sample website.

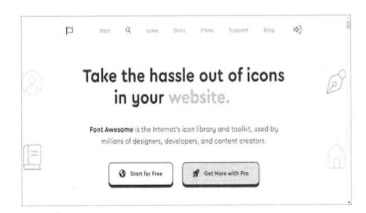

Figure: Font Awesome Has Become a Favourite of Web Designers

In the first step, you don't need to do anything but include the CSS file all.css in the HTML document, which you can do using the link element in the document header as follows:
...
<link href="css/all.css" rel="stylesheet">

That's all it takes. The included CSS file from Font Awesome handles the integration of the icon fonts with

@font-face as an additional font. The second step is to use Font Awesome's font icons anywhere in the HTML document using the <i> tag, but basically this works with any other tag as well. For example, you can insert and display a house icon in the HTML document as follows:

```
<i class="fas fa-home"></i>
```

You can adjust the size with font-size as you would with an ordinary font because basically, they are embedded font icons, for example:

```
<i class="fas fa-home" style="font-size:3em;"></i>
```

The font icons of Font Awesome have special classes included that allow you to increase the icon size with fa-2x, fa-3x, fa-4x, and fa-5x relative to their container, for example:

```
<i  class="fas fa-home fa-2x"></i>
```

You can also customize colors as you would with an ordinary font using the CSS feature color. For example, the following line uses the Twitter logo in Twitter's usual color:

```
<i class="fab fa-twitter fa-2x" style="color:#0084b4;"></i>
```

For symbols with a trade name or trademark, you must use the fab prefix instead of fas. The b of fab stands for brand, and the s of fas for solid. Font Awesome also offers a commercial version with even more icons and different styles, where you can use far (for regular) and fal (for light) as prefixes.

Here is a snippet of an HTML document with various font symbols from Font Awesome in use:

```
...
 <head>
...
   <link href="css/all.css" rel="stylesheet">    <style>
   ...
   <style>
 </head>
 <body>
  <header class="header">Use icon font</header>
  <nav>
  <a href="#">Home page <i class="fas fa-home"></i></a>|
  <a href="#">Blog <i class="fas fa-book"></i></a> |
  <a href="#">Links <i class="fas fa-anchor"></i></a> |
  <a href="#">About <i class="fas fa-user"></i> </a> |
 <a href="#">Contact <i class="fas fa-envelope"></i>
  </a>
  </nav>
  <main>
   <article>
    <h1><i class="fab fa-css3 fa-2x"></i> Article 1</h1>
    <p>Lorem ipsum dolor sit ... </p>
   </article>
   <article>
    <h1><i class="fas fa-html5 fa-2x"></i> Article 2</h1>
```

```
<p>Lorem ipsum dolor sit ... </p>
<ul class="fa-ul">
  <li><i class="fa-li fas fa-check-circle"></i>
     Done</li>
  <li><i class="fa-li fas fa-circle"></i>
      Not done</li>
  <li><i class="fa-li fas fa-ban"></i>
     Not possible</li>
  <li><i class="fa-li fas fa-spinner fa-spin"></i>
     In process</li>
 </ul>
  </article>
</main>
<footer class="footer">&copy; Name | <a href="#">Legal Notes</a><br><br>
<i class="fab fa-twitter fa-2x" style="color:#0084b4;"></i>
<i class="fab fa-google-plus fa-2x" style="color:red;"></i>
<i class="fab fa-facebook fa-2x" style="color:#3b5998;"></i>   <i class="fab fa-skype fa-2x"
style="color:#12A5F4;"></i>
 </footer>   </body> ...
```

You can see the example with the different icon fonts, including social media icons, from Font Awesome in
Figure.

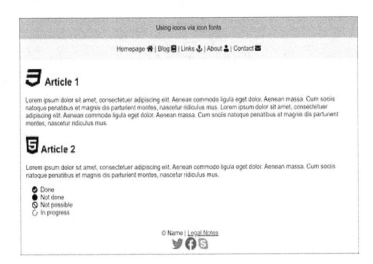

Figure: Various Icons without Graphics in Use Thanks to Font Awesome Icon Fonts

Besides Font Awesome, there are many other providers of such font icons, which can often be integrated and
used in a similar way.

Observing Licenses

The same applies here as with the downloadable fonts. Many of these icon fonts are free, but still have some
sort of license (GPL, Creative Commons, etc.) that you should be sure to read through before using and
embedding icon fonts on your website. Others are commercial and can be purchased.

Setting the Font Size Using "font-size"

The font size can be set using the CSS feature font-size. As a matter of fact, you might think it should be trivial to set the font size. But it already starts with the fact that the font size can be specified with pixels, points, percentages, em, or rem. The ideal font size will probably not exist anyway because there are too many different settings in the operating system and different large and small screens with different resolutions. In addition, the web browser allows you to scale the websites in different zoom levels.

Different screen sizes and resolutions, settings in the operating system or web browser, and different units of measure (UoM) make it truly complicated for the web designer to use the right font size and UoM. Nevertheless, in this chapter, you'll learn what you can use when and what you should not use.

No Specifications with "font-size": The Browser Standard

If you don't specify anything via font-size, the default value of the web browser will be used, which is often 16 pixels (= 100%, 1em, 1rem, or 16pt) as the base font size. Because default fonts are often displayed at different sizes, and users can change the size in the web browser, you should take control of the font size and not leave the display of text to chance.

Preset Keywords for the Font Size

CSS provides the predefined keywords small, x-small, xx-small, medium, large, x-large, and xx-large, where medium is the base font size. The other keywords decrease (small) or increase (large) the value of medium by a factor of 1.2 each. These values are absolute values. smaller and larger are two more keywords with relative values. Relative here means relative to the parent element. I personally have rarely made use of these keywords, as they allow only limited control over the actual font size. For this reason, I won't go into detail about those values.

Relative Font Sizes with "em"

An easy way to adjust the font size for the entire document is to set font-size for the body element. For example, if you set font-size for the body element to 1em or 100%, you'd have effectively used the default value of the web browser, which is the case in Figure.

If you want to increase the font size by 15% for the complete document, you only need to set font-size in the body element to 1.15em or 115%. This will automatically increase the font size of the other elements such as <h1> and <p> by 15%, and you don't have to worry about that. This is exactly what was done: the font was increased by 15% via the body element.

Due to the fact that a relative font size of the body element regulates the font size for all elements of the web page through inheritance, this option is widely used in practice to adjust the font size.

Setting the font size - font-size: 100% / 1em

Article 1

Lorem ipsum dolor sit amet, consectetuer adipiscing elit. Aenean commodo ligula eget dolor. Aenean massa. Cum sociis natoque penatibus et magnis dis parturient montes, nascetur ridiculus mus.

Article 2

Lorem ipsum dolor sit amet, consectetuer adipiscing elit. Aenean commodo ligula eget dolor. Aenean massa. Cum sociis natoque penatibus et magnis dis parturient montes, nascetur ridiculus mus.

© Name | Legal Notes

Figure: The Default Font Size Gets Preserved If You Set "font-size" to 100% or "1em" for the <body> Element

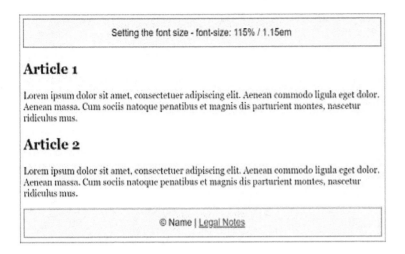

Figure: Here, the Font Size Has Been Increased by 15% via the <body> Element

But it's precisely this inheritance or, more accurately, cascading, that can make adjusting font sizes a little more complex if you don't act with caution here. Consider the following theoretical example:

body   { font-size: 0.95em; /* or 95% */ }   article { font-size: 0.8em; /* or 80% */ }   p   { font-size: 0.8em; /* or 80% */ } ...

Listing /examples/chapter/css/style.css

```
...
<body> <!-- 0.95em -->
...
  <article> <!-- 0.76em -->
   <h1> ... </h1>
   <p> <!-- 0.608em --> ... </p>   </article>
...
</body> ...
```

Listing /examples/chapter/index.html

For <body>, we set a smaller font size of 0.95em (or 95%). As mentioned earlier, this specification applies to the entire document, which has the side effect of reducing the article element by another 0.8em (or 80%) of this 0.95em (or 95%), thus setting it to 0.76em, since 0.96 × 0.8 = 0.76em.

In the example, the p element is still used inside an article element, which again reduces the set font size of 0.76em by 0.8em, so that a text inside the p element in an article element is set only in the font size 0.608em (0.76 × 0.8 = 0.608). The text in the p element would thus be displayed extremely small.

Setting the Font Size Using "rem"

The problem with inheriting relative values that occur if you use em or % for setting the font size can be avoided by using rem (rem = root em). Basically, rem is also just an em, the only difference being that when it inherits, it adheres to the highest root element, <html>, instead of the font size of the corresponding parent element. Let's take a look at the same section as before, but this time we use rem:

```
... html  { font-size: 100%; } /* Browser default */  body   { font-size: 0.9375rem; }  article { font-size: 0.8125rem; }  p    { font-size: 0.8125rem; } ...
```

Listing /examples/chapter/css/style2.css

```
...
<body> <!-- 0.9375em --> ...
  <article> <!-- 0.8125em -->
    <h1> ... </h1>
    <p> <!-- 0.8125em --> ... </p>  </article>
...
</body> ...
```

Listing /examples/chapter/index2.html

Here, you don't need any more math like in the example before with em because we've set the value of <html> to 100%, and on the basis of <html>, the root em, you can be sure that the subsequent font sizes with rem correspond to what has been written. Of course, the relationship of body text such as <p> to headings such as <h1>, <h2>, and so on will be preserved.

Fixed Defaults for the Font Size via Pixel and Point

For a long time, font sizes were specified in pixels. People were familiar with this UoM from the screen, and they could avoid the problem with the inheritance of relative values, as it was the case with percentages or with em. In addition, pixels can be used to implement a pixel-precise layout.

However, 12 pixels looks different on a 1,024 × 768 pixel 13-inch screen than on a 27-inch screen with a resolution of 2,560 × 1,440 pixels. In addition, it's no longer possible to say that a pixel is just a pixel. The days of uniform pixel densities of 72 ppi or 96 ppi are over. Newer devices such as smartphones often have 326 ppi, or various screens like the Retina of the iMac have a pixel density of 104 ppi. Without going too much into the complex details, this specifically means that with a higher pixel density on an inch, the pixels inevitably become smaller (and therefore the resolution becomes sharper). We hardly notice the individual pixels on a smartphone due to the high pixel density.

What about Points ("pt") as a Unit for Font Size?

The point value (pt) is better suited for printers or typesetters in the print sector. However, the different conversion factors of the pixel densities from 72 ppi up to 326 ppi result in different displays. The pt unit is more suitable for printing if you create a print version with CSS. It should be mentioned here that a specification of cm (for centimeters) is also possible. As with pt, it's also true for cm that it isn't possible to say whether the conversion to pixels has been performed correctly, and therefore the results of these specifications are relatively unpredictable.

For this reason, if a smartphone actually used 12 pixels for a font size at this high pixel density, you would have to use a magnifying glass to find the text. As a result, such mobile web browsers convert the device's pixels into a kind of pixel for CSS. Consequently, 12 pixels aren't always really 12 pixels. Thus, specifying pixels is rather unreliable with the extremely different sizes and resolutions of screens that exist today.

Responsive Units "vw" and "vh"

The font sizes with %, em, and especially rem are probably the most common units at the moment. These specifications are relative to the base font size or relative to the parent element. What's still missing here is a font size specification, which is relative to the screen dimensions. For this purpose, the W3C has introduced the viewport units, vw (for view width) and vh (for view height), which allow you to assign a size to an element that's calculated in relation to the width and height of the viewport.

For the width, you can use vw, and 1vw corresponds to 1% of the width of the viewport. Similarly, the same applies to the height where you can use vh, and 1vh corresponds to 1% of the height of the viewport. In addition, the units vmin and vmax are available, which refer to the height or width, using the smaller or larger value, respectively. Again, 1vmax corresponds to 1% of the width or height of the viewport. Here's a simple example of how you can adjust the font size without media queries based on the screen width with just a single specification:

```
html { font-size: 3vw; } ...
```

Listing /examples/chapter/css/style3.css

If you now run the example /examples/chapter/index3.html on different devices or scale the browser window, the font size will always be scaled by 3vw according to the screen width. This can be converted as follows if, for example, the screen width is 1,024 pixels:

1024px / 100 * 3vw = 30.72 pixels

This would have set the general font size of the web browser to 30.72 pixels for a screen width of 1,024 pixels. On a smaller screen width with a 480-pixel viewport this would be as follows:

480px / 100 * 3vw = 14.4 pixels

The example shows very nicely how you can achieve extremely responsive font specifications with the viewport unit, but in the example with 3vw, the font size in the html element is now much too large on large screens and barely legible on smaller screens.

```
html { font-size: calc(100% + 0.5vw); } ...
```

Listing /examples/chapter/css/style4.css

When you run the example with /examples/chapter/index4.html, you'll notice that everything is far from perfect, and the question remains how to specifically adjust individual elements with the viewport units. Just giving the vw or vh information seems to be too inaccurate. Further calculations with calc() might make everything a little too complicated. Probably the best solution is to set the viewport units only in the html element and use em or rem for everything else relative to it, as is also currently recommended by Zell Liew. This was just intended as a brief introduction to the newer viewport units related to font sizes. We'll probably encounter the new unit more often in the future.

General Relative Length Measure

The units vw and vh aren't limited to fonts, but were introduced as a general length measure, which you can already conclude from the names viewport width and viewport height. As mentioned previously, 1vw corresponds to 1% width of the web browser window. Thus, 100vw is the full browser width. This makes it easy, for example, to make sure that an element is always a certain size, no matter how big the screen is.

Here's an example:

```
.quarter {   width: 50vw;   height: 50vh;
}
```

The element with the .quarter class will now always cover a quarter of the browser window, no matter how large the device's screen is or whether you scale the browser window afterward.

Overview of the Common Methods for "font-size"

Table provides a brief overview of the common methods or units you can apply to the CSS feature font-size.

Unit	Example	Description
em	font-size: 1em;	Relative to the font size of the parent element
%	font-size: 100%;	Relative to the font size of the parent element
px	font-size: 16px;	Absolute font size
rem	font-size: 1rem;	Relative to the font size of <html>
smaller, larger	font-size: larger;	Slightly larger than the parent element
small-x, medium, …	font-size: small-x;	Uses exactly small-x (absolute font size)
vw	font-size: 3vw;	Adjusts the font size according to the width of the viewport (see next section)

Table Common Ways to Set the Font Size

Converting Pixels to "em" or "rem" with the 62.5% Trick

Richard Rutter's 62.5% trick is frequently encountered in responsive web design. Because most web browsers set the default font size to 16 pixels, and, based on that, 1 rem (or 1 em) always corresponds to the base font size, it makes sense to set the base font size to 10 pixels so that you can more easily set the relative values via em or rem. For example, if you want to set the text for an element to 18 pixels, you'd have to write a cumbersome specification such as 1.125em. Of course, you can also calculate this with 18 px ÷ 16 px = 1.125 em, but this is cumbersome in the long run. One option would be to use 1.8em right away for an 18-pixel font size. To do that, you just need to write the following definition:

body { font-size: 62.5%; /* base font size to 10 pixels */ } h1 { font-size: 2.4em; /* = 24 pixels */ } h2 { font-size: 1.9em; /* = 19 pixels */ }

Italic and Bold Fonts via "font-style" and "font-weight"

You can assign an italic font style by assigning the value italic to the CSS feature font-style. This will display the font in italic style. If a font doesn't have an italic style, the web browser will try to slant it using oblique, which is another value you can assign to font-style. The difference between italic and oblique isn't apparent at first glance, but italic uses real italics supplied by the font's manufacturer. With oblique, on the other hand, you can subsequently slant the fonts so that they look like real italic fonts. The default value of the CSS feature font-style is normal, with which the font gets displayed normally upright.

The CSS feature font-weight enables you to define the weight of the font. The term weight describes how thick or bold the letters will be displayed. The bold value allows you to define a bold font style. The default value of the normal font style is normal. In addition to bold, there are other weights such as bolder (bolder than bold), lighter (thinner than normal), and the numeric values 100, 200, and up to 900 (in increments of 100), where 400 is normal and 700 is bold. The question as to how strongly the font will be displayed with the values 100 to 900 depends on the computer platform and the web browser.

For Me, Only "bold" and "normal" with "font-weight" Works!

Most of the time, the web browser only recognizes the bold and normal font styles. Values such as lighter, bolder, or 100 to 900 can only be used if the font has these gradations.
In Figure, you can see a trivial example that demonstrates the CSS features font-style and font weight for adjusting the font style with CSS.

Demonstration

font-style: italic;

font-style: oblique;

font-style: normal;

font-weight: normal;

font-weight: bold;

Figure: Changing the Font Style with "font-style" and "font-weight" (Example in /examples/chapter/index.html)

Creating Small Caps Using "font-variant"

With font-variant and the single value small-caps, you can turn a letter into small caps. By means of a small cap, the text is converted to all uppercase, while maintaining the size of the lowercase letters. As a rule, true small caps, in which all letters have the same stroke width, aren't used unless the font used contains small caps. With the help of @font-face and an appropriate font, it's possible to use real small caps.

```
font-variant and text-transform

SMALL CAPS: FONT-VARIANT:SMALL-CAPS;

CAPITAL LETTERS: TEXT-TRANSFORM:UPPERCASE;
```

Figure: The Difference between (Fake) Small Caps and Capital Letters (Example in /examples/chapter/index.html)

Capital Letters
If you want to convert a text to uppercase, you can do this by using the CSS feature text-transform and the uppercase value.

Defining Line Spacing via "line-height"

The line spacing defines the distance from baseline to baseline and can be set using the CSS feature line-height. Line spacing is important for better readability of longer text passages. In practice, the default value on the monitor is almost always too small because this distance comes from the print area. For this reason, you're well advised to use a higher value. Most of the time, the following applies: the longer the lines of a text are, the larger you should choose the line spacing. A good value is often 120% (or 1.2em) up to 150% (or 1.5em). An increased line spacing helps your visitor "keep" the line while reading.

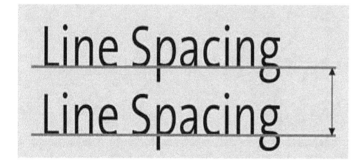

Figure: Line Spacing Is the Distance from Baseline to Baseline

Line spacing is often confused with the optical bleed-through shown in Figure.

Figure: Don't Confuse the Optical Bleed-Through with Line Spacing

In Figure, you can see how different values for the CSS feature line-height have a significant impact on the readability of the body text. You can also clearly see that a value below 100% reduces the line spacing and drastically worsens the readability of the continuous text because you can no longer keep the line as easily when reading.

Figure: Different Line Spacing Has a Drastic Effect on the Readability of the Text (Example in /examples/chapter/index.html)

A Short Notation for Font Formatting Using "font"

The CSS feature font is a short notation for all the features presented here in the order font-style, font variant, font-weight, font-size/line-height, and font-family. In practice, this short CSS notation is preferably placed in the <body> tag, and for individual elements such as headings or paragraph text, only the individual adjustments are made for it. For example:

```
body { font: 1.125em/150% Arial, sans-serif; } footer, header {
  ...
  font-size: 1.2em;
} h1 { font-style: italic; } article {   font-family: Georgia, Times, serif;   font-size: 1em;
}
```

Listing /examples/chapter/css/style.css

Here, the font size was set to 1.125em for the <body> tag, the line height to 150%, and the font to Arial or any existing serif font using the CSS feature font. By using this line, you've virtually defined the font for the website. For all other variations, as you can see in the example for the footer, header, h1, and article tags, you only need to adjust the individual characteristics for that font.

As you can see with the CSS feature font, you don't have to specify all properties. At least the font-size and font-family features must be present. In addition, if you use font-size and line-height, you must separate the two with a slash, where the first value is for font-size, and the second is for line-height. If only one value is used, it will apply to font-size. Here's a summary of the sequence that must be followed when using all features:

```
font: font-style        /* font style */    font-variant        /* font variant */    font-weight        /*
font weight */    font-size/line-height  /* font size/line spacing */    font-family;        /* font family */
```

A complete example in which all font features have been combined can look like the following:

```
p { italic normal bold 1.2em/120% Georgia, Times, serif; }
```

Specifying Letter and Word Spacing via "letter-spacing" and "word-spacing"

If you want to control the spacing between the letters, you can do this by using the CSS feature letterspacing. In your daily work, you shouldn't use letter spacing in regular body text because it tends to make the text less readable. This feature might be more useful for headlines or for texts that are written entirely in capital letters.

What letter-spacing does with individual letters, the CSS feature word-spacing can do with the spacing between individual words. By default, this kind of spacing is usually 0.25em, but as always, it depends on the default setting of the web browser. Here, too, a wider specification tends to worsen the reading flow and should therefore only be used sporadically.

You can see the effects of word-spacing and letter-spacing used after the heading for the corresponding paragraph text. The headlines here were also styled using letter-spacing. The example can be found in /examples/chapter/index.html.

Controlling the Width of the Individual Characters via "font-stretch"

The font-stretch feature can be used to change the width of the font by compressing or stretching the individual characters. However, this feature can't be applied to any font, but works only for fonts that contain appropriate subsets for it. Possible values in ascending order of font compression are semi condensed, condensed, extra-condensed, and ultra-condensed. Values that stretch the text, on the other hand, are semi-expanded, expanded, extra-expanded, and ultra-expanded. The default setting, which doesn't change the font width, is normal. There are fonts that can handle all nine values. Some fonts, on the other hand, can only be compressed via condensed and stretched via expanded. When this book went into print, all modern browsers were able to handle this feature, except for Safari for iOS. For an example, see /examples/chapter/index2.html.

Setting the Text Alignment Using "text-align"

Another important aspect for a good reading flow of texts (and also other inline elements) is the alignment —also referred to as font type—which can be set to one of the following four values using the CSS feature text-align:

left

This left-aligns the text, and is usually the default setting of the web browser. In a left-justified text with ragged margins, the line beginnings of all lines are in a perpendicular alignment to each other. This left justified alignment is most often used on websites because texts can be read best that way.

right

This aligns the text to the right.

center

This value is used to align the text centered (also called axial alignment). This is a uniform type setting in which the lines of a text are aligned exactly along a central axis. For ordinary and longer paragraph text, the center alignment is less suitable for reading. Centered text, on the other hand, can be useful for headlines, poems, or short texts.

justify

This aligns the text in justified type, with each line the same width and flush left and right. Justification is mainly used in book and newspaper typography. While justified text can look prettier than left-justified text with ragged margins, it can result in unsightly larger gaps between words because the web browser tries to keep the text flush on the right and left, which disrupts the flow of reading. CSS has introduced a hyphenation option via the CSS feature hyphens, but currently not all web browsers can handle it without any problem.

In Figure, you can see the different effects of text-align on a paragraph text; the best reading flow is achieved with a left-aligned or justified alignment. Because justified text can result in unsightly gaps, left justification is probably still the first choice for websites. For short texts or headlines, a centered alignment can be interesting. The example for this figure can be found in /examples/chapter/index.html.

Figure: Effects of "text-align" on Paragraph Text

Setting the Vertical Alignment via "vertical-align"

The CSS feature vertical-align can be used for the vertical alignment of inline elements and isn't intended for block elements such as <p> or <div>.

This makes it easy to align text or images in a table cell using a baseline, for example. For table cells, you can use the values top, middle, or bottom. In Figure, you can see these three values when executed in table cells that have been vertically aligned with the following rows:

```
.vtop { vertical-align: top; }
.vmiddle { vertical-align: middle; }
.vbottom { vertical-align: bottom; }
.vsuper { vertical-align: super; }
.vsub { vertical-align: sub; }
.vsub-05em { vertical-align: -0.5em; } ...
```

Listing /examples/chapter/css/style.css

Similarly, you can align inline elements in texts based on a baseline relative to the text by using vertical align. Here you align the text with the value baseline on the baseline, with sub below it and with super above the baseline. If aligning above or below the baseline doesn't suffice for you, you can use positive or negative values of percent, (r)em, or pixels to set the elements even higher or even lower. Here's an example where the inline elements <em> or <strong> have been set higher or lower, respectively, via vertical-align, which you can see in Figure:

<p>Lorem <em class="vsuper">**ipsum**</em>   dolor sit amet, consectetur adipisicing elit,   <strong class="vsub">**sed do**</strong> eiusmod   tempor incididunt ut labore et
  <strong class="vsub-05em ">**dolore**</strong>   magna aliqua.
</p> ...

Listing /examples/chapter/index.html

You can also use the CSS feature vertical-align for images with <img>. Note that a vertical alignment of the image at the top edge isn't the same as a float. In contrast to float, the image with vertical-align still occupies one line, as you can see clearly in Figure.

Setting the vertical alignment (table)

vertical-align: top;	vertical-align: middle;	vertical-align: bottom;
Lorem ipsum dolor sit amet, consectetur adipisicing elit, sed do eiusmod tempor incididunt ut labore et dolore magna aliqua.	Lorem ipsum dolor sit amet, consectetur adipisicing elit, sed do eiusmod tempor incididunt ut labore et dolore magna aliqua.	Lorem ipsum dolor sit amet, consectetur adipisicing elit, sed do eiusmod tempor incididunt ut labore et dolore magna aliqua.

Setting the vertical alignment (text)

Lorem ^{ipsum} dolor sit amet, consectetur adipisicing elit, **sed do** eiusmod tempor incididunt ut labore et $_{dolore}$ magna aliqua.

Figure: Vertical Alignment of Text in Table Cells and of Inline Elements in Text on the Baseline

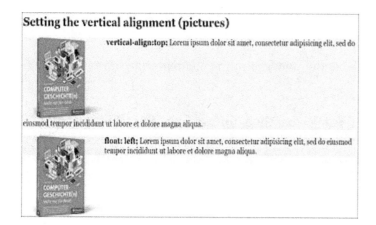

Figure: If You Align an Image with "vertical-align: top;" to the Top Edge of the Text, This Has Different Effects Than in the Lower Example with "float: left;"

Indenting Text Using "text-indent"

The CSS feature text-indent allows you to indent the first line of text with a positive value or drag it outward with a negative value. Such indentations are known mainly from books and the column typesetting of magazines, where the first line of a paragraph is indented to keep the reading flow smooth. On web pages, however, this kind of indentation occurs rarely. Here, the spacing from one paragraph to the next is more important, where the p element defaults to sufficient space from one paragraph to the next, and you can further adjust this using margin. In Figure, you can see such indentation of two paragraphs implemented with the following CSS statement:

.p-indent { text-indent: 1.2em; } ...

Listing /examples/chapter/css/style.css

Indenting text using text-indent

Lorem ipsum dolor sit amet, consectetur adipisicing elit, eiusmod tempor incididunt ut labore et dolore magna aliqua. Lorem ipsum dolor sit amet, consectetur adipisicing elit, eiusmod tempor incididunt ut labore et dolore magna aliqua.

Lorem ipsum dolor sit amet, consectetur adipisicing elit, eiusmod tempor incididunt ut labore et dolore magna aliqua. Lorem ipsum dolor sit amet, consectetur adipisicing elit, eiusmod tempor incididunt ut labore et dolore magna aliqua.

Figure: You Can Implement Text Indentation via the CSS Feature "text-indent"

Underlining Text and Striking Text Through Using "text-decoration"

To add an underscore to a text using CSS, you can use the CSS feature text-decoration. This allows you to draw a line under, above, or through the text. The values are underline, overline, and line-through.
By using none (default setting), you can remove this decoration. Removing an underscore with text decoration: none; can also be used to remove the underscore of a link (<a> tag).

Underlining text and striking text through using text-decoration

Lorem ipsum dolor sit amet, ~~consectetur adipisicing elit,~~ eiusmod tempor incididunt ut labore et dolore magna aliqua. Lorem ipsum dolor sit amet, consectetur adipisicing elit, eiusmod tempor incididunt ut labore et dolore magna aliqua.

Article from J.Wolf: (link)

C:/Users/wolf1/Documents/Buecher/HTML5-Englisch/8117_Zusatzmaterial_Codebeispiele/html-beispiele.promx.de/Beispiele/../index.html

Figure: Underlining (or Undoing the Underlining) or Striking Text Through Using the CSS Feature "text-decoration"

In Figure, you can see the use of text-decoration, where body text was underlined using the span element and the author information by means of text-decoration: underline; In addition, next to the author's name, the underline for the link was removed via text-decoration: none; and text was struck through using the span element in the body text via text-decoration: line-through.

.underline { text-decoration: underline; }
.a-no-underline { text-decoration: none; }
.line-through { text-decoration: line-through; } ...

Listing /examples/chapter/css/style.css

Underlining Using "border-bottom"

Because an underscore with text-decoration often crosses the letters g and y, you can use border bottom for an underscore of texts that aren't links. This means that the letters y and g won't be crossed.

Uppercase and Lowercase Text via "text-transform"

You can use the CSS feature text-transform to control the case of the text. For this purpose, you can use the values uppercase (for uppercase letters), lowercase (for lowercase letters), and capitalize (first letter as uppercase). Again, the default setting is none.

The capitalize value, which is used to represent each first letter of a word as a capital letter, is usually used only in English for titles. In languages such as German, for example, this value is less interesting.
In Figure, you can see how the h1 heading is displayed entirely in uppercase letters by means of text-transform: uppercase; . The paragraph, on the other hand, was set completely in lowercase via text-transform: lowercase; .

Uppercase and lowercase text via text-transform

UPPERCASE: LOREM IPSUM DOLOR SIT AMET, CONSECTETUR ADIPISICING ELIT. EIUSMOD TEMPOR INCIDIDUNT UT LABORE ET DOLORE MAGNA ALIQUA. LOREM IPSUM DOLOR SIT AMET, CONSECTETUR ADIPISICING ELIT. EIUSMOD TEMPOR INCIDIDUNT UT LABORE ET DOLORE MAGNA ALIQUA.

lowercase: lorem ipsum dolor sit amet, consectetur adipisicing elit, eiusmod tempor incididunt ut labore et dolore magna aliqua. lorem ipsum dolor sit amet, consectetur adipisicing elit, eiusmod tempor incididunt ut labore et dolore magna aliqua.

Figure: Uppercase and Lowercase Text via "text-transform"

```
.uppercase { text-transform: uppercase; }
.lowercase { text-transform: lowercase; } ...
```

Listing /examples/chapter/css/style.css

Small Caps

If you're not looking for continuous uppercase letters, but small caps, you should take a look at the CSS feature font-variant from Section.

Adding Shadow to Text via "text-shadow"

A popular effect is to add a shadow to the text using the CSS feature text-shadow. The use of text-shadow is also quite convenient:

```
text-shadow: 5px /* Horizontal offset  */ 5px /* Vertical offset    */ 4px  /* Gradient radius shadow */
gray;  /* Shadow color */
```

In Figure, you can see some variants of shadows used via the following CSS statements for headings:

```
.shadow-one { text-shadow: 3px 3px 5px gray; }
.shadow-two {    color: lightgray;    text-shadow: 0px -2px 1px black;
}
.shadow-three {    color: rgba(255, 0, 0, 0.7);    text-shadow:
```

```
        15px -15px 5px green,
        -5px 15px 8px blue;
    }
```

Listing /examples/chapter/css/style.css

In the example, you can see that it's possible to use several shadows at once for one text (up to six). To do that, you simply need to list the shadows separated by commas.

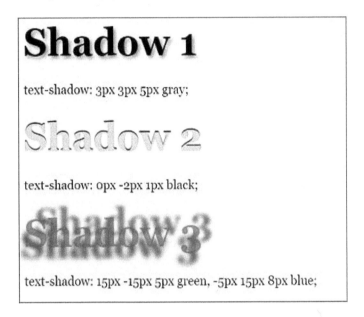

Figure: Different Variants of Shadows

Splitting Text into Multiple Columns Using "column-count"

One very useful feature for typography is the ability to automatically split a text into a multicolumn set using the CSS feature column-count and without any manual work with JavaScript. This function is especially useful for wide screens, so that lines which are too long can be split up into columns, increasing the readability of the text.

Here's how you can set up a two-column layout for the element used with .column:

```
.column {  column-count: 2;  column-gap: 1.5rem;
}
```

You can use column-gap to control the gap between the columns. In Figure, you can see the effect of these lines on an article element as a container with multiple p elements.

Figure: The Multicolumn Set Has Been Applied to an <article> Element as a Container

Instead of column-count, you can also use column-width and specify a width for a column. Depending on the value you specify for the width, this will automatically create as many columns as there is space in the viewport of the web browser. When the web browser can no longer split the columns in width, it will make one single column out of it, for example:

```
.column {   column-width: 250px;   column-gap: 1.5rem;
}
```

In Figure, the web browser has split the text into three columns of 250 pixels. In Figure, on the other hand, the browser window was reduced in size, and it was no longer possible to split the text into at least two columns of 250 pixels, so the text is now displayed in one column.

There's also a short notation available for the two properties column-width and column-count of the CSS feature columns:

```
.column {   columns: 20em 2;   column-gap: 1.5rem;
}
```

This way, you specify that two columns with a width of at least 20 em (320 pixels) should be used. If two columns of 20 em will no longer fit in the browser window, only one column will be used. This would be the case in the example if the viewport is less than 40 em or less than 640 pixels.

Other properties related to the multicolumn set are column-rule, which enables you to draw a line in the gap between columns, and column-span, which lets individual elements span multiple columns.

Figure: Three Columns with 250 pixels

Figure: If Two Columns No Longer Fit into the Width Specified with the CSS Property "column-width", Only One Column Will Be Displayed.

Designing Lists with CSS

Now you'll learn how to manipulate those lists using CSS. Strictly speaking, you can apply the CSS features list-style-type, list-style-image, and list-style-position to <ul> or <ol> for this purpose. A short notation for all three CSS features with list-style also exists. In the following sections, I'll go into a little more detail about these CSS features for styling lists.

Customizing Bullet Points Using "list-style-type"

The CSS feature list-style-type allows you to specify the bullet selection of unordered lists with <ul> and the type of numbering ordered lists with <ol>.
For unordered lists with <ul>, the following values are available: **none** No bullet. **disc**
Filled circle, also called bullet character, default setting. **circle**
Empty circle as bullet character. **square**
Square bullet sign.
For ordered lists with <ol> the following values are available, among others: **decimal**
Numbering in the form 1., 2., 3., 4., 5., 6., and so on. **decimal-leading-zero**
Numbering in the form 01., 02., 03., 04., and so on.

lower-alpha and lower-latin

Numbering in the form a., b., c., and so on.

upper-alpha and upper-latin

Numbering in the form A., B., C., and so on. **lower-roman**
Numbering in the form i., ii., iii., iv., v., and so on. **upper-roman**
Numbering like I., II., III., IV., V., and so on. **none** No numbering.

Numbering in Other Languages

There are other numberings in other languages such as Armenian (armenian), Hebrew (hebrew), Georgian (georgian), or Japanese (hiragana).

In Figure, you can see how a square bullet (square) was used instead of the filled circle (with disc) for an unordered list, and alphabetical numbering in capital letters was used instead of decimal numbering (decimal) for the ordered list. Only the following two lines were used as CSS statements:

... ul { list-style-type: square; } ol { list-style-type: upper-alpha; } ...

Listing /examples/chapter/css/style.css

Feel free to experiment with the values for <ul> and <ol> listed previously.

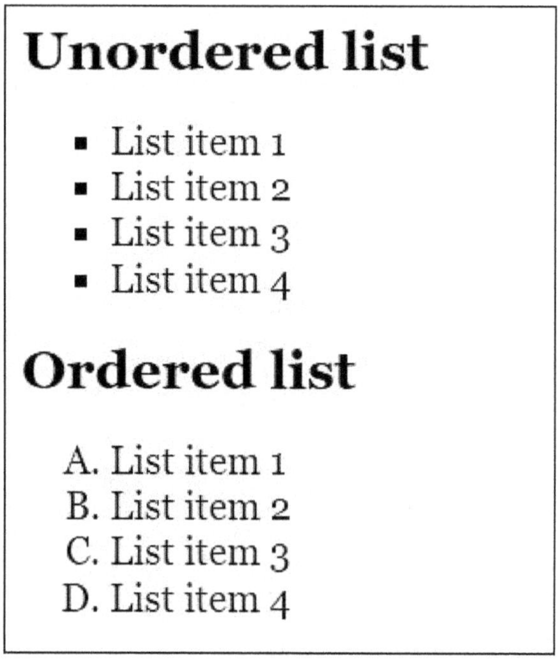

Unordered list

- List item 1
- List item 2
- List item 3
- List item 4

Ordered list

A. List item 1
B. List item 2
C. List item 3
D. List item 4

Figure: Designing Bullets with "list-style-type"

Using Images as Bullets via "list-style-image"

You can use the CSS feature list-style-image to add a custom graphic as an enumeration icon. The value you need to specify is url(path) with the path to a graphic.

In Figure, you can see such an example, where a simple graphic was used for the ul elements. The graphic was added with the following CSS line:

ul { list-style-image: url("../graphic/stern.png"); } ...

Listing /examples/chapter/css/style.css

Figure: You Can Use a Graphic as a Bullet Point with the CSS Feature "list-style-image"

Using a Special Character Instead of a Graphic

As an alternative, you can also use a special character instead of a graphic. To do that, you simply need to set list-style-type to none and define a special character as a list icon via li:before using content:
...
.myul { list-style-type: none; }
.myul li:before { content: '\2713'; color: green; } ...

If you want to know what is represented by the character '\2713', you should test this code (or look in /examples/chapter/index2.html). The advantage of using special characters instead of graphics is that you can adjust the size and color more easily.

Positioning Bulleted Lists via "list-style-position"

You can use the CSS feature list-style-position to set whether the bullet should be inside or outside the box that contains the entries. The default behaviour can be set using the outside value, which places the bullet point to the left of the text block. The counterpart to this value is inside, which places the bullet point inside the text block.

It's best to look at Figure, where you can see the difference between outside and inside. In the example, the box with the <li> tag was assigned a gray background color. The CSS statements for that were written as follows:

.outside { list-style-position: outside; }
.inside { list-style-position: inside; } ...

Listing /examples/chapter/css/style.css

Positioning bulleted lists (outside)

- List item 1: Lorem ipsum dolor sit amet, consectetuer adipiscing elit. Nullam ipsum.
- List item 2: Lorem ipsum dolor sit amet, consectetuer adipiscing elit. Nullam ipsum.

Positioning bulleted lists (inside)

- List item 1: Lorem ipsum dolor sit amet, consectetuer adipiscing elit. Nullam ipsum.
- List item 2: Lorem ipsum dolor sit amet, consectetuer adipiscing elit. Nullam ipsum.

Figure: You Can Use "list-style-position" to Define Whether the Bullet Points Should Be outside (Default Setting) or inside the Box with the Entries.

Short Notation "list-style" for Designing Lists

As is the case with several other CSS features, list-style is a short notation for the list-style-type, list-style-image, and list-style-position features, so you may be able to specify the shape, the graphic, and/or the bullet position in one go.

You can use any order and also enter only one or two entries. If you specify a graphic (list-style-image) with url(), the shape (list-style-type) will always be overwritten. list-style-type will only be used as an alternative if the graphic couldn't be loaded. Even if the order is arbitrary, it's recommended to maintain the order, as follows: list-type: list-style-type list-style-position list-style-image;

This can simplify any troubleshooting work. Here's another example to clarify this:

ul { list-style: disc url(mybullet.png) inside; }

This short notation corresponds to the following entries:

ul {
  list-style-type: disc;   list-style-image: url(mybullet.png);   list-style-position: inside;
}

Creating Navigation and Menus via Lists

To create a navigation with CSS, lists are commonly used. In this section, I'll describe a simple way to implement a navigation using lists and CSS. The following HTML code with a list is used for this purpose:
...
```
<nav>
  <ul class="menu">
    <li class="logo"><img src="graphics/logo.png" height="30"></li>
    <li class="menu-item"><a href="#">Home page</a></li>
    <li class="menu-item"><a href="#">News</a></li>
    <li class="menu-item"><a href="#">About me</a></li>
    <li class="menu-item"><a href="#">Contact</a></li>
    <li class="menu-item"><a href="#">Privacy</a></li>
    <li class="menu-item button"><a href="#">Sign in</a></li>
  </ul> </nav> ...
```

Listing /examples/chapter/index.html

The result of the list completely without styling is shown in Figure.

Figure: The Pure HTML Representation of the Navigation as a List

In Figure, on the other hand, I've already added basic styling to the individual elements in /examples/chapter/css/style.css. With regard to the lists, I've set list-style-type to none so that no bullet gets displayed.

```
... ul {    list-style-type: none;
}
```

Listing /examples/chapter/css/style.css

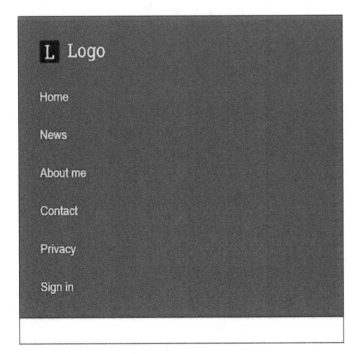

Figure: The List after a First Basic Styling

Creating the Mobile Navigation for the Smartphone

First of all, it's recommended to create the mobile navigation for smartphones. I chose a flexbox for this purpose because it allows me to lay out the menu and menu items without much effort. The important CSS lines for the mobile layout are as follows:

```
... .menu {    display: flex;    flex-wrap: wrap;    justify-content: space-between;    align-items: center; }
.menu-item.button {    order: 1; }
.menu-item {    width: 100%;    text-align: center;    order: 2;
}
```

Listing /examples/chapter/css/style.css

By using display: flex, you make the ul element a flex container, while align-items: center allows you to center the li elements (here, .menu-item) vertically on the cross axis. order enables you to sort the order of the flexbox elements. In the mobile version, I can thus position the button (order:1) in front of the navigation elements of the menu (order: 2). You can extend the individual li menu items across the entire width using width: 100%. You can see the mobile version of the vertical navigation menu with lists in Figure.

Figure: The Mobile Smartphone Version of the Vertical Navigation Menu with Lists

Creating the Vertical Navigation Menu for Tablets

I didn't change much for the vertical navigation menu for tablets. The logo can be extended using flex: 1 . The button next to it, on the other hand, only gets as much space as it needs (width: auto). The other menu items remain at width: 100% , as in the smartphone version and thus still extend across the entire width, placing each element in its own line.

...

```
@media all and (min-width: 37.5em) {
  .logo {        flex: 1;
  }
  .menu-item.button {        width: auto;        border-bottom: 0;
  }
}
```
...

Listing /examples/chapter/css/style.css

Figure: The Tablet Version of the Vertical Navigation with List Items

Expandable Menu with JavaScript for Mobile Versions

I didn't include an expandable menu for the mobile versions here because I would have had to anticipate JavaScript at this point. Instead, I created the example using a very simple expandable menu with jQuery, which you can find in /examples/chapter/index2.html

Figure: A Simple Expandable Menu with jQuery

Creating the Vertical Navigation Menu for Desktops

For the desktop version, I keep it very simple and set all menu items to width: auto, making them share the space behind the logo, which still uses flex: 1. If you want to provide all elements with equal space in the horizontal navigation, you could do this by setting the CSS feature flex to 1 in the menu-item class as well.
...

```
@media all and (min-width: 60em) {
    .menu-item {        width: auto;
    }   .logo {       order: 0;     }
    .menu-item {        order: 1;    }    .button {        order: 2;
    }
    .menu li.button {        padding-right: 0;
    }
}
```

Listing /examples/chapter/css/style.css

Figure: The Desktop Version of the Vertical Navigation with List Elements

Designing Appealing Tables with CSS

Tables are commonly used to present data in a clear way. Thanks to CSS, you can make a boring HTML table more attractive and appealing. You already know many CSS features for designing a table from other sections (but not yet in connection with tables). At this point, I only want to mention the CSS features that are particularly useful in the context of tables. To demonstrate this, we'll style the timetable shown in Figure from pure HTML with CSS in the following sections.

Time	Monday	Tuesday	Wednesday	Thursday	Friday	Saturday
8:00	English	English	German	Latin	Mathematics	Sport
8:45	Religion	Physics	Chemistry	English	English	Sport
9:30	French	Mathematics	English	German	Chemistry	Religion
10:15	Mathematics	Sport	Religion	Physics	free time	Sport
11:00	Sport	English	French	free time	free time	free time

Figure: A Boring Table in Pure HTML

Creating Fixed-Width Tables

You know that if width is too small, the contents of table cells without special specifications will take up the space they just need to get displayed. It doesn't matter if you want to reduce the table width explicitly via width to 500px, 300px, or 50px, the result will always look as shown in Figure because the table always tries to fit to the content.

It's still possible to use the CSS feature table-layout to assign a specified and fixed width to the table elements. The default value of table-layout is auto and provides the view you're used to. If, on the other hand, you use the value fixed for the CSS feature table-layout, then exactly the width you specified via width will be used. If the content doesn't fit into the table cell anymore, it will be wrapped, truncated (depending on the value of the overflow feature), or just written beyond the cell boundary. For example, with reference to Figure, I've limited the width of the table to 500 pixels and fixed the table layout as follows:

```
...
.table-fixed {   table-layout: fixed;   width: 500px;
}
...
```

Listing /examples/chapter/css/style.css

You can see the (not really appealing) result of this fixation in Figure.

Time	Monday	Tuesday	Wednesday	Thursday	Friday	Saturday
8:00	English	English	German	Latin	Mathema Sport	
8:45	Religion	Physics	Chemistr English		English	Sport
9:30	French	Mathema English		German	Chemistr Religion	
10:15	Mathema Sport		Religion	Physics	free time	Sport
11:00	Sport	English	French	free time	free time	free time

Figure: When You Use "table-layout: fixed;", Then No More Consideration Is Given to the Content

General Recommendation: Designing Appealing Tables with CSS

Because you may also look in this book for a general recipe for formatting a table properly with CSS, I'll discuss this briefly here and give you a few tips on how I would go about it. I summarize a table in HTML as usual. Then the table is assigned a width via width. I format the table header differently from the rest of the table cells. For a better overview, I color the individual table rows alternately with two different colors. Almost all table cells get padding by means of padding. When it makes sense, I use the CSS pseudo class :hover, which highlights a table row when the user hovers over it with the mouse. In summary, a basic layout of a table with CSS usually looks like this in my case:

```
... table {   width: 700px;
} th {   padding: 0.5em;   text-transform: uppercase;   border-top: 1px solid black;   border-bottom: 1px solid
black;   text-align: left;
} tr:nth-child(even) { background: lightgray; } td:nth-child(1) {   font-weight: bold;   width: 100px;
} td { padding: 0.5em; } tr:hover {   background: darkblue;   color: white;
}
...
```

Listing /examples/chapter/css/style.css

You can see the result of these few lines of CSS used to design a complete table in Figure.

TIME	MONDAY	TUESDAY	WEDNESDAY	THURSDAY	FRIDAY	SATURDAY
8:00	English	English	German	Latin	Mathematics	Sport
8:45	Religion	Physics	Chemistry	English	English	Sport
9:30	French	Mathematics	English	German	Chemistry	Religion
10:15	Mathematics	Sport	Religion	Physics	free time	Sport
11:00	Sport	English	French	free time	free time	free time

Figure: The Basic Formatting of an HTML Table with CSS Is Done with a Few Lines

Collapsing Borders for Table Cells Using "border-collapse"

The CSS feature border-collapse allows you to specify whether the borders of individual cells are displayed separately (border-collapse: separate; , default setting) or collapsed (border-collapse: collapse;). In Figure, you can see the use of the separate value, and in Figure the use of collapse.

table { border-collapse: separate; }

Time	Monday	Tuesday	Wednesday	Thursday	Friday	Saturday
8:00	English	English	German	Latin	Mathematics	Sport
8:45	Religion	Physics	Chemistry	English	English	Sport
9:30	French	Mathematics	English	German	Chemistry	Religion
10:15	Mathematics	Sport	Religion	Physics	free time	Sport
11:00	Sport	English	French	free time	free time	free time

Figure: Frames of Adjacent Elements Are Displayed Separately with "border-collapse: separate;" (= default setting)

table { border-collapse: collapse; }

Time	Monday	Tuesday	Wednesday	Thursday	Friday	Saturday
8:00	English	English	German	Latin	Mathematics	Sport
8:45	Religion	Physics	Chemistry	English	English	Sport
9:30	French	Mathematics	English	German	Chemistry	Religion
10:15	Mathematics	Sport	Religion	Physics	free time	Sport
11:00	Sport	English	French	free time	free time	free time

Figure: Due to "border-collapse: collapse;", the Borders of the Adjacent Elements Collapse (Example in /examples/chapter/index.html)

Setting the Spacing between Cells via "border-spacing"

If the CSS feature of border-collapse isn't equal to collapse, you can set the spacing of adjacent cells by using border-spacing. The specification for this is mostly in pixels, and you can also specify separately the values for a horizontal and vertical spacing. Compared to Figure, for the example in Figure, we used border-spacing: 5px 10px;, where the spacing in horizontal direction is 5 pixels and in the vertical direction 10 pixels to the adjacent table element.

"border-spacing: 0px;"

If you set border-spacing to 0, the borders won't collapse as they do with border-collapse: collapse; , but the cells will be positioned exactly next to each other.

table { border-spacing: 5px 10px; }

Time	Monday	Tuesday	Wednesday	Thursday	Friday	Saturday
8:00	English	English	German	Latin	Mathematics	Sport
8:45	Religion	Physics	Chemistry	English	English	Sport
9:30	French	Mathematics	English	German	Chemistry	Religion
10:15	Mathematics	Sport	Religion	Physics	free time	Sport
11:00	Sport	English	French	free time	free time	free time

Figure: You Can Adjust the Spacing between the Table Cells via "border-spacing" (Example in /examples/chapter/index.html)

Displaying Empty Table Cells Using "empty-cells"

If you have an empty table cell, you can use the CSS feature empty-cells to specify whether or not you want to draw a border around it. By default, the web browser usually displays a border around an empty table cell, as shown in Figure, which corresponds to the value show (empty-cells: show;).

table { empty-cells: show; }

Time	Monday	Tuesday	Wednesday	Thursday	Friday	Saturday
8:00	English	English	German	Latin	Mathematics	
8:45	Religion	Physics	Chemistry	English	English	Sport
9:30	French		English	German	Chemistry	Religion
10:15	Mathematics	Sport	Religion	Physics	free time	
11:00	Sport	English	French			

Figure: Showing Borders for Empty Cells Is the Default Setting, Which Can Also Be Written as "empty-cells: show;"

If you don't want a border to be drawn around a table cell with no content, you just need to assign the hide value to the empty-cells feature, as was done in the example in Figure. If you use the collapse value and not separate for the CSS feature border-collapse, the empty-cells: hide; specification will be ignored.

Empty Cells

A line feed, space, or tab feed is considered invisible content. On the other hand, if you write an enforced blank space with   in the table cell, this will be considered visible content, and a border will be drawn around it if you've used empty-cells: hide; .

table { empty-cells: hide; }

Time	Monday	Tuesday	Wednesday	Thursday	Friday	Saturday
8:00	English	English	German	Latin	Mathematics	
8:45	Religion	Physics	Chemistry	English	English	Sport
9:30	French		English	German	Chemistry	Religion
10:15	Mathematics	Sport	Religion	Physics	free time	
11:00	Sport	English	French			

Figure: If You Want to Hide the Border for Empty Cells, You Can Do This by Using "empty-cells: hide;" (Example in /examples/chapter/index.html)

Positioning Table Captions via "caption-side"

As you may already recognize from the title of the CSS feature caption-side, this feature sets the position of the table caption you used with the caption element. The default is usually a display above the table, which corresponds to the top value for caption-side. By means of bottom, you can position the caption below the table, as I did in Figure.

table { caption-side: bottom; }

Time	Monday	Tuesday	Wednesday	Thursday	Friday	Saturday
8:00	English	English	German	Latin	Mathematics	
8:45	Religion	Physics	Chemistry	English	English	Sport
9:30	French		English	German	Chemistry	Religion
10:15	Mathematics	Sport	Religion	Physics	free time	
11:00	Sport	English	French			

Table 1.1: Timetable for the class 7b

Figure: The Table Caption with <caption> Has Been Moved to the Bottom with "caption-side: bottom;" (Example in /examples/chapter/index.html)

Adjusting Images and Graphics Using "width" and "height"

Basically, you already know the CSS features you can use to customize images and graphics with CSS if you've read the book from the beginning. You can also set the size of the images using the CSS features, width and height. For example:

```
... .large {    width: 325px;    height: 267px; }
.medium {    width: 225px;    height: 184px; }
.small {    width: 125px;    height: 103px; } }
```

Listing /examples/chapter/css/style.css

For example, with these three classes, you can conveniently output the same image in three different sizes. Instead of width and height, you just need to specify the corresponding class name for the img elements. You can see the result of the following HTML lines in Figure:

```
...
   <img src="cover.png" alt="Computer History" class="small" />
```

```
<img src="cover.png" alt="Computer History" class="medium" />     <img src="cover.png"
alt="Computer History" class="large" /> ...
```

Listing /examples/chapter/index.html

You already know how to align images, namely by giving the CSS feature float the value left or right. If you
also want to center an image, you merely need to make a block element out of the img element via display:
block; , then you can use margin: 0px auto; or text-align: center; to center-align the image. Here are three
more classes you can use to align or center images with CSS:

```
...
img.align-left {    float: left;    margin: 0 0.6em 0.3em 0;
} img.align-right {    float: right;    margin: 0 0 0.3em 0.6em;
} img.align-center {    display: block;    margin: 0px auto;  }
```

Listing /examples/chapter/css/style2.css

Figure: One and the Same Image Was Put into a Class with the CSS Features "width" and "height" and
Used in Different Sizes

You can combine the classes created in this way with the classes for the appropriate size and have the
images output in the appropriate size and orientation for your website in no time at all. You can view the
result of the following HTML code in Figure:

```
...
<p>
  <img src="cover.png" alt="Computer History"       class="align-left medium">
  Lorem ipsum ...
</p>
<p>
  <img src="cover.png" alt="Computer History"       class="align-right small">
  Lorem ipsum ...
</p>
<p>
  <img src="cover.png" alt="Computer History"       class="small align-center">
  Lorem ipsum ...  </p> ...
```

Listing /examples/chapter/index2.html

Figure: Graphics Resized and Aligned with CSS

Transforming Elements with CSS

With CSS, it's also possible to change the position of HTML elements using the CSS feature transform. The possible actions are movements via translate(), an enlargement or reduction using scale(), a rotation by means of rotate(), the skewing of elements via skew(), and a distortion with matrix(). These transformations are supported by all currently available web browsers.

Although these transformations can be applied to other HTML elements as well, for demonstration purposes, we'll use images that have been placed side by side using a flexbox. You can see the starting point for the planned transformations in Figure.

```
...
<h1>Transforming images with CSS</h1>
<ul>
  <li>
    <img src="images/image01.jpg" alt="China photography tour 2019">
  </li>
  <li>
    <img src="images/image02.jpg" alt="China photography tour 2019">
  </li>
  <li>
    <img src="images/image03.jpg" alt="China photography tour 2019">
  </li>
  <li>
    <img src="images/image04.jpg" alt="China photography tour 2019">
  </li>
  <li>
    <img src="images/image05.jpg" alt="China photography tour 2019">    </li>
...
</ul> ...
```

Listing /examples/chapter/index.html

Figure: These Images Are Supposed to Be Transformed When Users Hover over Them (":hover")

Scaling HTML Elements via "transform: scale()"

You can enlarge (or reduce) elements using the CSS feature transform and the CSS function scale(). A value of scale(1.0) has no effect. If you use scale(1.25), the element will be enlarged by a factor of 1.25. Similarly, if you specify scale(0.75), an image will be scaled down by a factor of 0.75. The surrounding elements aren't affected by an enlargement or reduction and remain firmly in position.

Here's an example in which an image is to be enlarged by a factor of 1.25 when hovering. The results of the following CSS lines are shown in Figure:

```
...
img:hover {   transform: scale(1.25);
}
```

Listing /examples/chapter/css/style.css

Figure: The Images Are Enlarged by a Factor of 1.25 When You Move the Cursor over Them (":hover")

Rotating HTML Elements Using "transform: rotate()"

When you use rotate(), the respective element gets rotated by a specified number of degrees. The specification is in the form of rotate(15deg), which rotates the element clockwise by 15 degrees. A negative value rotates the element counterclockwise. You can see the result of the following CSS lines in Figure.

...

.trans a img:hover {   transform: rotate(15deg); }

Listing /examples/chapter/css/style.css

Figure: A Rotation on Mouseover Using "transform: rotate()"

Skewing HTML Elements Using "transform: skew()"

The skew() function can be used to skew an HTML element around the x-axis and y-axis. Here, too, two values are expected as degrees. The first value indicates the skew around the x-axis and the second one around the y-axis. For example, you can use skew(5deg, 10deg) to rotate the element 5 degrees around the x-axis and 10 degrees around the y-axis. You can view the results of the following CSS lines in Figure.

...
.trans a img:hover {   transform: skew(5deg, 10deg); }

Listing /examples/chapter/css/style.css

Figure: Skewing HTML Elements via "transform: skew()"

Additional Functions via "skewX()" and "skewY()"

If you want to skew an HTML element only around the x-axis or y-axis, the corresponding functions for these actions are skewX() and skewY(), respectively.

Moving HTML Elements Using "transform: translate()"

The translate() function enables you to move elements. For this purpose, you also need to specify two values to indicate by how much you want to move the element along the x-axis and y-axis. A specification such as translate(10px, 20px) moves the element 10 pixels to the right along the x-axis and 20 pixels down along the y-axis. Negative values move the element in the other direction. The following CSS snippet causes the movement shown in Figure when you halt the mouse cursor on the image:

```
...
#trans a img:hover {   transform: translate(30px, 20px); }
```

Listing /examples/chapter/css/style.css

Figure: Moving HTML Elements via "transform: translate()"

Combining Different Transformations

It's possible to combine several functions for the purpose of transforming. To do that, you only need to specify the respective functions separated by a space. Here's a simple example of this, in which an element gets enlarged by a factor of 1.25 and rotated clockwise by 10 degrees.

Figure: The Element Was Enlarged and Rotated

```
.trans a img:hover {   transform: scale(1.25) rotate(10deg); }
```

Listing /examples/chapter/css/style.css

Other HTML Elements

By the way, the transform functions presented here aren't limited to images or graphics and can be used for other HTML elements as well. Likewise, you can transform the HTML elements at any time and don't need to use hovering with the mouse to do so, although this is what people tend to prefer.

In Figure, for example, the articles were rotated or skewed via the rotate() and skew() functions. Of course, this isn't always useful, but my point is to show that these functions can be applied to other HTML elements too.

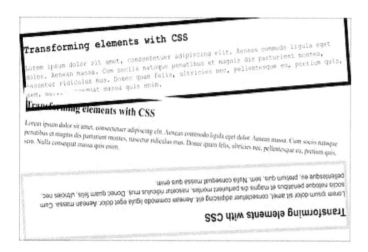

Figure: Other HTML Elements Can Also Be Transformed. Here, <article> Elements Were Rotated or Skewed (Example in /examples/chapter/index.html)

Other Functions for Transforming

I haven't mentioned transform-origin(x, y) yet, which allows you to move the origin point from the element to be transformed.

Creating Transitions with CSS

In the examples with mouse hovering and using transform, the transition of the effects was a bit messy after all. For example, in /examples/chapter/index.html, which is shown in Figure, if you place the mouse cursor over the image, the graphic gets immediately scaled up and rotated, just like a light switch, and then immediately returned to its normal position when you move the mouse somewhere else. If you find this transition a bit too abrupt, you can soften it using the CSS feature transition. This doesn't require much effort at all, as shown in the following CSS snippet:

```
... img {    max-height: 100%;    min-width: 100%;    object-fit: cover;    vertical-align: bottom;
transition: all 1s ease;
}
img:hover {    transform: scale(1.25) rotate(10deg);    border: 4px white solid;    transition: all 1s ease; }
```

Listing /examples/chapter/css/style.css

This example corresponds to the one in Figure, except that the image gets rotated and enlarged slowly (here exactly within 1 second) while you hover the mouse cursor over it. To ensure that the image gets moved back to the normal position just as slowly and not abruptly, the normal position was also defined using the same transition statement. More actions weren't necessary so that now there's no longer a jerky effect in conjunction with transform when you hover over the image. The best thing to do is to try out this example for yourself.

When looking at the transition feature, you'll notice that three values have been used here: all, 1s, and ease. Strictly speaking, transition is a short notation of the following features:

• transition-property

Allows you to specify the property to be animated during the transition. With all, you can specify that all properties are animated. You can also specify only individual properties here, such as background for animating.

• transition-duration

This specifies the duration of the transition in seconds. You can also determine the fraction of a second with, for example, 0.2s, which is two tenths of a second.

• transition-timing-function

This specification is a kind of temporal course of the transition. For example, the ease specification used here means that the transition starts slowly, speeds up a bit in the middle, and ends slowly again.
There are several such temporal progressions such as linear, ease-in, ease-out, or ease-in-out, which you can try for yourself.

Optionally, you could use transition-delay, which adds a delay at the start of the transition.

Consequently, you could alternatively write the short notation of transition used previously as follows:

```
img:hover {
transition-property: all;   transition-duration: 1s;   transition-timing-function: ease; }
```

Examples and Overview of "transition"

For some great demonstrations and examples of transitions using transition.

Styling HTML Forms with CSS

While you've seen HTML forms in action, I haven't yet described how to design forms with CSS. The following isn't meant to be the ultimate way, but rather a creative suggestion on how you can go about it. There are certainly countless ways to design a form with CSS. Here, I'll show you one of them.

Less Is More!

CSS now provides an extremely wide range of options for designing forms, which are only briefly touched on here. After these sections on forms, you should take a look at the many examples of HTML forms on the internet.

Please keep in mind that, despite the wide range of design options, forms are real functional elements of a website, and when designing them, you want to make sure that these elements remain recognizable as what they are intended for. A form is usually used to submit entered data to the web server via a web browser.

Neatly Structuring an HTML Form

The first step should be to create a structure with all necessary form elements in HTML. I decided to use the example of a simple HTML form that submits feedback or a simple message. Here's the HTML framework for it:

```
<form id="myForm" method="post">
 <fieldset>
  <div>
   <label for="name">Name:</label>    <input type="text" name="name" id="name"
placeholder="Your name">
  </div>
  <div>
   <label for="fname">First name:</label>    <input type="text" name="fname" id="fname"
placeholder="Your first name">
  </div>
  <div>
   <label for="mail">Email:</label>    <input type="email" name="mail" id="mail"
placeholder="Email address" required>
   <label for="mail"></label>
  </div>
  <div>
   <label for="born">Year of birth:</label>    <input type="number" name="born" id="born"
min="1920" max="2015" value="1990">
  </div>
  <div class="form_radio">
   <label>Gender:</label>
   <input type="radio" name="gender" id="male"        value="male" class="nobreak">
   <label for="male" class="nobreak">Male</label>    <input type="radio" name="gender" id="female"
value="female" class="nobreak">
   <label for="female" class="nobreak">Female</label>
  </div>
  <div>
   <label for="nachricht">Your message:</label>    <textarea name="message" id="message"
placeholder="Enter message here..." rows="8"        required>
   </textarea>
   <label for="message"></label>
  </div>
  <div>
   <input type="checkbox" name="reply" id="reply"        value="reply" class="nobreak">    <label
for="reply" class="nobreak">
    GDPR consent (<a href="#">Privacy policy</a>)
   </label>
  </div>
  <div>
```

```
        <input name="submit" type="submit" value="Submit" class="nobreak">     <input name="Reset"
type="reset" value="Reset" class="nobreak">
    </div>
    <p>(×) = Input required</p>
  </fieldset> </form> ...
```

Listing /examples/chapter/index.html

There isn't much more that needs to be said about this HTML form; you learned about all the individual
elements and attributes in detail.

If you want to make CSS life easier with HTML forms, you can place all input fields with their associated
labels between <div> and </div> right away, as shown in the example. This will display the related elements
directly in one line;

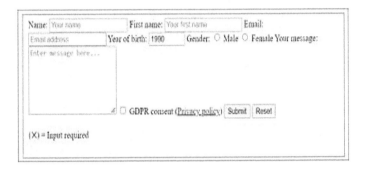

Figure: The Form without the <div> Elements

Likewise, it can only be recommended to use <fieldset> and <label> because these elements can be very
useful for design tasks.

Between <fieldset> and </fieldset>, you can group logically matching areas of form elements and at the
same time have another approach to use CSS to design this area.

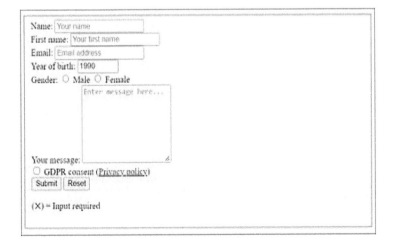

Figure: Here's the Form with the <div> Elements

The same applies to <label> because not only do you use it to create a connection to the form element with
the HTML attribute for, which means that when you click on the label, you immediately activate the form
element, but you also get a kind of grid in which elements are displayed next to each other as in a table by

specifying <label> and another form element such as <input>. Furthermore, you could design a <label> with an ID or class separately, which is more difficult with an empty text. Finally, screen readers help you show the relationship between text and form elements.

Aligning Form Elements with CSS

Once you've created the basic HTML framework with the relevant form elements, the first thing you should take care of is the alignment of the individual form elements. At the moment, everything is still a bit unordered.

Just take a closer look at the figure: what you need first is a uniform alignment and a width for the labels on the left of the HTML form. You need to decide whether you want to display the labels next to the form elements or above them. In this example, I decided to place the labels next to the form elements, which I write in the following CSS snippet:

```
label {    min-width: 8em;    display: inline-block;    text-align: left;
  }
```

Listing /examples/chapter/css/style.css

Here, I've used inline-block for display, which allows you to treat an element like a block element and use the width and height properties as well as margin without creating a paragraph (as would be the case with block). If, on the other hand, you want to place the labels above the form elements for input, you should use display: block; instead.

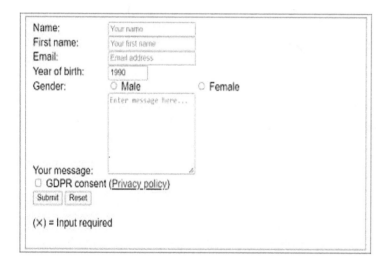

Figure: After the First Alignment of the HTML Element <label> with CSS

The first alignment of the label element looks good. Next, you'll probably want to write a uniform width for the input fields and the text area field. Again, not much is needed to do that, as the following CSS lines show:

```
... input {   width: 20em;   padding : 0.7em;   font-family: Arial;   color: gray;
} textarea {   width: 24em;   padding: 0.1em;   font-family: Arial;   color: gray;
}
```

Listing /examples/chapter/css/style.css

Because the radio buttons and the checkbox are input fields as well, and they would look strange with a width of 20em, we use an extra selector for them. In the example, I've therefore written the following:

```
input[type="checkbox"], input[type="radio"] {    width: auto;
  }
```

Listing /examples/chapter/css/style.css

This only cancels the length assignment of the input fields of type radio and checkbox. Let's take a quick look at Figure—the interim result looks impressive, doesn't it?

Figure: It's Starting to Look Neatly Arranged

What still doesn't look really appealing is the arrangement of the label in front of the multiline text field, the position of the checkbox below the text field, and the two buttons.

We should move the label in front of the multiline text field up as follows:

```
label:first-child { vertical-align: top; } ...
```

You can move the checkbox to the right by using a simple margin-left, and you can do the same with the submit button:

```
input[type="checkbox"], input[type="submit"] {    margin-left: 12em;
  }
```

Finally, a width specification for the two buttons is missing, which you can write as follows:

```
input[type="submit"], input[type="reset"] {    width: 12em;
  }
```

All in all, this completes the simple arrangement of the form elements with CSS. The result in Figure looks very nice.

Figure: Neatly Arranged Thanks to CSS

Designing Form Elements with CSS

After you've put everything in place, you can get down to styling the form visually with CSS. From the outside to the inside, the first thing to do is to design the field set and legend. In this example, I've used the following styles:

...
fieldset {   width: 90%;   padding-top: 1.5em;   padding-left: 1.5em;   background: rgb(240, 240, 240); }
...

This way, we've styled the area between <fieldset> and </fieldset> by setting the width, a background color, and a border.

In addition to the visual design of form elements, you can also include interactions for visitors, which will make the website not only more beautiful, but easier to use. You can implement such interactions using the CSS pseudo-class :hover or :active. Here are some practical examples:

... input:hover, textarea:hover {   background: #fffff0;   border: 2px solid #efe816;   box-shadow: 0 0 10px rgba(0,0,0,0.2);
 } input[type="submit"]:hover, input[type="reset"]:hover {   background: #c9c9c9;   border: 2px solid #6c6c6c;
 } input[type="submit"]:active, input[type="reset"]:active {   background: #8f8f8f;
 }
...

If you now hover the mouse pointer over one of the input fields or the multiline text area input field (:hover), this input field will be displayed with a different color and a different border. The box-shadow feature also gives the impression that this input field is glowing.

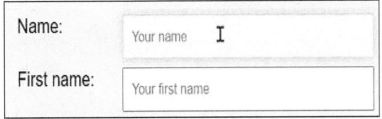

Figure: Interaction Help When the Mouse Pointer Is over an Input Field

The buttons in this example were also designed separately with CSS pseudo-classes, so that the background color changes when the mouse hovers over the button (:hover) or if you click on it (:active).

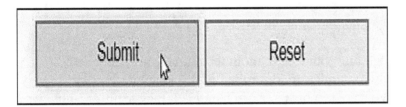

Figure: Hover Effect for Buttons with CSS

At the end of the example, I've created a version for smaller viewports. If the viewport width is less than 640 pixels, all label and input elements that aren't marked with the .nobreak class will be converted to block elements via display:block; and thus displayed one below the other. Here is the CSS for that:

```
...
/* Single column break at 640 pixels */ @media screen and (max-width: 40em) {   label:not(.nobreak) {
display: block; }   label{ padding-bottom: 0.4em; }   input:not(.nobreak) { display:block; }
input[type="checkbox"], input[type="submit"], input[type="radio"]  {    margin-left: 0;
 }
}
```

At this point, I could demonstrate and explain countless more options with CSS for HTML forms, but this would go beyond the scope of the book. The complete example for this section can be found in /examples/chapter/index.html.

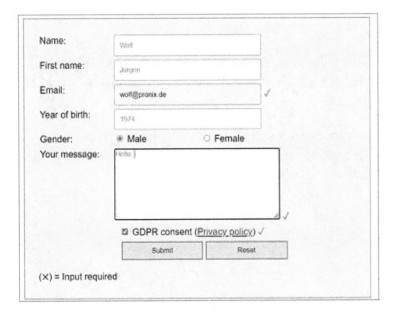

Figure: A Simple HTML Form Styled with CSS

Testing and Organizing

This chapter is more like a hodgepodge of different topics related to CSS and HTML. You'll learn specific things you still need to know in regards to testing and organizing websites.

In this chapter, you won't learn much about new features, but rather about techniques or tricks related to CSS and HTML that can be very useful. The following topics are described in this chapter:
 CSS and HTML are constantly evolving, and not every web browser can handle all new features right away. Here, you'll learn how to find out what a particular web browser is already capable of doing and what it isn't.
Because there are more and more different devices and hence different screen sizes, here you'll learn how to test and view websites in different sizes using online tools.
As projects get larger and longer, it can get confusing if you write everything in one CSS file. So, in this section, you'll learn how to use a central stylesheet to keep track of large projects.
I'll also describe the built-in style defaults of a web browser and how to reset or normalize all CSS defaults.

Web Browser Tests: What's Possible?

Today, most visitors are using modern web browsers. When this book went into print, Google Chrome was enthroned at the top, ahead of Safari. The remaining percentage points were shared between web browsers such as Firefox, Edge and Internet Explorer, Opera, and so on, although Firefox enjoys somewhat greater popularity in Germany than in the rest of the world. If you're serious about building websites, you'll be testing your work extensively in all major web browsers and on different devices. At this point, the question might arise which browsers you should use for testing and which functionality a web browser actually brings along. You'll get an answer to these questions in the following sections.

Validating HTML and CSS

The first step in testing a website should always involve validation. Many web browsers already provide a function for web developers to perform validation. Plug-ins are also often available for various browsers as well as HTML editors or development environments.

At this point, it's important to mention that a valid website doesn't mean that it's also perfect at the same time. Things like accessibility, usability, or speed won't get better just because the HTML or CSS is valid. Consequently, those validators are also just another bunch of tools for quality assurance.

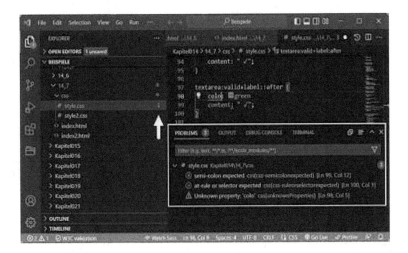

Figure: What's Indispensable for Me Is a Validation of HTML and CSS during the Writing Process of HTML and CSS, Like Here with Visual Studio Code from Microsoft

Which Browsers Are Visitors Currently Using?

First of all, you might be wondering which browsers you should use for testing. Of course, it would be best to test with all browsers right away, but this already raises the question of feasibility, especially considering that most visitors are now using mobile devices. For this reason, it makes sense to first look at a few statistics about which browsers are most commonly used nowadays.

Of course, you mustn't make the mistake of generalizing these kinds of statistics. For example, if you put a website online that contains mostly Apple articles, you're also likely to have mostly visitors with a Safari web browser. Then you'll probably study the statistics afterwards anyway, when the website has gone online, to see what your visitors came to your website with.

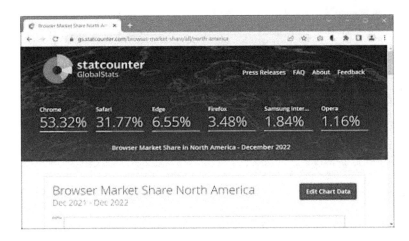

Figure: Web Browser Market in Germany

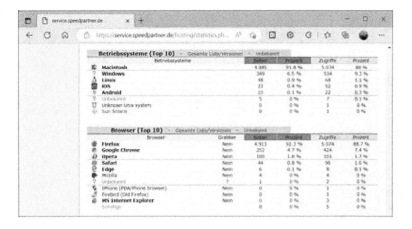

Figure: A Look at Your Own Statistics Then Reveals More Precisely What Your Visitors Really Use to Visit the Website

CSS Web Browser Test

Fortunately, modern CSS support is very good in all modern web browsers. To test the capabilities of the web browser with regard to CSS, there are several test systems available on the web. The advantage of those test systems should be that you can at least weigh up during the development of your website whether you should use a new CSS feature on your website at all or set up a fallback for certain web browsers that can't handle it.

A more specific test for CSS features was developed by Lea Verou. The latest web browsers currently manage around 50% to 67%, which isn't bad at all. It's also useful that the test lists the results for each individual area as well. Nice side effect of this test: you'll discover many new CSS features and also immediate links to the corresponding entries of the specification.

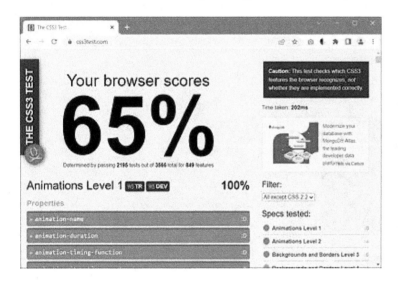

Figure: On https://css3test.com, You Get a Nice List of What the Web Browser Can and Can't (Yet) Do in Detail

HTML5 Web Browser Test

As for CSS, you can find an interesting overview of what the web browser can do and what it can't do (yet) compared to other web browsers in terms of HTML at https://html5test.com. Here, too, you'll find the latest

HTML features linked to the corresponding specification.

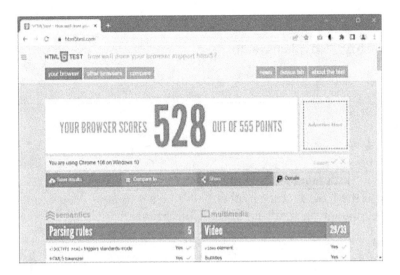

Figure: What the Web Browser Do in Terms of HTML

Can I Use That?

It's not easy to keep track of the different web technologies and what you can use of them with which web browser. Especially with newer CSS and HTML features, it can become quite a tedious matter to test what already works on which web browser without web browser prefixes.

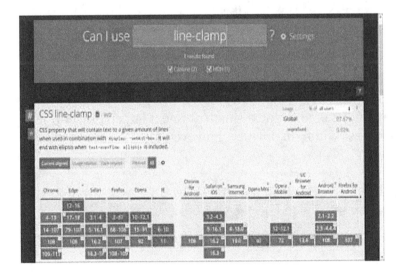

Figure: The Web Database www.caniuse.com Is Very Useful When It Comes to Determining Which Web Techniques Can Be Used with Which Web Browser

The web database at www.caniuse.com specializes in such cases and has proven its worth. The database takes into account the currently popular web browsers.

The website also features a very helpful continuing list of issues, notes, and resources on the topic you're looking for. Searching for a topic is comfortable and easy thanks to a dynamic search function.

Feature Query Using the "@supports" Rule

You can check whether a particular CSS feature is supported by a web browser using the CSS rule @supports. This feature query is also referred to as a CSS feature query. Here's an example:

```
...
@supports( hyphens: auto) {  p {    text-align: justify;    hyphens: auto;
 }
}
...
```

Listing /examples/chapter/css/style.css

Here, we use @supports to check if the web browser understands the hyphens: auto feature. If that's the case, the text in the p elements will be justified, and the CSS feature hyphens will be set to auto. You can use the CSS feature hyphens to enable the automatic hyphenation function of the web browser.

As an alternative, you can use the @supports rule with the not operator to check if the web browser doesn't support a specific CSS feature. For example:

```
@supports not( display: grid ) {
 /* CSS features in case the browser does not know display: grid */   float: right; /* e.g. float: right as alternative */
}
```

You can also combine multiple CSS features by using and or. Moreover, @media and @supports rules can be nested. Web browsers that don't understand the @supports rule will ignore anything inside the curly brackets.

Viewing Websites in Different Sizes

In addition to testing websites in different web browsers and validating CSS and HTML code, you should also view the website on screens of different sizes. If you've developed a website that responds to viewport width with media queries, you can also track a layout break to the next smaller or next larger viewport using the desktop browser by manually changing the browser width. In practice, however, this is somewhat inconvenient and imprecise in the long run.

For viewing websites in different sizes, almost all web browser manufacturers now offer their own tools for viewing websites in different sizes, some of which are integrated into the web browser:

• **Firefox**

In Firefox, for example, you can find the **Test Screen Sizes** command in the **Tools**

• **Web Developer** menu or use the keyboard shortcut (Ct rl) + (Shi f t) + (M) (Windows) or (Al t) + (cmd) + (M) (Mac), which also allows you to view the current web page in different screen sizes.

• **Chrome, Edge**

You can also find a corresponding tool in Chrome and Edge via the menu **Display**

• **More tools**

• **Developer tools**.

Again, the keyboard shortcut (Ct rl) + (Shi f t) + (M) (Windows) or (Al t) + (cmd) + (M) (Mac) will get you there faster.

. Safari

In Safari, you must first enable the **Developer** menu via **Safari**

• **Preferences** in the **Advanced** tab. Then, you'll find the item **Switch to "Responsive Design" mode** in the **Developer** menu. The shortcut (Al t) + (cmd) + (R) will also get you there.

Figure: Testing Screen Sizes Using Google Chrome

My personal favourite tool to test a website on different devices and with different screen resolutions is the commercial web browser Blisk, which is completely based on Chromium. This browser includes tools that make testing desktop and mobile versions during development even more efficient.

Figure: The Blisk Web Browser Allows You to Test a Website on Different Devices and Screen Sizes

Setting Up a Central Stylesheet

You may have seen CSS files on the web that you thought were pretty large. Especially if you're actively developing a more extensive website, it can be useful to initially distribute the various style statements across multiple CSS files.

The principle is simple: You use a central stylesheet, which you include in the HTML document as usual via the link element. In Figure, style.css is the central stylesheet. However, this central stylesheet doesn't contain any ordinary CSS content, but again only loads the other CSS files (e.g., reset.css, print.css, layout.css, navi.css, and iebrowser. css in the example of the figure) by using the @import rule. At first, this may sound a bit cumbersome, but during the development of extensive web projects, it's rather a relief to divide the stylesheets into meaningful units such as layout of header and footer, navigation, content, layout for printing, layout for old web browsers and so on—here you must decide by yourself according to sense and personal taste how (and if) you want to divide the stylesheets.

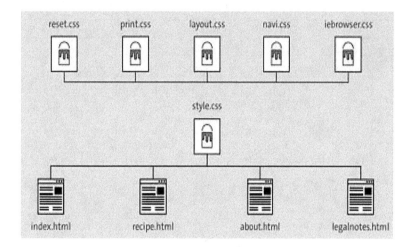

Figure: A Central Stylesheet Helps to Keep an Overview during Development and to Track Down Errors More Quickly

With reference to the example in Figure, such a central stylesheet style.css could look like the following:

```
/* Example of a central stylesheet, style.css */
/* Instead of reset.css, normalize.css would also work, which often makes more sense than reset.css. For
more information, see Section */
@import url("reset.css");
/* Basic design */
@import url("layout.css");
/* Navigation */
@import url("navi.css");
/* Print version */
@import url("print.css"); ...
```

CSS Files in a Separate Folder

In practice, it's also recommended to store CSS files generally in a separate directory. For this reason, you can often find the directory name CSS.

Combining Everything Back into One File to Shorten the Load Time

Keep in mind that the emphasis was on development. The disadvantage of multiple individual CSS files is that multiple server requests (one for each file) become necessary, which of course can increase the load time of the website significantly. So, when you're done with the website and want to make it public, you should combine the individual CSS files into one file for speed reasons. As in Figure, you can leave it at style.css because this file was included in the HTML document anyway.

Usually, you need to copy the style statements of each CSS file to the clipboard and paste them into style.css. However, if you use CSS statements for old web browsers, as in the iebrowser.css example, they should still be provided in a separate file.

If you want to avoid this kind of effort in the future and automate the development process a little more, you should take a look at the development tools Grunt (http://gruntjs.com) or Gulp (http://gulpjs.com).

CSS Compression

To reduce the file size of the CSS file again a bit and thus improve the load time, you could remove all superfluous lines of code with white spaces, line breaks, and comments. For such tasks, there are online tools available such as CSS Compressor (https://cssminifier.com) or YUI Compressor (http://refresh-sf.com). Before you do that, you should make a backup copy of your CSS file, which you'll need again if you want to change anything. The CSS file is no longer pleasant to read and edit after a CSS compression.

CSS Reset or Normalization?

The goal and purpose of a reset or normalization is to put the different basic browser settings on a common basis as much as possible, so that the website contains as few differences as possible in the different web browsers. To create such a CSS base, two ways have been established: reset and normalization.

Built-In Style Presets of the Web Browser and CSS Reset

When viewing the HTML document in different web browsers, you may have noticed that the display differs slightly. This is because all web browsers have built-in stylesheet defaults. One option would be to override the defaults with a CSS reset, so that when you start designing stylesheets, you're virtually doing everything yourself from the start.

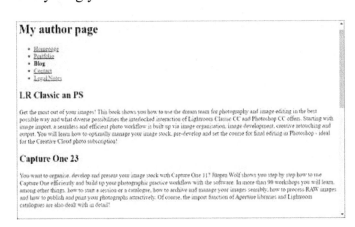

Figure: For Example, This Is What the Built-In Stylesheet Looks Like in the Chrome Web Browser

Figure: This Is What the Built-In Stylesheet Looks Like When You Use a CSS Reset to Override the Built-In Stylesheet

In Figure, the built-in stylesheet of the web browser was reset using the * selector (= universal selector) with the following CSS statements:

```
{    margin: 0;    padding: 0;
}
```

This removes all external and internal spacings and borders on all elements. In practice, this will have to be done at many points in a project anyway. Such a CSS reset is often a bit too radical because here even the lists are without indentation, and you have to set spacing again yourself for every smallest detail. However, because of the lists, it wouldn't be too much effort if you summarized the CSS reset as follows:

```
...
/* Minimal version of a CSS reset */
{    margin: 0;    padding: 0; } ul, ol {    margin-left: 1em;
}
```

Listing /examples/chapter/css/reset.css

Normalization: The Alternative to CSS Reset

The gentler and arguably better alternative to the hard CSS reset of the web browser's built-in stylesheet defaults is normalization. Although normalization overrides many built-in stylesheet defaults of the web browser, it does so while respecting useful CSS defaults. Fortunately, you don't have to start by thinking about what constitutes useful defaults yourself because others have already done that for you. You can find multiple normalization projects on the internet, which you can download and include in your project. And if you don't like some of the defaults, you can and should modify them and adapt them to your own needs. Probably the most famous normalization project is normalize.css by Nicolas Gallagher, which you can download from the website, https://necolas.github.io/normalize.css/. What's particularly nice about this project is that it fixes several web browser bugs right away.

The Evolution of Normalization: "sanitize.css"

From the normalization project with normalize.css, the sanitize.css project by Jonathan Neal has emerged. Unlike normalize.css, the project no longer takes into account older web browsers such as Safari 8 or Internet Explorer 10 and instead introduces constructs from newer web browsers.

CSS Reset, Normalization, or Leave Everything as It Is?

At this point, as with the central stylesheet setup, I should mention that these are all mere suggestions. Depending on their preferences, some web designers do a hard CSS reset and take over all tasks themselves, leaving nothing to chance or default settings, whereas others use one of the normalization projects and adapt the template to their own needs. Still others aren't fond of a CSS reset or normalization at all and prefer to work with their own styles.

There has been discussion about the need for a CSS reset for some time. Many web developers question the sense of first defining a complete CSS reset and then immediately overwriting it with their own styles. You'll come across a lot of pros and cons on the web and will probably have to ultimately decide for yourself what works best for you personally.

The CSS Preprocessor Sass and SCSS

A chapter on CSS preprocessors is almost mandatory in a book on CSS these days. You can use a CSS preprocessor to make writing CSS easier, for example, by eliminating repetitive writing. Code handling can also be simplified with a CSS preprocessor. This chapter contains a brief introduction to this topic; for this purpose, I chose Sass as the CSS preprocessor.

It may seem a bit inconvenient at first to pull another technology on top of CSS, which ultimately generates just another CSS file. But we're talking about CSS preprocessors. Sass is just one of many other CSS preprocessors that are now being used briskly by serious web designers on a daily basis. A preprocessor is used to automate tedious tasks and provide new functionality. A simple example is if, when creating a website with CSS, you assign a red color countless times to various CSS properties because that's the color a customer wants. However, the customer changes their mind and would rather have a shade of blue, so you have to assign the blue color to all red elements. This is where a CSS preprocessor such as Sass comes into play. Instead of constantly changing repetitive values, you can implement the change at only one central point according to the DRY principle (don't repeat yourself).

Other well-known representatives of CSS preprocessors are, for example, Less or Stylus. The special case or difference of Sass and SCSS will be explained in the following sections of this chapter. If you compare the CSS preprocessors with each other, you'll find that many things are pretty similar. I chose Sass because I use it a lot myself, and Sass is probably the CSS preprocessor with the biggest community.

The goal of this chapter is to familiarize you with the basics of Sass. The examples are therefore usually very simple and shorter in nature. But the advantage of using a CSS preprocessor to develop CSS code may not be immediately apparent to you. However, this will change significantly when you use Sass in more extensive projects.

Sass or SCSS Syntax

Because Sass and SCSS are often mentioned at the same time, it's beginners in particular who wonder whether these are two different CSS preprocessors. The answer is yes and no because both are Syntactically Awesome Style Sheet (Sass) after all. The difference between the two is that they're two different grammars. The original syntax was Sass syntax, and the syntax that was introduced afterward was Sassy CSS (SCSS). In this book, I use the newer SCSS syntax, which uses curly brackets and semicolons, unlike the Sass syntax. The following example in Table is intended to briefly explain the difference between the two syntaxes without going into too much detail.

SCSS Syntax (style.scss)	Sass Syntax (style.sass)

$but-size: 100%;
$color1: #fcfcfc;
$color2: #fafafa;
$spacing-p: 1em;
$spacing-m: 0.5em;
.button-form { width: $but-size;
  padding: $spacing-p; margin:
$spacing-m; background-color:
$color1;
  &:hover {
  background-color: $color2;
color: $color1;
  }
}
	$but-size: 100%
	$color1: #fcfcfc
	$color2: #fafafa
	$spacing-p: 1em
	$spacing-m: 0.5em
	.button-form width: $but-size
	  padding: $spacing-p margin:
	$spacing-m background-color:
	$color1
	  &:hover
	  background-color: $color2
	color: $color1

Table Differences between SCSS Syntax and Sass Syntax

The Sass syntax is always a bit shorter because, as already mentioned, it doesn't use curly brackets and semicolons. In Sass, nesting is done by means of indentation.

From Sass/SCSS to CSS

Of course, for styling purposes, the web browser can't do anything with the SCSS file shown on the left in Table. A file with the SCSS syntax has the extension *.scss (for the Sass syntax, it's *.sass). For this purpose, the CSS preprocessor must first convert (compile) the SCSS file into a CSS file, which you then also use for the web browser. On the right-hand side in Table, you can see the result of the SCSS file after the CSS preprocessor run as a CSS file.

SCSS File (style.scss)	CSS File (style.css)
$but-size: 100%; $color1: #fcfcfc;	.button-form { width: 100%;

$color2: #fafafa;
$spacing-p: 1em;
$spacing-m: 0.5em;
.button-form { width:
$but-size; padding:
$spacing-p; margin:
$spacing-m;
background-color:
$color1;
  &:hover {
  background-color:
$color2; color: $color1;
  }
}
	padding: 1em; margin:
	0.5em;
	  background-color:
	#fcfcfc; }
	.button-form:hover {
	background-color:
	#fafafa; color: #fcfcfc;
	}

Table From an SCSS File to a CSS File after the CSS Preprocessor Run

Installing and Setting Up Sass

Now that you know you need a CSS preprocessor that compiles a CSS file from the SCSS file, let's take a brief look at some possible options.

Online CSS Preprocessor without Installation

If you want to get started right away and aren't yet sure if you want to use Sass, or don't feel like installing and setting up an environment, you can take a look at the Sassmeister website (www.sassmeister.com). There you'll find an online compiler that compiles an SCSS syntax (and also the Sass syntax) to CSS.

Figure: The Sassmeister Website Provides an Online CSS Preprocessor

Setting Up Sass Using Visual Studio Code

My favourite solution is to set up Sass with Visual Studio Code. First, it can be done with a few clicks, and second, the Visual Studio development environment is available on all common systems and enjoys great popularity.

To install Sass with Visual Studio Code, you want to click on the icon with **Extensions** on the left. In the search bar, enter "Sass compiler", and select **Live Sass Compiler**. Then click **Install** in the description window. Restart Visual Studio Code.

Figure: Finding and Installing Live Sass Compiler in Visual Studio

Next, I created a new folder in which I created an index.html file and a styles folder with the style.scss file in it. I've deliberately kept the index.html file simple.

```
...
<head>
  <title>Sass during execution</title>
  <meta charset="UTF-8">
  <link rel="stylesheet" href="styles/style.css">
</head>
<body>
  <article class="my-article">
    <h1>Article 1</h1>
    <p>Lorem ipsum dolor … </p>
  </article>
  <article class="my-article">
    <h1>Article 2</h1>
    <p>Lorem ipsum dolor … </p>
  </article> </body> ...
```

Listing /examples/chapter/index.html

In the index.html file, I've already included the CSS file style.css, which doesn't exist yet. We now want to style the my-article class using Sass. In the style.scss file, I wrote the following content:

```
$color1: #6d6d6d;
$color2: #fff;
.my-article {    width: 30rem;    background-color: $color1;    color: $color2;    padding: 2rem; }
```

Listing /examples/chapter/style/style.scss

For the CSS preprocessor Sass to automatically make a CSS file named style.css out of it, all you need to do is enable the **Watch Sass** option at the bottom of the Visual Studio Code development environment. This enables a live translation from Sass or SCSS to CSS. Voilà, you've now created the CSS file from the SCSS file. That's all it took.

Figure: "Watch Sass" Allows You to Turn the SCSS File into a CSS File

No More Changes to the CSS File!

If you use Sass and have enabled the **Watch Sass** option, you shouldn't make any changes to the CSS file because you've now given the CSS preprocessor Sass control over it with the SCSS file. The changes to the CSS document would be overwritten when the Sass preprocessor is active and the SCSS file gets recompiled.

The great thing now is that as long as you have **Watch Sass** enabled, you don't have to worry about updating the CSS file. As soon as you make changes in the SCSS file, the CSS file will be automatically adjusted as well. You can recognize the active live translation when the **Watch Sass** label is replaced by the **Watching** label. The translation of the SCSS file takes place as soon as you save that file again.

Installing Sass for the Command Line

Of course, you can also install Sass from the command line. However, I'll only briefly describe this here. Before you can install Sass, you need Ruby on the computer. On macOS, Ruby is already integrated. On Windows, you must download and install the Ruby Installer from https://rubyinstaller.org/. On Linux, the following command on the command line is sufficient to install Ruby:

$ sudo apt-get install ruby

Once Ruby has been installed, you need to open the command line. On Windows, you open the **Start** menu and select **Start Command Prompt with Ruby**. On macOS and Linux, you want to launch the terminal. Then you must enter the following into the command line:

$ gem install sass

You may need to use sudo on macOS and Linux (sudo gem install sass). Then enter "sass -v" in the command line. If a version number gets displayed, you can be sure that Sass has been installed.

To compile a SCSS file, you need to change in the command line to the directory where you've saved the Sass file with the extension *.scss. Then you can use the following command to compile the SCSS file to get a CSS file:

$ sass style.scss:style.css

In this example, you compile the SCSS file style.scss and get the CSS file style.css.
In addition to the compilation of Sass files, you can also set up a monitoring service for files or directories in the command line, so that once a change has been saved in the SCSS file, it automatically gets compiled, as described in the preceding section with Visual Studio Code and the **Watch Sass** function. To monitor a single file, you need to use the following command in the command line:

$ sass --watch style.scss:style.css

This makes sure that when the SCSS file style.scss gets changed, it will automatically be compiled and the result will be saved in the CSS file, style.css.

You can monitor an entire folder via the following command:

$ sass --watch styles:styles

This will monitor all SCSS files in the styles directory and compile and save them as a CSS file in the same directory when a (saved) change occurs. For example, with an SCSS file named layout.scss, you would find a layout.css file in the styles directory after compilation. If you like it a bit neat, you can also create an scss folder and a css folder. In the scss folder, you store all SCSS files. Now, to save the CSS files in the css directory when compiling these SCSS files, you need to enter the following command:

$ sass --watch stylesheets/scss:stylesheets/css

Setting Output Styles for the CSS

You can also specify the output style for the CSS that Sass is supposed to create from the SCSS file. With the default value nested, everything is neatly nested. There are also expanded (indented), compact (everything in one line), and compressed (without spaces and line breaks) available. You can specify these output styles using --style. Here's how you can create a compressed style that's best suited for performance optimization:

$ sass --watch --style compressed stylesheets/scss:stylesheets/css

Using Variables with Sass

When you look at a larger CSS project, you'll notice that many values of CSS features, such as colors, spacing, dimension, and so on, are constantly repeated. If one wants to change these values afterward, an extensive search and replace of the values is often started. With variables in Sass, you can save yourself this work. They allow you to set a value for a CSS feature as a variable and then use it anywhere in the SCSS document. After compiling the SCSS file, these variables are replaced with the actual values in the CSS file. You introduce a variable with the dollar sign ($). This is followed by the name of the variable without spaces in between. You can assign a value to the variable via a colon and end the line with a semicolon —basically the same way you assign a value to a CSS feature.

The corresponding syntax looks as follows:

$variable-name: value;

Real-life examples could look like the following:

$color-primary: #5f5f5f;
$color-primary-font: #fff;
$font: 'Franklin Gothic','Arial Narrow',Arial,sans-serif;
$spacing-std: 1em;

You can then pass the variables defined in this way to a CSS feature using $variable-name. You're free to choose the name of the variable. Note, however, that you can't use any special characters. It's recommended to use a meaningful designation. A name like $heaven-blue isn't ideal because you might decide later to change the color from blue to yellow. Thus, a label like $color-primary is more appropriate. If you define a variable multiple times in the code, the last definition made always wins the deal when it comes to assigning a value to a CSS feature. You already know this from CSS as well.

Here's an example and what the CSS preprocessor makes of it.

SCSS File	CSS File

$color-primary: #5f5f5f;
$color-primary-font: #fff;
$font: 'Franklin Gothic',
  'Arial Narrow',Arial, sans-serif;
$spacing-std: 1em;
* {
  margin-top: 0;
}
body {
  font-family: $font; }
.my-article { width: 30rem;
  background-color: $color-primary;
color: $color-primary-font;
padding: $spacing-std; margin-
bottom: $spacing-std; }
	* {
	  margin-top: 0;
	}
	body { font-family: "Franklin
	Gothic", "Arial Narrow", Arial,
	sans-serif; }
	.my-article { width: 30rem;
	  background-color: #5f5f5f;
	color: #fff; padding: 1em;
	margin-bottom: 1em;
	}

SCSS file: /examples/chapter/style/style.scss	CSS file: /examples/chapter/style/style.css

Table The SCSS File and the CSS File after Compilation

The HTML file used is again /examples/chapter/index.html from Section.

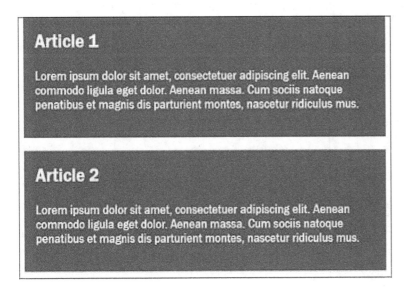

Figure: The HTML File /examples/chapter/index.html during Execution

Nesting with Sass

An enormous relief when writing SCSS documents is the use of a nesting of selectors (selector nesting), as they occur in the HTML document. However, it's important to keep the nesting within limits to avoid overloading the specificity of CSS, which can lead to a performance brake. I recommend a nesting of two to maximum three levels here. Here's a simple example of what such a nesting of selectors looks like and what the CSS preprocessor makes of it. Here, the selectors p and h1 are written inside the my-article class.

SCSS File	CSS File

...
.my-article { width: 30rem;
  background-color: $color-primary;
color: $color-primary-font;
padding: 0.1em;
  margin-bottom: $spacing-std;
border-radius: 5px; **h1 {**
  padding-left: 0.5em;
  } p {
  background-color: $color-
secondary;
 	
  color: $color-secondary-font;
padding: 1em;
  }
}
	...
	.my-article { width: 30rem;
	  background-color: #5f5f5f;
	color: #fff; padding: 0.1em;
	margin-bottom: 1em; border-
	radius: 5px; }
	.my-article h1 { padding-left:
	0.5em;
	}
	
	.my-article p { background-
	color: #fff; color: #000;
	padding: 1em;
	}

SCSS file: /examples/chapter/style/style.scss	CSS file: /examples/chapter/style/style.css

Table The SCSS File and the CSS File after the Preprocessor Run

I think this kind of nesting significantly facilitates my work and also the overview in the SCSS document. The HTML example is the same as in the previous sections and now looks as shown in Figure.

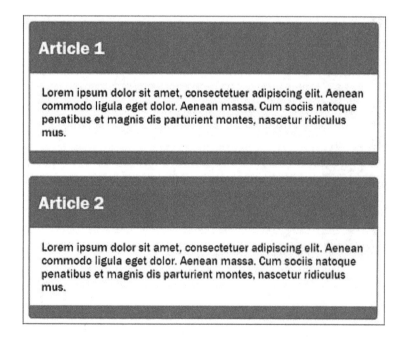

Figure: The HTML File /examples/chapter/index.html during Execution

Nesting is also useful for CSS properties (property nesting), which are grouped under a short name. For example, for the padding group, there are the individual properties padding-top, padding-bottom, padding left, and padding-right. You know the same from other CSS properties such as background-, margin-, border-, font-, and more. Returning to the padding example, you can implement this CSS property group as a nested property in SCSS as follows.

SCSS File	CSS File

.my-article { ...
  h1 { **padding: { left: 0.5em;
top: 0.1em;
  bottom: 0.1em;**
  }
  }
...
}
	...
	.my-article h1 { **padding-left:
	0.5em; padding-top: 0.1em;
	padding-bottom: 0.1em;**
	  }
	...

/examples/chapter/style/style2.scss	/examples/chapter/style/style2.css

Table The SCSS File and the CSS File after the Preprocessor Run

Mixins ("@mixin", "@include")

Besides variables, mixins represent the most commonly used feature of Sass. Mixins are entire blocks of CSS features you can reuse as a whole at any time. Creating and using them is just as easy. To define a mixin, you want to follow these steps:

@mixin mixin-name {

  ...

}

As usual, you need to write your CSS features between curly brackets. Then, you can use @include to access this code block at any time:

@include mixin-name;

For this purpose, we'll use our previous example from this chapter with mixins.

SCSS File	CSS File

...
**@mixin article-style {
  background-color: $color-
primary; color: $color-primary-
font; padding: 0.1em;
  margin-bottom: $spacing-std;
border-radius: 5px;**
}
	...
	.my-article { width: 35rem;
	  background-color: #5f5f5f;
	color: #fff; padding: 0.1em;
	margin-bottom: 1em; border-
	radius: 5px;
	}

```scss
@mixin article-content {
  background-color: $color-
secondary;  color: $color-
secondary-font;  padding: 2em;
} ...
.my-article {  width: 35rem;
@include article-style;  h1 {
padding-left: 0.5em;
  }
  p {
@include article-content;
  }
}
```

```css
.my-article h1 {  padding-left:
0.5em; }
.my-article p {  background-
color: #fff;  color: #000;
padding: 2em;
}
```

SCSS file:
/examples/chapter/style/style.scss

CSS file:
/examples/chapter/style/style.css

Table The SCSS File and the CSS File after the Preprocessor Run

Those mixins are perfect for entire blocks of code that you use over and over again. As you can see in the example, the mixins also work with the variables of Sass. In the context of the variables, the desire quickly arises to make the mixins themselves a bit more flexible, for example, to use a mixin code block with different color combinations or other different values such as the text size. This isn't a problem with mixins because you can use them with arguments. Such arguments must be written inside parentheses with variables. An example will demonstrate the mixins with arguments.

In the example, you can see that you can pass values for the arguments as Sass variables or also with valid CSS values. The HTML file /examples/chapter/index2. html has been adapted in the corresponding position as follows:

```html
...
  <article class="my-article">
    <h1>Article 1</h1>
    <p class="p1">Lorem ipsum ... </p>
  </article>
  <article class="my-article">
    <h1>Article 2</h1>
    <p class="p2">Lorem ipsum ... </p>    </article> ...
```

Listing /examples/chapter/index2.html

SCSS File	CSS File

```
...
@mixin article-content(
  $bg-color, $txt-color, $spacing) {
background-color: $bg-color;
color: $txt-color;  padding:
$spacing;
} ...
.my-article { ...
  .p1 {
  @include article-content(
  $color-secondary,
  $color-secondary-font,
  $spacing-std);
    }
  .p2 {
  @include article-content(
yellow,
  $color-secondary-font,
  0.5em);
    }
}
```

```
...
.my-article .p1 {  background-
color: #fff;   color: #000;
padding: 1em; }
.my-article .p2 {  background-
color: yellow;   color: #000;
padding: 0.5em;
}
```

SCSS file:
/examples/chapter/style/style2.scss

CSS file:
/examples/chapter/style/style2.css

Table The SCSS File and the CSS File after the Preprocessor Run

What's missing now are mixins with default values for the arguments to still be able to call and use the mixin without special values. You can do this by writing the default value after the variable separated by a colon:

```
...
@mixin article-content($bg-color:$color-secondary,
$txt-color:$color-secondary-font,  $spacing:$spacing-std) {
background-color: $bg-color;     color: $txt-color;     padding: $spacing;
}
...
.my-article {
...
  .p1 {
    @include article-content;
  }
  .p2 {
    @include article-content(yellow, $color-secondary-font, 0.5em);
  }
}
```

Listing /examples/chapter/style/style3.scss

In the example, I've used Sass variables as default values, which I can then adjust as needed. You can also just use a valid CSS value here. Now you can use the mixin with arguments and default values with and without values. If you don't set any values, the default values will be used. Here it's also possible that you call the mixin with one or two values. In that case, the default value will be used for the second and/or third value. For example, the following is also possible thanks to the default values:

@include article-content(green);
@include article-content(blue, yellow);

Extend ("@extend")

In addition to mixins, there's another way to avoid unnecessary repetitions, namely extends. It often happens with many selectors that they differ only by a few properties. The extends can be used in two different ways. First, I'll show you how to use @extend to split the CSS features of a selector and override or extend the necessary features in the new selector. In the example, we create the .my-article class selector as the base class for the other two class selectors, .my-article-top and .my-article-std, where we only change or override the color of the base class. Of course, you could also expand the two new classes. The extension is made here via @extends selector name. Any type of selector such as class selector, ID selector, element selector, and so on can be used as selector name.

SCSS File	CSS File

...
.my-article {   width: 35rem;
  background-color: $color-primary;
 	
  color: $color-primary-font;
padding: 0.1em;
  margin-bottom: $spacing-std;
border-radius: 5px;   h1 {
  padding-left: 0.5em;
  } p {
background-color: $color-secondary;   color: $color-secondary-font;   padding: 2em;
  }
}
.my-article-top { **@extend .my-article;**
  background-color: darkslategray;
}
.my-article-std { **@extend .my-article;**   background-color: darkred; }
	.my-article,
	.my-article-top, .my-article-std {
	width: 35rem;
	
	  background-color: #5f5f5f;
	color: #fff; padding: 0.1em;
	margin-bottom: 1em; border-radius: 5px; }
	.my-article h1,
	.my-article-top h1, .my-article-std
	h1 { padding-left: 0.5em; }
	.my-article p,
	.my-article-top p, .my-article-std
	p { background-color: #fff;
	color: #000; padding: 2em; }
	.my-article-top {
	  background-color:
	darkslategray; }
	.my-article-std {
	  background-color: darkred; }

SCSS file: /examples/chapter/style/style.scss	CSS file: /examples/chapter/style/style.css

Table The SCSS File and the CSS File after the Preprocessor Run

Especially in an example like this one, you can see very clearly that with the help of @extend, the code in the SCSS document remains very clear, in contrast to the generated code in the CSS document. This is immensely useful in development. In the HTML document, the two classes .my-article-top and .myarticle-std are used as follows:

```
...
  <article class="my-article-top">
    <h1>Article 1</h1>
    <p>Lorem ipsum ...</p>
  </article>
  <article class="my-article-std">
    <h1>Article 2</h1>
    <p>Lorem ipsum ...</p>
  </article> ...
```

Listing /examples/chapter/index.html

Because the base class .my-article doesn't appear at all in this example, we could have done without this selector because it unnecessarily inflates the CSS code. This takes us to the second option of using @extend. Instead of defining a selector that won't be used at all and would only serve the extension with @extend, you can also use a placeholder. You introduce such a placeholder with %. Here again is the same example, but now my-article is degraded to a placeholder and no longer appears in the CSS code. This requires only one change in the code.

SCSS File	CSS File
... **%my-article** { width: 35rem; background-color: $color-primary; color: $color-primary-font; padding: 0.1em; margin-bottom: $spacing-std; border-radius: 5px; h1 { padding-left: 0.5em; } p { background-color: $color-secondary; color: $color-secondary-font; padding: 2em; } } .my-article-top { **@extend %my-article;** background-color: darkslategray; }	.my-article-top, .my-article-std { width: 35rem; background-color: #5f5f5f; color: #fff; padding: 0.1em; margin-bottom: 1em; border-radius: 5px; } .my-article-top h1, .my-article-std h1 { padding-left: 0.5em; } .my-article-top p, .my-article-std p { background-color: #fff; color: #000; padding: 2em; }
.my-article-std { **@extend %my-article;** background-color: darkred; }	.my-article-top { background-color: darkslategray; } .my-article-std { background-color: darkred; }

SCSS file: /examples/chapter/style/style.scss	CSS file: /examples/chapter/style/style.css

Table The SCSS File and the CSS File after the Preprocessor Run

In contrast to the preceding example, the class selector .my-article no longer appears.

"@mixin or" and "@extend"

Now that you know about two techniques to make code more modular and reusable with mixins and extends, the question is which of the two is the better choice. As for the use in the SCSS file, both are very suitable. However, the CSS code which gets created from it is also likely to be decisive. Especially with mixins, the code gets significantly inflated if there are a lot of repetitions. However, if you want to pass arguments, then you'll prefer mixins over extends. My recommendation is to use @extend for SCSS code without arguments and to use @mixin for SCSS code with arguments. However, there are many different opinions on this. There are also developers who rely exclusively on mixins. This may also explain why mixins, along with variables, are often mentioned in an introduction to Sass, while the extends aren't mentioned at all. Again, the following also applies here: There isn't just one way of doing it. You now know two approaches.

Media Queries and "@content"

So that the mixins aren't too much overshadowed after the extend section, I still want to bring the media queries into play here, for which mixins with arguments are again perfect: You can define the breakpoints as variables and adjust them at any time. It's also useful that you can use inline media queries with Sass, which is an enormous help especially with extensive projects. The following example is intended to show how you can use media queries in Sass.

In this example, a mobile version (30em) and a desktop version (60em) were created. In the mobile version, the articles are displayed one below the other in the flexbox and side by side in the desktop version. In the created CSS code for the inline media query of Sass, you can also see that these media queries were created after compiling for each selector. This indeed means that there are a few more lines of code in the CSS file. But measured against the simplification and time saving of writing such media queries within the selector, the few bytes more than pay for themselves.

Besides the inline media queries, the use of variables with the mixins is also very useful, allowing you to customize the breakpoints quite comfortably. In addition, you can also apply arithmetic operators to the variables. I'll go into this separately.

You can also see in this example at display: flexbox that Sass also takes care of the browser prefixes.

SCSS File	CSS File

SCSS file: /examples/chapter/style/style.scss	CSS file: /examples/chapter/style/style.css
| ```scss
...
$mq-mobile: 30em;
$mq-desktop: 60em;
@mixin breakpoint($mq-width) {
  @media screen and (  min-width: $mq-width) {
  @content;
  }
}
.flex-container {  display: flex;  flex-flow: row wrap; }
.my-article {  font-family: $font;  font-size: 1em;  padding: 1em;
...
@include breakpoint($mq-mobile) {  font-size: 1.125em;  width: 90%;
  }
 @include breakpoint($mq-desktop) {  font-size: 1.25em;  width: 40%;
  }
}

h1 {
  margin-top: 0;
@include breakpoint($mq-mobile) {  font-size: 1.25em;
  }
@include breakpoint($mq-desktop) {  font-size: 1.5em;
  }
}
``` | ```css
.flex-container {  display: -webkit-box;  display: -ms-flexbox;  display: flex;
  -webkit-box-orient: horizontal;
  -webkit-box-direction: normal;
-ms-flex-flow: row wrap;  flex-flow: row wrap; }
.my-article {  font-family: "Franklin Gothic",  "Arial Narrow", Arial, sans-serif;  font-size: 1em;  padding: 1em; }
@media screen and (min-width: 30em) {
  .my-article {  font-size: 1.125em;  width: 90%;
  }
}
@media screen and (min-width: 60em) {
  .my-article {  font-size: 1.25em;  width: 40%;
  }
}

h1 {
  margin-top: 0; }
@media screen and (min-width: 30em) {  h1 {
  font-size: 1.25em;
  }
}
@media screen and (min-width: 60em) {  h1 {
  font-size: 1.5em;
  }
}
``` |

Table The SCSS File and the CSS File after the Preprocessor Run

In the example with the mixin breakpoint, I still smuggled in @content, which works a bit like magic here:

```scss
...
@mixin breakpoint($mq-width) {    @media screen and (          min-width: $mq-width) {
    @content;
  }
}
```

...

As the name @content already describes, you can insert a content (into a mixin) with it. This instructs the CSS preprocessor to insert the contents of the subsequent SCSS code block at this point when compiling.

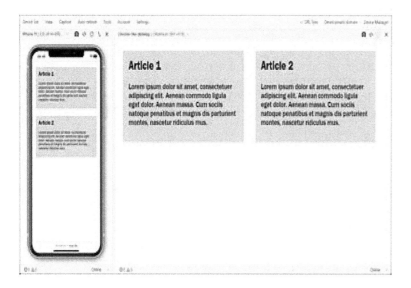

Figure: Example in Execution: The Mobile Version and the Desktop Version in the Blisk Web Browser

Operators

As briefly mentioned in the previous section, you can also use the calculation operators +, -, *, /, and % (modulo) with Sass. It can be quite useful to have the values calculated during the design and layout. Here's an example that demonstrates a few ways you can use operators in Sass. I used this example in the context of media queries and adjusted a few properties with simple calculations.

SCSS File	CSS File

...
 $article-width: 80%;
 $font-increase: 0.125em; $base-size: 1; ...
 .my-article {   font-family: $font;
 font-size: $base-size * 1em;
 padding: $base-size * 1em;
 background-color: lightgray;
 margin: 1em;
   @include breakpoint($mq-mobile) { **font-size: $base-size + $font-increase;**
 	
   width: $article-width;
   }
   @include breakpoint($mq-desktop) { **font-size: $base-size + ($font-increase * 2);**
 width: $article-width / 2;
   }
	.my-article { font-family: "Franklin Gothic", "Arial Narrow", Arial, sans-serif; font-size: 1em; padding: 1em;
	   background-color: lightgray;
	 margin: 1em; }
	 @media screen and (min-width: 30em) {
	   .my-article { font-size: 1.125em; width: 80%;
	   }
	 }
	
	 @media screen and (min-width: 60em) {
	   .my-article { font-size: 1.25em; width: 40%;
	   }
	 }

}

SCSS file:
/examples/chapter/style/style.scss

CSS file:
/examples/chapter/style/style.css

Table The SCSS File and the CSS File after the Preprocessor Run

These examples don't really need much more description. The usual rules such as "multiplication and division before addition and subtraction" apply here as well. You may be a bit surprised by the notation $base-size * 1em because it only calculates 1 × 1. This is necessary here because the $base-size variable has no unit, and this way we set the unit em. This wasn't necessary for $base-size + $font-increase because $font-increase was assigned the unit em.

Adjusting Colors and Brightness

Colors can be specified in Sass as usual in CSS with rgb(), rgba(), hsl(), hsla(), #fff, #ffffff, and of course the CSS keywords for color such as green, gray, red, and so on. In addition, Sass contains functions to adjust the brightness and saturation of colors. I've listed some of these functions for you in Table.

Syntax	Example	Description
lighten(color, [n]%)	background:lighten($color, 10%);	Lightens the color by n%
darken(color, [n]%)	background:darken($color, 10%);	Darkens the color by n%
desaturate(color, [n]%)	background:desaturate($color, 30%);	Reduces the color saturation by n%
saturate(color, [n]%)	background:saturate($color, 30%);	Increases the color saturation by n%
adjust-hue(color, [n]%)	background:adjust-hue($color, -90%);	Changes the hue of the color by n%
invert(color)	background:invert($color);	Inverts the color
complement(color)	background:complement($color);	Creates the complementary color to the specified color

grayscale(color)	background:grayscale($color);	Converts the specified color to grayscale

Table Some Useful Sass Functions for Manipulating Colors

The functions are relatively easy to use. To give you an impression, I want to create an example with buttons. In it, I'll just define a color for the button and adjust the rest using the Sass color-manipulation functions. This way, you only need to change that one color, while you've created an entire theme system for a simple button.

The effort of the SCSS example seems at first more extensive than necessary when looking at the CSS code. However, now you've also created a great template here that you can use to generate many more buttons in different colors. You just need to create more classes in the style of .my-btn. Especially helpful in this example are the functions for color manipulation when the hover effect is applied and when the button is deactivated. When hovering, the color is merely darkened (darken()) and desaturated (saturate()). If the button gets disabled, it will be lightened (lighten()).

SCSS File	CSS File

$btn-default: #3196cb;
$btn-color: white;
@mixin btn($btn-color:orange) {
background: $btn-color; **border-color: darken($btn-color, 10%); }**
@mixin btn-hover($btn-color:orange) {
$hover-color: saturate($btn-color, 10%); $hover-color: darken($hover-color, 10%);
background: $hover-color;
border-color: darken($btn-color, 20%); }
	.my-btn { margin-bottom: 1em; font-size: 14px; text-align: center; vertical-align: middle; cursor: pointer; padding: 0.5em 1em; border-radius: 4px; display: inline-block; border: 1px solid; color: white; }
	.my-btn {
	 background: #3196cb;
	
	border-color: #2778a2; }

SCSS file: /examples/chapter/style/style.scss	CSS file: /examples/chapter/style/style.css
| ```scss
@mixin btn-disabled($btn-color:orange) { background: lighten($btn-color, 20%) ; border-color: lighten($btn-color, 10%); }
%button-basic { margin-bottom: 1em; font-size: 14px; text-align: center; vertical-align: middle; cursor: pointer; padding: 0.5em 1em; border-radius: 4px; display: inline-block; border: 1px solid; color: $btn-color; }
.my-btn {
  @extend %button-basic;
  @include btn($btn-default);
  &:hover {
  @include btn-hover($btn-default);
  }
  &.disabled, &.disabled:hover {
cursor: not-allowed; opacity: .65;
  @include btn-disabled($btn-default);
  }
}
``` | ```css
.my-btn:hover { background: #1d7bac; border-color: #1d5979; }
.my-btn.disabled, .my-btn.disabled:hover { cursor: not-allowed; opacity: .65; background: #81c0e1; border-color: #58abd7; }
``` |

Table The SCSS File and the CSS File after the Preprocessor Run

In addition to the color manipulations, the ampersand character & was also placed in front of :hover, .disabled, and .disabled.hover in this example within the selector. The & is very useful when you use a nesting selector. For example, let's look at the following:

```scss
.my-btn {
  &.:hover {}
}
```

The CSS preprocessor turns this into the following:

```css
.my-btn:hover {}
```

Without the ampersand character &, the CSS preprocessor would do the following:

```css
.my-btn :hover {}
```

With this, the hover effect would not work. So, if you use the ampersand character inside a nested Sass selector, that selector will be appended to the parent selector instead of getting nested under it. This is especially popular in conjunction with the pseudo-class selectors such as :hover or ::after because they need to be linked to a selector. With the & you can easily reference the parent selectors.

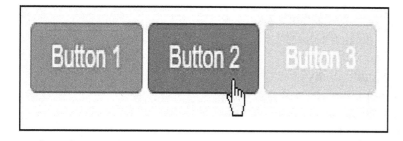

Figure: The HTML File /examples/chapter/index.html during Execution

Sass Control Structures

In the previous example, you created a kind of Sass template for buttons. Using control structures such as loops, you can automate the generation of CSS code for buttons in different colors. In the example, I want to use the @each loop for this purpose. This loop makes it possible to process a list of elements. With regard to the buttons, a list of color values should be used in the form of CSS keywords. This way you can create different buttons in different color schemes quite comfortably and with very little effort. Of course, this can be applied to any other element as well. I've highlighted in bold the changes to the /examples/chapter/style/style.scss file from the previous section.

SCSS File	CSS File

$btn-list: blue, darkred, darkgreen; ...
...
@each $btn-default in $btn-list {
  .my-btn-#{$btn-default} {
  @extend %button-basic;
  @include btn($btn-default);
 	
  &:hover {
  @include btn-hover($btn-default);
  }
  &.disabled, &.disabled:hover {
cursor: not-allowed; opacity: .65;
  @include btn-disabled($btn-default);
  }
  }
  }
}
	.my-btn-blue,
	.my-btn-darkred, .my-btn-darkgreen { ...
	}
	.my-btn-blue { ...
	
	}
	.my-btn-blue:hover { ...
	}
	.my-btn-blue.disabled, .my-btn-blue.disabled:hover { ...
	}
	.my-btn-darkred { ...
	}
	.my-btn-darkred:hover { ...
	}
	.my-btn-darkred.disabled, .my-btn-darkred.disabled:hover { ...
	}
	.my-btn-darkgreen { ...
	}
	.my-btn-darkgreen:hover { ...
	}
	.my-btn-darkgreen.disabled, .my-btn-darkgreen.disabled:hover { ...
	}

Table The SCSS File and the CSS File after the Preprocessor Run
The shortened CSS file demonstrates in a clear manner how further selectors for buttons with the different color schemes .my-btn-blue, .my-btn-darkred, and .my-btn-darkgreen, along with the hover and disable versions, were generated from the color specifications in the list. The comma-separated list $btnlist is passed through in the @each loop. The $btn-default variable is a placeholder and contains the respective color name of the $btn-list. On the first pass, $btn-default stands for blue, on the second pass for darkred, and on the third pass for darkgreen.

To ensure that the CSS color names are also attached to the selector, the $btn-default specification was interpolated with #{}. On the first pass, .my-btn-#{$btn-default} becomes .my-btn-blue, on the second pass .my-btn-darkred, and on the last pass .my-btn-darkgreen.

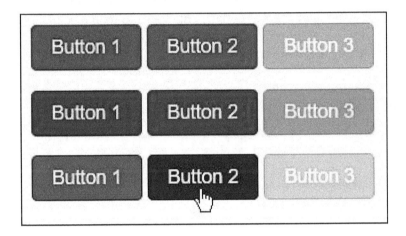

Figure: The HTML File /examples/chapter/index.html with the Different Button Color Schemes during Execution

Admittedly, at this point, the example looks a bit more complex for starters, but it does nicely demonstrate that you can be extremely productive with Sass the deeper you get into it. Besides the @each loop, Sass provides other control structures as well.

In addition to the list-based loop @each, you'll find the classic loop @for in Sass, which allows you to specify a certain number of repetitions for the code. The @for loop comes in two Flavors:

```
for $counter from 1 through 10 {
    // Code which gets executed 10 times    .my-class-#{$counter} {
      ...
    }
}
```

The loop is executed 10 times here. The current loop pass is stored in $counter. Due to the interpolation with #{}, 10 selectors (.my-class-1, .my-class-2, etc.) are generated here. Besides the option @for $ from [start] **through** [end], you can also use @for $ from [start] **to** [end] end here. With through, the final value is still executed, and, with to, the loop execution stops before it.

The @while loop is also available in Sass: such a loop is executed until the condition is false. However, you must be careful not to create an endless loop. Here's a pseudo-code for that:

```
$counter: 1;
$reply: 5;
@while $counter <= $reply {
  // Code that is executed until the condition is false, here 1<= 5
  // Increasing the $counter variable by 1
  $counter: $counter + 1;
}
```

Here, the loop is repeated as long as $counter is less than or equal to the value of $reply. Increasing the $counter variable at the end is very important because otherwise you would have an infinite loop.

Besides loops, there's also @if, which you can use to check a condition. The CSS preprocessor compiles a particular code only if the condition is true. To check conditions you can use different operators such as == (equal), != (unequal), > (greater than), < (less than), >= (greater than or equal), and <= (less than or equal). In the following example, I've changed the btn-hover mixin. Optionally, you can now have buttons created without a hover effect if you pass a value other than 1 as a second parameter in addition to the color.

```
...
@mixin btn-hover($btn-color:orange, $hover-effect: 1) {
  @if $hover-effect==1 {
    $hover-color: saturate($btn-color, 10%);
    $hover-color: darken($hover-color, 10%);
    background: $hover-color;       border-color: darken($btn-color, 20%);
  }
}
...
    @include btn-hover($btn-default, 0); ...
```

In this example, a CSS code block such as .my-btn-blue:hover {...} is only generated if $hover-effect is 1, which is the default value here.

Of course, there's also an alternative @else branch that gets executed when the @if condition doesn't apply. With regard to our example just shown, in the case of a disabled hover effect, the cursor should be changed to a stop symbol when you halt over the button with it. For example, you can use it to symbolize that this button can't be pressed.

```
...
@mixin btn-hover($btn-color:orange, $hover-effect: 1) {    @if $hover-effect==1 {
    ...
  }   @else {       cursor: not-allowed;
  }
}
```

Functions "@function"

Sass also provides a way to create real functions by using @function. Unlike mixins, which output a section of code, functions return a return value. Different data types such as numeric values (20, 1.125,

1.5em), strings ("text", 'text', text), colors (#fff, #ffffff, rgba (255, 255, 0, 0.75)), CSS value lists (1em, 1.5em, "Arial Narrow" , Arial, sans-serif;), Boolean values (false, true), or even a null value (null) can be returned. A function is introduced with @function followed by the name of the function. The arguments of the function must be written between parentheses. Curly brackets must contain the code of the function, while @return will return a value.

Here's a simple example that converts a pixel value to an em value:

```
$base-font-size: 16px;
@function px-to-em( $px-val ) {
    @return ( $px-val / $base-font-size ) * 1em;
}
```

You can use this function in the SCSS file as follows:

```
.my-article {    width: px-to-em( 960px );    font-size: px-to-em( 20px ); }
```

Then, the CSS preprocessor makes the following out of it:

```
.my-article {   width: 60em;   font-size: 1.25em;
}
```

Besides calculations, you can, of course, return other values from a function too. The following example uses a preferred color scheme such as Twitter or Facebook to return the color code. The list can be extended by any other color scheme.

```
@function select-color( $color:#fff ) {
    @if $color == facebook {
        @return #3b5998;
    }
    @if $color == twitter {
        @return #00acee;
    }

    @else {
        @return $color;
    }
}
```

I recommend you try out such mini samples directly in www.sassmeister.com. It's the ideal playground to learn Sass without immediately using the individual techniques in a project.

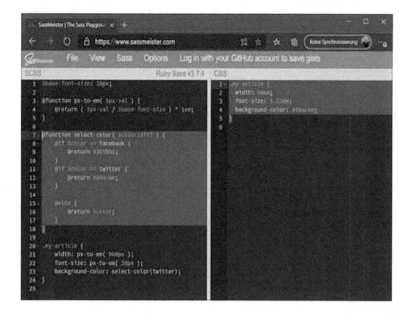

Figure: Sassmeister Is Perfect for Learning Sass without Having to Use It in the Project Right Away

"@import"

When the projects become more extensive, it isn't advisable to write everything in an SCSS file. As with CSS, in Sass, you can split SCSS files into meaningful sections such as reset, setup, layout, navigation, and so on; import them via @import; and compile all the spun-off sections into SCSS files to create a CSS file. As a web designer, you can still keep track of everything thanks to the individual SCSS files. For example, I personally use a style.scss file into which I import all other SCSS files. Here's an example of using @import:
@import "reset";
@import "layout";
@import "basic";

Listing /examples/chapter/style/style.scss

When importing with @import, the file name between "" is sufficient. In this example, the SCSS files _reset.scss, _layout.scss and _basic.scss are compiled, and the entire content is written to the CSS file, style.css. The underscore at the start of the individual SCSS file names is important so that they don't get compiled directly. If you didn't use an underscore, you would have generated the reset.css, layout.css, and basic.css files in addition to the style.css CSS file. However, this is superfluous here and can be bypassed quite elegantly with the underscore before the file name.

Of course, you can also specify the full file name when importing (even if it isn't necessary):

// File: style.scss -> style.css
@import "_reset.scss";
@import "_layout.scss";
@import "_basic.scss";

The order in which you write the SCSS documents when importing them is also of enormous importance, especially if you use variables that you also use in other documents. For a variable to be assigned correctly, it must also be known. For this purpose, it can be useful, for example, to write the variables in an extra

SCSS file and import that file right at the beginning:

```
@import "reset";
@import "setup"; // All variables go here
@import "layout";
@import "basic";
```

Comments

Finally, I want to share a few words about comments in Sass. Especially if the code becomes more extensive, you'll probably want to use comments. Here you can proceed like you would in CSS and add a comment like the following in the SCSS file:

```
/* I am a comment */
```

The CSS preprocessor will also include this comment in the CSS file. In addition, Sass still provides the option to write a comment as follows:

```
// I am a comment
```

However, this comment can only span one line. Furthermore, this comment won't be added to the CSS file by the CSS preprocessor. I find this useful as a method to separate comments that are significant for Sass from general comments for CSS.

Conclusion

CSS: The Backbone of Web Styling

CSS has been at the core of web styling since its inception, evolving through various versions to meet the demands of modern web design. From simple aesthetic enhancements to complex layouts, CSS has continually adapted to empower developers. Features like Flexbox, Grid Layouts, and CSS Variables have revolutionized the way we approach responsive design, enabling intuitive control over complex layouts and seamless theming capabilities.

The Critical Role of CSS in Modern Design

Modern web applications rely on user-friendly interfaces, and CSS bridges the gap between functionality and aesthetics. As more businesses shift online, creating visually appealing, responsive, and accessible websites becomes crucial. CSS's ability to define layout, typography, and animations plays a pivotal role in capturing user attention and enhancing usability.

Challenges in CSS Styling and Maintenance

While CSS is indispensable, scaling styles in large projects can be daunting. Issues such as specificity conflicts, inconsistent naming conventions, and redundant code often plague developers. To address these challenges, CSS introduces organizational methodologies like modular CSS, naming conventions (e.g., BEM), and tools for debugging and linting.

By adopting these practices, teams can mitigate complexities, ensuring that their stylesheets remain robust and maintainable even in large-scale applications.

Testing and Organizing CSS for Scalability

As web applications grow in size and complexity, ensuring consistent styling across browsers, devices, and user environments becomes imperative. Testing and organizing CSS isn't just about fixing bugs; it's about creating predictable, reusable, and scalable styles that can evolve with a project.

Key Testing Approaches

Cross-Browser Testing: Differences in browser engines (e.g., WebKit, Blink, Gecko) can result in varied rendering of CSS. Developers must test on multiple browsers using tools like BrowserStack or Sauce Labs.

Responsive Testing: With the rise of mobile-first development, designs must adapt gracefully to diverse screen sizes and orientations. CSS media queries, frameworks like Bootstrap, and responsive testing tools help achieve this.

Visual Regression Testing: Automated tools such as BackstopJS and Percy capture screenshots before and after changes, highlighting unintended visual differences. This is particularly useful in large projects where manual testing isn't feasible.

Strategies for Organizing CSS

Organizing CSS goes beyond file structure; it includes approaches to ensure readability, maintainability, and efficiency. Adopting modular CSS, leveraging CSS resets, and following established conventions like SMACSS (Scalable and Modular Architecture for CSS) or OOCSS (Object-Oriented CSS) can significantly streamline workflows.

Practical Example: Modular Organization

Consider a website with multiple sections—header, footer, and content. Each section can have its own stylesheet, imported into a main file:

```
/* main.css */
@import 'header.css';
@import 'footer.css';
@import 'content.css';
```

This approach prevents conflicts and allows team members to work independently on different parts of the application.

Sass/SCSS: Revolutionizing CSS Development

CSS preprocessors like Sass and SCSS have redefined how developers write and manage styles. By introducing programming-like features, they allow developers to create DRY (Don't Repeat Yourself) stylesheets that are easier to manage and scale.

Core Benefits of Sass/SCSS

Enhanced Readability and Maintainability: Nesting and modularization make stylesheets easier to read and maintain.
Reusability: Features like variables, mixins, and functions reduce redundancy and foster code reuse.

Dynamic Capabilities: Functions and logic allow for dynamic calculations, making styles adaptable and future-proof.

Example: Thematic Variables with Sass

Creating theme-based designs is a breeze with Sass variables:

```
$light-theme: #f9f9f9;
$dark-theme: #333;

body {
    background-color: $light-theme;
}
```

Switching themes requires only a change in the variable value, simplifying maintenance.

Advanced Features: A Game Changer

The flexibility of Sass extends to advanced concepts like inheritance, conditional statements, and loops. These features not only save time but also empower developers to handle complex projects with ease.

CSS and Sass/SCSS in the Context of Modern Web Development

The Rise of CSS Frameworks and Libraries

CSS frameworks like Bootstrap, Tailwind CSS, and Materialize have gained immense popularity for providing pre-styled components and responsive grids. While these frameworks are invaluable for rapid development, they often require customization to align with brand-specific aesthetics.

Sass plays a crucial role here by allowing developers to override framework variables and extend functionality. For instance:

```
// Overriding Bootstrap variables
$primary-color: #ff5722;
@import 'bootstrap';
```

CSS-in-JS: A New Paradigm

With the rise of JavaScript frameworks like React, CSS-in-JS has emerged as a powerful trend. Libraries like styled-components enable developers to write component-specific styles in JavaScript, ensuring encapsulation and avoiding global scope conflicts. While CSS-in-JS is not a replacement for Sass, the two can complement each other, with Sass used for foundational styles and CSS-in-JS for component-specific overrides.

Preprocessors in Serverless and JAMstack Architectures

In JAMstack (JavaScript, APIs, Markup) applications, precompiled assets play a critical role. Tools like Sass and PostCSS fit seamlessly into this architecture, enabling developers to preprocess styles during build time, ensuring optimal performance and smaller bundle sizes.

Future Directions for Styling in Web Development

CSS Evolution: A Glimpse into the Future

CSS is constantly evolving, with upcoming features promising even greater capabilities:

Container Queries: Enabling styles based on container size rather than viewport size.
CSS Nesting: Bringing native nesting capabilities, similar to Sass, directly into CSS.
Custom Media Queries: Allowing developers to define reusable media query rules.

The Enduring Role of Sass/SCSS

Despite advancements in CSS, preprocessors like Sass will remain relevant, especially in large-scale projects where modularization, reusability, and advanced features are critical. Sass continues to integrate seamlessly with modern tooling, from task runners like Gulp to module bundlers like Webpack and Vite.

Automation and AI in CSS Styling

With the advent of AI-driven tools, automated styling and suggestions are becoming a reality. AI can analyze designs and generate CSS, saving time and reducing manual errors.

Final Thoughts

The journey of web styling, from CSS basics to advanced concepts like testing and preprocessors, reflects the dynamic nature of web development. As tools and methodologies continue to evolve, mastering the foundational principles and staying adaptable to emerging trends remain key for developers.

By integrating the best practices of CSS and leveraging the power of Sass/SCSS, developers can create responsive, maintainable, and high-performing applications that meet the demands of modern users. The future of web styling is both promising and challenging, calling for a blend of creativity, technical expertise, and a commitment to continuous learning.

This holistic approach ensures that developers not only build beautiful websites but also push the boundaries of what's possible in web design and development.

8. The Future of HTML and CSS

Introduction

The web has undergone transformative changes over the past decades, driven largely by innovations in HTML and CSS. These foundational technologies shape how users interact with the internet and how developers bring ideas to life. As we approach 2025, both HTML and CSS continue to evolve, promising to redefine web development standards with new capabilities, enhanced performance, and greater inclusivity. This document delves into the upcoming trends, features, and shifts in HTML and CSS, highlighting their implications for developers, businesses, and users. From advanced semantic elements to state-of-the-art design tools, the future of these technologies is both exciting and transformative.

HTML

1. Semantic Enhancements

Semantic HTML remains a cornerstone of accessible and SEO-friendly web development. In 2025, new semantic elements are expected to enhance the structure and meaning of web content:

Proposed Elements: HTML5.3 and later iterations may introduce elements that further refine semantics for emerging use cases, such as immersive media or data visualization. For instance, new tags for defining VR/AR content (<xr> or <immersive-content>) could emerge.

Custom Elements: Developers will continue to leverage the power of Web Components, creating reusable and semantic custom elements that integrate seamlessly with existing HTML standards.

2. Accessibility by Design

Accessibility will no longer be an afterthought. With the rise of automated accessibility tools and improved support for ARIA roles, HTML standards will embed best practices to ensure inclusivity:

Native Support for ARIA Landmarks: Developers can expect more streamlined attributes for roles like banner, complementary, and region.

Enhanced Accessibility APIs: Direct integration with assistive technologies, ensuring real-time responsiveness and clarity for users with disabilities.

3. Integration with Web3 and Decentralization

As Web3 technologies grow, HTML will adapt to support decentralized applications (dApps):

Meta Tags for Blockchain Integration: Enhanced meta tags for blockchain identifiers and smart contract interactions.

Native Support for Peer-to-Peer Protocols: HTML will expand its scope to include elements and APIs that cater to decentralized networks like IPFS (InterPlanetary File System).

4. Performance Optimizations

Efficiency will be a key focus, with HTML enabling:

Declarative Shadow DOM: Simplified syntax to improve rendering performance and maintainability.

Native Lazy Loading Improvements: Built-in support for predictive preloading and improved lazy loading of images and iframes.

CSS

1. Container Queries Revolutionize Responsiveness

The introduction of container queries will address the limitations of traditional media queries:

Element-Based Queries: Instead of relying solely on viewport dimensions, container queries enable styles based on the dimensions of individual containers.

Dynamic Adaptability: This empowers developers to create truly modular and reusable components, enhancing the flexibility of design systems.

2. CSS Layers for Better Cascade Control

CSS Layers (@layer) are set to simplify cascade management:

Organized Styles: By assigning priorities to style layers, developers can ensure predictable and maintainable styling hierarchies.

Improved Collaboration: Teams can now collaborate on styles without fear of unintended overrides.

3. Native CSS Design Tokens

Design tokens are becoming a first-class citizen in CSS:

Syntax Standardization: Variables like --color-primary will evolve to be more integrated with tools and frameworks.

Interoperability: Native support for design tokens ensures seamless integration across tools like Figma, Sketch, and web development environments.

4. Advanced Visual and Interactive Features

CSS will continue to expand its design capabilities:

3D Transformations and Animations: Enhanced support for 3D effects, including realistic lighting, reflections, and perspective.

Subgrid Improvements: Grids will become even more flexible, with subgrid gaining new functionalities for nested layouts.

Style Queries: Allowing conditional styling based on computed styles of elements, adding another layer of interactivity.

5. Embracing AI and Machine Learning

CSS will begin leveraging AI to predict and suggest styles:

Auto-Generated Styles: AI tools can analyze content and propose optimal styling.

Responsive and Adaptive Design Suggestions: Machine learning algorithms will assist in creating designs that cater to diverse devices and preferences.

Emerging Trends in HTML and CSS

1. Integration with AR/VR and Immersive Web Experiences

With the rise of the Metaverse and immersive experiences:

HTML will adopt new elements and attributes for 3D and AR/VR content.
CSS will introduce properties for depth effects, spatial positioning, and responsive design in 3D environments.

2. Personalized and Adaptive Content

Websites will adapt to user preferences in real-time:

HTML will integrate attributes for dynamic content personalization.
CSS will support context-aware styles, dynamically adjusting based on user data like preferences or accessibility settings.

3. Green Coding Practices

Sustainability will influence web development practices:

Lighter HTML and CSS footprints to reduce data transfer and energy consumption.
Standardized tools for auditing and optimizing resource efficiency.

4. Enhanced Collaboration with JavaScript

While HTML and CSS become more capable on their own, they will also improve their synergy with JavaScript:

Declarative syntax for integrating animations and interactivity without heavy reliance on JavaScript.
APIs like Houdini will allow developers to extend CSS functionality with JavaScript, enabling greater customization and innovation.

Tools and Frameworks for 2025

1. Improved Browser DevTools

Browsers will enhance their development tools:

Real-time previews for container queries and style queries.
Accessibility simulators to test and improve inclusivity.

2. Frameworks Adapting to New Standards

Popular frameworks like React, Angular, and Vue will incorporate new HTML and CSS capabilities:

Support for CSS Layers and container queries.
Improved integration with native web components.

3. AI-Powered Design Platforms
AI will revolutionize web design:

Tools like GitHub Copilot for CSS will offer instant suggestions and refactor code.
Platforms will auto-generate HTML/CSS based on wireframes or mockups.

Challenges and Considerations

1. Backward Compatibility

While advancements are exciting, ensuring compatibility with older browsers and devices remains a challenge.

2. Learning Curve for Developers

New features introduce complexity:

Developers will need to stay updated through training and practice.
Educational resources must evolve to simplify adoption.

3. Performance Trade-offs

While new features enhance capabilities, they may also impact performance if not implemented carefully.

Let's Begin,

Throughout the previous chapters, you've learned a lot about the current state of HTML and CSS. Through the course of this chapter, we will attempt to cast our eyes to the future. We will look into the crystal ball of the web and see where these technologies are headed.

The nature of this chapter is going to be somewhat speculative, but we are going to look at some technology that is available through web browsers at the moment and may become available throughout the web ecosystem in the future.

The web moves fast, and keeping up with changes is a key skill to learn for those interested in technology and developing for the web. We hope to provide some really useful strategies and resources that can help you to do just that; to keep up with changes, to stay ahead of new web technologies, and to see what exciting and experimental features you may want to work with.

Before we experiment with the CSS Paint API and see what it allows web developers to do, we will consider some useful ways to help us, as developers, keep up with the everchanging environment of the web.

Keeping up with the Web

Keeping up with changes in web technology and the web as a platform is one of the toughest challenges you will face as a web developer or designer.

Design trends change and technologies evolve all the time. All of the browser vendors are continuously improving their browsers on desktop and mobile, bringing out new features and improving user and developer experience with new tools and capabilities.

Several browsers are made available to developers during their development cycles, and these can be useful to a developer as they let us use experimental features and see what is changing in the next release. We can keep an eye on upcoming changes and see what effect they may have on our websites, and we can act accordingly rather than having to react in an unplanned manner when the browser updates.

Chrome Canary

In this section, we will look at Chrome Canary, the nightly build of Google's Chrome web browser. There are versions of Chrome Canary available for Windows (32-bit and 64-bit), Mac, and Android, all of which can be downloaded from the Chrome Canary website.

Chrome Canary is a nightly build of the Chrome browser that may be unstable, but often contains experimental code and features that haven't been tested as thoroughly as they would be before being released in Google Chrome. This means there can be security issues, and such browsers should be used to assist development only. In other words, don't use them to store personal information such as credit card details and passwords.

Once you've downloaded and installed Chrome Canary, you can use it. It is very recognizable as it looks similar to the Chrome browser, though it does have a lot more yellow in the app's icon:

Figure: Chrome Canary (left) and Chrome (right)

You can also see from the About Google Chrome page that Chrome Canary will be running at least a few major versions ahead of Google Chrome.

In the following screenshot, you can see that Google Chrome is running major version 76:

About Chrome

Figure: About page for Google Chrome official build

In the following screenshot, you can see that Google Chrome Canary is running major version 78:

About Chrome

Figure: About page for Chrome Canary official build

We will look at some features that are only available in Chrome Canary later in this chapter when we look at the CSS Paint API and CSS Custom Properties API.

Nightly builds are also available for Firefox (from Firefox Nightly), Safari (Safari dev), and Edge (Edge Nightly). These browsers offer regular updates and are continuously improving the features they offer.

Experimental Flags

As well as new developments being available in the nightly builds of a browser, features are often released in the official build of the browser but behind a feature flag. This allows a developer to opt into a feature so that they can experiment or prototype a solution based on a cutting-edge browser feature while protecting the general public from a feature that is still being worked on and has not been standardized yet.

You can enable and disable flags in the Chrome browser by visiting **chrome://flags/** (to visit the page, type **chrome://flags/** in your browser's address bar and hit Enter). This page provides a list of available experiments that the current version of the browser is running and gives you the option to enable or disable these experiments.

The following screenshot shows you what the **chrome://flags/** page looks like. You can search for features and set them to disabled, enabled, or default. As the warning suggests, these are experimental features and should be treated as such. For example, there is always the potential that they can introduce an undetected security issue:

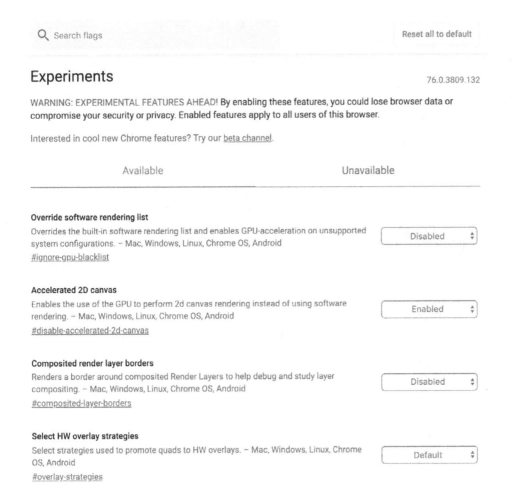

Figure: Chrome experimental flags page (chrome://flags)

These experiments relate to all aspects of the browser and can include experimental dev tools features, aspects of browser performance, and experimental web platform features such as HTML, CSS, and JavaScript. For example, in the past, this flag has included experiments relating to the new CSS grid layout and flexbox layout features, Structure and Layout.

Browser Vendor Status

While nightly builds of browsers can give you a chance to work with the latest features during their development and while they are still in an experimental state, browser vendors also provide useful resources for keeping up with the latest features and future roadmap of their browsers.

For the Chrome browser, you can keep up to date with current and future developments on the Chrome status website (https://packt.live/2qvpagS) and see what new features are being launched and how they are useful to web developers, The Chrome dev team's updates blog is also a great resource.

In the case of Google Chrome, information specifically about web dev tools improvements can also be accessed via the dev tools' "What's New" panel.

Caniuse

The browser landscape is a complicated one. Sometimes, a new feature will be accepted as standard and will be implemented in most or all browsers very quickly, but this is not always the case. Some features can appear in one browser and go through many iterations before a standard is agreed upon and they are implemented elsewhere.

For example, CSS Flexbox, Structure and Layout, first appeared way back in 2009 and went through several experimental versions before a recommendation for the CSS standards was agreed upon. The browser support is now quite good, but it has taken 10 years to get there.

We, as developers, often have to work to browser specifications (that is, a list of browsers the page must support), and we may need to know whether a browser feature is available for all of the browsers included in the specification. There are several sources for this information, and one of the most palatable is the caniuse website.

If we need to know if a browser feature is available in Edge we can check the caniuse website, and it will provide a breakdown of supported browsers.

For example, to check support for the CSS grid layout, which lets us create complex layouts and page structures without adding a lot of unwanted markups to a web page, The result is a map of browser support where green means full support, red means no support, and a lighter green means some support that is either behind a vendor prefix or is not the standardized version of the feature.

At the time of writing, the results for the CSS grid layout are as follows. As you can see, most of the current browsers support this feature with global support at around 91% with no prefix. IE 11 support has an older version of the specification, so it is supported with some caveats:

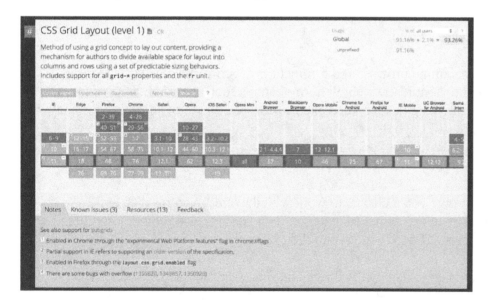

Figure: CSS Grid support

If we were to do the same for CSS grid layout level 2, that is, the CSS subgrid feature, the story would be very different. There is very little support for this feature at the moment, with the one glimmer of green being a future version of the Mozilla Firefox browser. The results, at the time of writing, are shown in the following screenshot:

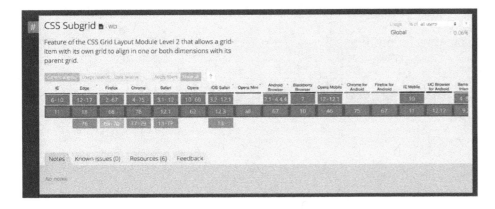

Figure: CSS Subgrid support

Using reference material such as caniuse.com, we are able to make educated decisions about whether a feature has sufficient support to be useful in our current or future web projects.

To compound our understanding, we will try using the caniuse.com website as a tool to check browser support in the next exercise.

Exercise: Verifying Browser Support for Web Pages Created Using CSS Grid

In this exercise, we will create a web page using CSS grid and check browser support and see if we can meet the browser requirements using this feature. Structure and Layout. Using the caniuse.com website as a tool, we will check the browser support for CSS grid and compare it to the browser requirements. Having checked the support, we will consider what we can do to match our requirements while still using a CSS grid layout.

Our browser requirements are as follows:

The latest version of browsers that update regularly, for example, Chrome, Firefox, Edge, and Safari Internet Explorer support from version 11 The steps are as follows:

Firstly, we will create a file called **Exercise.html**. Save this file.

Add the following code to the **Exercise.html** file. This code creates a simple web page with minimal styles to set box-sizing for all the elements, which will set the padding and margin to zero and the font to Arial:

```
<!DOCTYPE html>
<html lang="en">
  <head>
    <meta charset="utf-8">
    <title>Exercise: Browser support</title>
    <style>        body {        padding: 0;        margin: 0;        box-sizing: border-box;
font-family: Arial, Helvetica, sans-serif;        }
      *, *::after, *::before {        box-sizing: inherit;        }
    </style>
  </head>
  <body>
  </body>
</html>
```

We are going to use the CSS grid to create a layout like so:

```html
<div class="container grid">
    <header class="header">
      <h1>Browser support</h1>
    </header>
    <nav class="nav">
      <ul>
        <li class="current">Article 1</li>
        <li><a href="#">Article 2</a></li>
      </ul>
    </nav>
    <main class="main">
      <h2>Article 1</h2>
        <p>Lorem ipsum dolor sit amet, consectetur adipiscing elit. Duis sit amet porttitor dolor. Nunc sodales sodales risus. Donec vitae ex tempor leo blandit egestas sed sed odio. Vivamus nisi ligula, pharetra vel nisl sed, aliquam varius tellus. Maecenas vel semper eros, a pellentesque massa. Nullam rhoncus elit metus, sed rutrum ipsum malesuada sit amet. Maecenas nibh metus, fringilla vitae vulputate varius, consectetur nec ipsum. Suspendisse vitae fermentum felis, scelerisque imperdiet quam. Duis posuere maximus ex, tincidunt hendrerit dolor commodo id.</p>        <p>Aenean id laoreet ligula. Ut blandit odio arcu. Sed ex felis, auctor eget lobortis quis, iaculis in enim. Cras vehicula blandit odio. Aenean at imperdiet ex, sed lobortis dolor. Vivamus vehicula consectetur sem faucibus mollis. Pellentesque ac enim a velit ullamcorper varius in et dolor. Nam ultricies, urna at luctus feugiat, ante nisl maximus sapien, in rutrum dui dui at dolor. Fusce eu lorem ipsum.</p>        </main>
      <section class="advertisement">
        <h2>Advertise here</h2>
        <p>Want your product to be noticed?</p>
        <p>Advertise here!</p>
      </section>
    <footer class="footer">
      <p>Add Copyright info here</p>
    </footer>
  </div>
```

The following screenshot shows the result of adding this markup to the **body** element of **Exercise.html**:

Browser support

- Article 1
- Article 2

Article 1

Lorem ipsum dolor sit amet, consectetur adipiscing elit. Duis sit amet porttitor dolor. Nunc sodales sodales risus. Donec vitae ex tempor leo blandit egestas sed sed odio. Vivamus nisi ligula, pharetra vel nisl sed, aliquam varius tellus. Maecenas vel semper eros, a pellentesque massa. Nullam rhoncus elit metus, sed rutrum ipsum malesuada sit amet. Maecenas nibh metus, fringilla vitae vulputate varius, consectetur nec ipsum. Suspendisse vitae fermentum felis, scelerisque imperdiet quam. Duis posuere maximus ex, tincidunt hendrerit dolor commodo id.

Aenean id laoreet ligula. Ut blandit odio arcu. Sed ex felis, auctor eget lobortis quis, iaculis in enim. Cras vehicula blandit odio. Aenean at imperdiet ex, sed lobortis dolor. Vivamus vehicula consectetur sem faucibus mollis. Pellentesque ac enim a velit ullamcorper varius in et dolor. Nam ultricies, urna at luctus feugiat, ante nisl maximus sapien, in rutrum dui dui at dolor. Fusce eu lorem ipsum.

Advertise here

Want your product to be noticed? Advertise here.

Add Copyright info here

Figure: Markup without styles

The next step is to add markup for our layout that we can then style using CSS and apply a grid layout. The markup includes a container div on which we can apply the display, that is, the grid CSS property. Within the container, we create five elements – a header element with the page heading, a **nav** element with the navigation for the page, the main element for an article, a section for an advertisement, and a footer element that may contain legal information and site navigation. We can add some placeholder content to fill out the page.

We can now use the CSS grid to layout the elements of our page. We set the grid class to use **display: grid** and set the element's height to the entire viewport (100 vh). Here, we will make use of the **grid-template-areas** property to set out our layout with named areas. We'll create a map of what our layout will look like; for example, the header section spans two columns of the first row, starting in the first column:

```
<style> .grid { display: grid;  height: 100vh; grid-template-rows: 100px 1fr 100px; grid-template-columns: 100px 1fr 200px;          grid-template-areas:          "header header advert"
        "nav main advert"
        "footer footer footer";
   }
   .grid .footer {        grid-area: footer;       }
   .grid .header {        grid-area: header;       }
   .grid .main {        grid-area: main;       }
   .grid .nav {        grid-area: nav;       }
   .grid .advertisement {        grid-area: advert;       }
</style>
```

If you now right-click on the filename in **VSCode** on the left-hand side of the screen and select **open in default browser**, you will see the following screenshot that shows the result of applying the CSS grid layout:

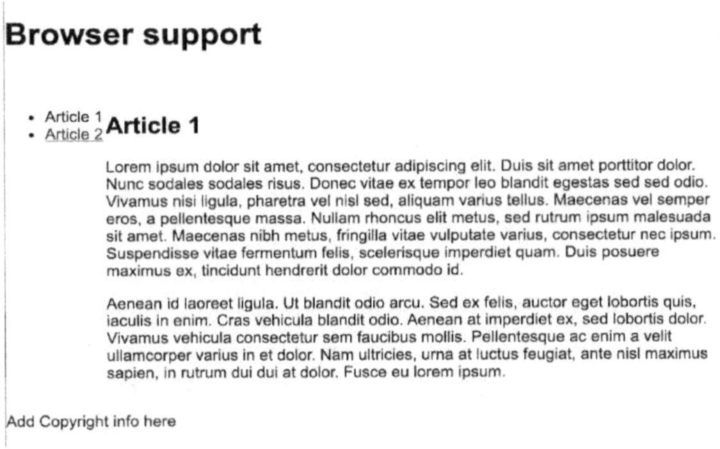

Figure: Grid layout applied

The layout now takes up the whole viewport. The header spans two columns, with the advert spanning two rows on the right. The footer spans the whole of the bottom of the page. The article expands responsively and takes up the middle section of the page.

Next, we will update the styles of the page to give each section a bit more differentiation. We will add some borders to distinguish between sections, style the nav, and use a background color to define the advertisement and footer elements.

We'll also apply some **padding** to give the content a bit of breathing space:

```
.header {           border-bottom: 1px solid gray;        }
.nav {              border-right: 1px solid gray;       }
.nav ul {           list-style-type: none;        margin: 0;       padding:0;        width: 100%;
}

.nav ul li {        width: 100%;        margin: 0;
   padding: 16px 8px;        }
.current {          background: lightgray;
   border-bottom: 1px solid gray;        }
.main {          display: block;        padding: 16px;
   overflow:auto;
}
.advertisement {            padding: 16px;        border-left: 1px solid gray;        background:
greenyellow;        }
.footer {          background: black;        color: white;        padding: 0 1rem;
}
```

The following screenshot shows the result of these changes:

Figure: Further styles applied to differentiate between sections of the layout

Our web page now has a layout defined with CSS grid template areas. CSS grids mean we don't have to use additional markup to control our layout and keep style and content separate. However, we have browser requirements to meet and the CSS grid, being relatively new, may give us some concerns. In this step, we will check support using caniuse.com.

We can see the result in Figure. It shows the caniuse.com support table for the CSS grid.
Looking at the support table, we can see a lot of green, which means support for the CSS grid in most major browsers is really good. There are a few red blocks for Opera Mini and Blackberry Browser, but neither of those is included in our requirements.
The one area that may concern us is IE, which only seems to have partial support for the CSS grid.
Hover the mouse over the IE 11 block so that we can see more details of what partial support means.

The following screenshot shows details of IE 11's partial support for the CSS grid:

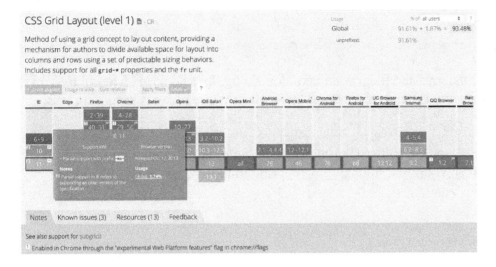

Figure: caniuse.com details of IE 11's grid layout support

The concerns we have are that the browser supports an older version of the CSS grid specification and it also expects the vendor prefix, that is, **-ms-**, to be used.

Checking the page in IE 11 shows us the issues that caniuse has flagged. In the following screenshot, we can see the result of opening the page in IE 11:

Figure: Result in IE 11

The result is that none of our layout code is working. We just get each element appearing one after the other. We aren't meeting our browser requirements at the moment but we now know that IE 11 can support some version of grid layout. To meet our browser requirements, we need to add some IE-specific CSS to solve the issues in IE 11. With CSS, the last rule that the browser recognizes will be the one that's been applied so that we can support both IE and modern browser implementations of the CSS grid.

Firstly, we apply the **-ms-** prefix for the grid and the row and column sizing. Instead of **grid-template-rows**, we apply the sizing to **-ms-grid-rows** and instead of **gridtemplate-columns**, we use **-ms-grid-columns**:

```
.grid {          display: -ms-grid;        display: grid;        height: 100vh;        -ms-grid-rows:
100px 1fr 100px;          grid-template-rows: 100px 1fr 100px;        -ms-grid-columns: 100px 1fr
200px;          grid-template-columns: 100px 1fr 200px;        grid-template-areas:          "header
header advert"
          "nav main advert"
          "footer footer footer";
    }
```

Because the IE version of grid does not support named grid areas and the **gridtemplate-areas** property, we need to set out each of our template areas with **-ms-grid-row** and **-ms-grid-column** to set the starting row and column position and then spans to control the amount of space the elements take up. Here is the code to do this:

```
    .grid .footer {
        -ms-grid-row: 3;
        -ms-grid-column: 1;
        -ms-grid-column-span: 3;          grid-area: footer;          }
    .grid .header {
        -ms-grid-row: 1;
        -ms-grid-column: 1;
        -ms-grid-column-span: 2;          grid-area: header;          }
    .grid .main {
        -ms-grid-row: 2;
        -ms-grid-column: 2;          grid-area: main;
    }
    .grid .nav {
        -ms-grid-row: 2;
        -ms-grid-column: 1;          grid-area: nav;          }
    .grid .advertisement {
        -ms-grid-row: 1;
        -ms-grid-column: 3;
        -ms-grid-row-span: 2;
grid-area: advert;
}
```

The result is a CSS grid layout that works in all modern browsers and IE back to version 10, which more than meets our browser requirements.

The following screenshot shows the resulting layout in IE 11:

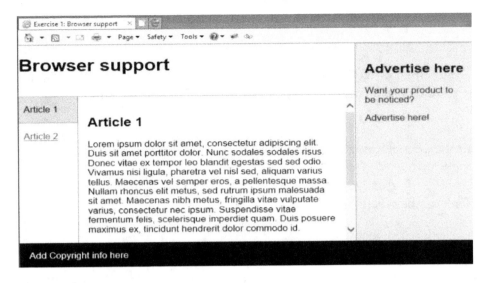

Figure: The result of making use of IE 11's CSS grid

As the preceding screenshot shows, we've solved the issues with our layout in IE 11 and now meet our browser support requirements.

By keeping track of the browser features we use on a web page and using tools such as caniuse.com, we can improve browser support and meet the requirements of our users and clients.

In the next part of this chapter, we will look at the CSS Paint API, which is a proposed specification that was created by the CSS Houdini Taskforce and designed to give developers more access to the CSS rendering pipeline and the CSSOM.

We will look at how we can use the technology of today by combining some of the techniques we've discussed in this chapter. We will also see how we can use progressive enhancement to provide a good user experience for those users who don't have access to the technology because it is not available in the browser they are using.

First, we will provide an explanation of the role of the CSS Houdini Taskforce and what it means for the future of web development.

CSS Houdini

The CSS **Technical Architecture Group** (**TAG**) Houdini Task Force (more prominently known as CSS Houdini) has been tasked with opening up the black box systems that make up browser rendering by providing APIs for developers to work with and for developers to change the behaviours of processes such as layout and paint.

The CSS Houdini group creates draft specifications to enhance CSS by giving developers more access to the render pipelines of the browser. We will look at two of these APIs: the CSS Paint API, which gives us greater control of the painting aspects of CSS such as background colors, gradients, and masks, and the CSS Properties and Values API, which you can use to register and define custom properties as being of a CSS type (such as a color or length). We will see how the two APIs can be used in unison.

By giving the web developer low-level access to the CSS render pipeline for layout, composition, and paint processes, developers are better able to control these processes and create more optimal scripts for rendering at the CSSOM level.

CSS Paint API

The first API from CSS Houdini to see the light of day, with an actual browser implementation, is the Paint API, which first appeared in Chrome 65 and is now available in Opera with the intent for Firefox, Safari, and Edge to implement it as well.

The Paint API gives us a way to control a 2D rendering context that we can programmatically draw to using JavaScript, Media – Audio, Video, and Canvas.

There are a couple of significant differences between the Paint API and the 2D rendering context of the Canvas:

The main difference is that the Paint API allows us to use the 2D image with any CSS property that accepts an image as a value. For example, we can create a 2D image and then use it as the value for a **background-image**, **border-image**, or **maskimage**.

The Paint API also makes use of a worklet, which is a bit like a worker, that is, a thread running parallel to the main browser thread. Essentially, this means that the worklet won't block the browser from doing other processes. The worklet has very restricted functionality, which means it can be heavily optimized for rendering.

To create a paint worklet, we will need to follow a few steps:

Firstly, we will create a simple JavaScript class with a **paint** method. The paint method will receive a 2D rendering context, a geometry object with the dimensions of the area in which we can paint, and, optionally, a set of properties.

We need to create this class in a separate file.

To be able to use the paint worklet, we must register it, which we will do with the **registerPaint** function. This function is only made available when we add the file to our web page as a paint worklet module. The **registerPaint** function takes two arguments: a unique key that you will use to identify the worklet and the JavaScript class with the paint method.

To add the module as a paint worklet, we'll use the **addModule** method on the **paintWorklet** object of CSS, which will look something like **CSS.paintWorklet. addModule("workletModule.js");**.

With the paint worklet registered and added to our web page, we can use it in CSS wherever we may expect an image. For example, to use a paint worklet as a background image for a paragraph element, we could call the paint worklet with a special CSS **paint** function:

```
<style>  p {    background-image: paint(paintWorklet);  }
</style>
```

Let's run through the creation of a very simple paint worklet to get a better idea of how all of this will tie together.

Exercise: Creating a Red Fill Paint Worklet

In this exercise, we will create our first very simple paint worklet. Our first iteration of a paint worklet will be limited to painting a rectangle, that is, the full size of the canvas, with the fill color red. This exercise will get us used to registering a paint worklet and applying it to CSS. Later, we will expand upon this simple paint worklet to develop some more sophisticated effects.

The steps are as follows:

Firstly, we want to create our worklet file. Create a new file and save it as **red-fillpaint.js**.
To be able to use the paint worklet, we will need a web page. In the same directory as our paint worklet file, create a file and save it as **Exercise.html**. Add the following code for a simple web page:

```
<!DOCTYPE html>
<html lang="en">
  <head>
    <meta charset="utf-8">
    <title>Exercise 13.02: A Simple Paint Worklet</title>
    <style>     body {     padding: 0;     margin: 0;     font-family: Arial, Helvetica, sans-serif;     }
    </style>
  </head>
  <body>

  </body>
</html>
```

Returning to **red-fill-paint.js**, we need to create a JavaScript class with a **paint** method. The behavior of our paint worklet will be defined in this **paint** method. The paint method will receive a context object that gives us access to drawing methods we can use to paint and a geometry object, which we can use to calculate the width and height of the area the worklet is applied to.

To fill the rectangle with red, use the following code:

```
class RedFillPaintWorklet {   paint(context, geometry) {     context.fillStyle = "red";     context.fillRect(0, 0, geometry.width, geometry.height);
  }
}
```

For this JavaScript class to be recognized as a paint worklet, we need to register it. We do that with **registerPaint**. We give the worklet a name and pass it the worklet class:

```
registerPaint("red-fill", RedFillPaintWorklet);
```

For now, we are done with the paint worklet module, but we need to add it to our web page. Returning to the **Exercise.html** file, we need to add a script and add the module. This will complete the registration of the paint worklet with our web page:

```
<script>
  CSS.paintWorklet.addModule("red-fill-paint.js"); </script>
```

Now, we can use the paint worklet. To do that, we will add a **div** element to the web page with the **red-background** class attribute:

```html
<div class="red-background"> This div should have a red background.
</div>
```

We will then use the paint function in our CSS and pass it the **red-fill** name that we have registered our paint worklet with. We'll use the following CSS to style the element, which we can add to the style element in the header of the web page:

```html
<style>
 .red-background {
  background: paint(red-fill);  color: white;  box-sizing: border-box;  width: 100%;  height: 100px;
padding: 16px;  }
</style>
```

If you now right-click on the filename in **VSCode** on the left-hand side of the screen and select **open in default browser**, you will see the result of this code to be similar to the following screenshot. We have painted a rectangle with the color red:

Figure: A red fill paint worklet applied to a div element

We could have simply created the same effect by applying the **background-color:**

red; style to the red-background class attribute. However, even with this very simple example, we can start to see some interesting features of paint worklets:

The worklet is integrated with CSS, meaning we can use it for various properties, such as **background-image**, **background-color**, and **mask-image**, as well as for shorthand properties such as **background**.

The dimensions of the worklet are dynamic and will repaint with the browser render pipeline, which means it is responsive by default.

In the next part of this chapter, we will look at how we can register properties that can be set in CSS and used in our paint worklet to make this background fill behaviour more flexible and controllable via CSS styling.

Custom Properties

With CSS custom properties (often called CSS variables), we have a way to store a value for use in several CSS declarations. We can change this value as we like.

The syntax for a CSS custom property is a name prefixed with two dashes (--). We can then use the value stored in the property with the CSS **var** function.

Here is an example of some CSS custom properties in use:

```
<style>
:root {
    --dark-text-color: #131313;
    --light-text-color: #cfcfcf;
}
p.dark {    color: var(--dark-text-color);  }
p.light {   color: var(--light-text-color);  }
</style>
```

The following screenshot shows the result of applying the preceding style rules to one paragraph element with the dark class attribute applied and one paragraph element with the light class attribute applied. The color variables we have created are set as the color style of the paragraph:

Lorem ipsum. Copy testing a LIGHT typography theme.

Lorem ipsum. Copy testing a DARK typography theme.

Figure: Custom properties for text color applied to paragraph elements

Custom properties can be used as inputs for a paint worklet, which allows us to reuse the paint worklet with different inputs (such as color), thereby making them a lot more flexible. For example, if we wanted to use more colors than red in our fill color paint worklet, we could use a **--fill-color** custom property to decide which color to fill the HTML element in with.

We can register properties with the paint worklet to allow CSS properties to affect the paint worklet. A static **input Properties** function can be added to our paint worklet JavaScript class and it will return an array of custom CSS properties the paint worklet expects as input, like so:

```
static get inputProperties() {
  return ["--fill-color"];
}
```

We can then access the property in our paint method via the properties argument. So, if we want to access the **--fill-color** property in our **paint** method, we can do the following:

```
paint(context, geometry, properties) {
    const color = properties.get("--fill-color");
```

Let's try an exercise to put what we've learned into practice and to see how we can use CSS properties to make a more flexible fill color paint worklet.

Exercise: The Fill Color Paint Worklet

In this exercise, we will create a new paint worklet that extends the red fill paint worklet to allow any color to be used to fill a rectangle. While still simple and easily achieved with standard CSS, this exercise will let us see how we can use properties with our paint worklets. The steps are as follows:

Make a copy of **red-fill-paint.js** from Exercise, Browser Support, and rename it color-fill-paint.js. We will change the name of the class to **ColorFillPaintWorklet**.

The paint worklet for the fill color paint worklet will be very similar to the red fill paint worklet, although we will take the color value from the **--fill-color** property, thus allowing us to change the color dynamically. To do this, we need to add a static **inputProperties** function that returns an array with the **--fill-color** property:

```
class ColorFillPaintWorklet {   static get inputProperties() {
return ["--fill-color"];   }
```

We can then access the properties in the paint worklet through the **properties** argument of the **paint** method. We will get the **--fill-color** property and set the context's **fillStyle** to that value:

```
class ColorFillPaintWorklet {   static get inputProperties() {
    return ["--fill-color"];
  }   paint(context, geometry, properties) {
      const color = properties.get("--fill-color");
    context.fillStyle = color;
    context.fillRect(0, 0, geometry.width, geometry.height);
  }
}
```

To complete the work on the paint worklet, we need to register it as **"color-fill"**:

```
registerPaint("color-fill", ColorFillPaintWorklet);
```

To make use of the paint worklet, we will make a copy of the **Exercise.
html** file and rename it **Exercise.html**. We'll change the title of the HTML document to Exercise, Fill Color Paint Worklet:

```
<head>
    <meta charset="utf-8">  <title>Exercise: Fill Color Paint Worklet</title>
      <style>  body { padding: 0; margin: 0; font-family: Arial, Helvetica, sans-serif;
}
      </style>
    </head>
```

Also, in the same document, change the paint worklet module to **color-fill-paint.**

js:
```
    <script>
        CSS.paintWorklet.addModule("color-fill-paint.js");
      </script>
    </body>
</html>
```

Next, we will replace the **.red-background** style with a **.fill-background** style that uses color-fill instead of red-fill. We'll also set up two new class attributes – **.green** and **.orange** – that will set the **--fill-color** property:

```
    <style>
      .green {
          --fill-color: #05a505;
      }
      .orange {
          --fill-color: #ff9900;
      }
      .fill-background {
box-sizing:border-box;  background: paint(color-fill);
color: white;
width: 100%;
height: 100px;
```

```
  padding: 16px;
}
</style>
```

Finally, we'll replace the div element with the **.red-background** class attribute with two div elements, both with the **.fill-background** class attribute applied. However, one will have the **.green** class attribute applied to it, while the other will have the **.orange** class attribute applied to it:

```
<div class="fill-background green">
```

This div should have a green background.

```
    </div>
    <div class="fill-background orange">
```

This div should have an orange background.
```
</div>
```

If you now right-click on the filename in **VSCode** on the left-hand side of the screen and select **open in default browser**, you will see the following screenshot that shows the color fill paint worklet being applied to two different divs with green and orange background fills:

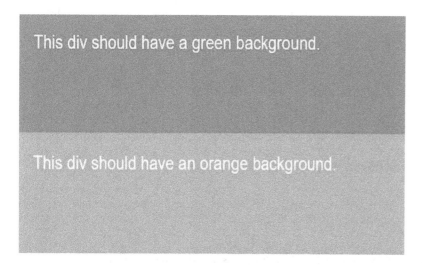

Figure: Fill color paint worklet applied with different parameters

Custom properties allow us to create more flexible worklets. We can easily apply different parameters using CSS selectors. An added advantage is that because paint worklets are intrinsically tied to the CSS rendering system, we can take advantage of properties such as CSS transition to animate a paint worklet.

Next, we will look at how we can use multiple properties and work with user input to update the custom properties. This can make our paint worklet much more interactive and opens up some more possibilities regarding what we can do with a paint worklet.

Input Properties

Using some JavaScript, we can do even more with these custom properties. For example, we can listen to a mouse or touch input and pass the x and y coordinates to a paint worklet. With these values, we can paint an element based on the point where the pointer is moving or the point where the pointer enters and leaves the element.

In the next exercise, we will introduce a few more custom properties and update them based on the movement of the mouse. In so doing, we will create a paint worklet that is a bit more complex but also goes beyond what is easily done with standard CSS properties (such as **background-color**).

Exercise: Paint Worklet with Mouse Input

In this exercise, we will create a new paint worklet that paints a circle that follows the mouse as it moves over an element that the paint worklet is associated with. Using CSS pseudo-classes, we will then update the custom properties when the user clicks the element in order to paint a clicked state for the element.

The steps are as follows:

Create a new file and name it **pointer-input-paint.js**. We will create a new paint worklet in this file. In pointer-input-paint.js, we want to create a JavaScript class called **PointerInputPaint**. This will encompass the behaviour of our paint worklet. We will register the paint worklet as **"pointer"** so that we can use it in our document's CSS:

```
class PointerInputPaint {    paint(context, geometry, properties) {    }
} registerPaint("pointer", PointerInputPaint);
```

Next, we can define a set of input properties, which is the set of CSS custom properties we will set via CSS. We want to know the x and y positions of the mouse, so we will store those positions as the **--position-x** and **--position-y** properties. We also want to customize the size and color of our mouse follower and for that, we will store properties for size and two different colors in the following properties:

--size, **--primary-fill-color**, and **--secondary-fill-color**:

```
static get inputProperties() {
    return ["--position-x", "--position-y", "--primary-fill-color", "--secondaryfill-color", "--size"];
}
```

In the paint method of our paint worklet, we are going to need to do two things:

read the values from our CSS input properties and use the values to draw a gradient onto the element the paint worklet is attached to.

First, we need to read the input properties. We do this in the paint function, where the properties argument gives us access to each of the input properties. We can use the get function to get a property by its name. We get each property, that is, the x and y coordinates of the mouse, the primary and secondary colors, and the size property:

```
paint(context, geometry, properties) {
const x = properties.get("--position-x");
const y = properties.get("--position-y");
const primaryColor = properties.get("--primary-fill-color");
const secondaryColor = properties.get("--secondary-fill-color");
const size = properties.get("--size");
```

Then, we draw a radial gradient based on the input properties. In the preceding code, we use the x and y coordinates to create a circle of the size of our size input. We then add the primary and secondary colors as color stops to the gradient. We learned about creating gradients on a canvas context in Chapter, Media – Audio, Video, and Canvas. This technique is the same as it is for a paint worklet because that uses a version of a canvas:

```
var gradient = context.createRadialGradient( x, y, 0, x, y, geometry.width * size );
gradient.addColorStop(0.24, primaryColor);
gradient.addColorStop(0.25, secondaryColor);
gradient.addColorStop(1, secondaryColor);
```

The gradient here is positioned at the x and y values, which will be defined by the mouse position. We use this gradient as a fill style and fill the whole rectangle for the element, like we did in the previous exercises:

```
context.fillStyle = gradient;
context.fillRect(0, 0, geometry.width, geometry.height);     }
```

That is the whole of the paint worklet.

Next, we will create an HTML document so that we can make use of our paint worklet. Create a new file and name it **Exercise.html**. Copy the following markup into that file. This markup creates a web page with a single button centered on the page. The button is styled to create a large button:

```
<!DOCTYPE html>
<html lang="en">
  <head>
    <meta charset="utf-8">
    <title>Exercise 13.04: Mouse Input Worklet</title>
    <style>          body {
padding: 0;
margin: 0;
font-family: Arial, Helvetica, sans-serif;          }
    </style>
  </head>
  <body>
    <div class="centered-content">
      <button class="button pointer centered-content">          Click me!
      </button>
    </div>
    <style>
      .centered-content {          display: flex;          align-items: center;          justify-content:
center;          }
        .button {          outline: none;          user-select: none;
          -webkit-appearance: none;
          appearance: none;          margin: 16px;          width: 375px;          height: 150px;
padding: 16px;          font-size: 24px;          }
    </style>
  </body>
</html>
```

As shown in the following screenshot, this simple HTML document creates a single button with some CSS classes and the text **Click me!**. We have added a few styles to replace the default button styles and to center the content:

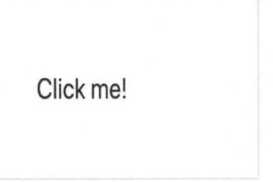

Figure: A "Click me!" button

In a script tag, we'll add our paint worklet to this page so that we can use it in our CSS:

```
<script>
   CSS.paintWorklet.addModule("pointer-input-paint.js");
</script>
```

Next, we need to create our CSS custom properties so that we can store the values that our paint worklet will read from. We will create these in a CSS declaration targeted at the **:root** pseudo-class so that they are defined globally for all CSS:

```
<style>
   :root {
      --position-x: 0;
      --position-y: 0;
      --primary-fill-color: #7200ca;
      --secondary-fill-color: #12005e;
      --size: 0.1;
   }
```

We can now add the pointer class definition to the CSS. This will use our paint worklet as a background to any element the pointer class attribute is added to. When the button is active (or clicked), we will change the values of two of our CSS properties, that is, the secondary fill color (**--secondary-fill-color**) and the size (**--size**). We do this by setting the properties using the CSS pseudo-classes for **:visited** and **:active** (which we learned about in Chapter, Introduction to HTML and CSS):

```
   .pointer {               background: paint(pointer);               color: white;               }
   .pointer:visited,
    .pointer:active {
      --secondary-fill-color: #12005e;
      --size: 10;
   }
</style>
```

The result is a dark purple button, as shown in the following screenshot. There is a small light purple dot in the top left corner of the button. At the moment, this will not move around:

Figure: The button with the pointer paint worklet applied

When the button is clicked, it will turn a lighter shade of purple, as shown in the following screenshot:

Figure: The active state of the button with the pointer paint worklet applied

To get the mouse follower working correctly, we need a little bit of JavaScript. Let's add a **mousemove** event listener to our button element. An event listener will trigger when something happens; in this case, when the mouse is moved by the user. When the mouse is moved, we will set the **--position-x** and **--position-y** properties with the new x and y coordinates of the mouse pointer over the element. We'll use the **setProperty** function to set a property on the style object of the document element of the HTML DOM. This is equivalent to setting the CSS properties inline on the HTML element or using the **:root** selector in CSS.

We add this to our script tag:

```
const mouseInput = document.querySelector(".pointer");
mouseInput.addEventListener("mousemove", () => {
document.documentElement.style.setProperty("--position-x", event.
offsetX);
document.documentElement.style.setProperty("--position-y", event. offsetY);
});
```

If you now right-click on the filename in **VSCode** on the left-hand side of the screen and select **open in default browser**, we should have a pointer that follows the mouse position correctly, as seen in the following figure:

Figure: The button with pointer following the mouse

In this exercise, we have used the mouse position to update CSS custom properties and used these properties in a paint worklet to draw a mouse follower on an element.

We can begin to see some of the benefits of using a paint worklet here as we haven't had to add any extra elements or pseudo-elements to the HTML to handle the pointer.

In the next section, we will look at another CSS Houdini API, the CSS Properties and Values API, and we will see how we can use this API to register CSS custom properties and how we can have even more control of them in a paint worklet.

CSS Properties and Values API

The CSS Properties and Values API allows us to register custom CSS properties and define their initial value, the syntax they are based on, and whether the value inherits down the HTML DOM tree (as, for example, a font size or family property value would).

To register CSS properties, we need to use JavaScript. The API provides us with a method so that we can register CSS properties with the **registerProperty** method, which is available on the global CSS object.

Let's have a look at an example:

```
CSS.registerProperty({
name: "--primary-fill-color", syntax: "<color>", inherits: false, initialValue: "white" });
```

The **registerProperty** method expects an object that defines our CSS custom property. We need to give the property a name, for example, **--primary-fill-color** or **--size**, and define whether it inherits – in other words, whether the value is inherited by DOM elements that are children of the element the property is associated with.

We can also define the syntax that the property follows. If we define the syntax that the property follows, we also need to provide an initial value for the property. There are quite a few different syntax types that we can choose from, including **<length>**, **<angle>**, **<color>**, **<number>**, and **<time>**, which define different parts of the CSS syntax.

In the preceding example, we defined a color property that follows the **<color>** syntax and has an initial value set as white. The benefit of defining a property in this way is that we can tell if the value will make sense in a CSS rule and we can use it as a value in a CSS transition where interpolation from one value to another can be calculated.

At the time of writing, this API will only work in Chrome Canary, which presents a further problem that we will discuss in the next section when we talk about progressive enhancement as a technique for developing for the web, where not all users will have the same browser or a browser with the same capabilities.

In the next exercise, we will do just that. We will take the fill color paint worklet from our previous exercise and animate it by changing a custom property with the CSS transition and animation properties.

Next, we will look at how we can use CSS animations or transitions to control custom properties. We will use animation to further improve our pointer paint worklet.

Animating Custom Properties

Remember that our paint worklet is integrated into CSS and its rendering pipeline. This means that it will repaint if the style properties change. Because we can provide an input property and the paint worklet will call the paint method if the property changes, we are able to use CSS to animate the custom property. This means that we can easily animate a paint worklet with CSS using the CSS animation and transition properties.

There is one caveat that makes this more difficult, though. The problem is that the type of CSS custom property is not easily recognized. What we need is a way of telling CSS what type of property we are passing it. In other words, we need to be able to tell CSS if we are giving it a percentage value, a number, a color value, a length value (**px**, **em**), or an angle value (**deg**, **turn**, **rad**).

We can use the CSS Properties and Values API to solve this problem. In the next exercise, we will do just that.

Exercise: Animating a Paint Worklet

In this exercise, we will animate the paint worklet we created in Exercise, Paint Worklet with Mouse Input. We do not need to make any changes to our paint worklet for this exercise, but we will need to register custom properties so that they can be animated using the CSS transition property.

The steps are as follows:

Make a copy of the **Exercise.html** file from our previous exercise. Rename the copied file **Exercise.html** and update the title of the web page document:

<title>Exercise: Animated Paint Worklet</title>

We want to add a transition to our pointer class declaration, which will transition the custom properties for **--size**, **--primary-fill-color**, and **--secondary-fillcolor**. This will cause the values for these properties to transition to the values that have been set when the element with the pointer class is clicked:

```
.pointer {background: paint(pointer);
color: white;
transition: --size 1s, --primary-fill-color 0.5s, --secondary-fill- color 0.5s;
}
```

The transition will not work yet because the custom properties have not had their syntax type defined and the CSS engine does not know how to transition from one value to another without knowing the type of the value.

To get the transitions to work, we need to register the properties. We do that with the **registerProperty** method:

```
CSS.registerProperty({
name: "--primary-fill-color", syntax: "<color>", inherits: false, initialValue: "#7200ca" });
CSS.registerProperty({
name: "--secondary-fill-color", syntax: "<color>", inherits: false, initialValue: "#12005e" });
CSS.registerProperty({ name: "--size", syntax: "<number>", inherits: false, initialValue: 0.05
});
```

If you now right-click on the filename in **VSCode** on the left-hand side of the screen and select **open in default browser** to see the result in a browser. Now that we've registered the properties for the two-color values and the size of the pointer, we can see the animation working when we click the button with the pointer class attribute attached, as shown in the following screenshot:

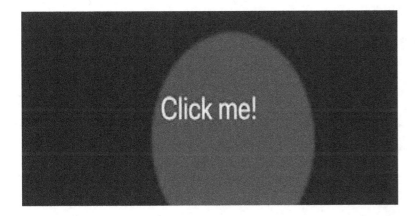

Figure: The button with a pointer following the mouse and animated CSS transitions

This exercise will work in Chrome Canary, where the CSS Properties and Values API is currently available. However, it will cause some problems in browsers where that feature is not available.

In the next part of this chapter, we will examine the support for the APIs we have used in browsers. With this information to hand, we can form a strategy for progressive enhancement with which we can deal with browsers that have not yet implemented this feature.

Current Browser Support

We can check the current browser support for the CSS Paint API feature. The following screenshot shows which browsers support the feature at the time of writing. Browser support is still mostly limited to Chrome, Opera, and Android browsers. There is still a lot of red in the screenshot, but it is worth bearing in mind that Chrome makes up a good percentage of browser users:

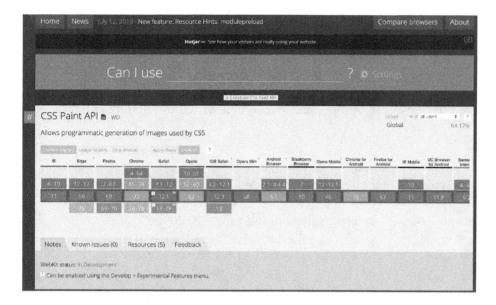

Figure: caniuse.com browser support data for the CSS Paint API

It shows where APIs have already been implemented but also where there is interest in implementing the APIs or where the APIs are currently in development:

Figure: Current state of various CSS Houdini APIs

As we can see from the preceding screenshot, many of the seven APIs that have been developed and specified by the CSS Houdini task force has seen interest from browser developers, and several have seen implementations shipped in major browsers. In particular, the **Paint API** and **Typed OM** have been actively developed and shipped in Chrome, Opera, and Samsung Browser, with Firefox and Safari showing interest in actively developing those features.

We can also see that the Properties and Values API has partial support such as that found in the Chrome Canary browser.

As we can see, the features we are using are not yet available in all the browsers we would want our web pages to work in. It is always a good idea to get as good support as we can, but it is possible to mitigate this issue with the strategy of progressive enhancement, which we will learn about in the next part of this chapter.

Progressive enhancement is really important for helping developers produce web pages that work for as wide a variety of users as possible while allowing us to use the latest technologies and giving us the freedom to experiment.

As a technique, it lets us provide our base content to any user on any device while enriching and enhancing the user experience for those with more capable browsers and devices.

Progressive Enhancement

There are several approaches that we can use when we are working with the web to make sure our websites provide the best experience possible for the greatest number of users. Unlike some closed systems, we cannot trust that all users will have the same capabilities or devices. What we can do is work from a baseline set of features and then enhance the experience for more capable browsers. This is called Progressive Enhancement.

An example of this technique is providing a simple, functional web page with text and links and then adding JavaScript to enhance the experience.

One particular challenge is CSS custom properties, or CSS variables because they are useful when used throughout your CSS declarations and are not available in IE 11. They are difficult to polyfill without having to restrict what they can do. One way of handling CSS variables is with the user of a CSS preprocessor and the build tools that replace the CSS variables at build time to create CSS that works in IE 11. We covered the use of build tools and CSS preprocessors in Chapter 10, Preprocessors and Tooling. This could then be served to the restricted browser while more capable browsers make use of CSS variables.

In the case of the CSS Paint API, we can provide a decent experience without a paint worklet, and there are often JavaScript polyfills to reach a similar experience. In the next exercise, we will apply some of these techniques to make our paint worklet example from Exercise 13.04, Paint Worklet with Mouse Input, work across more browsers.

Exercise: Progressive Enhancement

If we take a moment to analyze the code, we created in Exercise, animating a Paint Worklet, we will see that it presents a few difficulties as code we may want to use on a live website.

If you open the **Exercise.html** page in a browser that doesn't support either the CSS Paint API or CSS Properties and Values API, you will experience none of the stylings we expect and also some JavaScript errors.

The following screenshot shows the result of running **Exercise.html** in the Chrome browser, which does not support the CSS Properties and Values API. The dev tools console panel is open and shows a JavaScript error caused by a lack of support for **CSS.registerProperty**. The button is difficult to use as it appears with none of the expected styles:

Figure: Unsupported features running in Chrome

In this exercise, we will make our code more robust and provide a decent experience for those browsers that do not support the features we want to use. We will see how we can start from a working version and can then enhance the experience depending on the availability of new features.

Here are the steps:

Make a copy of the **Exercise.html** file from our previous exercise. Rename the copied file **Exercise.html** and update the title of the web page document:

<title>Exercise: Progressive Enhancement</title>

One of the benefits of cascade in CSS is that unrecognized CSS rules will be ignored, and so the last rule to be defined in the CSS, that is, a recognized rule, will be the style that's applied. We can use this technique to progressively enhance CSS. We can set background colors for the pointer class for normal and active states of the button when paint worklets are not recognized:

```
.pointer {background: #12005e;
background: paint(pointer);
color: white;
transition: --size 1s, --primary-fill-color 0.5s, --secondary-fill-color 0.5s;
}
.pointer:visited, .pointer:active {
background-color: #7200ca;
        --secondary-fill-color: #7200ca;
        --size: 10;
}
```

As a baseline experience for the button, this is enough functionality for browsers without the CSS Paint API. The button still works and there is visual differentiation between the active click state and the normal state. We still have some issues to deal with to stop errors being thrown, which we will handle next.

The next step is to prevent some errors being thrown when we register properties and the paint worklet in JavaScript. In this exercise, we can handle any issues well enough with some feature detection. Using an **if** statement, we can check whether a property exists in the browser. We can check that the CSS object is found on the window object, and if so, we run the rest of the code. We do the same to check for the existence of the **registerProperty** method, which is used for registering properties, and the **paintWorklet** property, which is used for adding paintlet modules to our CSS. This protects our code from throwing errors that will prevent further code from running:

```
if (window.CSS) {
if ("registerProperty" in CSS) {
CSS.registerProperty({
name: "--primary-fill-color", syntax: "<color>", inherits: false, initialValue: "#7200ca"});
CSS.registerProperty({
name: "--secondary-fill-color", syntax: "<color>", inherits: false, initialValue: "#12005e"});
CSS.registerProperty({ name: "--size", syntax: "<number>", inherits: false, initialValue: 0.05});
}if ("paintWorklet" in CSS) { CSS.paintWorklet.addModule("pointer-input-paint.js");
    }
}
```

We have now prevented any JavaScript errors from being thrown, which could prevent other scripts on the page from functioning. In this simple case, we have done enough to make the button function and look OK and then enhanced it as browser capabilities improved.

If you now right-click on the filename in **VSCode** on the left-hand side of the screen and select **open in default browser**, you will see the following screenshot that shows the button hover state on a browser that does not support the CSS Paint API or CSS Properties and Values API. The button style is still visible and the button is functional, but we can't see the mouse following the circle. The button is usable but does not have an enhanced experience:

Figure: Hover state of unsupported features but with improved progressive enhancement

The following screenshot shows the button click state on a browser that does not support the CSS Paint API or CSS Properties and Values API. The click state has no animation but has a color fill and shows that the user is clicking the button:

Figure: Click state of unsupported features but with improved progressive enhancement

In the following screenshot, we can see the hover state of the button in a browser with full support for the CSS Paint API and the CSS Properties and Values API, along with the mouse follower:

Figure: Overstate in a browser that supports CSS Houdini features

In the following screenshot, we can see the click state of the button in a browser with full support for the CSS Paint API and the CSS Properties and Values API. The click state is animated:

Figure: Click state in a browser that supports CSS Houdini features

Having looked at some of the features of the CSS Paint API and CSS Properties and Values API, we have considered a small subset of the CSS Houdini APIs that will provide a lot of low-level controls of the CSS render pipeline and browser layout. We have also considered how to handle experimental browser features in our current web development processes.

We will end this chapter with an activity where we will create our own paint worklet before we summarize our learning.

Activity: Button Library

You have been asked to build a library of buttons that can be used as part of a design system for consistent designs across the whole of the site you are working on. To begin with, the client is requesting four button types – default, secondary, ghost, and a special button.

The steps are as follows:

Create a directory called **design_system_activity** for the project.

Create a new file in that directory and name it **index.html**. Copy the following markup into the file:

```html
<!DOCTYPE html>
<html lang="en">
  <head>
    <meta charset="utf-8">
    <title>Activity: Buttons</title>
    <style>        body {        padding: 0;        margin: 0;        font-family: Arial,
Helvetica, sans-serif;        }
        .button {        outline: none;        user-select: none;        -webkit-appearance: none;
appearance: none;        margin: 16px;        min-width: 128px;        min-height: 32px;
padding: 8px 16px;        font-size: 24px;        border: 2px solid #fcfcfc;        box-shadow: 0
0 5px 0 rgba(0, 0, 0, 0.2);        border-radius: 3px;        cursor: pointer;        }
    </style>
  </head>
  <body>
    <div class="actions">
      <button class="button button--primary">
        Primary
      </button>
      <button class="button button--secondary">
        Secondary
      </button>
      <button class="button button--ghost">
        Ghost
      </button>
      <button class="button button--special">
        Special
      </button>
    </div>
    <script>
    </script>
  </body>
</html>
```

We have added markup for four button types: primary, secondary, ghost, and special.

Create styles for the primary button with the text color as white, the font-weight as bold, and the background color with a hex value of #f44336. When hovered over, the button's background color will change to #ff9900.

The following screenshot shows the expected primary button design:

Figure: Primary button designs for normal and hover states

Create styles for the secondary button with the text color as white, the font-weight as normal, and the background color with a hex value of #9e9e9e. When hovered over, the button's background color will change to #7c7c7c.

The following screenshot shows the expected secondary button design:

Figure: Secondary button designs for normal and hover states

Create styles for the ghost button with the text and border color as #9e9e9e, the font-weight as normal, and the background color as white. When hovered over, the button's background color will change to #efefef. The following screenshot shows the expected ghost button design:

Figure: Ghost button designs for normal and hover states

Finally, create a style for the special button. This button will have a linear gradient background with the primary color value #f44336 and the secondary color value #ff9900. The gradient will transition when hovered over since the color values are being swapped. You can use a paint worklet for this button, which you can create in a file called **gradient-paint.js**. The worklet name should be animated-gradient.

The following screenshot shows the expected special button design:

Figure: Special button designs for normal and hover states

To draw the gradient of the special button, we will create a gradient paint worklet by creating a JavaScript file called **gradient-paint.js** and copying the following JavaScript code into it:

```
class GradientPaintWorklet {    static get inputProperties() {
    return ["--primary-fill-color", "--secondary-fill-color"];
  }    paint(context, geometry, properties) {
    const primaryColor = properties.get("--primary-fill-color");
const secondaryColor = properties.get("--secondary-fill-color");        const gradient =
context.createLinearGradient(0, 0, geometry.        width, geometry.height);
    gradient.addColorStop(0, primaryColor);        gradient.addColorStop(1.0, secondaryColor);
    context.fillStyle = gradient;
    context.fillRect(0, 0, geometry.width, geometry.height);
  }
} registerPaint("animated-gradient", GradientPaintWorklet);
```

We have now completed the activity and started creating a design system by including the use of a paint worklet with the CSS Paint API and CSS Properties and Values API.

Conclusion: The Path Ahead for HTML and CSS

As we look toward the future of HTML and CSS, it's clear that these cornerstone technologies of the web are evolving to meet the demands of modern development. The innovations on the horizon promise not only to simplify the lives of developers but also to create more inclusive, accessible, and efficient experiences for users across the globe.

Embracing Change While Preserving Fundamentals

HTML and CSS have always thrived on a balance between innovation and stability. HTML's semantic structure remains a foundational element of web development, even as new elements and APIs enrich its capabilities. CSS, with its declarative approach, continues to provide developers with the power to shape the web's visual and interactive dimensions.

In 2025, this dynamic remains unchanged, but the tools and methodologies are more sophisticated than ever. The advent of container queries, CSS custom properties, and logical properties signals a maturity in CSS that prioritizes developer ergonomics and user-centric design. Similarly, the integration of native Web Components and declarative shadow DOM in HTML allows developers to create reusable and maintainable interfaces, ensuring scalability and efficiency in large projects.

Key Trends Shaping the Future

Several overarching trends are shaping how we approach HTML and CSS in 2025. These include:

Accessibility by Default

Accessibility has shifted from being an afterthought to a non-negotiable aspect of web development. Developers and designers are leveraging the semantic power of HTML and the customization abilities of CSS to craft experiences that are inclusive for everyone. Tools like ARIA, combined with better browser support for assistive technologies, are making it easier to build accessible websites without requiring extensive additional effort.

Responsive and Adaptive Design

The focus on responsive and adaptive design has reached new heights. With the rise of container queries, developers can design components that adapt to their container's size rather than relying solely on the viewport. This revolutionizes modular design, allowing for greater flexibility and consistency across varied devices and layouts.

Performance and Optimization

As users demand faster load times, HTML and CSS are evolving to prioritize performance. Lazy loading, optimized font-display options, and CSS subgrid are just a few examples of how these technologies address performance bottlenecks. Additionally, the integration of edge computing and advanced browser optimizations ensure that websites deliver content with minimal latency.

Design Systems and Standardization

Design systems have become a core strategy for maintaining visual consistency across digital ecosystems. HTML and CSS play a central role in these systems, providing reusable, styleable components that ensure cohesion. Standardization through tools like CSS-in-JS libraries and preprocessors is bridging the gap between design and development.

Interoperability and Collaboration

Modern web development demands collaboration between developers, designers, and other stakeholders. Tools that integrate HTML and CSS with design software—such as Figma or Adobe XD—are facilitating smoother workflows. This ensures that design prototypes translate seamlessly into production code.

Emerging Challenges and Opportunities

Despite these advancements, challenges remain. The rapid evolution of HTML and CSS introduces a steep learning curve for newcomers and experienced developers alike. Balancing innovation with backward compatibility is a constant struggle, as legacy systems can limit the adoption of new features.

However, these challenges also create opportunities. As tools and frameworks abstract the complexity of raw HTML and CSS, developers can focus on crafting unique experiences rather than reinventing the wheel. Community-driven efforts, open-source contributions, and comprehensive documentation are helping to democratize access to the latest features.

Beyond 2025: The Next Frontier

Looking beyond 2025, we can anticipate even more transformative changes. The rise of AI and machine learning is likely to influence how HTML and CSS are authored and optimized. For example, AI-powered tools can analyze user behaviour to recommend layout adjustments or predict accessibility issues before they arise.

Furthermore, the integration of immersive technologies such as AR and VR into web development will demand new standards and best practices. HTML and CSS will play a critical role in defining how 3D elements and spatial interfaces are rendered and styled within web browsers.

A Call to Action for Developers

As stewards of the web, developers hold the responsibility to shape its future thoughtfully. Embracing the latest advancements in HTML and CSS while adhering to best practices ensures that the web remains a universal and equitable platform. This involves:

Staying Informed: Regularly exploring updates from W3C and browser vendors.
Advocating for Accessibility: Prioritizing inclusivity in every project.
Building Sustainably: Designing for performance, scalability, and maintainability.
Contributing to Standards: Engaging with the community to shape the future of web technologies.

Final Thoughts

The journey of HTML and CSS from their humble beginnings to their present-day sophistication is a testament to the web's resilience and adaptability. As we move forward, these technologies will continue to empower developers and designers to push the boundaries of what's possible online. By leveraging the advancements of 2025 and beyond, we can build a web that is not only more functional and beautiful but also more equitable and sustainable for all.

The future of HTML and CSS is not just about the code—it's about the impact it creates. As developers, we have the privilege and responsibility to harness these tools to build experiences that inform, inspire, and connect people worldwide. The possibilities are as limitless as the web itself.

Final Thoughts

As we reach the end of our journey through the world of HTML and CSS, I hope you've gained not only a deeper understanding of the intricacies behind web design but also a newfound appreciation for the art of coding. In today's digital age, mastering these foundational technologies opens the door to creating websites that are not only functional but also visually captivating.

In this book, we've explored the core concepts, modern techniques, and best practices that will help you design responsive, accessible, and aesthetically pleasing websites. The power of HTML and CSS lies in their ability to work together, transforming your ideas into dynamic, interactive experiences on the web.

Remember, web development is an ever-evolving field, and your learning doesn't end here. Stay curious, experiment with new features, and continue to push the boundaries of what's possible with these essential tools. Whether you're building a simple personal website or crafting complex web applications, the skills you've acquired in this book will serve as a solid foundation for your continued growth as a web developer.

I encourage you to keep practicing, learning, and embracing the ever-changing landscape of web technologies. There's always something new to discover, and with HTML and CSS, the possibilities are limitless.

Thank you for embarking on this exploration of modern web design techniques. I look forward to seeing the amazing websites and projects you will create in the future!

Wishing you success in your coding journey. Happy designing!
Mike Zephalon

www.ingramcontent.com/pod-product-compliance
Lightning Source LLC
LaVergne TN
LVHW081750050326
832903LV00027B/1885